POWER RESOURCES THEORY
A CRITICAL APPROACH

Edited by Julia S. O'Connor and Gregg M. Olsen

This collection of essays looks at power resources theory (PRT), a ground-breaking approach to political theory that builds upon the existing strengths of Marxist theorizing while addressing its weaknesses. Rather than simply asserting that all social policies in all capitalist societies exist to maintain capitalism and serve the long-term interests of the capitalist class, PRT examines the nature and impact of social policies and the level and types of social inequality in a variety of advanced capitalist nations. Approaches to social policy and the impacts of these policies vary significantly from nation to nation. It is these variations that PRT seeks to account for, focusing on the strengths and organization of the labour movements in various nations.

The editors have compiled essays that examine the PRT approach, as well as essays that offer critical analysis of PRT. As existing summations of state theory literature largely omit PRT, this anthology is essential reading for anyone interested in social policy and radical approaches to social welfare.

JULIA S. O'CONNOR is Director of the National Economic and Social Council in Dublin, Ireland.
GREGG M. OLSEN is Associate Professor of Sociology at the University of Manitoba.

EDITED BY JULIA S. O'CONNOR
AND GREGG M. OLSEN

Power Resources Theory and the Welfare State: A Critical Approach

Essays collected in honour of Walter Korpi

UNIVERSITY OF TORONTO PRESS
Toronto Buffalo London

© University of Toronto Press Incorporated 1998
Toronto Buffalo London
Printed in Canada

ISBN 0-8020-0809-7 (cloth)
ISBN 0-8020-7171-6 (paper)

Printed on acid-free paper

Canadian Cataloguing in Publication Data

Main entry under title:

Power resources theory and the welfare state: a critical approach

ISBN 0-8020-0809-7 (bound) ISBN 0-8020-7171-6 (pbk.)

1. Welfare state — Philosophy. 2. Power (Social sciences).
I. O'Connor, Julia Sile, 1947– . II. Olsen, Gregg Matthew, 1956– .

HV31.P68 1998   361.6'5'01   c98-930020-x

The editors of this volume are listed in alphabetical order.

University of Toronto Press acknowledges the financial assistance to its publishing program of the Canada Council for the Arts and the Ontario Arts Council.

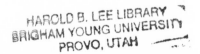

Contents

PART II: POWER RESOURCES THEORY:
A CRITICAL APPROACH

The Iceberg of Power below the Surface: A Preface to Power Resources Theory

WALTER KORPI

During the major part of our adult lives we are involved with the production and distribution of worldly goods. Our efforts result in varying degrees and different types of inequalities among citizens, inequalities reflecting what, in broad terms, can be referred to as 'life chances.' In the social sciences the role of power in these distributive processes is a contested one. The issues here concern the overall relevance of the concept of power as well as how power is to be conceptualized. Many social scientists, especially economists, often ignore the concept of power or assume that differences in power are small enough to be largely negligible. Among political scientists and sociologists, however, the relevance of power is recognized, and debates instead have focused on the most useful ways of conceptualizing the role of power. The power resources approach assumes that, in the analysis of distributive processes, power is an indispensable concept. This preface briefly discusses the context for the development of the power resources approach, its position in contemporary debates, and the challenges which it is currently facing.

The power resources approach developed gradually since the late 1960s in debates with major strands of social scientific thought, such as structural-functionalism, ideas of pluralist industrial society generated by the logic of industrialism and modernization, different versions of neo-Marxism, and different approaches to the study of power. These various strands of thought all assume that the distribution of power in Western societies has been relatively stable, although they sometimes disagree on whether this distribution is relatively equal or grossly unequal. The power resources approach, in contrast, advances the hypothesis that the distribution of power resources varies, shifting over time and between countries.

In the debates on the conceptualization of power, scholars within the so-called behavioural approach want to restrict the concept of power to cases involving clearly visible conflicts, such as when demands by Actor A are resisted by Actor B, who is forced to yield to the demands made. Other students of power, however, have seen such a limitation as unfortunate. While the use of power in manifest conflict naturally is of major significance, such cases may only reflect the visible part of what could be called the iceberg of power. In less easily discernible ways – so to speak, below the surface – power may play other and crucial roles in distributive processes. The power resources approach therefore focuses not only on the direct, but also on the indirect consequences of power, indirect consequences mediated through various alternative strategies and actions available to holders of power resources. This approach assumes bounded rationality in the sense that actors not only attempt to do as well as they can under the structural conditions in which they find themselves, but also to change these structures to their long-term advantage. From this perspective, it is important to acknowledge and distinguish between conflicts which result in open clashes (e.g., strikes and lockouts) and those which generate other types of strategies to affect distributive processes.

The 'frustration-relative deprivation' view holds that conflicts burst out when the gap between expectations and actual achievements becomes intolerable, that is, when relative deprivation increases actors' frustrations beyond certain critical levels. Assuming actors to be rational, the power resources approach indicates that, where differences in power resources between actors are large, the weaker party may find it to be in its best interests, at least in the short term, not to attempt to resist the claims of the stronger actor and is likely, in the long run, to modify its levels of aspiration (Korpi, 1974). In distributive processes involving differently empowered actors, power thus may have important consequences without being associated with manifest conflict. The behavioural approach largely overlooks those situations where differences in power between actors are large because it focuses explicitly on manifest conflict generated through decision making. It concentrates, instead, on cases where these differences are relatively small.

In the Western countries, the major part of distributive processes take place in three institutional sectors or spheres of society – markets, democratic politics, and the family. Socio-economic class is of major importance for structuring distributive processes in markets and democratic politics. According to what could be called a logic of choice of action spheres, wage- and salary-earners who are relatively disadvantaged in terms of economic resources to be used on the markets can be expected to attempt – with varying degrees of success – to act collectively via democratic politics, where the universal and equal right to vote, at least in principle, is the most important power resource. From such a perspective, the power resources approach has been used to analyse levels and changes of industrial conflict in the Western nations. Contrary to what has been argued by many, a high level of industrial conflict in a country need not necessarily reflect a strong working class. In some countries, political parties on the left have been in positions of power which have enabled them to redirect important parts of distributive conflicts from the labour market into democratic politics, thereby making industrial conflict temporarily 'wither away' (Korpi, 1978; Korpi and Shalev, 1980).

In the analysis of the role of power in distributive processes, it is necessary to consider the costs of power. These costs are generated in three stages of the power process – that is, the mobilization of resources, the maintenance of resources in a 'liquid' form (i.e., ready for use), and the application of resources to reward or punish other actors.[1] Situations of potential conflict necessitate the keeping of resources ready for use, generating liquidity as well as (potential) application costs. Prudent managers of power resources therefore are likely to attempt to decrease these costs of power through reliance on indirect ways of affecting distributive processes. Central in this context is the emergence of formal and informal societal institutions. This strategy thus involves a move – often a conflictual one – from distributive action to distributive institutions, which routinize distributive processes. These institutions can be expected to differentiate distributive outcomes in ways which reflect the prevailing distribution of power while decreasing both liquidity and application costs of power.

The power resources approach therefore helps to account for the emergence and development of institutions, a preoccupation within the new 'institutionalism,' or polity-centred, school in the social sciences in Western societies since the 1980s. From the latter approach, the emergence of institutions often has been viewed from a 'horizontal' perspective, as attempts to coordinate cooperation among symmetrically positioned actors in 'Prisoners' Dilemma' type of conflicts. The power resources approach, in contrast, suggests that institutions also must be viewed from a 'vertical' perspective, with differently empowered actors attempting to generate differential distributions of rewards. This facilitates the understanding of the micro–macro links central in social science analysis.

In Western societies, laws regulating the rights and duties of citizenship constitute formal institutions of basic importance for distributive processes. As formulated by T.H. Marshall, citizenship has civil, political, and social dimensions. A focus on changes in the distribution of power resources between major interest groups has proved fruitful in the analysis of the emergence and development of citizenship rights. In Western societies the welfare state has gradually come to expand the scope of social citizenship. The welfare state was, of course, not created for any single purpose or by any single party or class. During the period after the Second World War, parties representing workers, farmers, and salaried employees, as well as coalitions between them and more religiously oriented parties, have used democratic politics in attempts to influence distributive processes via the size and shape of welfare states (see, for example, Esping-Andersen, 1985, 1990; Esping-Andersen and Korpi, 1985; Huber, Ragin, and Stephens, 1993; Kangas, 1991; Korpi, 1983, 1989; Myles, 1989; Palme, 1990; Stephens, 1979; Wennemo, 1994). Welfare state institutions, in turn, have been found to influence distributive processes as well as the formation of identities and coalitions among citizens (Korpi, 1980; Korpi and Palme, in press).

Until the 1980s the role of gender was by and large neglected in analyses of distributive processes and welfare states. This neglect also has characterized work within the power resources approach, which has primarily been used in attempts to analyse the role of socio-economic stratification and class in the development of social rights. Gender and class generate cross-cutting cleavages. Classes are thus constituted by men and women, but women as well as men are distributed among different classes. Yet within the family, which typically is taken as the nucleus of the class or stratification systems in Western societies, we find varying degrees of gender-related differences in the division of labour as well as in control over resources.

Men have been direct participants in the distributive processes generating socio-economic stratification, while women, responsible for the major part of unpaid caring work, have played more marginal roles in this basic stratification process. The long arm of gendered patterns in the use of labour power thus reaches into the family in terms of differences in control over economic resources, status, identities, decision making within the family, and personal autonomy, especially dependence on the spouse (see, for example, Clement and Myles, 1994; Hernes, 1987; Leira, 1992; Lewis, 1993; O'Connor, 1996, and chapter 7, this volume; Orloff, 1993). In this context, Pateman (1989) has pointed to what she has termed

'Wollstonecraft's Dilemma': should a wife's unpaid caring work form the base for her rights, as does her husband's participation in the labour force, or should a variety of social services (e.g., day care, care for the elderly and the sick) be developed and put in place to allow women to participate in the labour force on equal terms with men? It would appear that an analysis of this dilemma in terms of what types of power resources are generated in paid and unpaid work is a useful starting-point for discussing alternative policy strategies.

In the power resources approach, race and ethnicity also have received little attention. Again, however, this need not imply that these factors cannot be brought into the power resources perspective. Thus, for example, systems of inequality based on race and ethnicity typically have their origins in the exercise of means of violence – wars, colonization, and enslavement. These historical roots have been perpetuated via strategies of closure, defining racial and ethnic characteristics as marks of inferiority, inequalities to which differentially distributed rewards have been added. As argued by William J. Wilson (1978), race has a close relationship to class.

The borders of the nation-state traditionally have circumscribed the arena within which distributive processes take place, but it has long been recognized that the international setting is of significance for constellations of power relations and strategies of distributive conflict within nation-states. During the last quarter of the twentieth century, the cross-border mobility of financial assets has been facilitated by various forms of deregulation, thereby opening up new action alternatives for holders of economic power resources. Actors whose main resources are based on labour power and the right to vote have not benefited in the same way from the decreasing significance of national borders. Furthermore, in the Western countries mass unemployment has returned. In combination, these changes have reshaped relations of power, markedly improving the position of actors who control economic resources (cf. Korpi, 1991; Olsen, 1992, and chapter 12, this volume). However, through its focus on distributive strife and the relations of power among actors, the power resources approach can be invaluable in our attempts to understand the causes and consequences of economic globalization. As noted above, this approach assumes that, in the Western countries, relations of power between major societal actors are shifting, not stable. During the first three-quarters of the twentieth century – although with significant variation between countries and over time – there was a trend towards decreasing inequalities in the distribution of power within the Western countries. Of course, this decreasing inequality did not reflect immutable laws, but was, instead, the outcome of factors such as changing possibilities for collective action within the labour force, destabilization following the two world wars, institutional structures, and policy inventions. The focus on changing relations of power makes the power resources approach central for an understanding of the reversals as well as the expansion of the welfare state, of increasing as well as of decreasing inequality.

This volume contains a very fine array of articles by leading representatives and critics of the power resources approach. It covers most of the important aspects of welfare states, including welfare state models and social expenditures as well as the major social policy areas, such as pensions, family policy, unemployment insurance, and health care. It also discusses challenges to the power resources approach and stresses the necessity for closer analyses of issues related to gender, race, and globalization. This volume thus points to some of the achievements of the power resources approach as well as areas of ongoing research and continued debates. The power resources approach is a work in progress, not an arrival.

Note

1 Parallel to the development of the power resources approach, what have been called 'resource mobilization theories' have focused especially on the mobilization of resources for collective action in the emergence 'new' social movements.

References

Clement, Wallace, and John Myles. 1994. *Relations of Ruling: Class and Gender in Postindustrial Societies.* Montreal: McGill-Queen's University Press.
Esping-Andersen, Gøsta. 'Power and Distributional Regimes.' *Politics and Society* 14(2): 223–56.
Esping-Andersen, Gøsta. 1990. *The Three Worlds of Welfare Capitalism.* Cambridge: Polity Press.
Esping-Andersen, Gøsta, and Walter Korpi. 1985. 'Social Policy as Class Politics in Post-War Capitalism: Scandinavia, Austria, and Germany.' In *Order and Conflict in Contemporary Capitalism*, ed. John H. Goldthorpe, pp. 179–208. Oxford: Oxford University Press.

Hernes, Helga Maria. 1987. *Welfare State and Woman Power: Essays in State Feminism.* Oslo: Norwegian University Press.

Huber, E., C. Ragin, and J.D. Stephens. 1993. 'Social Democracy, Christian Democracy, Constitutional Structure, and the Welfare State.' *American Journal of Sociology* 99 (3): 711–49.

Kangas, Olli. 1991. *The Politics of Social Rights.* Swedish Institute for Social Research, Stockholm University, Stockholm, Dissertation series no. 19.

Korpi, Walter. 1974. 'Conflict, Power and Relative Deprivation.' *American Political Science Review* 68 (4): 1569–78.

Korpi, Walter. 1978. *The Working Class in Welfare Capitalism: Work, Unions and Politics in Sweden.* London: Routledge & Kegan Paul.

Korpi, Walter. 1980. 'Social Policy and Distributional Conflict in the Capitalist Democracies: A Preliminary Comparative Framework.' *West European Politics* 3 (3): 296–316.

Korpi, Walter. 1983. *The Democratic Class Struggle.* London: Routledge & Kegan Paul.

Korpi, Walter. 1989. 'Power, Politics, and State Autonomy in the Development of Social Citizenship: Social Rights during Sickness in Eighteen OECD Countries since 1930.' *American Sociological Review* 54: 309–28.

Korpi, Walter. 1991. 'Political and Economic Explanations for Unemployment: A Cross-National and Long-Term Analysis.' *British Journal of Political Science* 21 (3): 315–48.

Korpi, Walter, and Joakim Palme. Inpress. 'The Paradox of Redistribution and the Strategy of Equality: Welfare State Institutions, Inequality and Poverty in the Western Countries.' *American Sociological Review.*

Korpi, Walter, and Michael Shalev. 1980. 'Strikes, Power and Politics in the Western Nations, 1900–1976.' *Political Power and Social Theory* 1: 301–34.

Leira, Arnlaug. 1992. *Models of Motherhood: Welfare State Policy and Scandinavian Experiences of Everyday Practices.* Cambridge: Cambridge University Press.

Lewis, Jane. 1993. 'Introduction: Women, Work, Family and Social Policies in Europe.' In *Women and Social Policies in Europe,* ed. Jane Lewis. Aldershot: Edward Elgar.

Myles, John. 1989. *Old Age in the Welfare State: The Political Economy of Public Pensions,* Rev. ed. Lawrence: University Press of Kansas.

O'Connor, Julia S. 1996. 'From Women in the Welfare State to Gendering Welfare State Regimes.' *Current Sociology* 44(2): 1–130.

Olsen, Gregg M. 1992. *The Struggle for Economic Democracy in Sweden.* Aldershot, UK: Avebury.

Orloff, Ann Shola. 1993. *The Politics of Pensions : A Comparative Analysis of Britain, Canada, and the United States, 1880–1940.* Madison: University of Wisconsin Press.

Palme, Joakim. 1990. *Pension Rights in Welfare Capitalism: The Development of Old-Age Pensions in 18 OECD Countries 1930 to 1985*. Swedish Institute for Social Reasearch, Stockholm University, Stockholm, Dissertation series no. 14.

Pateman, Carole. 1989. *The Disorder of Women: Democracy, Feminism and Political Theory*. Cambridge: Polity.

Stephens, John D. 1979. *The Transition from Capitalism to Socialism*. London: Macmillan.

Wennemo, Irene. 1994. *Sharing the Costs of Children: Studies on the Development of Family Support in the OECD Countries*. Swedish Institute for Social Research, Stockholm University, Stockholm, Dissertation series no. 25.

Wilson, William J. 1978. *The Declining Significance of Race: Blacks and Changing American Institutions*. Chicago: University of Chicago Press.

Acknowledgments

We wish to acknowledge the following authors and publishers for permission to include articles originally published by them:

Chapter 1 is reprinted from Walter Korpi: 'Power Resources Approach vs. Action and Conflict: On Causal and Intentional Explanations in the Study of Power,' *Sociological Theory* 1985, vol. 3, no. 2, pp. 31–35, by permission of the American Sociology Association.

Chapter 2 is reprinted from Irene Wennemo: 'The Development of Family Policy: A Comparison of Family Benefits and Tax Reductions for Families in Eighteen OECD Countries,' *Acta Sociologica* 1992, no. 3, pp. 201–217, by permission of Scandinavian University Press, Oslo, Norway.

Chapter 3 is reprinted from Evelyne Huber and John D. Stephens: 'Political Parties and Public Pensions: A Quantitative Analysis,' *Acta Sociologica* 1993, no. 4, pp. 309–325, by permission of Scandinavian University Press, Oslo, Norway.

Chapter 4 is reprinted from Gøsta Esping-Andersen: 'Three Political Economies of the Welfare State,' *Canadian Review of Sociology and Anthropology* 1989, vol. 26, no. 1, pp. 10–36, by permission of the Canadian Sociology & Anthropology Association.

Chapter 5 is reprinted from Julia S. O'Connor: 'Welfare Expenditure and Policy Orientation in Canada in Comparative Perspective,' *Canadian Review of Sociology and Anthropology* 1989, vol. 26, no. 1, pp. 127–150, by permission of the Canadian Sociology & Anthropology Association.

Chapter 6 is reprinted from Gregg M. Olsen: 'Locating the Canadian Welfare State: Family Policy and Health Care in Canada, Sweden, and the United States,' *The Canadian Journal of Sociology* 1994, vol. 19, no. 1, pp. 1–20, by permission of the journal.

Chapter 7 is reprinted from Julia O'Connor: 'Gender, Class, and Citizenship in the Comparative Analysis of Welfare State Regimes,' *British Journal of Sociology* 1993, vol. 44, no. 3, pp. 501–518, by permission of the journal.

Chapter 8 is reprinted from J. Lewis: 'Gender and the Development of Welfare Regimes,' *Journal of European Social Policy* 1992, vol. 2, no. 3, pp. 159–173, by permission of Sage Publications Ltd.

Chapter 9 is reprinted from Jill Quadagno: 'Race, Class, and Gender in the U.S. Welfare State: Nixon's Failed Family Assistance Plan,' *American Sociological Review* 1990, vol. 55, pp. 11–28, by permission of the American Sociological Association.

Chapter 10 is reprinted from Bo Rothstein: 'Labour Market Institutions and Working Class Strength,' in Sven Steinmo, Kathleen Thelen, and Frank Longstreth, eds., *Structuring Politics: Historical Institutionalism in Comparative Analysis* 1992, pp. 33–56. Reprinted with the permission of Cambridge University Press.

Chapter 11 is reprinted from Peter Baldwin: 'The Scandinavian Origins of the Welfare State,' *Comparative Studies in Society and History* 1989, vol. 31, no. 1, pp. 3–24. Reprinted with the permission of Cambridge University Press.

Chapter 12 is reprinted from Gregg M. Olsen: 'Re-modelling Sweden: The Rise and Demise of the Compromise in a Global Economy,' *Social Problems* 1996, vol. 43, no. 1, pp. 1–20, by permission of the Society for the Study of Social Problems.

Contributors

Peter Baldwin is Professor of History at the University of California, Los Angeles.

Gøsta Esping-Andersen is Professor of Political Science at the University of Trento.

Evelyne Huber is Morehead Alumni Professor of Political Science and Director of the Institute of Latin American Studies at the University of North Carolina, Chapel Hill.

Walter Korpi is Professor of Social Policy at the Swedish Institute for Social Research, University of Stockholm.

Jane Lewis is Professor of All Souls College, Oxford University.

Julia S. O'Connor is Director of the National Economic and Social Council, Dublin, Ireland, and Associate Professor of Sociology at McMaster University.

Gregg M. Olsen is Associate Professor of Sociology at the University of Manitoba.

Jill Quadagno holds the Mildred and Claude Pepper Eminent Scholars' chair in Social Gerontology at Florida State University, Tallahassee.

Bo Rothstein is August Rohss Professor in Political Science at the University of Göteborg.

John D. Stephens is Professor of Political Science at the University of North Carolina, Chapel Hill.

Irene Wennemo is a researcher at the Swedish Trade Union Confederation (LO), Stockholm.

POWER RESOURCES THEORY AND THE WELFARE STATE

Introduction
Understanding the Welfare State: Power Resources Theory and Its Critics

GREGG M. OLSEN and JULIA S. O'CONNOR

The 1970s witnessed an outpouring of competing theoretical accounts of the origin, development, character, and impact of modern welfare states. One of the most fruitful approaches to emerge during this period of expansion was the power resources perspective advanced by a Scandinavian school of researchers and closely associated with the pioneering work of Walter Korpi (1978, 1980, 1983, 1985), Gøsta Esping-Andersen (1985a, 1985b, 1990; also Esping-Andersen and Korpi, 1985, 1987), and John Stephens (1980; see also Ulf Himmelstrand et al, 1981). Although the approach was not without shortcomings and blind spots, the emphasis power resources theory (PRT) placed on comparative and quantitative studies of the relationship between social policy and labour mobilization enabled it to provide a more satisfying explanation for wide variations in the development and outcome of welfare states across the industrialized nations than that of many other accounts. While other approaches, conservative and radical alike, tended to ignore or minimize such diversity, PRT attempted to order the welfare states of Scandinavia, Western Europe, and North America on the basis of salient characteristics and their impact on social inequality. In particular, such models often highlighted differences between the generous, comprehensive, universal, and coordinated social policies which comprise welfare states like Sweden's, and their relatively underdeveloped counterparts found in, for example, the American welfare state. This article provides an introduction to PRT; critically examines its contribution to the development of (welfare) state theory, as well as its flaws; and evaluates its usefulness in the current era of globalization and welfare retrenchment.[1]

The Origin and Growth of Welfare States: From Structural–Functional Imperatives and Interest Groups to Labour Mobilization

Prior to the dramatic expansion of the welfare state in advanced capitalist nations in the late 1960s and early 1970s, most accounts of its origins and growth stemmed from only a few broad theoretical traditions. Structural functionalism, associated with the work of pre-eminent macrosociologists such as Emile Durkheim and Talcott Parsons, and the pluralist theory of Robert Dahl and Charles Lindblom were two of the most predominant schools, holding sway for over two decades. However, while both approaches came to prominence during roughly the same period and explicitly or implicitly served to legitimate the status quo, they began from rather different assumptions.

Writing around the turn of the century, Durkheim argued that political institutions arose in response to universal stresses and needs which emerged as simple societies evolved into more complex entities. Much later, Parsons also acknowledged the restoration of equilibrium in changing societies in this way, but placed more emphasis on the need for 'shared values' among society's members in order for it to set and realize its goals. New institutions allowed for such 'goal attainment' and for the maintenance of 'consensus' among the citizenry. Structural-functionalists, then, saw the development of the welfare state as a society's way of adapting gradually to the changes brought about by modernization, industrialization (with its impact on employment levels and workplace health), urbanization, and population growth, rather than as the result of philanthropy, innovation, or political machination.

Much of the work in this tradition tended towards descriptive accounts of public intervention focusing on economic development and/or dominant values (e.g., individualism vs collectivism) in particular nations (Lipset, 1963, 1969, 1990; Tomasson, 1970). However, a number of researchers attempted to provide more empirical support for some of the central functionalist tenets. Examining a multitude of advanced and less-developed nations, they demonstrated that welfare programs emerged and expanded primarily in those countries which had experienced high levels of economic growth, industrialization, and demographic change – especially the dramatic expansion of the elderly population which resulted from increasing longevity and lower rates of infant mortality (cf. Cutright, 1965; Rimlinger, 1966; Wilensky, 1975, 1976; Wilensky and Lebeaux, 1965). More important, they noted that it was the most-developed nations which had the highest levels of *expenditure* on social welfare programs.[2] From this perspective, politics were not seen as the primary determinant of the welfare state. Moreover, as the logic of industrialism, or modernization, continued to spread, nations would grow increasingly similar (convergence theory) and political ideologies of the left and right would become irrelevant (end-of-ideology theory) (Galbraith, 1967; Kerr et al, 1964; Kuznets, 1965; Lipset, 1960).

Rooted in liberal political philosophy, pluralist accounts of welfare-state development take a fundamentally different tack from that of functionalist approaches. Rather than emphasizing structural imperatives, pluralism focuses on agency or the role of various actors in bringing about change. Contrary to the central premises of elite theory and Marxism, Dahlian pluralism maintained that power is widely diffused among a variety of competing interest groups and not held by ruling elites or classes. While highlighting conflict rather than consensus, pluralists stressed the fact that individuals are often members of several different associations and organizations (cross-cutting cleavages) and maintained that no one particular group predominates at all times over all issues. From this perspective, social welfare policies and programs are viewed as the state's response to the demands of various lobbies representing women, the elderly, small business, farmers, and numerous other pressure groups (e.g., Fox, 1981; Janowitz, 1976). More recently, attempts have been made to combine the logic of both functionalism and pluralism. These studies maintain that both the size of the aged population and the actions of interest groups are the strongest determinants of *welfare spending* (Pampel and Williamson, 1988, 1989).

Amidst the radicalism of the 1960s and 1970s, neo-Marxist theories were among the first to take issue with central planks of both theoretical traditions, castigating their conservative and false presentation of societal stability.[3] Consensus, if it existed at all – and labour disputes, strikes, demonstrations, and other frequent outbursts of radicalism and dissatisfaction belied such a suggestion – was seen as enforced through economic and political domination. Neo-Marxists maintained that, far from diffuse, power was concentrated in the hands of a capitalist class which was thereby largely able to control a state that was anything but neutral. One strand of neo-Marxist theory, so-called instrumentalism, attempted to demonstrate this state bias empirically by highlighting the many direct or indirect personal, social, and professional ties between capitalists and political elites (e.g., Domhoff, 1983; Miliband, 1969). Instrumentalists concluded that welfare programs emerged because capitalists wanted them – a notion often referred to as 'corporate liberalism.' Enlightened and far-sighted capitalists thus oversaw and hastened the introduction of poor relief, unemployment insurance, educational reform, and other public and private social welfare policies in a conscious effort to increase output, stabilize or revitalize the economy, and pre-empt or defuse working-class militancy (cf. Brody, 1980; McQuaid, 1978; Weinstein, 1968). Structuralist versions of neo-Marxist theory were better able to explain those instances when welfare programs were implemented against the wishes of particular prominent and powerful capitalists by referring to the long-term interests of the entire capitalist class and by stressing that the state was 'relatively autonomous' from direct manipulation and much more structurally determined (Poulantzas, 1969, 1976, 1978). Ironically, its focus on the state's functions – including almost automatically responding to the needs of the capitalist system and restoring social order – gave this latter approach a rather functionalist cast.[4]

Power resources theory (PRT) emerged in the late 1970s and early 1980s in an attempt to redress some of the problems with existing mainstream and radical accounts of the welfare state. Despite the central role of class conflict in Marx's work, both earlier neo-Marxist theories tended to ignore or depreciate the efforts of the working class in the creation of various social programs and largely failed to acknowledge significant variation in the growth and development of welfare states across nations.[5] Like instrumentalism and structuralism, PRT rejected the pluralist notion that power was widespread, and viewed the capitalist class as, by far, the most powerful actor in society by virtue of its control over economic resources (the means of production). However, unlike these radical approaches, it maintained that the balance of power between labour and capital was fluid, and therefore variable. While capital would always have the upper hand within a capitalist framework, labour had potential access to political resources which could increase its power, and thereby allow it to implement social reform and alter distributional inequalities to a significant degree. Creating a political party and mobilizing its numerical majority in the party's support was one way the working class could increase its power. However, the success of social-democratic, labour, or other parties of the left would depend upon a well-organized labour movement. High rates of unionization and the organization of unions into a cohesive labour central or confederation were therefore crucial (Korpi, 1980, 1983). It was also acknowledged that labour strength could be augmented if the working class was able to form coalitions with other classes, such as agrarian or white-collar workers (Esping-Andersen, 1990; Esping-Andersen and Friedland, 1982). PRT maintained that welfare states would develop the farthest in nations where labour was strongest as measured along such dimensions.

Such suggestions, of course, contradicted the functionalist research which had concluded that it was economics, not politics, which mattered most to welfare development. Power resources theorists maintained that, while a high level of economic development was necessary in order to fund expensive welfare programs – partially explaining the bifurcation in welfare spending between advanced and underdeveloped nations reported in the functionalist studies discussed above – it was not a sufficient explanation. After all, the commitment to social welfare was much greater in Sweden than in the United States, although both were rich, developed nations. Without politics, there was nothing compelling rich nations to commit resources to the development of a welfare state. Power resources theorists limited their studies to twenty-four or fewer advanced capitalist nations.[6] Controlling for level of economic development in this manner, they demonstrated substantial variation among the advanced nations which had been missed by overly inclusive functionalist studies of sixty or more nations at various developmental stages and with various types of political systems, and found the indicators of power resources to have a significant relationship to levels of welfare *expenditure* (Cameron, 1978; Hicks and Swank, 1984, 1992; O'Connor, 1988; Stephens, 1980).[7]

Power resources theorists have also taken issue with functionalist and structuralist explanations for the *introduction* of major welfare programs. From these perspectives, the emergence of a number of early social insurance programs, such as workers' compensation, sickness and maternity benefits, and old-age pensions, was closely related to the level of economic development (functionalism) and/or to political unrest and the consequent need to integrate workers (structuralism). According to the latter view, early welfare programs selectively targeted the working class in an attempt to co-opt it (Alber, 1988; Schneider, 1982). However, this overemphasis on economic development or the ulterior and pre-emptive actions of the state depreciates the role and demands of organized workers. As Esping-Andersen and Korpi (1985) point out, the nations in which social insurance programs emerged first, such as Germany and Austria, were often also those in which labour was mobilized and relatively strong, prompting reaction from the state. [8]

The politicians who pioneered the introduction of social insurance in the 1880s, Otto von Bismarck in Germany and Eduard von Taaffe in the Habsburg Empire, did not see themselves as reacting to factors such as demographic changes and increasing economic resources in their nations. Instead, taking warning from the Paris Commune, they consciously used state power to develop social policy as the second leg of a strategy to undercut the threat to the existing social order from *the growing organizational strength of an emerging industrial working class*; the first leg of the strategy was the use of repressive measures. (Esping-Andersen and Korpi, 1985: 179; emphasis added)

In addition, it is clear that some welfare programs, such as unemployment insurance and family allowances, emerged long after industrialization had taken place in most nations, contrary to the logic of functionalist explanations (see table 1). Moreover, power resources theorists maintained that it was much more important to examine the impact and character of welfare states than the early introduction of particular social insurance programs or welfare expenditures alone.

TABLE 1
Introduction of Social Programs in Eighteen Nations

	Workers' compensation	Sickness & maternity	Old-age pensions	Unemployment insurance	Family allowances
Austria	1887	1888	1906	1920	1948
Belgium	1903	1894	1924	1920	1930
Canada	1908[1]	1957	1927	1940	1944
Denmark	1894	1892	1891	1907	1952
Finland	1893	1963	1937	1917	1948
France	1898	1928	1910	1905	1932
Germany	1884	1883	1889	1927	1954
Great Britain	1897	1911	1908	1911	1945
Greece	1914	1922	1934	1945	1958
Ireland	1897	1911	1908	1911	1944
Italy	1898	1912	1912	1919	1937
Luxembourg	1902	1901	1911	1921	1947
Netherlands	1901	1913	1913	1916/49	1939
Norway	1895	1909	1936	1906	1946
Portugal	1913	1935	1935	1975	1942
Spain	1932	1932	1919	1919	1938
Sweden	1901	1891	1913	1934	1947
United States	1910[1]	1965[2]	1935	1935	–

[1] Subnational (state or provincial programs).
[2] The United States does not have a national health care system.
Source: Schneider, 1982.

The Impact of Welfare States: Acknowledging the Variation

Complementing their research on welfare spending, functionalists had argued that there was a positive, linear relationship between a nation's level of economic development and its level of social equality. Not surprisingly, they found that material rewards – especially income – were more equally distributed in the more economically advanced, industrialized nations (Kuznets, 1955; Cutright, 1967). In later research they discovered that the relationship was more curvilinear, suggesting that a threshold is reached in the later phases of economic development, after which the impact of industrialization on social inequality becomes progressively weaker and nations become much more alike (Jackman, 1974; Branco and Williamson, 1988).

However, as the data presented in table 2 indicate, income inequality and poverty levels varied greatly among advanced, industrialized nations in the early 1980s. The Gini index – a measure of income distribution – indicates that income inequality was much lower in the Scandinavian countries (Norway and Sweden) and Germany than in it was in the Anglo nations (the United States, Canada, the United Kingdom, and Australia) examined here. An identical pattern emerges when poverty levels are analysed. The poverty rate, defined as the percentage of all persons whose income was less than half the median national income of the population, was more than twice as high in the Anglo nations as it was in Scandinavia and Germany in 1982. Poverty rates among some of the most vulnerable groups, such as single-parent families and the elderly, followed a similar pattern across these nations.

A measure of the poverty gap, presented in the last two columns of table 2, directly indicates the impact of the welfare state on poverty. Column 5 indicates how much income, measured as a percentage of each nation's GDP, it would take to bring those persons living in poverty up to the poverty-line income prior to receiving their transfer payments. Column 6 provides a measure of the poverty gap after transfers have been paid out. A comparison of the figures in both columns suggests that the impact of the welfare state has been weakest in the Anglo nations (with the exception of the United Kingdom) and strongest in Scandinavia and Germany, where poverty rates were reduced by 90 per cent or more via welfare measures.[9]

Given such variation, power resources theorists rejected functionalist accounts of declining social inequality among industrialized nations. Again

TABLE 2

Income Inequality and Poverty in Nine Industrial Nations circa 1980

		Poverty Rate[2] % of Poor			Poverty Gap as a % of GDP, early 1980s	
	Gini index[1]	All persons[3]	Lone parent with children[4]	Single elderly persons (65–74) (years)	Pre-transfer	Post-transfer
Australia	.292	11.4	55.4	30.1	4.5	0.4
Canada	.290	12.3	46.3	32.0	4.2	1.3
Germany	.249	4.9	7.2	12.9	6.4	0.6
Netherlands	.291	7.5	21.0	2.0	6.5	1.4
Norway	.222	4.8	8.1	4.9	4.6	0.5
Sweden	.197	5.0	9.8	0.9	4.1	0.4
Switzerland	.275	8.2	21.2	16.9	4.9	1.2
United Kingdom	.275	11.7	29.3	51.5	3.3	0.2
United States	.315	16.6	54.0	39.6	5.6	2.3

[1] The Gini index is the most commonly used measure of income inequality. It varies between zero (perfect equality) and one (perfect inequality). The index here has been adjusted for family size.

[2] The poverty rate is defined here as the percentage of all persons whose income was less than half the median national income. Poverty rates have been adjusted for family size. Poverty rates are actually higher in some countries, such as the United States, than listed here because of the existence of a large, unregistered homeless population which does not show up in statistical reports.

[3] All persons includes all persons in families.

[4] Lone parent includes children living in families with one adult under age sixty-five and no other adults in the household.

Sources: Mitchell, 1991; Osberg, 1992; and Smeeding, 1991.

they argued that, when analyses are restricted to the economically advanced nations, labour strength provides the best explanation for reductions in income inequality and for the variation observed across countries (Dryzek, 1978; Hewitt, 1977; Hicks, 1991; Korpi, 1980; Stephens, 1980).[10] Moreover, they demonstrated that, in Scandinavia and other nations where labour was more highly mobilized, the character of welfare states differed significantly; they were generally more generous (with higher income-replacement rates, greater coverage, and fewer waiting days) and more preventative in nature than elsewhere (Kangas, 1991; Olsen, ed., 1988, article 6 in this volume). These programs have tended to mitigate numerous forms of inequality (Erikson and Åberg, 1987), including those associated with, for example, old age (Myles, 1989; Palme, 1990) and gender (Ruggie, 1984; Sundström, 1991).

Included in part I of this volume ('The Power Resources Perspective: Labour Strength and Welfare Regimes') is an early article by Walter Korpi which critically assesses dominant definitions and analyses of power extant in the social science literature and introduces and sets out the rationale for a power resources approach. PRT, according to Korpi, 'indicates that the distribution of power resources between collectivities or classes and the changes in this distribution are of crucial importance for societal processes and social change.' This article is followed by five more recent studies which examine various programs and dimensions of the welfare state. In two of these studies, an attempt is made to identify factors that moderate the direct and linear relationship between welfare state development and level of power resources assumed in the early PRT studies.[11] For example, Irene Wennemo also specifies the relationship between labour mobilization and social welfare in her examination of the introduction and nature of family policy in eighteen OECD nations. She suggests that one power resource – the strength of left (labour or social democratic) parties – has a significant impact on the level of benefits provided through family allowances, but very little impact on fiscal welfare (tax deductions). Similarly, Evelyne Huber and John D. Stephens, leading exponents of the PRT tradition, show that social democratic party rule is more closely associated with the *quality* of old-age pensions and lower levels of inequality among the elderly than it is with overall expenditures on pensions. The latter, they conclude, appears to be more closely related to Christian democratic-party incumbency associated with high levels of transfer payments. They also challenge the pluralist notion that interest groups are primarily responsible for explaining cross-national variation in welfare provision for the elderly.

The Character of Welfare States: From Bipolar Models to Welfare State Regimes

The proliferation of research on social policy in the 1970s led not only to debates over the origins and impact of various social programs but also to attempts at distinguishing among types of welfare states. Given the focus on welfare spending, government outlay on social programs originally played a central role in the determination of whether a nation was labelled as a 'welfare leader' or a 'welfare laggard,' but it was not the only consideration. Welfare typologies were usually conceptualized as bi-polar and linear. At one end of the continuum was the 'residual' welfare state, characterized by lower spending, a restricted range of provision, targeted programs (through means- and/or needs-testing), meagre support, and a tight connection between welfare benefits and paid labour. Misfortune and need are the basis for welfare provision here when private alternatives (the family, the market, and charities) have been exhausted. The American welfare state comes closest to this description. At the other end of the continuum was the 'institutional' welfare state, characterized by a wide range of generous, universal, public social programs provided as a right of citizenship, and by a reluctance to set fixed boundaries on the provision of welfare (cf. Esping-Andersen and Korpi, 1987; Jones, 1985; Furniss and Tilton, 1977; Titmuss, 1958, 1974). Sweden approximates this ideal type most closely. Other nations were situated somewhere between these two poles.

By the 1980s, it already was evident that bipolar, linear models of social welfare provision could not represent adequately the many dimensions of the welfare states of several nations. Expenditure levels alone were clearly unsatisfactory as a means of understanding and classifying welfare states. High levels of spending on particular labour market, old-age, or medical programs, for example, might simply reflect high levels of unemployment (Britain in the 1980s), the provision of lavish pensions for civil servants (Germany and France), or an attempt to provide health care in a huge country where the population is widely dispersed (Canada).

A more meaningful way to distinguish among welfare-state types, based upon T.H. Marshall's (1964) well-known work on the rights of citizenship, was developed by Esping-Andersen.[12] He drew attention to welfare states' variable capacity to reduce people's reliance upon the market through the provision of public alternatives which allow them to maintain a normal and socially acceptable standard of living. 'Decommodification,' or protection from total dependence on the labour market for survival, highlighted the distinction between weak and strong welfare states, but it did not identify important differences among those nations which provided expensive, universal, public programs. Following Wilensky and Lebeaux (1965) and Titmuss (1974), among others, Esping-Andersen (1990) thus developed a tripolar typology describing three 'worlds' or 'regimes' of welfare capitalism: (1) the social-democratic world, best exemplified by Sweden and Norway; (2) the liberal world, typified by the United States, Canada, Australia, and the United Kingdom; and (3) a conservative or status-based world comprising nations such as Germany, Austria, France, and Italy.

The welfare state regime concept – a key theoretical construct in the PRT tradition – is detailed by Gøsta Esping-Andersen in part I of this book. It links decommodification to the various types of social rights that predominate in different industrialized nations. While all welfare states make use of three different criteria of eligibility for social programs and benefits – means and/or income testing, social insurance contributions, and citizenship – the dominance of one criterion over the others serves to differentiate types of welfare states. In the social-democratic welfare state, the citizenship criterion predominates, whereas the liberal welfare state is characterized by a strong emphasis on means-tested programs, and the conservative welfare state is distinguished by its variety of class and status-based social insurance schemes. Welfare state regimes, Esping-Andersen notes, also vary in the primacy they accord to the state, the market, or the family. While the social-democratic regime largely utilizes the state to meet social needs, the liberal regime depends mostly on the market, and the conservative regime is heavily reliant upon the family.

The liberal and social-democratic regimes identified by Esping-Andersen resemble the residual and institutional welfare states, respectively, of earlier welfare typologies discussed above, but the conservative regime cannot easily be placed at a mid-point on a continuum. While the nations in the conservative welfare world often assume an intermediate position between the other two worlds with regard to total welfare spending, their welfare states possess unique features. Influenced heavily by the Church, conservative or status-based welfare states seek to maintain traditional institutions, hierarchies, and roles. For example, unlike those in the social-democratic world, family policies in the conservative regime are designed to preserve the public and private spheres as the domains of men and women, respectively. And, unlike those found in the liberal world, benefits provided in the conservative world often are relatively generous, publicly administered, and provided as a right. However, they are constructed through a variety of social insurance schemes to preserve status and income differentials among classes and occupational groups. The social-democratic and liberal welfare states play an equally important role in structuring the stratification systems extant in their respective worlds.

Using a broader compass than the articles by Wennemo, and Huber and Stephens – each of which focused on only one key policy component of the welfare state – Julia S. O'Connor examines overall 'welfare effort' and policy orientation in Canada from a comparative perspective. Canadian patterns over the 1960–90 period are considered in the context of seventeen other OECD countries, with a focus on four key dimensions of welfare effort associated welfare regimes: decommodification, solidarity, redistribution, and full employment.

Although the welfare regime approach has, in many ways, proven more useful than previous dichotomous leader–laggard models, it has also garnered criticism. For example, the welfare world triad cannot properly accommodate the 'Latin rim' nations (Spain, Portugal, Greece) which, it has been argued, constitute a separate, fourth welfare world (Leibfried, 1992). On the grounds that strong labour movements and high-benefit equality distinguishes Australia and New Zealand from other members of the liberal world such as Canada and the United States, Castles and Mitchell (1992) have also put forth an alternative four-world welfare model. However, as Gregg M. Olsen argues in part I of this volume, distinct differences within the liberal world also exist between the U.S. and Canadian welfare states when social services (particularly health care), rather than just transfer programs, are examined closely. He points out that welfare states in each regime are not necessarily very uniform or coherent, and may concurrently possess programs which can be categorized into more than one regime. Moreover, he suggests that any specific social program or policy (e.g., health care) may simultaneously possess qualities or features associated with more than one of the welfare state regimes.

Articles 2 to 6 in part I point to some problems with PRT and/or the closely associated welfare worlds model, and suggest, after a closer examination and armed with new empirical evidence, certain theoretical modifications. Most of the authors, however, remain largely, if cautiously, committed to the perspective.[13] In part II ('Power Resources Theory: A Critical Approach'), more serious charges are brought to bear against PRT's almost exclusive focus on labour strength and the three-regime typology. Emphasizing gender, race, political institutions, and class, these six articles suggest that the PRT/welfare worlds approach needs to be seriously overhauled if it is to remain relevant – especially in an era of globalization.

Bringing Gender and Race In

Gender, Class, and Citizenship

One of the most well-developed critiques of Esping-Andersen's three-regime typology has been made by scholars interested in a more gender-sensitive welfare state analysis. Until the early 1990s, feminist studies of the welfare state and PRT research developed in parallel, rather than in recognition of one another.[14] Research in the PRT tradition tended to emphasize class over gender and was usually comparative and quantitative.[15] Most feminist research, however, has been country-specific and qualitative. The focus on welfare state regimes by power resources analysts and the relatively recent interest in more comparative research by several feminist theorists has afforded an opportunity for dialogue between these two streams of research.

While recognizing the innovative character of the welfare regime concept, feminist critics of the model focus on its emphasis on the class-citizenship aspect of social rights, its minimal attention to other bases of stratification, and its tendency to ignore the family in the state–market–family triad (O'Connor, 1996). Some analysts have argued not only for a gendered understanding of decommodification, stratification, and state/market/family relations, but also for the need to supplement these dimensions with additional ones, including access to paid work and the associated services to facilitate this (e.g., daycare), personal autonomy, and the capacity to form an autonomous household(e.g., Orloff, 1993a).

In this vein, Julia S. O'Connor argues in article 7 that the incorporation of gender into a comparative analytical framework must entail a reassessment of the conventional conception of citizenship, a broadening of conventional definitions of political mobilization and participation, and a modification of the welfare state regime model. The concept of decommodification, or insulation from total dependence on the labour market, must be supplemented by the concept of personal autonomy, or insulation from involuntary personal economic dependence on family members and/or public reliance upon on state agencies. The idea of personal autonomy relates directly to the articulation of the relations of production and reproduction, or activities within the labour market and the family. It addresses the issue of services that facilitate labour market participation and points to the welfare state as an important mechanism of gender stratification. The emphasis upon personal autonomy is predicated upon the recognition that benefit structures may facilitate independence for some people while creating or perpetuating dependence for others. It also highlights the fact that it is necessary to be a participant in the labour market before decommodification can occur.

Ann Orloff (1993a) has suggested that a measure of the capacity to form and maintain an autonomous household is necessary to capture the effects of state social provision on gender relations. Her rationale for this dimension is as follows: 'If decommodification is important because it frees wage earners from the compulsion of participating in the market, a parallel dimension is needed to indicate the ability of those who do most of the domestic and caring work – almost all women – to form and maintain autonomous households, that is, to survive and support their children without having to marry to gain access to breadwinners' income' (Orloff, 1993a: 319). The objective of such a measure is to identify how benefits, such as those for lone mothers, contribute to a capacity to maintain autonomous households and enhance women's power *vis-à-vis* men within marriages and families. And it would need to capture variation in the extent to which welfare states meet the needs of those who are not in the labour market (i.e., non-commodified) and whose economic dependence is on male breadwinners. Orloff envisages two ways of conceptualizing this capacity. First, a new, broader, and more generic measure of self-determination or autonomy could be created by merging Esping-Andersen's notion of decommodification with the concept of individual independence from markets and marriage. Second, the concept of decommodification could be supplemented with a separate dimension that measures the level of success that women's movements have had in securing economic independence for women through, for example, increasing access to the paid labour force, creating services that ease the burden of caring on individual households, and ensuring secure incomes for women engaged in full-time domestic work. The focus on women's agency in fostering such independence would be analogous to PRT's emphasis on the role labour movements have played in securing protection from the market for workers.

The studies considered in this section so far are complementary to Esping-Andersen's welfare-worlds approach, arguing for the gendering of key components of the model and bolstering it with specifically gendered dimensions to construct an approach that recognizes the importance of class and gender and their interaction. Other analysts suggest alternative bases for gender-sensitive welfare state analysis. In her critique of the welfare regime model (article 8 in this volume), Jane Lewis agrees that the Esping-Andersen typology is gender-blind because it ignores women's segregation (or partial segregation) in the unpaid domestic sphere, their consequently limited opportunity for decommodification, and their subsequent reliance upon meagre, means-tested benefits or coverage provided through a spouse's insurance. She thus proposes a new model which evaluates and categorizes welfare states on the basis of their commitment to the concept of a 'male breadwinner.' She argues that, although it has varied by degree, a male-breadwinner family arrangement has historically cut across established typologies of welfare states.[16]

All of these analyses build upon earlier work on women and the welfare state, most of which was directed towards identifying the impact of the welfare state on women and making women visible in welfare state analysis (e.g., Wilson, 1977). Consequently, there are a number of common themes in feminist analyses of welfare states, irrespective of country of origin. These include the following: women's pivotal position within the welfare state, not only as paid workers but as unpaid community caregivers; the centrality of the welfare state for women as clients, consumers of services, and political citizens; issues of patriarchy, social reproduction, social control, and dependency; and the relationship among women's roles as unpaid carers, paid workers, and political citizens. Less common themes include the role of women as political activists in welfare state development, and the welfare state as a mechanism of empowerment for women (Skocpol, 1992; Gordon, 1994; Hernes, 1987).[17]

A significant problem with some of the early work on women and the welfare state is that its conclusions tend to be generalized to *the* welfare state, even though they are based on studies of individual countries. This is problematic, since it cannot be assumed that what is evident about the welfare state in one country can be generalized across all welfare states, or over time in any particular nation. While there are common issues across welfare states, such as the gendered nature of caring and dependency, the connotation of terms and the salience of issues vary across countries. Differences in emphasis coincide in part with the theoretical framework of the researcher and, to a large extent, with the particular welfare state regime under scrutiny (O'Connor, 1996).

For the most part, single-country studies based on U.K., U.S., or Canadian experience tend to emphasize the oppressive characteristics of the welfare state for women and the role of the welfare state in the reproduction of patriarchy (e.g., Wilson, 1977; Nelson, 1984; Fraser, 1989; Dickinson and Russell, 1986), whereas comparative studies and those based on Scandinavian experience, while recognizing the subordination of women, emphasize the possibility for the empowerment of women through the welfare state (e.g., Ruggie, 1984; Borchorst and Siim, 1987; Dahlerup, 1987; Hernes, 1987; Norris, 1987). This difference is not surprising when women's experience with welfare state institutions in different countries is considered. Women's experience is more negative in nations where they encounter the welfare state primarily as social assistance clients rather than as consumers, employees, or political citizens.

This also explains, in part, the concentration on women's dependence and powerlessness in much of the Anglo-American literature.

In contrast to their experience in liberal welfare states, women in social-democratic welfare states are less likely to be welfare or social assistance clients. This difference in experience is reflected in a relatively optimistic view of state potential. For example, Helga Hernes, a Norwegian analyst, discusses the possibility of creating a 'woman-friendly state,' that is, 'a state where injustice on the basis of gender would be largely eliminated without an increase in other forms of inequality such as among groups of women' (Hernes, 1977: 15). Comparative analysis affords an opportunity to identify the factors that are conducive to the development of such a state.

Race, Gender, and Citizenship in Welfare State Analysis

Theories and typologies which incorporate gender into their analyses are still inadequate to explain the complexity of mechanisms which structure welfare states. Race, in particular, is central to the development and formation of many welfare states, perhaps most notably that in the United States. In article 9, Jill Quadagno argues that class struggle has been emphasized as the central dynamic in the formation of the U.S. welfare state, while race and gender as major factors in its organization commonly have been overlooked. She supports this argument through a historical examination of a Family Assistance Plan proposed during the Nixon administration. Her analysis suggests that, while social policy may be used to increase female dependence, under certain historical conditions it also may enhance gender and racial equality (cf. Piven, 1984). Quadagno's article in this volume and her recent book (1994) are part of a burgeoning body of scholarship which attempts to integrate race, gender, and class. Not surprisingly, much of this work has emanated from the United States (e.g., Gordon, 1994; Mink, 1990, Boris, 1995).[18] However, this literature largely involves country-specific, historical studies which have received little attention in the PRT debates.

More recently, Fiona Williams (1995) has proposed a framework more sensitive to race and the interrelationship among gender, race, class, and welfare states which *is* comparative. She calls for an examination of states' relationship, via social policies (or welfare states), to the family, work, and the nation. The last dimension includes an account of systems of migration, colonialism and imperialism and processes of inclusion and exclusion from the nation-state as reflected in citizenship rights. Williams maintains that such considerations are necessary in order to grasp the diversity of welfare settlements in different nations.

The absence of a comparative body of work incorporating class, gender, and race is not surprising. Clearly, with the inclusion of each additional dimension, the complexity of the analysis and the difficulty of large-scale comparative research increase. But the use of quantitative and qualitative historical approaches affords an opportunity for a more multifaceted analysis which can better inform our understanding of social policy as a potentially liberating force. In the 1990s, however, this potential appears increasingly undermined by the ongoing restructuring of welfare states and the consequent impact upon women and others intimately linked to them.

Power Resources Theory in an Era of Globalization: Identifying Actors and Structures

In the mid-1980s, PRT and other critical and mainstream 'society-centred' theories rightfully were taken to task for largely overlooking the state, or treating it as epiphenomenal. Neo-Weberian 'state-centred' theorists argued that state officials might pursue their own distinctive goals, rather than those of interest groups or capitalists – indeed, sometimes challenging the wishes or demands of such actors. State structures, for example, administrative systems and bureaucracies, rules of electoral competition, party systems, constitutional frameworks, relations among levels of government and governmental agencies, and historical patterns of democratization, also were viewed as important determinants of social policy from this perspective (e.g., Evans, Rueschmeyer, and Skocpol, 1985; March and Olsen, 1989; Skocpol and Amenta, 1986; Steinmo, Thelen, and Longstreth, 1992). More recently, the role of 'social policy feedback' and a variety of other political factors have been highlighted by this 'neo-institutional' or polity-centred, approach (cf. Weir, Orloff, and Skocpol, 1988; Orloff, 1993b).[19] The central role of state structures and their interaction with other variables is appearing increasingly in comparative social welfare research (e.g., Olsen and Brym, 1996). In article 10, Bo Rothstein seeks to combine the strengths of PRT and the neo-institutional approach. He highlights the impact of labour-market institutions upon working-class strength and argues that, in nations where unemployment insurance has been administered by unions or their representatives (the

'Ghent System') rather than by the state, union density, and hence labour strength, has been reinforced. Rothstein's article helps clarify the relationship between political structures and agency.

If PRT underplayed the role of the state in shaping social programs and the expansion of the welfare state, its overemphasis on unions and social-democratic/labour parties also eclipsed the impact of other political and class actors in the construction and shaping of welfare states. While agreeing that 'politics matter,' Francis Castles (1978; Castles, ed., 1982; Castles and McKinlay, 1979), for example, pointed out early on that the degree of unity or division among political parties on the right is an important determinant of whether left-wing parties will succeed in their attempts to implement social programs and reduce inequality. In his historical examination of the welfare state in Scandinavia (article 11), Peter Baldwin also suggests that the impetus for the development of the welfare state was not provided by only the working class and social-democratic/labour parties, because it emerged long before they came to power. He highlights, instead, the important role played by the agrarian class.[20] While Baldwin undoubtedly overstates his case, reaching conclusions about the 'welfare state' while examining only its social insurance component (and only one social insurance policy at that – pensions), his work is important because it draws attention to other important social actors often neglected by PRT.[21]

Despite its valuable contribution to our understanding of welfare states and its dominant position in the social policy literature over the past decade, PRT appeared rather less persuasive by the 1990s. It is true that, in those nations where workers are more organized and the welfare state is most deeply entrenched, labour has been somewhat more insulated from the introduction of the new workplace technologies and practices associated with 'lean production,' the intense competition from newly industrializing nations, and over two decades of persistently sluggish growth. Unlike in the United States, for example, where a more flexible economy has encouraged the proliferation of low-wage jobs, dramatically swelling the numbers of the working poor, many European countries have sought to preserve their high-wage economies. This strategy, however, has become increasingly associated with chronically high levels of unemployment. Moreover, poverty and income inequality have risen steadily on both sides of the Atlantic in recent years. Although the United States has easily maintained its long-standing reputation as one of the most inegalitarian of the advanced capitalist nations, the occurrence of such developments in countries where labour's power resources were greatest was an eventuality which PRT had some difficulty explaining.

While purportedly examining a 'balance of power,' power resources theorists concentrated almost exclusively on the power resources of labour while largely ignoring structural developments which were rapidly and decisively increasing the strength of capital (Olsen, 1991a, 1992). The transformation of the 'capitalist world economy' into a 'world capitalist economy' – characterized by the emergence of new patterns of production, consumption, and distribution, and by new or modified supranational agreements and organizations (e.g., the North American Free Trade Agreement, European Union, and World Trade Organization) – left labour in a much weaker position *vis-à-vis* capital in every advanced capitalist nation. This shift in the balance of power between capital and labour is, as Gregg M. Olsen argues in article 12, one of the most important aspects of 'globalization.'[22]

In the new, more global environment, financial capital, transnational corporations, and other actors play a significantly greater role in determining what is desirable, or even possible, with little if any regard for 'strong' national labour movements. This may be done purposefully or, as with the actions of bond traders, currency speculators, credit-rating agencies, and others who buy, sell, and deal in capital markets, more unintentionally. Keynesian policies, protective regulations, social programs, and other progressive distributional policies associated with the 'golden age of welfare capitalism,' thus soon were defined as market 'rigidities.' They have given way to deregulation, massively regressive shifts in taxation policy, balanced-budget legislation, and the dismantling or downgrading of welfare states. In this global environment, all governments – even incumbent social-democratic or labour governments with an 'institutionalized commitment to full employment' (Therborn, 1986) – have much less room to manoeuvre. This is reflected in mass unemployment and/or the increasingly frequent use of part-time work, contingent employment, subcontracting, and self-employment today.[23]

Olsen documents the impact of globalization in Sweden, a nation renowned as a labour stronghold and welfare leader, where, only two decades ago, blueprints to transform Swedish capitalism were enthusiastically drafted from within the Swedish labour movement. By the late 1980s and early 1990s, however, Swedish labour had long abandoned radical proposals for industrial and economic democracy and was scrambling to halt the erosion of its welfare state and industrial relations system, which were under attack – an effort which has been spectacularly unsuccessful to date (Olsen, 1995).

Labour's inability to preserve the Swedish model was also due to fracturing from within the Swedish labour movement. New fault lines emerged and grew between the social-democratic party (SAP) and the blue-collar labour confederation (LO), as well as between and within the blue-collar and white-collar (TCO) labour centrals (Olsen, 1991b, 1992). PRT's quantitative measures of labour strength, such as unionization rates or the electoral durability of parties of the left, can mask potentially serious rifts and fractures to the labour movement and, consequently, provide a misleading reading of labour strength.[24] If it is to remain useful, PRT clearly must address the growing asymmetry in power between capital and labour and the structural developments upon which it is based, and identify the 'power resources' which are most salient in the new, more global market economy.

Few studies today would assert the primacy of any monocausal determinant of social policy, although they are sometimes still geared towards finding the 'best' theoretical approach. However, in light of all of the valuable, critical appraisals of PRT cited above and elaborated upon in this volume, most researchers are now concerned with identifying the interactions among a wide range of factors of varying significance, dependent upon the nation, historical period, and specific social policy under scrutiny. The difficult work of identifying these variables and interactions remains to be done.

Notes

1 Power resources theory is also referred to as the 'Social Democratic Model,' the 'Working Class Mobilization Model,' or 'Political Class Struggle' theory.
2 The conventional index of welfare spending focuses upon total government expenses allocated to welfare programs ('transfers' and/or services) expressed as a proportion of GDP (gross domestic product) rather than as a percentage of total government expenditures. This measure indicates the amount of resources committed to welfare in relation to total national resources.
3 Despite their inherent conservatism, functionalist explanations can and have been used to defend welfare states against attacks on expenditure levels, as evident in the conclusion reached in a study by Coughlin and Armour

(1983: 195): 'In contrast to the popular notion that irresponsible "big spenders" or the "shiftless" poor are at the root of the fiscal crisis of the welfare state, our analysis reveals that large, impersonal forces – demographic and economic – are more proximate causes of the continuing expansion of the two largest sectors of social security [old age and public health].'

4 Structuralist accounts which suggest, for example, that the introduction of factory legislation to protect women in several industrialized countries in the late 1800s was *really* about preserving capitalism by ensuring the reproduction of a future labour force bear a strong resemblance to the functionalism of Robert Merton, with its concept of manifest and latent functions. Similarly, in their study of the welfare state in the United States, Piven and Cloward (1971) maintain that the primary objective of social welfare programs was to restore, maintain, and enforce social order. However, unlike many others in the structuralist tradition, they view the emergence of these programs as largely a response to civil disorder and outbursts of protest by the poor.

5 When variation was acknowledged, it made little difference to their analysis. Structuralists, for example, alternately argued that highly developed and decidedly underdeveloped welfare states served to maintain the capitalist system.

6 These studies commonly focused on the eighteen nations which have been consistently democratic in the post–Second World War period (Australia, Austria, Belgium, Canada, Denmark, Finland, France, Germany, Ireland, Italy, Japan, the Netherlands, New Zealand, Norway, Sweden, Switzerland, the United Kingdom, and the United States).

7 The significance of the sample used for the conclusions reached is pointed out by Uusitalo (1984: 405). 'By including countries from the whole range of developmental sequence, from least to most advanced, you maximize the variance of economic level and thereby create statistical conditions for its explanatory power. If the sample includes only developed countries, the variance of their economic performance is much smaller, and it cannot be expected to have much explanatory power.' However, later functionalist studies by Wilensky (1975, 1976), who focused on a limited number of advanced nations, still found support for the 'logic of industrialism' thesis. The contrary conclusions reached by Wilensky and power resources theorists such as Stephens (1980) were due to the different measures of 'welfare effort' (spending) they used. While the former focused on 'social security expenditures' furnished by the ILO (International Labour Organization), the latter used 'civil public expenditure.' Both measures are problematic, as O'Connor and Brym (1988) note, because they are either too limited,

largely focusing on 'transfer payments' while excluding spending on other central elements of the welfare state such as social services (e.g., Wilensky), or too broad, including all non-military forms of public expenditure (e.g., foreign affairs, internal security, research, road construction, and municipal services) (e.g., Stephens). Problems of measurement and other methodological issues are addressed in Gilbert and Moon (1988), Huber, Ragin, and Stephens (1993), Janoski and Hicks (1994), O'Connor and Brym (1988), and Uusitalo (1984).

8 Neo-Marxist structuralist accounts of the emergence of social security programs in Germany, for example, are not necessarily at odds with PRT. While the latter highlights labour mobilization, the former has tended to focus on the state's response to that threat. Interestingly, German chancellor Otto von Bismarck's oft-quoted justification for the introduction of old-age security in the late 1800s ('One who can look forward to an old-age pension is far more contented and much easier to manage' – quoted in King, 1983: 14) is routinely taken at face value by structuralists – a courtesy rarely granted to contemporary rulers and politicians.

9 The United Kingdom was also extremely successful in reducing its poverty rate, but, because its initial level of poverty was so high, its post-transfer poverty rate remained rather high. Many more recent studies also have demonstrated that poverty levels and income inequality is much lower in Scandinavia and other north European nations such as Germany and the Netherlands (e.g., Atkinson, Rainwater, and Smeeding, 1995).

10 However, the ongoing debate between functionalism and PRT is far from clear cut. For example, Jackman (1980) notes that, while socialist parties may have redistributed income away from the most-privileged income quintile, they have not effected any significant redistribution in favour of the bottom 40 per cent of income-earners. In his comparative study of public assistance in the United States and (West) Germany, Leibfried (1978: 60) also concludes that 'social democracy does not ... guarantee a clear difference with respect to welfare policy "outcomes."' Of course, like many others, these studies examine the effects of only one indicator of labour mobilization – 'socialist' political parties.

11 This also is done by Göran Therborn (1986). He argues that low rates of unemployment over the long term are as dependent upon the establishment of an 'institutionalized commitment to full employment' as they are on labour mobilization, although these factors are often closely linked to one another. This helps explain why a nation such as Japan, where labour has not been very strong, has had one of the most successful employment records in the industrialized world in recent decades.

12 Marshall (1963, 1964) argued that the process of modernization over the past three centuries involved an expansion of the rights of citizenship and an increase in the numbers of inhabitants given status as citizens. He identified three different types of rights which emerged progressively: 'civil rights' (e.g., freedom of speech, thought, and faith), 'political rights' (e.g., the right to vote), and 'social rights' (e.g., education and the welfare state).

13 In light of some of the criticisms of the welfare worlds approach, Korpi and Palme (1998) have recently constructed a more elaborate model.

14 'Feminist' here refers to work that recognizes gender as a fundamental structuring mechanism in all societies and as crucial to understanding welfare states. Despite considerable diversity in theoretical orientation among feminist analysts, this is the common orientation that unites them. The particular aspect of gender difference that is emphasized varies by theoretical orientation (see Williams, 1989: 82–5).

15 Important exceptions were the analysis by Pippa Norris on the comparative position of women in OECD countries (Norris, 1987) and Mary Ruggie's analysis of the state and working women in Britain and Sweden (1984).

16 Diane Sainsbury (1994) has extended this analysis by contrasting the 'male breadwinner' model with an 'individual' model and identifying ten dimensions of variation that differentiate them (e.g., familial ideology, the basis of entitlement, the unit of benefits and contributions, the gendered priority of employment and wage policies, the public or private provision of care, and whether caring work is unpaid or has a paid component). She suggests that the male-breadwinner model is inadequate as an exclusive model for gendering welfare states, and demonstrates the usefulness of comparison across a broader range of dimensions.

17 Several of these issues are discussed by Caroline Andrew in her analysis of women and the Canadian welfare state. She highlights the role of women's organizations in the development of welfare state services as well as the roles of women as workers and women as clients (Andrew, 1984).

18 One of the earliest proponents of such an approach, however, was Fiona Williams (1989), whose work has focused on Britain.

19 It should be acknowledged that PRT did not totally ignore the state or policy feedback. State structures were seen as the 'residue' of class struggle, which, in turn, would have an impact on future struggles (see, e.g., Esping-Andersen, Friedland, and Wright, 1976; Korpi, 1980). However, this aspect was not usually highlighted.

20 This argument is more fully developed in Baldwin (1990). Here Balwin argues that coalitions of middle-class interests were the central catalyst for the emergence of 'solidaristic' social policies (comprehensive social insurance).

26   Gregg M. Olsen and Julia S. O'Connor

21 For a critique of Baldwin, see Olsson (1990). Although he does not focus
   on the emergence of the welfare state, Gordon Laxer (1989) highlights the
   role of agrarian movements in the Canadian scene during the period of
   industrialization.
22 'Globalization' is often understood in a very narrow sense, i.e., the integration of nations into the global economy through increased trade. This
   circumscribed definition, however, fails to address directly the impact of the
   changing imbalance of power among class forces on social inequality and
   the welfare state.
23 See Walter Korpi (1991) for an explanation for the emergence of mass unemployment from a PRT perspective.
24 Other useful critiques of the measures of labour strength utilized by PRT
   have been put forward by Keman (1990) and Shalev (1983, 1992).

References

Alber, Jens. 1988. 'Continuities and Changes in the Idea of the Welfare State.'
   Politics and Society 16/4: 451–68.
Andrew, Caroline. 1984. 'Women and the Welfare State.' *Canadian Journal of
   Political Science* 17/4: 667–83.
Atkinson, Anthony B., Lee Rainwater, and Timothy M. Smeeding. 1995. *Income
   Distribution in OECD Countries: Evidence from the Luxembourg Income Study.* Paris:
   OECD.
Baldwin, Peter. 1990. *The Politics of Social Solidarity: Class Bases of the European
   Welfare State, 1875–1975.* Cambridge: Cambridge University Press.
Borchorst, Anette, and Birte Siim. 1987. 'Women and the Advanced Welfare State
   – A New Kind of Patriarchal Power?' In *Women and the State: The Shifting Bound-
   aries of Public and Private,* ed. Anne Showstack Sassoon. London: Hutchinson.
Boris, Eileen. 1995. 'The Racialized Gendered State: Constructions of Citizen-
   ship in the United States.' *Social Politics* 2/2: 160–80.
Branco, Kenneth J., and John B. Williamson. 1988. 'Economic Development
   and Income Distribution: A Cross-National Analysis.' *American Journal of
   Economics and Sociology* 47/3: 277–97.
Brody, David. 1980. 'The Rise and Decline of Welfare Capitalism.' In *Workers in
   Industrial America.* New York: Oxford University Press.
Cameron, David. 1978. 'The Expansion of the Public Economy: A Comparative
   Analysis.' *American Political Science Review* 72: 1243–61.
Castles, Francis G., 1978. *The Social Democratic Image of Society.* London:
   Routledge and Kegan Paul.

Castles, Francis G. ed. 1982. *The Impact of Parties: Politics and Parties in Democratic Capitalist States*. London: Sage.

Castles, Francis G., and Robert D. McKinlay. 1979. 'Does Politics Matter? An Analysis of the Public Welfare Commitment in Advanced Democratic States.' *European Journal of Political Research* 7: 169–86.

Castles, Francis G., and Deborah Mitchell. 1992. 'Identifying Welfare State Regimes: The Links between Politics, Instruments and Outcomes.' *Governance: An International Journal of Policy and Administration* 5/1:1–26.

Coughlin, Richard M., and Philip K. Armour. 1983. 'Sectoral Differentiation in Social Security Spending in the OECD Nations.' *Comparative Social Research* 6: 175–99.

Cutright, Phillips. 1965. 'Political Structure, Economic Development, and National Security Programs.' *American Journal of Sociology* 70/4: 537–50.

– 1967. 'Inequality: A Cross-National Analysis.' *American Sociological Review* 32: 562–78.

Dahlerup, Drude. 1987. 'Confusing Concepts – Confusing Reality: A Theoretical Discussion of the Patriarchal State.' In *Women and the State*, ed. Anne Showstack Sassoon. London: Hutchinson.

Dickinson, James, and Bob Russell, eds. 1986. *Family, Economy and State: The Social Reproduction Process under Capitalism*. Toronto: Garamond.

Domhoff, G. William. 1983. *Who Rules America Now? A View for the '80s*. Englewood Cliffs, NJ: Prentice-Hall.

Dryzek, John. 1978. 'Politics, Economics and Inequality: A cross-national analysis.' *European Journal of Political Research* 6: 399–410.

Erikson, Robert, and Rune Åberg. 1987. *Welfare in Transition: A Survey of Living Conditions in Sweden, 1968–1981*. Oxford: Oxford University Press.

Esping-Andersen, Gøsta. 1985a. *Politics against Markets: The Social Democratic Road to Power*. Princeton, NJ: Princeton University Press.

– 1985b. 'Power and Distributional Regimes.' *Politics and Society* 14: 223–56.

– 1990. *The Three Worlds of Welfare Capitalism*. Princeton, NJ: Princeton University Press.

Esping-Andersen, Gøsta, and Walter Korpi. 1985. 'Social Policy as Class Politics in Post-War Capitalism.' In *Order and Conflict in Contemporary Capitalism*, ed. John H. Goldthorpe. Oxford: The Clarendon Press.

– 1987. 'From Poor Relief to Institutional Welfare States: The Development of Scandinavian Social Policy,' In *The Scandinavian Model: Welfare States and Welfare Research.*, ed. Robert Erikson, Erik J. Hansen, Stein Ringen, and Hannu Uusitalo. Armonk, NY: M.E. Sharpe.

Esping-Andersen, Gøsta, and Roger Friedland. 1982. 'Class Coalitions in the Making of West European Economies.' *Political Power and Social Theory* 3: 1–52.

Esping-Andersen, Gøsta, Roger Friedland, and Erik Olin Wright. 1976. 'Modes of Class Struggle and the Capitalist State.' *Kapitalistate* 4/5: 186–220.

Evans, Peter B., Dietrich Rueschemeyer, and Theda Skocpol, eds. 1985. *Bringing the State Back In*. Cambridge: Cambridge University Press.

Fox, Richard G. 1981. 'The Welfare State and the Political Mobilization of the Elderly.' In *Aging: Social Change*, ed. Sara B. Kiesler, James N. Morgan, and Valerie Kincade Oppenheimer. New York: Academic Press.

Fraser, Nancy. 1989. 'Women, Welfare, and the Politics of Need Interpretation.' In *Unruly Practices: Power, Discourse and Gender in Contemporary Social Theory*, ed. Nancy Fraser. Minneapolis: University of Minnesota Press.

Furniss, Norman, and Timothy Tilton. 1977. *The Case for the Welfare State: From Social Security to Social Equality*. Bloomington: Indiana University Press.

Galbraith, John K. 1967. *The New Industrial State*. Boston: Houghton Mifflin.

Gilbert, Neil, and Ailee Moon. 1988. 'Analyzing Welfare Effort: An Appraisal of Comparative Methods.' *Journal of Policy Analysis and Management* 7/2: 326–40.

Gordon, Linda. 1994. *Pitied But Not Entitled: Single Mothers and the History of Welfare*. New York: The Free Press.

Hernes, Helga Maria. 1987. *Welfare State and Woman Power: Essays in State Feminism*. Oslo: Norwegian University Press.

Hewitt, Christopher. 1977. 'The Effect of Political Democracy and Social Democracy on Equality in Industrial Societies: A Cross-National Comparison.' *American Sociological Review* 42 (June): 450–64.

Hicks, Alexander. 1991. 'Unions, Social Democracy, Welfare and Growth.' *Research in Political Sociology* 5: 209–34.

Hicks, Alexander, and Duane Swank. 1984. 'On the Political Economy of Welfare Expansion: A Comparative Analysis of 18 Advanced Capitalist Democracies, 1960–1971.' *Comparative Political Studies* 17/1: 81–119.

– 1992. 'Politics, Institutions, and Welfare Spending in Industrialized Democracies, 1969–1982.' *American Political Science Review* 86: 658–74.

Himmelstrand, Ulf, Göran Ahrne, Leif Lundberg, and Lars Lundberg. 1981. *Beyond Welfare Capitalism: Issues, Actors and Forces in Societal Change*. London: Heinemann.

Huber, Evelyne, Charles Ragin, and John D. Stephens. 1993. 'Social Democracy, Christian Democracy, Constitutional Structure, and the Welfare State.' *American Journal of Sociology* 99/3: 711–49.

Jackman, Robert W. 1974. 'Political Democracy and Social Equality: A Comparative Analysis.' *American Sociological Review* 39: 29–45.

– 1980. 'Socialist Parties and Income Inequality in Western Industrial Societies.' *The Journal of Politics* 42: 135–49.

Janoski, Thomas, and Alexander M. Hicks, eds. 1994. *The Comparative Political Economy of the Welfare State*. Cambridge: Cambridge University Press.

Janowitz, Morris. 1976. *Social Control of the Welfare State.* Chicago: University of Chicago Press.

Jones, Catherine. 1985. 'Types of Welfare Capitalism.' *Government and Opposition* 20/3: 328–42.

Kangas, Olli. 1991. 'The Bigger the Better? On the Dimensions of Welfare State Development: Social Expenditures versus Social Rights.' *Acta Sociologica* 34/1: 33–44.

Keman, Hans. 1990. 'Social Democracy and the Politics of Welfare Statism.' *The Netherlands' Journal of Social Sciences* 26/1: 17–34.

Kerr, Clark, John T. Dunlop, Frederick H. Harbison, and Charles A. Myers. 1964. *Industrialism and Industrial Man.* New York: Oxford University Press.

King, Anthony. 1983. 'The Political Consequences of the Welfare State.' In Shimon E. Spiro and Ephraim Yuchtman-Yaar, eds., *Evaluating the Welfare State: Social and Political Perspectives.* New York: Academic Press.

Korpi, Walter. 1978. *The Working Class in Welfare Capitalism: Work, Unions and Politics in Sweden.* London: Routledge and Kegan Paul.

– 1980. 'Social Policy and Distributional Conflict in the Capitalist Democracies: A Preliminary Comparative Framework.' *West European Politics* 3/3: 296–316.

– 1983. *The Democratic Class Struggle.* London: Routledge and Kegan Paul.

– 1985. 'Power Resources Approach vs. Action and Conflict: On Causal and Intentional Explanation in the Study of Power.' *Sociological Theory* 3: 31–45.

– 1991. 'Political and Economic Explanations for Unemployment: A cross-national Long-term Analysis.' *British Journal of Political Science* 21: 315–48.

Korpi, Walter, and Joakim Palme. 1998. 'The Paradox of Redistribution and Strategies of Equality.' *American Sociological Review.*

Kudrle, Robert T., and Theodore R. Marmor. 1984. 'The Development of Welfare States in North America.' In *The Development of Welfare States in North America,* eds. Peter Flora and Arnold J. Heidenheimer. London: Transaction.

Kuznets, Simon. 1955. 'Economic Growth and Income Inequality.' *The American Economic Review* 45/1: 1–28.

– 1965. *Economic Growth and Structure.* New York: Norton.

Laxer, Gordon. 1989. *Open for Business: The Roots of Foreign Ownership in Canada.* Toronto: Oxford University Press.

Leibfried, Stephan. 1978. 'Public Assistance in the United States and the Federal Republic of Germany.' *Comparative Politics* 11/1: 59–76.

– 1992. 'Towards a European Welfare State: On Integrating Poverty Regimes into the European Community.' In *Social Policy in a Changing Europe,* ed. Zsuzsa Ferge and Jon Eivind Kolberg. Boulder, CO: Westview.

Lipset, Seymour Martin. 1960. *Political Man: The Social Bases of Politics.* Garden City, NY: Doubleday.
– 1963. *The First New Nation: The United States in Historical and Comparative Perspective.* New York: Basic.
– 1969. *Revolution and Counter-Revolution.* London: Heinemann Educational.
– 1990. *Continental Divide: The Values and Institutions of the United States and Canada.* New York: Routledge.
March, James G., and Johan P. Olsen. 1989. *Rediscovering Institutions: The Organizational Basis of Politics.* New York: Macmillan.
Marshall, T. H. 1963. *Sociology at the Crossroads.* London: Heinemann.
– 1964. *Class, Citizenship and Social Development.* Chicago: University of Chicago Press.
McQuaid, Kim. 1978. 'Corporate Liberalism in the American Business Community, 1920–1940.' *Business History Review* 52/3: 342–68.
Miliband, Ralph. 1969. *The State in Capitalist Society.* New York: Basic.
Mink, Gwendoline. 1990. 'The Lady and The Tramp: Gender, Race, and the Origins of the American Welfare State.' In *Women, The State, and Welfare,* ed. Linda Gordon. Madison: University of Wisconsin Press.
Mitchell, Deborah. 1991. *Income Transfers in Ten Welfare States.* Aldershot: Avebury.
Myles, John. 1989. *Old Age in the Welfare State: The Political Economy of Public Pensions.* Lawrence: University Press of Kansas.
Nelson, Barbara. 1984. 'Women's Poverty and Women's Citizenship,' In *Women and Poverty,* ed. Barbara C. Gelphi, Nancy C.M. Hartsack, Clare C. Novak, and Myra H. Strober. Chicago: University of Chicago Press.
Norris, Pippa. 1987. *Politics and Sexual Equality The Comparative Position of Women in Western Democracies.* Boulder, CO: Rienner and Wheatsheaf.
O'Connor, Julia S. 1988. 'Convergence or Divergence? Change in Welfare Effort in OECD Countries 1960-1980.' *European Journal of Political Research* 16: 277–99.
– 1996. 'From Women and the Welfare State to Gendering Welfare State Regimes.' *Current Sociology* 44: 2.
O'Connor, Julia S., and Robert J. Brym. 1988. 'Public Welfare Expenditure in OECD Countries: Towards a Reconciliation of Inconsistent Findings.' *The British Journal of Sociology* 39/1: 47–68.
Olsen, Gregg M. 1991a. 'Labour Mobilization and the Strength of Capital: The Rise and Stall of Economic Democracy in Sweden.' *Studies in Political Economy* 34: 109–46.
– 1991b. 'Swedish Social Democracy and Beyond: Internal Obstacles to Economic Democracy.' In *Regulating Labour: The State, Neo-Conservatism and*

Industrial Relations, ed. Larry Haiven, Stephen McBride, and John Shields. Toronto: Garamond Press.

– 1992. *The Struggle for Economic Democracy in Sweden*. Aldershot: Avebury.

– 1995. 'The Search for a New Model: Industrial Relations in Sweden.' In *Labour Gains, Labour Pains: 50 Years of PC1003*, ed. Cy Gonick, Paul Phillips, and Jesse Vorst. Halifax: Fernwood.

– 1995. 'The Search for a New Model: Industrial Relations in Sweden.' In *Labour Gains, Labour Pains: 50 Years of PC1003*, ed. Cy Gonick, Paul Phillips, and Jesse Vorst. Halifax: Fernwood.

Olsen, Gregg M., ed. 1988. *Industrial Change and Labour Adjustment in Sweden and Canada*. Toronto: Garamond.

Olsen, Gregg M., and Robert J. Brym. 1996. 'Between American Exceptionalism and Social Democracy: Public and Private Pensions in Canada.' In *The Privatization of Social Policy: Occupational Welfare and the Welfare State in America, Scandinavia and Japan*, ed. Michael Shalev. London: Macmillan.

Olsson, Sven E. 1990. *Social Policy and Welfare State in Sweden*. Lund: Arkiv.

Orloff, Ann Shola. 1993a. 'Gender and the Social Rights of Citizenship: The Comparative Analysis of Gender Relations and Welfare States.' *American Sociological Review* 58 (June): 303–28.

– 1993b. *The Politics of Pensions: A Comparative Analysis of Britain, Canada, and the United States, 1880–1940*. Madison: University of Wisconsin Press.

Osberg, Lars. 1992. 'Canada's Economic Performance: Inequality, Poverty and Growth.' In *False Promises: The Failure of Conservative Economics*, ed. Robert C. Allen and Gideon Rosenbluth. Vancouver: New Star.

Ostner, Ilona, and Jane Lewis. 1995. 'Gender and the Evolution of European Social Policies.' In *European Social Policy between Fragmentation and Integration*, ed. Stephan Liebried and Paul Pierson. Washington, DC: The Brookings Institute.

Palme, Joakim. 1990. *Pensions Rights in Welfare Capitalism: The Development of Old-Age Pensions in 18 OECD Countries, 1930 to 1985*. Stockholm: University of Stockholm Press.

Pampel, Fred C., and Robin Stryker. 1990. 'Age Structure, the State, and Social Welfare Spending: A Reanalysis.' *British Journal of Sociology* 41/1: 16–24.

Pampel, Fred C., and John B. Williamson. 1988. 'Welfare Spending in Advanced Industrial Economies.' *American Journal of Sociology* 93/6: 1424–56.

– 1989. *Age, Class, Politics and the Welfare State*. Cambridge: Cambridge University Press.

Piven, Frances Fox. 1984. 'Women and the State: Ideology, Power, and the Welfare State.' *Socialist-Feminism Today:* 4: 11–19.

32   Gregg M. Olsen and Julia S. O'Connor

Piven, Frances Fox, and Richard A. Cloward. 1971. *Regulating the Poor: The Functions of Public Welfare.* New York: Vintage.

Poulantzas, Nicos. 1969. 'The Problem of the Capitalist State.' *New Left Review* 58: 67–78.

– 1976. 'The Capitalist State.' *New Left Review* 95: 63–83.

– 1978. *Political Power and Social Classes.* London: Verso.

Quadagno, Jill. 1994. *The Colour of Welfare: How Racism Undermined the War on Poverty.* New York: Oxford University Press.

Rimlinger, Gaston V. 1966. 'Welfare Policy and Economic Development: A Comparative Historical Perspective.' *Journal of Economic History* 26: 556–71.

Ruggie, Mary. 1984. *The State and Working Women: A Comparative Study of Britain and Sweden.* Princeton, NJ: Princeton University Press.

Shalev, Michael. 1983. 'The Social Democratic Model and Beyond: Two "Generations" of Comparative Research on the Welfare State.' *Comparative Social Research* 6: 315–51.

– 1992. 'The Resurgence of Labour Quiescence.' In *The Future of Labour Movements,* ed. Mario Regini. London: Sage.

Sainsbury, Diane. 1994. 'Women's and Men's Social Rights: Gendering Dimensions of Welfare States.' In *Gendering Welfare States,* ed. Diane Sainsbury. London: Sage.

Schneider, Saundra K. 1982. 'The Sequential Development of Social Programs in Eighteen Welfare States.' *Comparative Social Research* 5: 195–219.

Skocpol, Theda. 1992. *Protecting Soldiers and Mothers: The Political Origins of Social Policy in the United States.* Cambridge, MA: Belknap.

Skocpol, Theda, and Edwin Amenta. 1986. 'States and Social Policies.' *Annual Review of Sociology* 12: 131–57.

Smeeding, Timothy M. 1991. 'Cross-National Comparisons of Inequality and Poverty Position.' In *Economic Inequality and Poverty: International Perspectives,* ed. Lars Osberg. Armonk: M.E. Sharpe.

Steinmo, Sven, Kathleen Thelen, and Frank Longstreth, eds. 1992. *Structuring Politics: Historical Institutionalism in Comparative Perspective.* Cambridge: Cambridge University Press.

Stephens, John. 1980. *The Transition from Capitalism to Socialism.* Atlantic Highlands, NJ: Humanities.

Sundström, Marianne. 1991. 'Sweden: Supporting Work, Family and Gender Equality.' In *Child Care, Parental Leave and the Under 3's: Policy Innovation in Europe,* ed. Sheila Kamerman and Alfred J. Kahn. Westport, CT: Auburn House.

Therborn, Göran. 1986. *Why Some Peoples Are More Unemployed Than Others.* London: Verso.

Titmuss, Richard M. 1958. *Essays on the Welfare State.* London: Allen and Unwin.

− 1974. *Social Policy: An Introduction.* London: Allen and Unwin.

Tomasson, Richard F. 1970. *Sweden: Prototype of Modern Society.* New York: Random House.

Uusitalo, Hannu. 1984. 'Comparative Research on the Determinants of the Welfare State.' *European Journal of Political Research* 12: 403–22.

Weinstein, James. 1968. *The Corporate Ideal in the Liberal State, 1900–1918.* Boston: Beacon.

Weir, Margaret, Ann Orloff, and Theda Skocpol. 1988. *The Politics of Social Policy in the United States.* London: Allen and Unwin.

Wilensky, Harold L. 1975. *The Welfare State and Equality.* Berkeley: University of California Press.

− 1976. *The 'New Corporatism,' Centralization and the Welfare State.* London: Sage.

Wilensky, Harold L., and Charles N. Lebeaux. 1965. *Industrial Society and Social Welfare.* New York: The Free Press.

Williams, Fiona. 1989. *Social Policy: A Critical Introduction: Issues of Race, Gender and Class.* Cambridge: Polity.

− 1995. 'Race/Ethnicity, Gender, and Class in Welfare States: A Framework for Comparative Analysis.' *Social Politics: International Studies in Gender, State and Society* 2/2: 127–59.

Wilson, Elizabeth. 1977. *Women and the Welfare State.* London: Tavistock.

PART I
THE POWER RESOURCES PERSPECTIVE:
LABOUR STRENGTH AND WELFARE REGIMES

1

Power Resources Approach vs Action and Conflict: On Causal and Intentional Explanations in the Study of Power

WALTER KORPI

One of the most controversial concepts in social sciences is power. Among social scientists we find diametrically opposed views – explicit or implicit – on its relevance, nature, and distribution. While many economists as well as other social scientists exclude differences in power from their areas of study, throughout the centuries others have made power the fulcrum for the understanding of their societies. Antithetical views on the nature of power underlie the 'consensus' and 'conflict' models of society, which compete in several disciplines. A fundamental issue in the social sciences today is to what extent the free-enterprise or capitalist democracies are to be understood as systems of powers in balance or as hierarchies of power. The controversy over the role of power is perhaps most clearly evident in relation to the classical questions about the causes of inequalities in the distribution of man's worldly goods. The predicament of social scientists – that they are themselves actors in the systems which they attempt to explain and thus likely to become victims of different types of biases in their work – finds one of its clearest expressions in the debate on power.

In spite of its highly controversial subject matter, the power debate has been rather muted in recent years. The many contradictory views have reached a rather uneasy co-existence, largely based on ignorance of or contempt for the standpoints of others. The great controversy in the 1950s and 1960s between 'pluralists' and 'elitists' on the conceptualization of and methods for the study of power petered out without having been resolved in any clearcut way. Although often prefatory and incomplete in its formulations, the pluralist–elitist debate raised issues which remain central for the understanding of power. These issues have been sharpened by later 'neo-elitist' and 'three-dimensional' critics of the pluralist positions.

In my view a crucial limitation in the approaches of the pluralists as well as of their neo-elitist and three-dimensional critics is the focus on the exercise of power. The effort to focus on observable behavior reflects a strong reliance on the causal mode of explanation in the analysis of power. In this area, however, causal analysis must be supplemented by the mode of analysis unique to the social sciences: intentional explanation, in which the desires and beliefs of actors are taken into account and action is seen as rational and directed to bring about some goal.

By now the writings on power constitute a vast and highly heterogeneous literature characterized by considerable conceptual confusion. The purpose of this essay is to attempt to clarify some of the conceptual issues in this area and to indicate how the controversies between the pluralists and their later critics can be analyzed and understood in terms of an alternative approach to the study of power, one which takes its starting-point in power resources, or the bases of power, rather than in the exercise of power. Such a power resources perspective invites us to supplement the prevailing causal approach to the study of power with an explicitly intentional mode of explanation, the power resources approach clarifies some of the complex relationships between power and conflict. It facilitates the analysis of the role of power in the context of exchange, an area from which power as well as differences in power often are excluded. This approach also sheds light on the role of social structure in transmitting the consequences of power. It provides a conceptual basis for the rational explanation of the indirect and disguised consequences of power, which the critics of the pluralist approach have drawn attention to but which they have been less successful in clarifying.

The Behavioral Tradition and Its Critics

Although the pluralist or behavioral[1] tradition includes quite different voices, the leitmotif in this body of thought has been the programatic claim that the essence of power and its consequences are revealed and can be studied primarily in situations where power is actually exercised. 'Pluralists concentrate on the power exercise itself' (Polsby 1980: 119). In this approach power tends to be conceived of in terms of behavior more or less closely associated with manifest conflict, sometimes with the added restriction that the exercise of power involves only punishments (negative sanctions). This tradition has one of its intellectual roots in the well-known and often misinterpreted definition, erroneously ascribed to Weber (1947: 152), that power is 'the probability that one actor within a social relationship will be in a position to carry out his own will despite resistance.'[2] With its implication of action and conflict, Dahl's (1957: 202) 'intuitive notion' that 'A has power over B to the extent that he can get B to do something that B would not otherwise do' has been central to the behavioral tradition.[3]

Writers in the behavioral tradition have argued that the empirical study of power must focus on the analysis of concrete decision-making involving key issues rather than routine decisions (e.g., Dahl 1958; Merelman 1968; Rose 1967: 52–3). They have tended to claim that power is revealed primarily in conflicts related to the making of such decisions (e.g., Dahl 1958: 466; Merelman 1968: 457). A central tenet of the behaviorists has been that the identification of who prevails in decision-making 'seems the best way to determine which individuals and groups have "more" power in social life, because direct conflict between actors presents a situation most closely approximating an experimental test of their capacities to affect outcomes' (Polsby 1980: 4). However, some of them have recognized that power can also be exercised in situations without overt conflict (e.g., Wolfinger 1971: 1102; Polsby 1980: 192–3, 217).

In its program but not always in its practice, the behavioral approach thus limited itself to a traditional causal mode of explanation, where the exercise of power via participation in decision-making constituted the observable explanans. The association of power with manifest conflict presented unambiguous evidence for the counterfactual argument of conflicting interests and made it possible for the behaviorists to lean back on the old dictum that each man is the best judge of his own interests. The phenomena that were subjected to study in the behavioral approach were unquestionably manifestations of power. However, as C.J. Friedrich (1963: 203) has noted, it is often the case that 'power hides.' The troubling question which its critics came to raise was if these phenomena in fact included the major consequences of power or if they perhaps only constituted the visible part of the iceberg of power.

The behavioral approach thus came under attack for concentrating itself on observable participation in decision-making. The critics – labelled elitist or neo-elitists by defenders of the behavioral tradition – wanted to extend the focus of study to include activities which precede actual decision-making. As is well known, they introduced the concepts 'non-issues' and 'non-decision-making' to refer to such processes neglected in the behavioral tradition. However, these critics remained close to the behavioral tradition in conceptualizing power as behavior tied to manifest conflict (Bachrach and Baratz 1962, 1963, 1970; cf also Frey 1971).[4] The neo-elitist approach thus largely remained limited to the causal mode of explanation, while extending the explanans – the exercise of power – to include also less easily observable behavior.

In a significant contribution to the study of power, Lukes (1974) criticized both the behavioral and neo-elitist conceptualizations, labelling the former as a 'one-dimensional' and the latter as a 'two-dimensional' view of power. In his own 'three-dimensional' perspective on power, Lukes went beyond the two-dimensional view primarily by explicitly assuming that power need not be connected with manifest conflicts. Instead, he associated power with the presence of conflicts of interest, i.e., latent conflicts, which he defined as 'a contradiction between the interests of those exercising power and the *real interests* of those they exclude' (Lukes 1974: 24–5).[5]

Also Lukes, however, remained confined to the view that power must be studied in and through its exercise. In fact, Lukes (1974: 27) recognized that all these 'three views ... can be seen as alternative interpretations and applications of one and the same underlying concept of power, according to which *A exercises power over B when A affects B* in a manner contrary to B's interests' (italics mine). Like the 'two-dimensional' critics of the pluralist position, Lukes also largely retained the causal mode of explanation and attempted to extend the definition of the explanation – the exercise of power. Thus he elaborated on the concept 'non-decisions' and 'non-issues' by including in the exercise of power inaction as well as action, and unconscious as well as conscious exercises of power (Lukes 1974: 39–42 and 50–5). In the resulting cross-classification based on the degree of action and the degree of consciousness we can thus potentially discern ways of exercising power which involve unconscious action as well as unconscious inaction, concepts which are unlikely to appear inviting to empirically inclined social scientists.

While the 'two- and three-dimensional' critics of the behavioral school have succeeded in drawing attention to the serious limitations in this approach, they have thus been less successful in conceptually clarifying the issues involved and in developing a theoretical base for alternatives to the approach which they have attacked. The above discussion indicates that it is necessary to escape from the confines of the behavioral approach through other routes than by extending the definition of the explanations – the exercise of power – into obscurity. Instead, we must supplement the causal mode of explanation in the study of power with intentional explanation, where we explicitly try to take account of the capacity of human beings for strategic action in the pursuit of goals. According to Elster (1983, chap. 3), an action by an individual is explained intentionally when we can specify the future state it was intended to bring about. An intentional actor chooses to act in ways which he believes will be means to his goal. What he regards as means towards the goal will, in turn, depend on his beliefs about the factual environment and its interrelations. Thus intentional explanation comes to involve 'a triadic relation between action, desire and belief' (Elster 1983: 70). The emergence of desires and beliefs can, in turn, be explained causally.

Intentional action is related to the future. The intentional actor is seen as making conscious choices, as attempting to take account of his environment in pursuing his goal, and as being capable of strategic behavior, also indirect strategies such as 'taking one step back' in order to be able to take 'two steps forward' at a later point in time. His environment includes other actors who can also be assumed to be intentional and rational. The intentional mode of explanation thus leads to an analysis of interdependent choices, an approach which is presently best formalized in game theory, where the decision of each is seen as dependent on the decisions of all.

The intentional mode of explanation of interdependent choices involves as key elements an actors' expectations about the actions of other actors as well as his expectations of the expectations of other actors. Each actor must try to foresee the decisions of other actors, knowing that they are trying to foresee his decision. In such situations of interdependence, the capacities for action as well as the expectations of actors can be assumed to depend on and to reflect their relative power resources. In the perspective of the making of interdependent choices, the distribution of power resources among actors is thus brought into the focus of interest. The intentional mode of explanation therefore suggests that we should reverse the behavioral approach and begin the study of power with power resources rather than with the exercise of power.[6] By starting the analysis with power resources and their characteristics, we can facilitate the understanding of the rational motives for the differing uses and consequences of power. The power resources approach outlined below provides a conceptual framework for the understanding of the relationships of power to conflict, exchange, and inequality. It enables us to incorporate in the same theoretical framework not only the exercise of power, but also its more indirect and hidden consequences, 'the other face' of power, and allows us to see familiar phenomena in a somewhat different light. To provide a background for the discussion of the implications which the view of power as a dispositional concept has in an intentional mode of analysis, we will now turn to a discussion of the diverse characteristics of different types of power resources.

Power Resources and Their Consequences

As indicated above, students of power have often made the distinction between power as a dispositional concept; i.e., as an ability or capacity, and power in use or the exercise of power (e.g., Blalock 1967: 110; Gamson 1968: chap. 5; cf. also Rogers 1974, Wrong 1978: chap. 1, and Benton, 1981). The view that power is primarily a capacity or an ability has old traditions. Thus more than three centuries ago Thomas Hobbes (1651, 1962: 72) defined the power of a man as 'his present means to obtain some future apparent good.' A century later, Adam Smith followed Hobbes in treating power as a capacity (Smith 1776, 1970: 134). In the first quarter of the 19th century James Mill (1816, 1939: 864–5) also defined power as a capacity: 'Power is a means to an end ... Power, in its most appropriate signification, therefore, means security for the conformity between the will of one man and the acts of other men ... There are two classes of [securities] by which the conformity between the will of one man and the acts of other men may be accomplished. The one is pleasure, the other pain.'

To delimit the concept of power so that it does not become equated with all types of social causation, we will here define power resources as the attributes (capacities or means) of actors (individuals or collectivities) which enable them to reward or to punish other actors.[7] Since power is a relational concept, the attributes of actors become power resources only among two or more interdependent actors who have at least some interests in the attributes of the other actor.[8] From the power resources perspective, power is not a zero-sum concept. Power in use, or the exercise of power, can be defined in terms of the activation of power resources in relation to other actors. As will be discussed below, however, power resources can have important consequences even without being activated.

Power resources differ in terms of a multiplicity of dimensions. An aspect often considered significant in this context is the domain of a power resource, i.e., the number of actors who are receptive to rewards or punishments via this resource. Another is its scope; i.e., the range of activities of other actors that can be rewarded or punished via the resource. As noted above, power resources can also be classified according to whether they reward or punish other actors, that is, if the resource is an inducement or a pressure resource.[9]

The costs involved in using a power resource are crucial characteristics of power resources. Costs can be defined in terms of opportunity costs (Harsanvi 1962; Baldwin 1971b) and can result from two different sources: mobilization and application. Mobilization costs concern the relative ease with which a resource can be mobilized or made ready for use.[10] Thus, for instance, partly because of the 'free rider' problem, resources which require coordination or collective action by a large number of actors to become ready for use tend to be more costly to mobilize than resources which can put into use by a single actor or a small group of actors. Application costs derive from the actual use of a power resource. Application costs partly depend on whether it is possible for an actor to use promises or threats to attempt to affect others and if these commitments have to be redeemed.

Application costs depend to a significant extent on the orientations or attitudes held by those affected by the use of a power resource towards the actor using the resource. Etzioni (1961: 4–6) has suggested a classification of power resources from this latter point of view.[11] Coercive power resources which involve physical sanctions generate alienation among persons subject to them; i.e., a strongly negative attitude towards the actors using these resources. Renumerative power resources involving control over material rewards tend to create a calculative orientation; i.e., a mildly negative or positive attitude. Normative power resources, which involve the allocation or manipulation of symbolic rewards and deprivations, generate positive orientations among those subject to them. The costs involved in the application of power resources (e.g., in terms of the need to monitor activities of those subject to power) tend to be highest for coercive and lowest for normative power resources.

Some types of power resources can be described as basic in the sense that they in themselves provide the capacity to reward or to punish other actors. Through processes of conversion, from basic power resources actors can derive other power resources, which, however, ultimately depend on the basic power resources for their effectiveness. The distinction between basic and derived power resources is not easy to draw but appears fruitful. Thus, for instance, normative power resources can be assumed to be ultimately based on resources which provide the capability to apply coercive or renumerative sanctions.

Tentatively some additional aspects of power resources can be briefly suggested. Scarcity refers to the extent to which a resource is available. Centrality reflects the extent to which a resource is necessary for the daily life of other actors. Concentration potential indicates the extent to which a resource can be concentrated to one or a few actors. Storage potential refers to the extent to which a resource can be preserved over time. Liquidity refers to the degree to which a resource is ready to be used.

Although power resources refer to particular relations between actors in specific situations, some types of power resources will be much more significant than others. This is because they apply to relations and situations of many different kinds, or to a kind that is very common. For the following discussion we should note that, in Western societies, such major types of basic power resources include means of violence, property, and labor power.

In terms of the aforementioned dimensions, means of violence have a large domain, wide scope, and high concentration potential, as well as a relatively high convertibility. Although the legitimate use of violence is typically reserved for the state, resources for violence are not scarce. Their essential drawback is the high costs associated with their use.

Economists often use the concept of property to refer to a very heterogeneous array of power resources, including physical capital and 'human capital.' The differences in the characteristics of the different types of power resources subsumed under the concept of property provide starting points for an understanding of the nature of capitalist democracy. Physical capital in the form of control over the means of production is a very significant power resource with a large domain and a wide scope. It has high centrality, since it involves control over people's livelihood. Furthermore, it has a high concentration potential and involves relatively low application costs. Money is also a significant power resource with a large domain, high concentration potential, as well as high convertibility, liquidity, scarcity, and storage potential.[12] It has been necessary to restrict its wide scope; e.g., through laws against bribery.

'Human capital' (e.g., labor power, occupational skills, and education) clearly includes important power resources. In contrast to money and physical capital, however, human capital generally has a much smaller domain as well as a narrower scope. It cannot be concentrated to a very high degree, is often difficult to preserve over time, and is generally not a scarce resource. Furthermore, it has a relatively low convertibility, and its mobilization involves relatively high costs. Of particular significance in this context is the fact that human capital cannot be divested from its owner. It can thus not be sold, only rented.

The relative strength of the power resources of different actors can be tested in contests or manifest conflicts. In real life as well as in the social sciences, however, it is often difficult to evaluate the relative power positions of two contending actors in advance, since their power resources can differ not only quantitatively, but also qualitatively. The contending parties may also attempt to present more or less distorted pictures of their resources. Benton (1981: 177) hints that if actors 'A and B are assumed to utilize their capabilities and resources in whatever conflicts develop between them, then the outcome is predictable and unvarying.' Hindes (1982) is right in arguing against such a deterministic view and in underlining the importance of indeterminacy introduced by the arenas of struggle and the course of struggle itself. Thus the patterns of coalition formation that may develop in the course of such struggles are important for the outcome but difficult to predict. In real life situations a varying degree of uncertainty will therefore often surround the actors' estimation of the distribution of power resources as well as of likely outcomes of power contests. The relationship between the distribution of power resources as well as of likely outcomes of power contests. The relationship between the distribution of power resources and the outcome of conflicts must therefore be seen as a probabilistic one, where the degree of indeterminacy will covary negatively with the degree of difference in power resources between actors.

Traditional causal analysis leads us to focus on those consequences which result when power resources are activated or exercised. The intentional mode of explanation, however, sensitizes us additionally to other, more indirect but important consequences of power resources, consequences which reflect the diverse characteristics of power resources discussed above. We assume here that in the making of interdependent choices rational actors are likely to allow their own expectations, their expectations of the expectations and actions of others, as well as their evaluations of the different means available to themselves and to actors to be affected by their perceptions of the distribution of power resources among actors. Intentional actors are also likely to develop long term strategies and indirect strategies, designed to increase the effectiveness of their power resources. Intentional analysis of actors who control power resources can thus help to clarify the relationship of power to conflict and to exchange.

Power and Conflict

If manifest conflict often has been viewed as more or less closely associated with power, exchange, on the contrary, has frequently been regarded as the antithesis to power (e.g., Simon 1953; Homans 1961: 77–8; Blau 1964: 116–17; Eckstein 1973: 1161; Barry 1975: 92; Martin 1977: 42). Interaction based on exchange is thus seen as voluntary, balanced, and symmetrical, whereas interaction involving power is seen as enforced, imbalanced, and asymmetrical. However, Baldwin (1978) and Hernes (1975) have argued that there are important advantages in treating power as a kind of exchange.

These positions reflect conceptual unclarities and contribute to an underestimation of the role of power in social affairs. Power is involved in exchange as well as in conflict, but it is a concept on a different level from the latter ones. The use of power resources by actor A may generate a response by actor B, who also engages power resources. The resulting interaction can be described according to whether it involves rewards and/or pressure resources according to the four-fold table below.

Interaction where both parties activate pressure resources constitutes manifest conflict, whereas interaction involving the mutual use of rewards traditionally is called exchange. Interaction where one party activates pressure resources, but the other party reward resources, can be described as a type of exploitation.[13] Conflict, exchange, and exploitation are thus different types of interaction involving the use of power resources.

Because of its tendency to associate power with conflict, the behavioral approach makes it difficult to analyze the role of power in exchange and in other contexts where conflict is not manifest. While the two- and three-dimensional critics of the behavioral tradition have asserted that this leads to an underestimation of the role of power in social life, they have not provided a satisfactory theoretical account of why this is the case. The intentional mode of explanation indicates that this underestimation arises because in the making of interdependent choices, the dis-

		Type of power used by B	
		Reward	Pressure
Type of power resource used by A	Reward	Exchange	Exploitation
	Pressure	Exploitation	Conflict

tribution of power resources influences the extent to which rational actors will allow conflicts of interests between them to generate manifest conflicts, i.e., interaction where both parties activate pressure resources. The difference in power resources affects the evaluation of the means available to the actors as well as their expectations about the actions of the other party, and a rational actor will take this difference into consideration before he activates his pressure resources (Korpi 1974).[14]

The probability that an actor will activate pressure resources can be seen as a multiplicative function of his expectancy of success and of his motivation for (or the subjective utility of) reaching the goal. Both these factors are likely to be affected by the perceived deference in power resources between actors. The probability of success which an actor estimates that the use of pressure resources will have can thus be expected to decline with an increasing disadvantage in power resources between the actor and his adversary. The perceived difference in power resources will, however, affect also the motivation of the weaker actor for reaching the goal. This effect is produced along two different routes. Firstly, the costs associated with reaching the goal will depend on the difference in power resources. The greater an actor's disadvantage in power resources, the greater is the probability that the adversary will oppose his action, something which increases his estimated costs for reaching the goal and decreases his 'net' reward. Secondly, at least in the long run, the distribution of power resources will affect the level of aspiration of an actor and thereby also the degree of relative deprivation he experiences in relation to another actor. Thus the greater the difference in power resources between two actors, the lower is also the motivation of the weaker actor to exercise pressure resources in relation to the stronger one.

The intentional mode of explanation thus indicates that, where the difference in power resources between two interdependent actors is great, the weaker actor is unlikely to exercise pressure resources. The stronger actor, however, is likely to use pressure resources, if necessary, to reach his goal. But since manifest conflict requires that both actors use pressure resources, between actors with great power disparities conflicts of interest are relatively unlikely to turn into overt conflicts. In such situations, the weaker actor may not reveal his preferences and various forms of 'non-decision-making' and exploitation are likely to occur. Where the difference in power resources between two actors is relatively small, however, the probability of success and the motivation of the weaker party are higher, something which increases the probability of overt conflicts. The power resource approach thus indicates that, since the probability

of manifest conflicts decreases with increasing differences in power resources between actors, to focus the study of power on situations
involving manifest conflicts considerably increases the likelihood of
discovering 'pluralist' power structures.[15] The face validity which the behavioral approach acquires through its tendency to associate power with
conflict therefore exacts the price of potential bias in results.

Power, Exchange, and Inequality

While the debate between the pluralists and their two- and three-dimensional critics totally has bypassed the role of power in exchange, the power
resources approach invites to an analysis of this area, which remains one
of the most confounded in power theory. Since exchange forms the very
base of economic life in the free-market or capitalist democracies, it is a
crucial area for the understanding of the role of power in, and thus the
nature of, these societies.

The opposition of power to exchange is generally based on the unwarranted exclusion of inducement resources from the definition of power.
Exchange situations involving the mutual use of inducement resources
can be regarded as cases of 'positive sum' conflicts. The parties have a
common interest in reaching an agreement; i.e., they can both derive
what we heuristically can call utility from the exchange relationship, but
they have opposed interests in setting the terms for the exchange.

Among the social sciences, economics is the discipline which has spe-
cialized in the analysis of exchange relationships. The basic theoretical
tool for the analysis of exchange in the presently dominant neo-classical
school of economics is the model of perfect competition. One of the
crucial assumptions in this model is that all actors on the market are
price takers; i.e., each actor is so small in relation to the market that it
cannot affect market prices. Thus, in effect, significant differences in
power resources between actors are defined out of the model of perfect
competition. Although the theories of monopoly, oligopoly, and monop-
sony provide models for analyzing exchange relationships where the power
resources of the parties are unequal, it would appear that the views of
neo-classical economists on the functioning of markets in Western societies are often premised on the model of perfect competition (Morgenstern
1972).[16] This tendency contributes to the assumption especially widespread among neo-classical economists that capitalist democracies are
based on a balance of powers.

For example, Milton Friedman takes the primitive market as the fulcrum for his analysis of the functioning of markets in Western societies which he contrasts with the functioning of politics. In the simplest form, a society consists of independent households, where each household retains the alternative of producing for itself rather than entering into exchange with other households. 'Since the household always has the alternative of producing directly for itself, it need not enter into any exchange unless it benefits from it. Here, no exchange will take place unless both parties do benefit from it. Cooperation is thereby achieved without coercion ... As in that simple model, so in the complex enterprise and money-exchange economy, co-operation is strictly individual and voluntary *provided:* (a) that enterprises are private, so that the ultimate contracting parties are individuals and (b) that individuals are effectively free to enter or not to enter into any particular exchange relationship, so that every transaction is strictly voluntary' (Friedman 1962: 13–14). Although his arguments are partly circular, Friedman tacitly assumes that in Western societies market exchange tends to be voluntary as well as mutually satisfying and benefitting to both parties. Politics, on the contrary, he sees as involving coercion and concentration of power.

In neo-classical economics, theories of the firm are also often premised on the assumption of perfect competition and thus on the absence of differences in power in the relationship between sellers and buyers of labor power. Thus in developing the contractual theory of the firm, widely accepted among economists, Alchian and Demsetz (1972: 777) write: 'The firm ... has no power of fiat, no authority, no disciplinary action any different in the slightest degree from ordinary market contracting between any two people ... What then is the content of the presumed power to manage and assign workers to various tasks? Exactly the same as one little consumer's power to manage and assign his grocer to various tasks. The single consumer can assign his grocer to the task of obtaining whatever the customer can induce the grocer to provide at a price acceptable to both parties. That is precisely all that an employer can do to an employee. To speak of managing, directing, or assigning workers to various tasks is a deceptive way of noting that the employer continually is involved in renegotiation of contracts on terms that must be acceptable to both parties.'

The power resources approach indicates that the widespread views among neo-classical economists that exchange on markets and in firms in the Western nations is voluntary, equal, and equitable is valid only in special cases. Standard sociological theory indicates that, in analyzing exchange between two actors, A and B, we can compare the outcome or utility which an actor receives from this exchange with the utility he can receive in his best alternative exchange relationship and with his level of aspiration with respect to utility. Actor A will not continue an exchange with actor B unless A's utility in this exchange relationship is equal to or greater than the utility he can receive in his next-best exchange alternative. The difference between A's utility here and the utility which he can receive in his next-best exchange option indicates his degree of dependence on this particular exchange relationship, or B's power over A in this relationship. The extent to which an actor is satisfied or dissatisfied depends on the difference between his level of aspiration and the utility which he receives. Because of the lack of better alternatives, an actor can thus be obliged to continue an exchange which he finds dissatisfying.

A situation of perfect competition, by definition, implies that both actors will have many and about equally good exchange alternatives. In perfect competition the dependence of both actors on a particular exchange relationship is therefore small and of about the same size. Here exchange can be assumed to be voluntary and of about equal benefit to both parties and to reveal the preferences of the actors.

But in exchange situations where the parties have different power resources, the exchange process is likely to work out quite differently. Here it is important to view exchange as a process over time involving bargaining. In a situation where actor A is much less dependent on this particular exchange relationship that is actor B, actor A is likely to initiate a bargaining process by which he can decrease the utility of actor B until both became equally dependent on their mutual exchange relationship. Because of his lack of better exchange options, actor B will continue the exchange despite the fact that he is likely to be dissatisfied with the decreasing returns.[17] It is not meaningful to describe actor B's deliberate choice between the lesser of two evils as voluntary. Unlike the standard mode of neo-classical economic analysis, the power resources approach thus leads to the hypothesis of 'the Matthew effect' in exchange: to him that hath shall be given.

The crucial question raised by the foregoing discussion is whether it is fruitful to assume that markets in Western societies tend to be characterized by perfect competition in the sense that actors cannot affect their terms of exchange. Of central relevance in this context is the labor market. The classical writers had a much less idyllic view on these matters than their neo-classical followers. Thus when discussing the setting of wages, Adam Smith (1776, 1970: 169) observed: 'The workmen desire to get as much, the masters to give as little as possible. The former are disposed to combine in order to raise, the latter in order to lower the wages of labour. It is not, however, difficult to foresee which of the two parties must, upon all ordinary occasions, have the advantage in the dispute, and forces the other into a compliance with their terms ... In all such disputes, the masters can hold out much longer.'

The institutional structures of Western societies have, of course, changed much since the days of Adam Smith. But is the power relationship between the employer and the employee equivalent to that between the customer and his grocer, something which many neo-classical economists as well as others maintain? A significant fact which speaks this interpretation is that, in the Western societies, labor law expresses and institutionalizes a disadvantage in power resources of the employees by recognizing and supporting, through state power, the basic managerial prerogatives of hiring and firing and the employers' right to issue orders to employees during working time as well as the employees' duty to obey these orders. Thus in the situation where labor and capital are most directly confronted in the capitalist democracies – the place of work – labor is clearly accorded a subordinate role. No similar or parallel legal rights support the customer's relationship to the grocer.

When it comes to views and assumptions concerning the power relationship between employers and employees in the Western nations, what is a self-evident axiom for one social scientist can be a value-distorted misrepresentation for another. A focus on the nature of the power resources available to business interests and to wage earners can provide a basis for an evaluation of the potential fruitfulness of the differing assumptions. In view of the differences between the characteristics of capital and 'human capital' as power resources, it would appear to be a fruitful hypothesis that, in capitalist democracies, business interests and employers generally have greater power resources than employees. Differences in the initial distribution of power resources can also be assumed to affect the degree of inequality generated through exchange.[18]

Indirect Strategies and Power Resource Investments

When power resources are mobilized and exercised, some part of them are consumed in the process and the use of power resources always involves opportunity costs. The continuous *ad hoc* engagement of resources in repeated controversies related to decision-making also involves high costs for the maintenance of liquidity of resources. Furthermore, the application of pressure resources can increase uncertainty and the potential for uncontrollable change. The power resources approach thus indicates that prudent managers of power resources have strong incentives to avoid the exercise of power, which constitutes the very explanans in the causal analysis of power and which has been in the focus of attention in the behavioral tradition of power studies. There are especially high premiums attached to avoiding uses of power resources which are likely to elicit controversies, the most favored object of behavioral power studies. In this context intentional analysis of the relative advantages of the courses of action available to rational managers of power resources opens up ways for the understanding of phenomena related to indirect consequences of power and to 'the other face' of power. In the following we will focus on the ways in which rational managers of power resources are likely to attempt to decrease their costs by trying to find strategies for the generalized and routine handling of decision-making and potential controversies.

The indirect strategies for an economical management of power resources involve processes which we can refer to as investments of power resources; i.e., present sacrifices through the conversion of resources in ways which can increase future benefits. At least four major forms of such investment processes can be discerned: development of channels for the mobilization of power resources, creation of institutions for decision-making and conflict regulation, conversion of power resources from more costly to less costly types, and the fostering of anticipated reactions. An analysis of such investment processes can thus give rational explanations of the 'hidden' consequences of power, parts of which the critics of the behavioral approach have attempted to include in the explanans of causal explanation under such headings as 'non-issues,' 'non-decision-making,' and 'inactive or unconscious exercises of power.'

Mobilization Channels

Investments intended to develop routines and institutions to facilitate the mobilization of power resources can decrease the costs of mobilization and augment the effectiveness of power resources by increasing their liquidity. The creation of organizations – in Schattschneider's (1960) term 'the mobilization of bias' – is perhaps the single most important type of investment of this type. The capacity to act collectively tends to increase the effectiveness of most power resources. The growth of 'juristic persons' and corporate actors throughout the past centuries (cf.

Coleman 1974: chap. 1) can be seen as a reflection of this fact. However, organizations play especially important roles in facilitating the mobilization of power resources which require collective action to be of major importance, such as the mobilization of 'human capital' through union organizations and of numbers through political parties.

Institutionalization of Power

Through processes of investment, power resources can be used to structure the conditions and the situations in which action and decision-making take place as well as to create institutional structures for decision-making and conflict resolution.[19] By determining the context and conditions as well as the methods, principles, and structures *for* decision-making, power resources can have major consequences without being directly or continuously exercised in decision-making. Differing views on the role of power are found in the prevailing theoretical approaches to the existence, origin, and role of societal institutions such as the state, political democracy, collective bargaining, and the welfare state.

The presently most influential type of model in the social sciences, the celebrated general equilibrium models of the Arrow-Debreu variety in neo-classical economics, define out the very existence of societal institutions such as the state. The only institution we find in the world re-created in these models is the perfect or competitive market, but there is no state, no money, no interest organizations. The absence of societal institutions in the general equilibrium models of the economy is the ultimate consequence of the model's disregard for differences in power resources between actors.

In sociology and political science, the functionalist perspective on societal institutions is presently represented in two different versions. Thus the structural functionalists tend to regard institutions such as the state as originating in the needs of the whole society and as serving the interests of different groups in relatively unbiased ways (e.g., Kerr et al. 1973; Parsons 1966). Those who have made a structuralist or functionalist interpretation of Marx tend to view the state as originating in and as serving the needs of the economically dominant class – in the capitalist societies, the bourgeoisie (e.g., Althusser 1971; Poulanzas 1978). According to Elster (1982: 460), in 'Marxist social science proper, we find that functionalism is rampant.'[20]

The power resources approach, however, leads us to view societal institutions largely as the residues of previous activations of power resources, often in the context of manifest conflicts which for the time being have been settled through various types of compromises. The development of institutions, bureaucracies, structures, and rules for the making of decisions and for the distribution of rewards and punishments can limit the need to continuously activate power resources.[21] In comparison with an unregulated situation, these various forms for the 'creation of order' can give some benefits to both parties, at least in the short run, by decreasing uncertainty and the costs of mobilizing and activating power resources as well as the costs of keeping resources liquid. However, the benefits of order can be unequally distributed. My hypothesis is that the distribution of power resources between the parties may thus have unequal gains from their operation. The conflictual background to such institutions and structures need not be manifest in their day-to-day operations.[22] The power resources approach thus resolves the actionist–structuralist dispute in power analysis by indicting that actors can invest power resources in structures and institutions which, in the long run, affect and constrain the behavior of others.

Of central importance of our interpretation of the consequences of the operation of institutional structures such as the state now becomes the question of the distribution of power resources and its stability in the capitalist democracies. In view of the importance which organizations for collective action can play for increasing the effectiveness of wage-earners' power resources in relation to those of business interests, it would therefore appear to be a fruitful hypothesis that the degree of the subordination of wage-earners can vary over time as well as between countries as a result of the extent to which employees are organized for collective action in unions and in political parties based on the working class. Variations in the difference in power resources between classes can be assumed to have significant consequences for distributive processes, levels of aspiration, and patterns of conflict, as well as for institutional structures and for the functioning of the state and of various state organs. In contrast to the pluralist perspective as well as to the functionalist interpretations of Marxism, which assume that the state in capitalist democracies is more or less a constant, and basically reflects either the interests of the plurality of pressure groups in society or the interests of the economically dominant class, the power resource approach leads to the hypothesis that the extent of bias in the functioning of the state can vary considerably as a reflection of the distribution of power resources in these societies and thus that politics can be expected to matter; e.g., for the distributive processes in society.

In this context the institution of political democracy, created in most countries as a residue of serious conflicts, is of particular significance. It limited the legitimate use of the means of violence in societal conflicts and based control over the government, in principle, on numbers rather than on economic resources. At the same time, it formed the basis for the gradually increasing tensions between markets and politics arising from the fact that unequally distributed power resources on the markets are confronted with – at least in principle – equally distributed power resources in politics.

In the recent debate on the origins of the welfare state, some 'pluralist' writers have claimed that the rise of the welfare state primarily reflects the needs of the citizens generated by demographic changes as well as the increasing resources of industrializing societies (e.g., Wilensky 1975), whereas some neo-Marxist writers have tended to see the welfare state as arising from the needs of capital to stabilize its positions (e.g., Ginsburg 1979). Both views assume that party politics and parliamentary conflicts have played insignificant roles in this context. The power resources approach, however, leads us to expect that the welfare state in its modern version reflects the distribution of power between the contending classes or collectivities and that its development is significantly affected by the extent to which power based on universal and equal suffrage has made inroads into the power resources on the markets.[23]

Conversion and Consciousness

One of the classical issues in the debate on power concerns the potential role of ideologies and preferences as potential mediators of power. These issues are often considered under such labels as 'false consciousness' and 'real interests.' In the intentional mode of explanation, this problem emerges in questions concerning the factors affecting motivational structures and beliefs concerning the actor's environment. Elster (1983: 84–5) argues that, in the social sciences, causal analysis is the proper mode of explanation of variations in motives and beliefs. In spite of its reliance on causal analysis, the behavioral tradition has confronted major problems in recognizing the role of power in the formation of the social consciousness of citizens, including levels of aspirations, norms of fairness, values, and ideologies.[24] Writers in this tradition have sometimes dismissed the question of 'false consciousness' as 'a label for popular opinion that does not follow leftist prescriptions and a shorthand of saying that 'the people do not know what is good for them' (Wolfinger 1971: 1066). Although they have admitted the existence especially of historical cases of 'false consciousness' where the 'real interests' of large groups of citizens were not articulated, the analysis of the role of ideologies and beliefs in the context of power cannot be easily incorporated into the behavioral approach to the study of power.[25]

The power resources approach invites us to apply the intentional mode of explanation in analyzing the rational considerations of managers of power resources, which can lead them to use indirect strategies involving attempts to affect ideologies, motives, and beliefs of other actors. Because different types of power resources are associated with differing costs, rational managers of power resources have strong incentives to invest in the conversion of high-cost power resources into low-cost ones. Since normative power resources generally have the lowest costs, we can expect much investment efforts to be directed to the conversion of coercive and renumerative power resources into normative resources. To put it in Weberian terms (Weber 1922, 1980: 12), one can say that such a conversion of power resources changes the basis and orientation of action from the rational weighting of the relative utilities of alternative courses of action (*Zweckrationalität*) to the pursuit of an internalized value (*Wertrationalität*), an activity which largely constitutes its own reward. Attempts to develop and to spread ideologies and to cultivate legitimacy can be regarded as conversion techniques for decreasing the costs of power. Contrary to Dahrendorf (1968: 26), the power resources perspective indicates that, among actors with conflicting interests, power has to be understood as anterior to social norms.

It must be remembered, however, that the creation of ideologies serves similar purposes also in broadly based collective action. By defining rational action narrowly in terms of individual and material benefits, economists have found it very difficult to find rational explanations to ubiquitous actions for a public good; e.g., voting and joining a union. From this starting-point, collective action for a public good is seen as inhibited because of the 'free rider' problem (Olson 1965). By creating internalized values, the development of ideologies in social movements can help to overcome the free-rider problem and form the bases for *wertrational* collective action.

Anticipated Reactions

Friedrich (1963: 203) noted that 'the inclination of all persons exposed to influence to anticipate the reactions of him who has power to issue commands, bestow benefits, offer advantages of all sorts, constitutes a general rule in politics.' This well-known 'rule of anticipated reactions' draws attention to large areas where power resources have consequences without being activated or exercised. The focus on conflict and participation in decision-making in the behavioral tradition has tended to divert attention away from anticipated reactions.[26]

The difficulties which the behavioral approach creates for the recognition of consequences of power which are not associated with the exercise of power are illustrated by Nelson W. Polsby (1980) in his discussion of Crenson' study of the potential role of steel companies in inhibiting citizens' protests against air pollution in middle-sized American cities (Crenson 1971). On the same page where Polsby argues that pluralists do not neglect anticipated reactions, he maintains that, in the absence of evidence that the steel company had actively suppressed community protests against air pollution, the lack of such protests can be interpreted as reflecting a 'genuine consensus' based on a conscious trade-off by the citizens of air pollution against employment (Polsby 1980: 217). Polsby does not appear to recognize the possibility that this very trade-off could be a consequence of citizens' awareness of the power resources of the steel company, which may be seen as able to move its production without serious costs to communities where pollution is accepted.

Anticipated reactions are also difficult to incorporate in the neo-elitist approach, with its continued focus on the exercise of power. While in the 'three-dimensional' approach anticipated reactions perhaps can be taken as examples of the 'unconscious or inactive' exercise of power, this way of conceptualizing the phenomenon becomes unnecessarily awkward.

The power resources approach indicates that the fostering of anticipated reactions can be seen as an important strategy of investments to increase the economical use of power resources. One area of significance in this context is the credibility of threats of punishment. If threats are effective, the costs associated with the use of pressure resources can be considerably decreased. Therefore, managers of power resources have incentives to invest resources to increase the credibility of threats; e.g., by the staging and setting of examples and through attempts to bind themselves to the carrying out of threats if necessary.[27] The idea of general deterrence in legal thought is based on the strengthening of anticipated reactions.

Summary and Conclusions

While especially neo-classical economists typically define away differences in power resources from their analyses of Western democracies, the behavioral paradigm started in the observation that in these societies 'knowledge, wealth, social position, access to officials, and other resources are unequally distributed' (Dahl 1961: 1) and asked the question: who then actually governs? The answer of the pluralists was that, in spite of these seemingly unfavorable initial positions, something approximating a pluralist democracy can exist if resources are spread at least to some extent. Their argument 'entails not perfect equality of resources and not that everyone or every group has some resources but only that political resources not be monopolized by one group or closely held by a few' (Polsby 1980: 195). The conclusion was thus that the differences in power resources presently existing in the Western societies did not have very significant consequences for functioning of pluralist democracy. The pluralists arrived at this conclusion through the proven methods of causal analysis and relied on empirical research having a high face validity.

If the pluralists are guilty of rushing too hastily to their conclusions, it is not as much a result of sins of commission as of sins of omission.[28] I can agree with the pluralists that, in the Western democracies, power resources, and especially political power resources, are not literally monopolized by any one group, but are instead less unequally distributed than in any other type of past or present complex society. Yet we must ask if the research methodology relied upon in the behavioral approach can adequately account for the consequences of the inequalities of power resources still remaining in these societies.

The conclusion of this paper is that the existing inequalities in the distribution of power resources in Western democracies are great enough to be of crucial importance for the functioning of these societies. Furthermore, the differences in the degree of inequality in the distribution of power resources between countries and between time periods provide a fruitful base for the understanding of variations among the western democracies.[29] To be able to appreciate the consequences of the distribution of power resources, we must complement traditional causal analysis with the intentional mode of explanation. In interdependent decision-making the distribution of power resources among rational actors is likely to be crucial for their choice of strategies. Since power resources provide the *sine qua non* for the consequences of power, by starting the analysis from the perspective of power resources we are in a strategically good position to chart the diverse types of consequences of power.

In combination with the intentional mode of explanation, the power resource approach outlined here provides conceptual tools for incorporating into the same theoretical framework not only the direct exercise of power resources focused upon in the behavioral tradition, but also the more disguised consequences of power which the critics of the pluralist approach have tried to handle by inflating their major explanans – the concept of the exercise of power. The power resources approach enables us to see familiar aspects of power in a partly new light. It explains why a focus on behavior and conflictual issues in the study of power is likely to introduce a systematic bias into the results in favor of the discovery of 'pluralist' power structures. The widespread opposition of power to exchange has not only disguised the relationships between power and exchange but has also been very important for the current underestimation of the role of power; e.g., in market relationships.

Phenomena which the critics of the behavioral approach have labelled 'the other face' of power, and inactive or unconscious uses of power, can be incorporated into the power resource approach as indirect strategies for the rational deployment of power resources. The intentional mode of explanation indicates that because of the costs involved in the exercise of power, thrifty managers of power resources have rational motives for avoiding the very explanans central in the behavioral tradition; i.e., participation in non-routine decision-making related to controversial issues. Power resources managers are instead likely to develop indirect strategies for the more efficient long-run use of their resources, strategies involving the investment of power resources. The intentional mode of explanation makes it possible to analyze the rational background to such investments and the less readily visible consequences of power. Important among the different forms the investments of power resources may take are the development of channels or organizations for the mobilization of power resources, the creation of institutions for decision-making and conflict resolution, the conversion of high-cost resources into low-cost ones, and the fostering of anticipated reactions.

The power resources approach indicates that the distribution of power resources between collectivities or classes and the changes in this distribution are of crucial importance for societal processes and for social change. In capitalist democracies capital and 'human capital' form the major types of basic power resources. Because of differences in the characteristics of their power resources, a fruitful hypothesis is that, in comparison with employers and business interests, wage-earners are generally at a disadvantage with respect to power resources, but that, through their capacity for collective action, the extent of their disadvantage can vary over time as well as between countries. These hypotheses are contrary to pluralist as well to functionalist Marxian assumptions.

Like several other concepts in the social sciences, the interpretation of the concept of power is closely associated with the moral and political values of the social scientist. This connection has stimulated an interesting philosophical debate on whether or not power is an 'essentially contested' concept (e.g., Lukes 1979; Bloch et al. 1979; Smith 1980). In practice, however, the study of power is severely hampered also by the disciplinary and intellectual separation between scholars who work with more or less sharply opposed assumptions about power and its distribution in the Western nations. If judged by their views and beliefs about power, the different communities of social scientists in the Western democracies often appear to be studying and living in disparate worlds. By its focus on empirically observable power resources and on the clarification of strategies generated by rational motives to use power resources efficiently, the power resources approach can provide an arena for a fruitful debate among social scientists and may contribute to the narrowing of the area of disagreement over power.

A focus on the distribution of power resources also invites and encourages a comparative approach in the empirical study of power. We may never agree on what the 'real' interests of people are, but we can compare similar persons in situations where their relative power resources differ significantly. The empirical comparison of the conditions, consciousness, and actions of similar persons in differing power resource contexts can provide fruitful avenues for furthering the study of power.

Notes

This paper is part of a comparative study of the development of social policies and welfare states in eighteen OECD countries during the period 1930–80. The project is supported by the Swedish Delegation for Social Research, the Bank of Sweden Tercentennial Foundation and the German Marshall Fund of the United States. I wish to thank all those (including an anonymous referee) who have provided valuable comments on the paper in its different incarnations.

1 As Frey (1971: 1081) notes the labels 'elitist' and 'pluralist' used in the debate carry heavy evaluative overtones. Mills' 1956 study, *The Power Elite*, appears to have influenced the choice of labels. This is somewhat ironic since Mills' formal definition of power is quite pluralist and is phrased in terms of participation in decision-making (Mills 1963: 23).

2 In *Wirtschaft und Gesellschaft*, Weber (1922, 1980: 28) defined power (*Macht*)
    in the following way: 'Macht bedeutet jede Chance, innerhalb einer sozialen
    Beziehung den eigenen Willen *auch* [my italics] gegen Widerstreben
    durchzusetzen, gleichveil worauf diese Chance beruht.' Weber's definition
    of power does thus not see manifest conflict in terms of the undoing of resis-
    tance as a *necessary* condition for the exercise of power. The word *auch*
    (even) also appears in Weber's similar definition of power on p. 531 in the
    same book. Wrong (1979: 262) is therefore wrong in making Weber himself
    potentially responsible for the lack of this word in translations that have
    been available in English. This responsibility rests with the translators. Since
    Weber defined power in terms of the *probability* of actors' realizing their will,
    his definition is a dispositional rather than a behavioral one. This becomes
    clear in his comments (in which I substitute my own translation in place of
    Henderson and Parsons' erroneous one): 'The concept of "power" is socio-
    logically amorphous. All conceivable qualities of a man and all conceivable
    constellations can put someone in the position to carry out his own will in a
    given situation.' (In this context it can be noted that Henderson and
    Parsons translate 'amorf' as 'highly comprehensive.')

3 Through its stress on conflict in combination with actual rather than poten-
    tial exercise of power, also Wolfinger's (1971: 1079) statement that 'power
    is a relationship in which A gets B to do something that B would not other-
    wise do' gives an indication of how power has tended to be viewed in this
    approach. Definitions of power in similar terms also include Lasswell and
    Kaplan 1950: 75–6; Deutsch 1963: 111; Blau 1964: 117; Bierstedt 1950;
    Kahn 1964; and Polsby 1980: 4.

4 The behavioral perspective with a focus on the exercise of power was thus
    retained in the view that a 'non-decision' is 'a decision that results in sup-
    pression and thwarting of a latent or manifest challenge to the values or
    interests of the decision maker,' while the tie to manifest conflict reappeared
    through the assumption that non-decisions can occur only in situations
    where grievances, conflicts, or power struggles are present (Bachrach and
    Baratz 1970: 44, 46, 49–50). Critical treatments of the behavioral tradition
    include Barry 1975 and Nagel 1975. Alford and Friedland (1975) criticize
    also the 'neo-elitist' approach in the study of power in ways which resemble
    the criticism presented here.

5 By defining conflicts of interests in terms of 'real' interests, Lukes 'maintains
    that men's wants may themselves be a product of a system which works
    against their interests, and relates the latter to what they would want and
    prefer, were they able to make a choice' (Lukes 1974: 34). The association

of power with 'real' interests has generated a vivid debate (for references see, e.g., Benton 1981).

6   Also Alford and Friedland (1975) and Benton (1981: 174–8) argue for the study of power from the resource side rather than through its exercise. I have myself developed this approach (Korpi 1974, 1978, and 1983).

7   It is important to note that not all factors of social causation are power resources (cf., e.g., Abell 1977).

8   Other discussions of the resource concept can be found, e.g., in Coleman 1971a, 1971b and 1974, and Clark 1975. As Lukes (1974: 26–35) has observed the definition of the interests of actors is of relevance for the conceptualization of power. He excludes from the concept of power those relations where there are no conflicts of interest between actors. I am inclined to include in the definition of power both situations where conflicts of interests are present and situations where they are not. In the former case we can talk about 'vertical' power, in the latter case about 'horizontal' power. The following discussion is limited to 'vertical' power.

9   The limitation of the concept of power to punishment resources is not warranted (e.g., Baldwin 1971a: 28; Barry 1975: 92).

10 In analyses of power the term 'mobilization' is used interchangeably to refer to the processes whereby an actor acquires control over power resources and makes them ready for use as well as for the actual use of power resources; i.e., the exercise of power. I have here chosen to use it in its former meaning.

11 Etzioni's classification must be seen as a preliminary one. It is not clear how information is to be placed in this typology, which also appears to have a built-in distinction between pressure and reward resources.

12 Parsons (1967) has argued that, in the political sphere, power is a medium of exchange similar to what money is in the economic sphere. This parallel is, however, not a fruitful one.

13 The term 'exploitation' has also been used to characterize 'unfair' exchange relations, something which assumes that we can determine what is a fair exchange relation. No such assumptions are involved in the present use of the term, which is not intended to cover all the possible forms of exploitation. Some writers use the term 'exchange' very broadly to also include the use of pressure resources (e.g., Lively 1975: 12; Oppenheim 1978: 596–7).

14 During the postwar period, the dominant tradition in conflict analysis has seen manifest conflict primarily as a response to an increasing gap between expectations and actual achievements; i.e., increasing relative deprivation (e.g., Davies 1962; Gurr 1970; for an alternative view, see Korpi 1974). From this perspective the association of power and manifest conflict can be interpreted to mean that, when conflicts of interest increase in intensity, the

likelihood increases that power will be used to settle such conflicts. The behavioral tradition in power analysis appears to be premised on such an interpretation.

15 This approach indicates that the absence of manifest conflict in a decision-making process cannot be taken as sufficient proof that all the concerned parties have an equal influence on it. Thus when Dahl (1961: 75) observes that there were no overt conflicts between the longtime leader to the Democratic party in New Haven and the Economic Notables in the city, nor between the party leader and the factory hands, the former observation is more telling than the latter, since those having great power resources are much more likely than the factory hands to take action if their interests are hurt.

16 For discussions of the role of power in economics Rotschild (1971) and Lindblom (1977) compare politics and markets without assuming perfect competition. In this context it should be noted that the behavioral approach does not assume equally distributed power resources (cf. e.g., Dahl 1961: 4–5).

17 In his later treatments of exchange, Homans (1974: 88) recognizes that the power distribution between the actors affects the outcome of bargaining. See also Emerson 1976: 354–5 on exchange ratios. One example of the effects of variations in distribution of power resources on the outcome of exchange is the covariation long observed between changes in unemployment, a rough indicator of the relative power position of sellers and buyers of labor power, and the rate of change of money wages; i.e., the Phillips curve (Phillips 1957).

18 In arguing that the genesis of power resources is to be found in imbalanced exchange relations, Blau (1964) and Homans (1961, 1974) assume that power derives from a unilateral provision of services which is matched or balanced by approval, conformity, etc. This view has been criticized by Birnbaum (1975) and Lively (1975) on the grounds that it neglects the extent to which social power derives from a position within a structure of distribution as well as the extent to which exchange is governed by rules imposed by the larger society. It appears that what Blau and Homans regard as the genesis of power resources often is the establishment of particular power relationships on the initiative of the weaker actors. The notion of 'secondary exchange' (Blau 1964: 157–8) assumes that powerful actors abstain from using power resources to their full advantage in exchange for the social approval of the weaker actors. Social approval by weak actors, however, is not a very efficient power resource and must therefore be assumed to have only marginal effects on exchange rates.

19 Alford and Friedland (1975) refer to the former as 'systemic power' and to the latter as 'structural power.'

20 It must be noted, however, that classical Marxists, including presumably Marx himself as well as Gramsci, and numerous 'neo-Marxist' writers, have not ascribed to this functionalist view of the state (cf., e.g, Gough 1979; Holloway and Picciotta 1978; and Jessop 1982).

21 This perspective puts in a new light the programmatic claim by scholars in the behavioral tradition to study controversial issues of extraordinary importance and to avoid the routine varieties of decision-making. The critics of this tradition have often questioned the choice of issues on the grounds that these scholars may not have achieved their goal in the selection of key issues. However, the goal itself, involving the exclusion from attention of the institutionalized and routine forms of decision-making, has rarely been criticized. Yet this goal itself involves a crucial limitation in the study of power.

22 Institutionalization of decision-making and conflict regulation are not limited to the governmental or public sector, which has been the focus of study in the behavioral tradition. The labor market, collective bargaining, industrial technology, and physical planning are other examples of such investments.

23 In the 1970s this tension became evident, for example, in the confrontation between 'Keynesian' and 'monetarist' economic policies. The central issue in this conflict is whether the citizens through the government can and should take responsibility for the level of employment crucial for their welfare, or if the level of employment should be left to be an outcome of market forces.

24 Writers in the behavioral tradition of power analysis have argued that ideologies and values are not power resources on the grounds that we apparently cannot discover any consensus on elite values or any internally consistent, unidimensional body of beliefs in the population (e.g., Merelman 1968: 453–4; Wolfinger 1971: 1072–3). However, to have consequences for social behavior, the cultivation of values, ideologies, and legitimacy need not meet with complete success. As Mann (1970) has pointed out, the cohesion of liberal democracy is not based on the normative acceptance by the great majority of the population of the values of a 'ruling class.' Instead, the compliance of large segments of the population can be based more on a pragamatic acceptance of specific roles and on the absence of a shared ideology questioning the basic working of their society (cf. Abercrombie and Turner: 1978).

25 Dahl (1961: 17) thus notes that in the 18th and 19th centuries, the New Haven 'elite seems to have possessed that most indispensable of all characteristics in a dominant group – the sense, shared not only by themselves but

by the populace – that their claim to govern was legitimate.' Also other historical examples of 'false consciousness' and manipulation through values, levels of aspirations, and institutional practice – e.g., the long period of acquiescence by the blacks in the American South – are widely recognized (Wolfinger 1971: 1077).

26 Writers in the behavioral tradition have not been unaware of the role of anticipated reactions. But such reactions often tend to enter their analyses in a reversed version (reminding of the concept of 'secondary exchange') and 'indirect influence,' which makes 'elected leaders keep the real or imagined preferences of constituents constantly in mind in deciding what policies to adopt or reject' (Dahl 1961: 164; cf. also Wolfinger 1971: 1067–8). While Merelman (1968: 455) correctly points out that anticipated reactions can be found among the stronger as well as among the weaker actors, the power resource approach indicates that the consequences of anticipated reactions will depend on the difference in power resources between actors and tend to be greater among the weaker than among the stronger actors.

27 Cf. Schelling (1960, part I) for a discussion of techniques for making threats credible.

28 While a high standard characterizes empirical research in the behavioral tradition, in this context it can be noted that, in the study of community power, researchers relying on the behavioral approach have come out with results which predominantly indicate that power is not hierarchically distributed, whereas those using the 'stratificationist' approach have found results which are closer to 50–50 distribution between 'pyramidal' and 'other' power distributions (Polsby 1980: 146, 148). While these results can reflect a number of different factors, such as choice of communities and reliability of research methods, there is also the possibility that this may reflect a tendency towards bias in research methodology.

29 For attempts to use differences in the internal distribution of power resources among OECD countries as explanatory variables in explaining phenomena such as patterns of industrial conflict, social policy, and welfare states, cf. Korpi 1983; chaps. 8 and 9, and Esping-Andersen and Korpi 1984.

References

Abell, Peter. 1977. 'The Many Faces of Power and Liberty: Revealed Preferences, Autonomy, and Teleological Explanation.' *Sociology* 15 (January): 3–24.

Abercrombie, Nicholas, and Brian S. Turner. 1978. The Dominant Ideology Thesis. *British Journal of Sociology* 29 (no. 2): 149–170.

Alchian, Armen A., and Harold Demsetz. 1972. Production, Information Costs, and Economic Organization. *American Economic Review* 62 (no. 5): 777–95.

Alford, Robert A., and Roger Friedland. 1975. Political Participation and Public Policy. Pp. 429–79 in *Annual Review of Sociology,* edited by Alex Inkeles. Palo Alto: Annual Reviews, Inc.

Althusser, L. 1971. *Lenin and Philosophy and Other Essays.* London: New Left Books.

Bachrach, Peter, and Morton S. Baratz. 1962. Two Faces of Power. *American Political Science* Review 56 (December): 947–52.

– 1963. Decision and Non-Decisions: An Analytical Framework. *American Political Science Review* 57 (September): 632–42.

– 1970. *Power and Poverty Theory and Practice.* New York: Oxford University Press.

Baldwin, David A. 1971a. The Power of Positive Sanction. *World Politics* 24: 19–38.

– 1971b. The Costs of Power. *Journal of Conflict Resolution* 15: 145–55.

– 1978. Power and Social Exchange. *American Political Science Review* 72 (December): 1229–42.

Barry, Brian. 1975. Power: An Economic Analysis. Pp. 67–102 in *Power and Political Theory,* edited by Brian Barry. New York: Wiley.

Benton, T. 1981. Objective Interests and the Sociology of Power. *Sociology* 15 (May): 161–184.

Bierstedt, Robert. 1950. An Analysis of Social Power. *American Sociological Review* 15 (December): 730–8.

Birnbaum, Pierre. 1975. Power Divorced From its Sources. A Critique of the Exchange Theory of Power. Pp. 15–32 in *Power and Political Theory,* edited by Brian Barry. New York: Wiley.

Blalock, Herbert M. 1967. *Toward a Theory of Minority Group Relations.* New York: Wiley.

Blau, Peter M. 1964. *Exchange and Power in Social Life.* New York: Wiley.

Bloch, Michael, Bryan Heading, and Philip Lawrence. 1979. Power in Social Theory: A Non-relative View. Pp. 243–60 in *Philosophical Disputes in the Social Sciences,* edited by S.C. Brown. Hassocks, Sussex: Harvester.

Clark, Terry N. 1975. Community Power. Pp. 271–95 in *Annual Review of Sociology,* edited by Alex Inkeles. Palo Alto: Annual Reviews, Inc.

Coleman, James S. 1971a. *Resources for Social Change: Race in the United States.* New York: Wiley.

– 1971b. Foundations for a Theory of Collective Action. Pp. 27–46 in *Social Choice,* edited by Bernhard Lieberman. New York: Norton.

— 1974. *Power and the Structure of Society*. New York: Norton.

Crenson, Matthew. 1971. *The Unpolitics of Air Pollution*. Baltimore: Johns Hopkins University Press.

Dahl, Robert A. 1957. The Concept of Power. *Behavioral Science* 2: 201–15.

— 1958. A Critique of the Ruling-Elite Model. *American Political Science Review* 52 (June): 463–9.

— 1961. *Who Governs? Power and Democracy in an American City*. New Haven, Connecticut: Yale University Press.

— 1963. *Modern Political Analysis*. Englewood Cliffs, N.J.: Prentice-Hall.

Dahrendorf, R. 1968. *Essays on the Theory of Society*. Stanford, Calif.: Stanford University Press.

Davies, James C. 1962. Toward a Theory of Revolution. *American Sociological Review* 27 (February): 5–18.

Deutsch, Karl W. 1963. *The Nerves of Government*. New York: Free Press.

Eckstein, H. 1973. A Structural Basis for Political Inquiry. *American Political Science Review* 67 (December): 1142–61.

Elster, Jon. 1982. Marxist, Functionalism and Game Theory. *Theory and Society* 11: 453–82.

— 1983. *Explaining Technical Change*. Cambridge: Cambridge University Press.

Emerson, Richard M. 1976. Social Exchange Theory. Pp. 335–62 in *Annual Review of Sociology*, edited by Alex Inkeles. Palo Alto: Annual Reviews, Inc.

Esping-Andersen, Gøsta, and Walter Korpi. 1984. Social Policy as Class Politics in Postwar Capitalism: Scandinavia, Austria and Germany. In *Order and Conflict in Contemporary Capitalism: Studies in the Political Economy of West European Nations*, edited by John H. Goldthorpe. Oxford: Oxford University Press.

Etzioni, Amitai. 1961. *A Comparative Analysis of Complex Organizations*. New York: Free Press.

Frey, Frederick W. 1971. Comment: On Issues and Nonissues in the Study of Power. *American Political Science Review* 65 (December): 1081–101.

Friedman, Milton. 1962. *Capitalism and Freedom*. Chicago: University of Chicago Press.

Friedrich, Carl J. 1963. *Man and His Government*. New York: McGraw-Hill.

Gamson, William A. 1968. *Power and Discontent*. Homewood, Ill.: Dorsey.

Ginsburg, Norman. 1979. *Class, Capital and Social Policy*. London: Macmillan.

Gough, Ian. 1979. *The Political Economy of the Welfare State*. London: Macmillan.

Gurr, Ted R. 1970. *Why Men Rebel*. Princeton: Princeton University Press.

Harsanyi, J.C. 1962. Measurement of Social Power, Opportunity Costs, and the Theory of Two-Person Bargaining Games. *Behavioral Science* 7 (January): 67–80.

Hernes, Gudmund. 1975. *Makt og Avmakt.* Oslo: Universitetsforlaget.

Hindess, Barry. 1982. Power, Interests and the Outcomes of Struggles. *Sociology* 16 (November): 498–511.

Hobbes, Thomas. 1962. *Leviathan.* London: Collier Macmillan.

Holloway, J., and S. Picciotta. 1978. *State and Capital.* London: Edward Arnold.

Homans, George C. 1961. *Social Behavior: Its Elementary Forms.* New York: Harcourt & Brace.

– 1974. *Social Behavior: Its Elementary Forms.* (Revised Edition). New York: Harcourt Brace Jovanovich.

Jessop, Bob. 1982. *The Capitalist State.* Oxford: Martin Robertson.

Kahn, Robert. 1964. Introduction. In *Power and Conflict in Organizations,* edited by R.L. Kahn and E. Boulding. New York: Basic Books.

Kerr, C., et al. 1973. *Industrialism and Industrial Man.* Harmondsworth: Penguin.

Korpi, Walter. 1974. Conflict, Power and Relative Deprivation. *American Political Science Review* 68 (December): 569–78.

– 1978. *The Working Class in Welfare Capitalism. Work, Unions and Politics in Sweden.* London: Routledge & Kegan Paul.

– 1983. *The Democratic Class Struggle.* London: Routledge & Kegan Paul.

Lasswell, Harald D., and Abraham Kaplan. 1950. *Power and Society: A Framework for Political Inquiry.* New Haven: Yale University Press.

Lenski, Gerhard. 1966. *Power and Privilege.* New York: McGraw-Hill.

Lindblom, Charles D. 1977. *Markets and Politics.* New York: Basic Books.

Lively, Jack. 1975. The Limits of Exchange Theory. Pp. 1–14 in *Power and Political Theory,* edited by Brian Barry. New York: Wiley.

Lukes. Stephen M. 1974. *Power: A Radical View.* London: Macmillan.

– 1979. On the Relativity of Power. Pp. 261–74 in *Philosophical Disputes in the Social Sciences,* edited by S.C. Brown. Hassocks, Sussex: Harvester.

Mann, Michael. 1970. The Social Cohesion of Liberal Democracy. *American Sociological Review* 35 (3): 423–39.

Martin, Roderick. 1977. *The Sociology of Power.* London: Routledge & Kegan Paul.

Merelman, Richard M. 1968. On the Neo-Elitist Critique of Community Power. *American Political Science Review* 62 (June): 451–60.

Mill, James. 1816, 1939. An Essay on Government. Pp. 857–89 in *The English Philosophers from Bacon to Mill,* edited by Edwin A. Burtt. New York: The Modern Library.

Mills, C. Wright. 1956. *The Power Elite.* New York: Oxford University Press.

– 1963. *Power, Politics and People.* New York: Oxford University Press.

Morgenstern, Oskar. 1972. Thirteen Critical Points in Contemporary Economic Theory: An Interpretation. *Journal of Economic Literature* 10 (4): 1163–89.

Nagel, Jack H. 1975. *The Descriptive Analysis of Power.* New Haven: Yale University Press.

Olson, Jr, M. 1965. *The Logic of Collective Action.* Cambridge, Mass.: Harvard University Press.

Oppenheim, Frederic E. 1978. Power Revisited. *Journal of Politics* (August): 549–621.

Parsons, T. 1966. *Societies: Evolutionary and Comparative Perspectives.* Englewood Cliffs: Prentice-Hall.

– 1967. On the Concept of Political Power. Pp. 297–354 in T. Parsons, *Sociological Theory and Modern Society.* New York: Free Press.

Phillips, A.W. 1957. The Relation between Unemployment and the Rate of Change of Money Wage Rates in the United Kingdom, 1861–1957. *Economica* 25 (November): 283–99.

Polsby, Nelson W. 1980. *Community Power and Political Theory. A Further Look at Problems of Evidence and Inference* (Second, enlarged edition). New Haven: Yale University Press.

Poulantzas, Nicos. 1978. *State, Power, Socialism.* London: Verso.

Rogers, Mary F. 1974. Instrumental and Infra-Resources: The Bases of Power. *American Journal of Sociology* 79 (May): 1418–33.

Rose, Arnold M. 1967. *The Power Structure.* New York: Oxford University Press.

Rotschild, K.W. 1971. *Power in Economics.* Harmondsworth: Penguin.

Schattschneider, E.E. 1960. *The Semisovereign People.* New York: Holt, Rinehart and Winston.

Schelling, Thomas C. 1960. *The Strategy of Conflict.* New York: Oxford University Press.

Simon, Herbert A. 1953. Notes on the Observation and Measurement of Political Power. *Journal of Politics* 15: 500–16.

– 1957. *Models of Man.* New York: Wiley.

Smith, Adam. 1776, 1970. *The Wealth of Nations.* Harmondsworth: Penguin.

Smith, G.W. 1981. Must Radicals Be Marxists? Lukes on Power, Contestability and Alienation. *British Journal of Political Science* 11: 403–25.

Weber, Max. 1922, 1980. *Wirtschaft und Gesellschaft. Grundriss der Verstehende Soziolgoie* (Fifth revised edition). Tübingen: J.C.B. Mohr.

– 1947. *The Theory of Social and Economic Organization.* New York: Oxford University Press.

Wilensky, Harold. 1975. *The Welfare State and Equality. The Roots of Social Expenditures.* Berkeley: University of California Press.

Wolfinger, Raymond E. 1971. Nondecisions and the Study of Local Politics and Rejoinder to Frey's 'Comment.' *American Political Science Review* 65 (December): 1063–80 and 1102–4.

Wrong, Dennis H. 1979. *Power: Its Forms, Bases, and Uses.* New York: Harper.

2

The Development of Family Policy:
A Comparison of Family Benefits and
Tax Reductions for Families in OECD
Countries   IRENE WENNEMO

In the course of the postwar period, universal family support has been introduced in most industrialized nations. Governments may introduce such support in order to attain two policy objectives, raising fertility and increasing the economic well-being of families. There have been two major types of universal support to families: different types of family tax reductions on the one hand and cash benefits on the other. In this paper, predictors of the growth of family benefit levels in these systems will be examined.

The results indicate that benefit levels are influenced by national political trends. Left party strength has a significant impact on the level of cash benefits, but a weak negative one on tax reductions, the latter type of benefit being more advantageous for earners of high incomes. Religious party strength also has a rather strong influence on family support. In contrast, measures linked to modernization and industrialization do not exercise any strong effect on the extension of family support. Neither measures of economic development nor fertility demonstrates any consistent impact on benefit levels.

1. Introduction

Towards the end of the 1940s, general income transfers to families with children were introduced in many industrialized countries. Forty years later, nearly all developed nations had extended some type of targeted economic support to families. There are two major types of universal family support: tax reductions for families with children and cash benefits. Nearly all OECD countries have provided some kind of tax deduction for families, and most of them introduced cash benefits during the postwar period. However, despite the similarities in systems of family support, the volume of economic transfers to families has varied markedly between countries.

Family policy has been influenced by two different policy traditions of the welfare state, social and population policy. Their effects converge on family policy with mixed effects, since the goals pursued in these two policy arenas are somewhat contradictory. Social policy has the double purpose of expanding the rights of social citizenship and evening out the distribution of resources between social groups. Population policy, on the other hand, has as its main aim the stimulation of population growth (Kälvemark 1980). Introduction of public transfers to families did not give rise to the same kinds of political conflicts as did the introduction of other social insurance programmes (Marklund 1982: 73–5). This is partly explained by the twofold purpose of family policy. However, this relative lack of political conflict is also linked to the fact that family support programmes, with the exception of maternity insurance, may not directly affect the labour market and the bargaining power of the negotiating social interest groups in society.

The purpose of this paper is to analyse the development of rights to family support and the differences between industrialized countries in that respect. The study will concentrate upon legislated family support to which all parents are universally entitled. An explanation which accentuates the importance of both social and population policy will be discussed and analysed. In the context of the 'social policy approach,' two major types of explanation will be discussed. The first of these views industrialization as the driving force for the evolution of social policy. Development leads to new, unsatisfied needs, but also creates new economic resources, which make social reforms for relieving these demands possible (cf. Wilensky 1975). The second perspective stresses the importance of conflicts between different interest groups. The outcome of these conflicts is assumed to shape differences between countries. The most important competing interests involve labour, business and the state (Korpi 1985; Esping-Andersen 1985; Skocpol 1985).

In the next section, the theoretical perspectives sketched above are examined in greater detail. In section 3 of the paper a description is presented of the development of universal family support in the countries under study. Lastly, we analyse the factors which influence the size of family cash benefits and family tax deductions respectively.

2. Theoretical Perspectives

2.1. The Effect of Fertility

A connection between fertility and family benefits is taken for granted from a population policy point of view. Economic support for families with children has, according to this perspective, the purpose of directing the reproductive behaviour of citizens. A low fertility rate, with government action as a mediating factor, will lead to high levels of support of families. We will discuss this relation below, but we will also discuss a contradictory one, whereby the effect of fertility on family support is assumed to be positive instead of negative.

The relative cost of having children in industrial societies is often assumed to be greater than the cost thus incurred in mainly agricultural societies. This depends on urbanization and the movement of labour from families into markets and the public sector. The introduction of compulsory schooling and legislation against child labour had the same kind of effect. The development of contraceptive methods led to a greater ability to control fertility. Together, these phenomena may have led to a decrease in the average number of children per family, and thereby to a higher standard of living (Wilensky and Lebeaux 1965; Heinsohn et al. 1982; Rausing 1986). The decline in fertility might in the long run lead to an insufficiently large labour force in comparison with the number of elderly, especially when it is taken into account that average life expectancy has greatly increased in the industrialized countries during the 20th century. A contradiction between rational actions of the individual and long-run collective welfare arises in this situation, which very much resembles a 'prisoner's dilemma' (Elster 1979: 8). One way to solve this problem is to introduce economic transfers to families, which reduce the cost of having children and thereby make it less costly to act in the interests of society.

Some social researchers have viewed the regulative effects of social policy and the reproductive function of the welfare state as important for explaining its development (Therborn 1987, 1989). Proponents of this approach view family policy as a significant example of the social steering of fertility and reproduction. In Sweden, the family reforms proposed by the Myrdals in 'Crisis in the population question' (1934) are often used as illustrative support for such arguments. It has further been pointed out in several studies that economic support to families has been introduced with the intention of raising low rates of fertility (Alestalo and Uusitalo 1986: 212; Gordon 1988: 282f).

Kälvemark (1980) proposes that the intentions of legislatures can be classified as population policy or family policy. This is, however, seldom possible, because political solutions to social problems are often based upon compromises between groups and parties, which might have different motives for supporting the same political reform. In this study, a less precise method will be used to distinguish between these policies. In the population policy arena, the aim of regulating individual reproduction determines the amount of support to families. Universal support to families decreases the cost of having children, but does not regulate the parents' behaviour in any detail. The assumption is that low fertility should lead to high levels of family support and high birth rates should be followed by low levels of economic support. This assumption is valid as long as the regime's goal is not markedly to increase the size of the population.[1] The hypothesis also requires the assumption that there exists a rather strong state, which has the ability to force through political reforms that aim to steer the actions of its citizens.

The alternative hypothesis predicts an opposite effect of fertility on support for families. According to Downs (1957), government policies may be seen as methods for maximizing the number of votes in elections. An introduction of, or an increase in, universal family support favours a large proportion of the voters and is unlikely to meet strong resistance in any minority group, partly because it does not intervene in labour markets. This approach to the state is totally different from the former one. Here the actions of the government are directed not towards realizing long-run utility but rather towards consolidating short-term advantages for the ruling party.

According to the Downsian perspective, high fertility leads to a high proportion of the parents among the electorate who must be taken into consideration when policy and political platforms are outlined. Thus, high fertility is assumed to lead to an increase in economic support to parents and fertility is therefore positively, rather than negatively, linked to the level of family benefits.[2]

2.2. The Effect of Industrialization

The 'logic of industrialism' perspective singles out industrialization and economic developments as the most important causes of welfare state expansion (Kerr et al. 1960). According to this perspective, economic development affects, among other things, the age distribution of the population; yet it also creates new economic resources, which makes it possible for the nation to develop sociopolitical programmes. Partisan politics and conflicts between interest groups are, according to this perspective, of subordinate importance (Wilensky 1976).

Consequently, the industrialization approach leads to the prediction that a high level of industrialization makes it possible to afford improvements in family policy. Industrialization also leads, as pointed out earlier, to increases in the cost of having children and to the rise of family support as necessary means of ensuring the reproduction of the working-age population. These results hypothesized of industrialization are rather similar to those hypothesized within approaches highlighting the significant of fertility rates for expansion of family support. The additional factor here is the importance of economic resources for increases in family support.

2.3. Social Rights and Family Support

The type of explanation that emphasizes the role of conflicts between important interest groups is also applicable to the arena of family policy. These conflicts often take place over the emergence and extension of social policy measures. Groups with weak market resources have a much greater interest in policies that decrease individual dependence upon the market. According to this approach, economic development is thought to provide the basic framework for decisions taken in the policy arena. Industrialization is not seen as a sufficient explanation for the growth of social policy, however.

This approach further builds on the assumption that there is an uneven distribution of power resources in society. The control of capital and the means of production are essential unequally distributed resources. Other resources include the control of human capital and labour, which are relatively evenly divided among the population. Those with only a small amount of power resources, have the possibility of advancing their interests through collective organizations. Through these organizations, they may intervene in the political process and control the supply of labour on the market (Korpi 1978, 1985).

Several studies have emphasized the importance of left parties and trade unions for explaining differences in social policy development between countries (Castles 1978; Shalev 1983; Esping-Andersen 1985; Korpi 1989). The explanatory significance of the strength of these organizations for the expansion of social rights in sickness and old age has recently been demonstrated (Korpi 1989; Palme 1990).

In case studies of the political process by which early family policy was formulated, the importance of left-wing women's organizations has been pointed out. These women's groups played a role early on in the political struggle for legislated support during maternity, especially for single mothers (Ohlander 1989; Seip and Ibsen 1989; Skocpol and Ritter 1991). In the working-class movement, particularly its women's organizations, there was great scepticism about the purpose of population policy. In most countries, strong tension existed between the social and the population aspects of family policy until the mid-1930s. The universal family benefit was seen as an award for fecundity and as a method of keeping women out of the labour market (Hatje 1974; Carlson 1990).

A problem was solved for left organizations when they changed their attitudes towards universal family support during the late 1930s and the 1940s. In a situation where the individual has total economic responsibility for reproduction, the easiest way to increase your economic well-being is to avoid having any children (Rausing 1986). But this individualistic strategy might harm the working-class movement, given that the responsibility for increasing the family's economic well-being is laid upon the individual. According to the neo-Malthusian view, which was shared by the majority of left organizations in the early 20th century, the economic stratification arising between those with a few children and those with many children was not a political issue but instead an issue of education and morality. If this process of stratification continues, the working class may be divided into an enlightened upper stratum on the one hand, and on the other hand a lower stratum whose members have many children and therefore a worse economic situation. To let the state subsidize reproduction would lead to a more homogeneous working class and, in addition, politicize the question of responsibility for the reproduction of the nation's population (Wennemo 1991).

2.4 The Effects of Family Policy on Income Distribution

Two major arguments for developing family support programmes have been advanced. On the one hand it is argued that economic support to families with children will increase the fertility rates, as we have previously hypothesized. The other argument states that the level of economic well-being for families should be increased in relative terms by redistributing means from the childless to families with children. The purpose in some cases has also been to target income redistribution to families with limited economic resources, which is meant to intensify the equalizing effect of such redistributive measures (Hatje 1974; SOU 1946).

All programmes of family support redistribute income between households with and without children. The cash benefit also has a redistributive effect between income groups. This is due to the fact that while taxes are paid on a proportional or progressive basis, the benefit is paid so that an equal amount is distributed to all children (Åberg 1989). However, the redistributive effect per monetary unit is relatively low compared with that of means-tested benefits that target families with low income (Tobin 1968).

Tax reduction variants of family policy normally do not have such equalizing effects. We can see why this is the case through a detailed examination of the two major methods whereby family tax reduction is implemented. The first of these tax reduction methods, tax allowances, implies a reduction of taxable income by a given amount per child. With a progressive tax system, this means that those with the highest incomes get the greatest tax reductions, whereas those with low or no income either will not get any tax reduction or will get a very small one. In the second method of tax reduction, tax deductions, the income tax payment itself is reduced by a given amount per child. This means that those who do not pay any (or a very low) income tax will not get any family support, but that families above this income level will get equal support.[3]

The tax deductions are, in most, cases only horizontally redistributive. The system equalizes income between people with and without children on the same level of income. The universal family benefit also achieves some vertical redistributive effect, by equalizing household incomes between different income strata. On these grounds, it is reasonable to assume that the strength of left parties should influence the level of child benefits positively and the level of family tax deductions negatively, or at least not positively. Such relationships have been found in studies in Finland and Sweden. Left parties do indeed make legislative proposals for cash benefits, while right parties propose policies mandating various kinds of tax cuts (Kangas 1986; Hinnfors 1992).

2.5 Religion and Family

Esping-Andersen (1990) has presented a categorization of welfare states, which expands upon Titmuss' (1974) classification of social policy programmes. Esping-Andersen categorizes welfare states as liberal, conservative/corporatist, or social democratic with respect to their regime types. In the conservative type, which I will concentrate upon, the family is seen as a very important component of society. In these countries economic support for families favours maternity and actively encourages the creation of families with only one employed adult (Esping-Andersen 1990: 27). The aim of sanctioning families with one wage-earner can be seen as a third motive for the introduction of support for families. The reasons for focusing on the other two motives in this study are that the motive of supporting families with one wage-earner has not been used in the family policy debate as often as the other two, that this motive is very interwoven with the motive of increasing fertility, and lastly that the importance of this motive is rather difficult to estimate empirically.[4]

More generally, the problem with this typology of welfare states is that the way in which a given country is classified depends on the characteristics of its social insurance system. The trichotomy therefore does not explain the divergences it highlights. In this study I will therefore try to find an indicator for which countries with different regime-types demonstrate divergent patterns in accordance with the categorization.

Esping-Andersen classifies Belgium, France, Germany, Italy, and Austria as countries with a high degree of conservatism (1990: 74). In four of these countries, there exist strong and stable religious parties. France is the exception; in this country, religious parties have been very small or non-existent throughout the postwar period. In most of the countries that Esping-Andersen classifies as having a lower or medium degree of conservatism religious parties are either non-existent or very small. Exceptions to this pattern include the Netherlands and Switzerland.

In a study of Pampel and Adams (1990), it was demonstrated that the share of Catholics in the population (which is strongly related to the existence of religious parties) has a great impact on the level of expenditure on family support. Other studies have emphasized the role of the religious element in politics in more structural institutional terms, by demonstrating that strong Catholic parties lead to a strong state and thereby to greater possibilities of enforcing social policy (Wilensky 1981; Kersbergen 1991).

It is of course difficult to draw any firm conclusions about causal relationships between the size of religious parties and such phenomena as Catholicism or corporatist relations. In this study I will use the degree of religious party participation in government and the electoral share of votes received by such parties for measuring the strength of church and religion. The advantage of using these variables is that they closely index religious groups' direct influence on political decisions, and also reflect attitudes at the individual level. I assume that it is the existence of political parties, rather than Catholicism as such, that indicates and channels the strength of religious attitudes in society and thereby shapes differences in family policy. I further assume that these parties have a positive impact on the levels of all kinds of economic family support.

3. The Development of Family Support

3.1. The Introduction of Family Support

There are two major types of universal economic support for families, family benefits and tax reductions. The family benefit system can be further divided into two groups, universal systems and employment-based systems. The universal system is the most common family benefit system, dominant in Scandinavia and in the Anglo-Saxon countries. The universal family benefit is conditional upon permanent residence in the country and is often paid to the mother. The latter is at least the case for the Scandinavian countries, Australia and United Kingdom since 1978 (Knudsen 1990: 133; Parry 1986: 175; US Social Security Administration). Benefits in the employment-based systems are based on either one of the parents' employment. In these countries, family benefits often started out as a wage supplement for workers in given industries. The coverage of family support increased over time to include the self-employed and farmers and later also the unemployed and groups outside the labour force. In virtually no case was any benefit system abolished during the period studied, nor was the nominal amount of money reduced in any country (Swedish Institute for Social Research data; US Social Security Administration).[5] This gives some support to the assumption that universal social policy measures are difficult to cut back because so high a proportion of the population is favoured by them and has interest in them (Korpi 1981: 205ff). Listed in table 1 are types of family benefits systems with the year of introduction for each of the 18 countries studied in the period 1930–85.

France became the first country among these studied here to introduce a benefit to families with two children. Some other countries had already introduced some form of child benefit by this time, but the significance of these benefits was qualified by substantial legislative limitations. In countries with employment-based systems, some classification problems emerged for the early period. For example, France had already introduced a wage supplement for parents in some industries in the second decade of this century. Legislation that mandated employers' contributions to family benefit funds was introduced in 1932, but the breakthrough came as late as 1938 (Questiaux and Fournier 1978). A family benefit system was also introduced early in Belgium. A select group of employers organized the first benefit fund as early as 1921, but the coverage of this legislation was not extended to all wage-earners and self-

TABLE 1

The System of Family Benefits and the Number of Children Required for Receiving Benefit in Eighteen OECD Countries, 1930–1985

Country	System	1st child	2nd child	3rd child	4th child
Australia	Universal	1947	1941		
Canada	Universal	1944			
Denmark	Universal	{ 1977m 1961 1952m			
Finland	Universal	1948			1943
Ireland	Universal	1963	1952	1944	
New Zealand	Universal	{ 1946 1941m	1940m	1926m	
Norway	Universal	1969	1946		
Sweden	Universal	1948			
United Kingdom	Universal	1977	1945		
The Netherlands	Dual system	1946e		1951u	
West Germany	1973: Employment 1974: Universal	1974	1961	1954	
Austria	Employment based	1948 (1921)			
Belgium	Employment based	1939 (1921)			
France	Employment based		1938 (1932)		
Italy	Employment based	1955 (1929)			
Switzerland	Employment based	1952			
Japan	Means-tested			1971m	
United States	No system				

m = means-tested.
( ) = to some groups.
e = employment based.
u = universal.
Sources: Swedish Institute for Social Research data; US Social Security Administration, 1949–88.

employed until 1938–9 (Berghman et al. 1987). Large religious parties exist in all the countries (except France) that have had employment-based benefit systems throughout the period under study, as well as in the Netherlands (which has had a dual system) and Germany (which changed system in 1974). This supports the hypothesis that religious parties can play an important role in setting family policy. The countries with employment-based systems of family support often established them earlier than countries with universal systems, especially if the timing of the initial selective legislation is used as an index. The universal benefit system is the most common, and is often preceded by legislation covering only families with more than a given number of children at the beginning of the period. This is the case for Australia, Finland, Ireland, New Zealand, Norway, and the United Kingdom. Moreover, Japan and the USA have no universal benefit systems at all.

Differences in institutional structure may affect benefit levels and the amount of tax reductions mandated, independently of political or other variables. A study of differences in unemployment insurance show that its institutional character may affect such aspects of social organization as union membership density (Rothstein 1990). Palme (1990) has further shown that differences in the structure of the old-age pension system can affect benefit levels. In this case, differences in how the benefit levels get set and how the benefit is financed may influence the level of benefits and potentially also the level of tax reductions. Details about such divergences between the characteristics of systems are outside the scope of this study, but we could certainly assume that such differences may affect levels of family support.

Table 2 shows the development of legislation regulating tax reductions during the period 1930–85. The number of countries with tax allowances peaked in 1965. However, systems of tax allowances halted in many countries during the period. The high frequency of abolition of tax allowances and tax deductions might be explained by the low visibility of the systems, and that withdrawals of reductions were compensated for by increases in family cash benefits in all cases (SSIB data). Family tax allowances were available for a time in all of the countries under study. In most countries, the introduction of tax allowances actually preceded the introduction of cash benefits. In half of the countries the system has been abolished, although it was later reintroduced in some countries. The tax deduction system, which is the most equalizing type of tax reduction, seems to be more common in the later period, yet as late as 1985 this type of reduction was still less frequently in use than were tax allowances.

3.2. The Extension of Family Support

This study is based not, as is usual with studies of policy outputs, upon state expenditure, but instead on families' rights to economic support. This makes it possible to discriminate between different types of economic support, such as, for example, between universal support and

TABLE 2: The Legislation of Tax Reductions for Families with Two Children in Eighteen OECD Countries, 1930–1985

Country	1930	1933	1939	1947	1950	1955	1960	1965	1970	1975	1980	1985
Australia	A	A	A	A	A	A	A	A	A	A		
Austria			A	A	A	A	A	A	A	D		
Belgium			A	A	A	A	A	A	A	B	B	B
Canada				A	A	A	A	A	A	A	A	B
Denmark	A	A	A	A	A	A	B					
Finland	A	A	A	B	A	A	A	A	A	B	B	A
France								A	A	A	A	A
Germany						A	A	A	A		A	A
Ireland								A	A	A	A	A
Italy											D	D
Japan				A	A	A	A	A	A	A	A	A
The Netherlands						A	A	A	A	A	A	A
New Zealand	A	A	A	A	A	A	A	A	A		D	D
Norway	A	A	A	A	A	B	B	B			D	D
Sweden	A	A	A	A								
Switzerland	A	A	A	A	A	A	A	A	A	A	A	A
United Kingdom				A	A	A	A	A	A	A		
USA				A	A	A	A	A	A	A	A	A
Number of countries A	7	7	9	13	13	14	14	15	14	11	10	10
D				1		1	2	1		3	5	5

A = Tax allowances.
D = Tax deductions.
B = Both types of system.
Source: Swedish Institute for Social Research data.

different types of means-tested support. It also allows us to study the effect of different types of family tax reductions.

The benefits and tax reductions have been calculated for a family with two pre-school-aged children and one parent employed full-time and receiving an average industrial worker's wage. The family benefits and the tax reductions are measured in terms of annual means. Only economic support that is given on the basis of children present in the family is included. Benefits and tax deductions provided solely for housewives are excluded from the statistics for countries in which such benefits are provided.[6] The level of benefits is defined as the proportion of total benefits to the total net income for the above-defined family type. The net income is defined as the family's income after taxes and including family benefits. These measures of the level of family support are used to improve comparability between the countries and over time.[7]

Figures 1 and 2 depict the level of cash benefits and tax reductions as a proportion of net family income in the countries under study for the years 1950 and 1985. These points in time are chosen to cover as large a share of the postwar period as possible: 1950 is the first year by which family benefit systems had been introduced in most of the countries under study, while 1985 is the last year included in the data set upon which this study is based. The countries are clustered according to the system of family benefits in the country.

As indicated above, all countries except Italy and Ireland had implemented some form of universal family support system by 1950. However,

FIGURE 1
The Share of Family Benefits, Tax Reductions, and Tax Allowances in the Average Industrial Wage in Eighteen OECD Countries in 1950

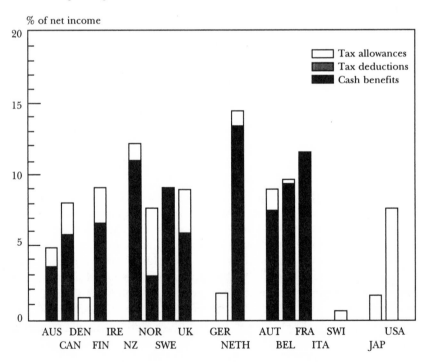

FIGURE 2
The Share of Family Benefits, Tax Reductions, and Tax Allowances in the Average
Industrial Wage in Eighteen OECD Countries in 1985

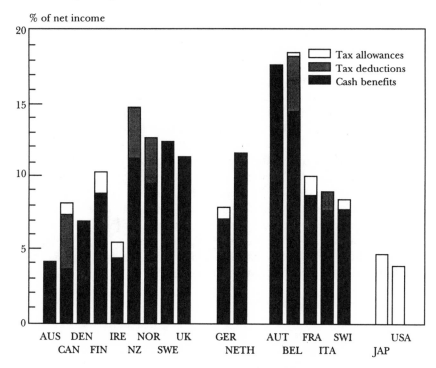

only 11 of the 18 countries had introduced a system of cash benefits to families with children. The USA, Germany, Denmark, Japan, and Switzerland had only tax reductions for families at this time. Sweden and France had only cash benefits, and the remaining nine countries made available a combination of cash benefits and tax reductions.

Figure 1 also demonstrates that, in most countries with both cash benefits and tax reductions (Norway being the only exception here), the economic importance of the benefits was greater than that of the tax reduction. However, this is the case only for families with one parent earning an average industrial wage. If household income is higher, then the effect of tax reduction can also be much more significant. It is further demonstrated that the level of support varies a lot between countries. The Netherlands, New Zealand and France had benefit levels of more than 10 per cent of the total net household income, while six countries had a benefit level of less that 3 per cent.

By 1985, all countries had implemented some form of universal family support system and all countries except Japan and the USA had introduced cash benefits for families. Austria, Sweden, the Netherlands, the United Kingdom, Denmark, and Australia gave no tax reductions to families in 1985. Again, as in 1950, the level of cash benefits was higher than that of tax reductions in those countries offering both systems, with Canada being the exception. The figures also demonstrate a secular growth trend in family support during the postwar period. As noted previously, in 1950 only three countries provided family support at a level higher than 10% of net family income. By 1985, eight countries were providing economic support of this magnitude. Nearly all the overall growth in family support is explained by increases in the size of cash benefits, even if that is not the case for every country.

Three countries – the Netherlands, France, and the USA – decreased their level of family support by more than 1 percentage point. The countries with cash benefits did not explicitly reduce their level of family support. The relative value of this support decreased because it did not increase as fast as family income did. Belgium, Austria, Italy, and Switzerland increased their level of family support by more than 8 percentage points in the course of the postwar period.

4. The Determinants of Family Support

4.1. Methods

The different models of economic family support can be ordered according to their equalizing effects between different income strata. This aspect of family support is important for testing out hypotheses, especially our prediction that emphasizes the role of left parties. Therefore, tests will be made separately for two types of family support: cash benefits and tax allowances.[8]

The data have been collected from 18 OECD countries for the period 1930–85 as part of a greater project, the purpose of which is to examine the development of social rights in industrialized countries. The countries in the sample have been democratically ruled since World War II and have populations above 1 million. They are Australia, Austria, Belgium, Canada, Denmark, Finland, France, West Germany, Ireland, Italy, Japan, the Netherlands, New Zealand, Norway, Sweden, Switzerland, the United Kingdom, and the United States. Information about these countries' forms of economic family support were collected for 1930, 1933, 1939, 1947, 1950, and every subsequent fifth year up to 1985.

In the preceding discussion, some mechanisms producing variation in the level of family support have been proposed. In this section, indicators for measuring their effects will be discussed. The values of the independent variables are calculated as averages over each of the five-year periods preceding the year for which the level of family support is measured. For example, for 1960 the values of the independent variables are calculated as averages for the period 1955-9. For 1947 the relevant period is 1939-46, and for 1950, 1947-9. Measuring the effect of the independent variables after such a time-lag will strengthen our case for ascribing causal significance to these variables.

Fertility is measured by the gross reproduction rate, which, in short, means the average number of girls born to a woman during her entire fertile period. It might be objected that the net reproduction rate, which takes into consideration mortality among women of childbearing age, is a more reliable measure of fertility. In most of the countries, however, this measure is not available for the whole period. Economic growth and development are measured by two indicators. The first is the level of GDP/capita, which indicates the level of economic development and industrialization in the country.[9] The other indicator is economic growth, which is measured by the relative annual percentage increase in GDP/capita. This variable indicates the amount of new economic resources the country generates during a given year and thereby, it is assumed, the nation's capacity to carry out expensive social reforms.

Two different kinds of indicators are used as gauges of the strength of the left and religious parties. The first includes measures of political parties' participation in the government, or, more precisely, the parties' average shares of cabinet portfolios during a period. This gauges the parties' ability to influence the process of national political decision-making. However, parties and organizations excluded from the government may also influence social policy-making. In situations where the opposition has strong support from the public, it may be necessary for parties in the government to make political compromises or allow their policies to be influenced by the opposition's programme in order to preserve their political influence. Duverger (1954) calls this 'contagion from the left,' but this phenomenon might involve pressure from religious parties as well as from left ones. To measure such pressure I use the share of votes for left and religious parties.

The countries can be divided into sub-groups according to their family benefit system. I have previously indicated that the type of family support system a country has may possible have an independent effect on benefit levels and the levels of tax allowances. Therefore, two dummy variables are included, one for countries with an employment-based system and one for countries without a family benefit system (Japan and the USA). A trend variable is also used in the regression analysis to screen out relations that result from strong trends in dependent and independent variables. Country dummies are, however, not introduced in the model. The reason for this is that some of the independent variables, namely the shares of left and religious votes and the two system variables, remain constant or fairly invariable over time within the countries but differ significantly between the countries. An introduction of country dummies leads to a misspecification of the effects of the variables that are specific for some of the countries.

The model has been specified in terms of the following multivariate OLS equation:

$$\text{Family support} = a + b_1\,\text{economy}_{it} + b^2\,\text{fertility}_{it} + b_3\,\text{left}_{it} + b_4\,\text{religious}_{it} + b_5\,\text{system1}_{it} + b_6\,\text{system2}_{it} + b_7\,\text{trend}_t + e_{it}$$

Economy   = (a) relative level of GDP/capita measured in 1975 US dollars; (b) relative level GDP/capita growth.

Fertility = average gross reproduction rate.

Left   = (a) average share of cabinet portfolios for left parties; (b) average share of electoral votes for left parties.

Religious = (a) average share of cabinet portfolios for religious parties; (b) average share of electoral votes for religious parties.

System1   = 0 for countries with a universal system, 1 for countries with an employment-based system.

System2   = 0 for countries with a system of cash benefits, 1 for countries with no such system.

Trend   = year.

The data are analysed for the period 1947–85.[10] The interwar period is excluded, primarily because the causes of development of social policy during this period may differ dramatically from the causes of such development in the postwar period (Korpi 1989; Palme 1990; Väisänen 1991). Inclusion of this period would be problematic also because universal family benefits were not common until after World War II.

The trend variable and the two dummy variables that discriminate between different benefit systems are inserted in the model to avoid some of the problems that may arise when using a sample with changes taking place both over time and between units. Tests of significance are displayed along with slope estimates and their standard error in tables 3

TABLE 3
The Effects on Family Benefits' Share of Income of Economic Development and Growth,
Fertility, Left Strength, Religious Party Strength, System Variables, and a Trend

Variables				
Level of economic	0.00	0.00		
development	(0.00)	(0.00)		
Economic growth			−0.06	−0.11
Fertility	1.53	2.24	1.44	1.62
	(1.23)	(1.31)	(1.20)	(1.23)
Left participation	4.34***		4.37***	
in government	(1.05)		(1.05)	
Religious parties'	3.55*		3.59*	
participation in govt.	(1.94)		(1.92)	
Left votes		8.76***		8.06***
		(2.62)		(2.55)
Votes for religious		7.27**		7.09**
parties		(2.71)		(2.72)
Employment-based	2.95**	1.70	2.98**	1.73
system	(1.04)	(1.05)	(1.03)	(1.05)
No universal	−3.67***	−3.40**	−3.57***	−3.25**
system	(1.05)	(1.11)	(1.04)	(1.13)
Trend	0.09*	0.05	0.10***	0.10***
	(0.04)	(0.04)	(0.03)	(0.03)
Constant	−180.79*	−102.70	−196.75***	−194.55***
	(86.96)	(84.99)	(56.36)	(56.59)
Adjusted R^2	0.408	0.408	0.409	0.404
Degrees of freedom	161	161	161	161

Standard error in parentheses.
*** = $p < 0.05$
** = $p < 0.01$
* = $p < 0.001$

and 4. A two-tailed test is used for fertility and for variables that discriminate between the different benefit systems. For the other variables, one-tailed tests are used. The sample can of course not be seen as a random one, so the test is used here simply to provide some indications of the robustness of the estimates.

4.2. Findings

Table 3 depicts the effects of the independent variables on the level of cash benefits. The fit of the model is fairly good. The share of explained variance ranges between 40 and 41 per cent.

TABLE 4

The Effects on Tax Allowances' Share of Net Income of Economic Development and Growth, Fertility, Left Strength, Religious Party Strength, System Variables, and a Trend

Variables				
Level of economic development	0.00** (0.00)	0.00** (0.00)		
Economic growth			0.00 (0.06)	0.01 (0.06)
Fertility	1.85** (0.64)	2.19** (0.68)	1.48* (0.64)	1.61* (0.65)
Left participation in government	−0.69 (0.54)		−0.64 (0.56)	
Religious parties' participation in govt.	1.39 (1.00)		0.95 (1.02)	
Left votes		−0.18 (1.37)		−1.08 (1.35)
Votes for religious parties		1.65 (1.42)		1.16 (1.44)
Employment-based system	−1.09* (0.54)	−0.85 (0.55)	−1.01 (0.55)	−0.86 (0.56)
No universal system	1.43** (0.54)	1.71** (0.58)	1.64** (0.55)	1.66** (0.60)
Trend	−0.06** (0.02)	−0.5* (0.02)	−0.01 (0.01)	−0.01 (0.01)
Constant	111.54** (44.96)	94.29* (44.36)	19.07 (29.85)	14.00 (29.98)
Adjusted R^2	0.218	0.204	0.181	0.174
Degrees of freedom	153	153	153	153

Standard error in parentheses.
*** = $p < 0.05$
** = $p < 0.01$
* = $p < 0.001$

Neither the level nor the annual growth rate of GDP/capita seems to have any significant effects on the level of benefits. The signs of the coefficients are not as predicted for economic growth, but the estimates are in any case not significant. Fertility exercises positive, but insignificant, effects on the level of family benefits. The relationship found lends no support to the claim that family benefits are used to regulate fertility in a systematic way. By contrast, our results provide weak support for the alternative hypothesis, which assumed that a large proportion of parents among voters leads to increases in benefit levels.

The measures of the strength of left parties exercise strong positive effect on family benefits. Here relations are significant for both left participation in government and the electoral share of votes for left parties. The strength of religious parties also has a strong influence on the level of family benefits. The relationship is weaker than that exercised by left strength, especially in the cabinet equations, but it is still significant.[11]

Countries with an employment-based system have higher benefit levels than other countries. In one of the models this difference is significant. The reasons may have something to do with the institutional structure of the employment-based systems, as was assumed earlier. There is a significant difference between countries with and without a cash benefit system even after all the independent variables are brought into the model. The difference between these groups of countries is possibly the result of a threshold effect. Once a benefit system is introduced it is seldom abolished, even if the political situation which led to it may have changed. The fact that it is easier for a political party to introduce family benefits than it is to abolish them leads to a situation where countries may have a family benefit system that is dependent on the earlier political situation and not on the current one. This fact can make a difference between countries with and without a cash benefit system, which is not dependent on differences in the other independent variables in the model.

The effects of the independent variables on tax allowances for families are analysed in table 4. The explained variance ranges between 17 and 22 per cent, which indicates a rather low degree of fit for the tax allowance models.

The level of GDP/capita has a positive and significant effect on the level of tax allowances. Economic growth, on the other hand, has no demonstrable effect. Fertility exercises a positive and significant effect. This supports the conclusions we have derived from the analysis of family benefits; in other words, that family support is not used for the purpose of regulating reproduction.[12] Even if the intention of family support programmes has been to increase birth rates, this goal does not seem to have been achieved. Instead, fertility has a positive effect on family support, which indicates support for the hypothesis derived from the 'Downsian' approach.

The results further show that the strength of left parties has a weak negative impact on the level of tax allowances. According to the hypothesis we have advanced, left party strength should have positive impacts on family benefit levels and negative ones on tax allowances, owing to their different income-equalizing effects. The first hypothesis is strongly confirmed by our data, whereas the second one is confirmed to more limited extent. The strength of religious parties also exercises a weak positive effect. Together with the results presented above, this leads us to the conclusion that the strength of religious parties seems to have an overall positive impact on economic support for families.[13]

Countries with an employment-based system have lower levels of tax reductions than other countries; in one model the difference is significant. The countries without any benefit systems have significantly higher tax reductions, suggesting that these systems are alternative rather than complementary means of family support.[14]

5. Summary and Conclusions

In analysing the effect of the independent variables on family support, we have found that economic growth and the level of economic development have no substantial positive effect on the extent of family support. In addition, a weak positive relationship between fertility and family support indicates that such support is not used as a means of directing the reproduction of the population in any systematic way. The results give us reason to question views of social policy measures as methods whereby the behaviour of citizens is efficiently regulated or steered. The reason for this can be either that most governments do not intend to regulate fertility with family policy, or that it is impossible to use social policy measures for this purpose.[15] Instead, the results give weak support to the alternative hypothesis that a high proportion of parents among voters seem to have a positive impact on the level of benefits. This indicates that the political parties in government are to a greater extent driven by vote-maximizing in the short run than to optimize long-term utility for society.

The hypothesis derived from the power resources approach is rather strongly confirmed by the data. The two indicators used for the strength of left parties exercised a strong positive impact on family benefits and a weak negative one on tax allowances. These results are consistent with previously cited studies on the impact of left party strength on the development of social rights. (Studies which have demonstrated this effect on rights to sickness insurance, old-age pensions and workmen's compensation are Korpi 1985, Palme 1990, and Väisänen 1991.) Religious party strength also seems to have positive effects on both types of family support, but the effects on the level of tax allowances are weak. These results support the previously presented hypothesis emphasizing the 'familism' of the religious parties, which was assumed to lead to improved economic support for families.

Finally, the two variables which discriminated between different systems of family benefit show that employment-based systems have slightly higher benefit levels and lower levels of tax reductions, even taking into account differences in the countries' rates of economic growth and level of development, rates of fertility and domestic political configurations. These results may indicate that differences in institutional structures, such as the financing of benefits or the decision-making process, exercise an independent impact on the level of family benefits.

It was further demonstrated that the independent variables examined here could not explain all of the differences between the group with and without family benefit systems. This is probably due to some sort of threshold effect. The results from both the descriptive and analytic part of this study shows that it is rather difficult to abolish a system of family benefits once it is introduced in a nation. A possible way of reducing the level of cash benefits is to withhold increases in benefit levels, thereby allowing inflation to erode their value.

In conclusion, we can state that the trends we observed cannot be accounted for by theoretical approaches that identify partisan politics as less relevant for the level of family support and ascribe an independent causal role to industrialization and declining fertility rates. Instead, the results have given strong support to approaches that emphasize the importance of partisan politics in determining the course of social policy development. The strength of both left and Christian parties has a significant impact on the extent of family support. Furthermore, the hypothesis that accentuated the importance of the proportion of parents in the population is confirmed to a limited extent.

As has been shown in this study, the level of family support is best predicted by the indicators reflecting the domestic political situation. The universal introduction of a family support structure probably results from the rising cost of having children, which is itself affected by industrialization, and from problems with decreasing fertility during the 20th century, even if the extension and form of this structure is determined by national partisan politics. It is highly probably that the two different theoretical perspectives on social policy focus on different and complementary aspects of the growth of the welfare state.

92   Irene Wennemo

Notes

I want to thank Alex Hicks, Johan Fritzell, Olli Kangas, Walter Korpi, Joakim Palme, Theda Skocpol, and two referees for their useful comments and Eero Carroll for correcting my English.

1   The assumption implies that countries with below-average rates of fertility should be providing more extensive family benefits that nations with above-average fertility rates. The validity of this assumption can be questioned when the aim of the ruling elite is rapidly to increase the size of the population. Family policies intended to realize this aim were implemented in Germany and Italy in the interwar period and during World War II, as well as in the USSR and some East European countries in the postwar period. These countries and periods, however, are excluded from the scope of study.
2   If high fertility rates instead indicate that fewer families are having more children, the proportion of parents is smaller than in the previous case. But this may instead lead to greater demand for economic support to families. This may lead to family support issues acquiring more importance higher on the policy agenda for families in this case, and therefore to the same effect as in the previous case.
3   Since 1980 a system of tax reductions whereby parents who do not benefit from the tax reduction are compensated with a cash benefit of the same amount of money has been implemented in Norway.
4   The problem with estimating this effect is that it is difficult to find a predictor reflecting this motive. The share of women in the labour force cannot be used as a predictor, even if it can be an effect of this policy. This is because policies arising from this motive can exist in countries with low female labour force participation as well as in those with high. It is possible, however, that religious parties have these kinds of family policy goals.
5   Denmark, Australia, and Italy are, however, exceptions to this rule. Denmark reintroduced a means-tested system in 1977; this system turned into a universal system again in 1987, a very small share of the population with very high incomes were excluded from the benefit (Vedel-Petersen 1978). Denmark is therefore included in the analysis. Australia introduced a means-tested system to replace its universal system in 1987, with Italy following in 1988. These changes occur, however, outside the period under study.
6   At one time there existed a system in France which provided economic support to families with both a non-working housewife and children. This system is included in the analysis.

7 Because of variations in the proportion of working mothers with pre-school children between countries, this measure is not totally applicable for the purposes of ascertaining the economic importance of support to families. In Scandinavian countries, female labour force participation was very high during the 1970s and 1980s. This led to an overestimation of the support's share of income, because the family's average income gets higher when both parents are employed. During the same period, Scandinavian countries strongly increased the amount of support for other types of family support, primarily public child care. In 1980, expenditure on public child care was higher than that on family benefits in Denmark, Finland and Sweden (Olson 1986; Kuhnle 1986; Johansen 1986; Alestalo and Uusitalo 1986).

8 Tax deductions will not be dealt with here, partly because this system does not discriminate clearly between the hypotheses and partly because this type of support is relatively rare and does not last long in any country.

9 It has been argued that the share of the agricultural labour force reflects the level of a nations's industrialization better than GDP/capita. The multi-collinearity between these variables is however very high ($r = 0.79$), and it is therefore reasonable to believe that these indicators measure the same phenomena.

10 West Germany is excluded from the analysis for 1947 because of the untypical postwar political situation.

11 Analysing the country residuals of the equations indicates that Germany and Switzerland provide a lower level of benefits than the model would predict, whereas Belgium and New Zealand provide a higher level of benefits than predicted. The benefit levels for these cases vary by about 4 percentage points on either side of the predicted level.

12 If fertility has only a delayed effect on the level of family support, the coefficients can be wrongly estimated. To test this possibility, fertility from the previous period was used (for 1960, 1950–4). This leads to weaker effects than those exercised by unlagged fertility rates, but the coefficients still remain positive.

13 Here the residuals indicate that the UK provides more extensive family allowances than the model would predict, whereas Italy does worse than predicted. The difference between the predicted and actual value is around 2 percentage points.

14 If both types of tax reductions are used in the regressions the amount of explained variance decreases by half. The effect of the left party becomes weaker as assumed, and reaches values very close to zero. The effect of fertility decreases a little.

15   This result attains additional significance when considered in the context of anti-Keynesian political criticism. In Keynesian political thought, the capacity for and the positive effect of state intervention in the economy are stressed. However, in recent decades, doubts about the ability of the state to deal with macroeconomic conjunctural shifts has been raised.

References

Åberg, R. 1989. Distributive Mechanisms of the Welfare State – A Formal Analysis and an Empirical Application. *European Sociological Review* 5(2).

Alestalo, M. & Uusitalo, H. 1986. Finland. In P. Flora, *Growth to the Limits vol 1*. Berlin: Walter de Gruyter.

Berghman, J., Peters, J. & Vranken, J. 1987. Belgium. In P. Flora, *Growth to the Limits vol 4*. Berlin: Walter de Gruyter.

Carlson, A.C. 1990. *The Swedish Experiment in Family Politics – The Myrdals and the Interwar Population Crisis*. New Brunswick, NJ: Transaction Publishers.

Castles, F. 1978. *The Social Democratic Image of Society*. London: Routledge.

Downs, A. 1957. *An Economic Theory of Democracy*. New York: Harper.

Duverger, M. 1954. *Political Parties: Their Organizations and Activity in the Modern State*. New York: Wiley.

Elster, J. 1979. *Ulysses and the Sirens – Studies in Rationality and Irrationality*. Cambridge: Cambridge University Press.

Esping-Andersen, G. 1985. *Politics against Markets. The Social Democratic Road to Power*. Princeton, NJ: Princeton University Press.

Esping-Andersen, G. 1990. *Three Worlds of Welfare Capitalism*. Cambridge: Polity.

Gordon, M. 1988. *Social Security Policies in Industrial Countries – A Comparative Analysis*. Cambridge: Cambridge University Press.

Hatje, A. 1974. *Befolkningsfrägan och välfärden, Debatten om familjepolitik och nativietsökning under 1930-och 1940-talen*. Stockholm: Allmänna förlaget.

Heinsohn, G., Kineper, R. & Steiger, O. 1982. *Människoproduktionens historia. Allmän befolkningsteori för den nya tiden*. Lund: Arkiv.

Hinnfors, J. 1992: *Familjepolitik – Samhällsförändringar och partistrategier, 1960–1990*. Stockholm: Almquist & Wicksell International.

Johansen, L.N. 1986. Denmark. In P. Fora, *Growth to the Limits vol 4*. Berlin: Walter de Gruyter.

Kangas, O. 1986. *Luokkaintressitja Hyvinvointivaltio*. Helsinki: Helsingin Hauppakorkeakoulin Julkaisuja D-84.

Kerr, C. et al. 1973. *Industrialism and Industrial Man*. Cambridge, Mass.: Harvard University Press.

Kersbergen K. 1991. *Social Capitalism – A Study of Christian Democracy and the Post War Settlement of the Welfare State.* Florence: European University Institute.

Korpi, W. 1978. *Working Class in Welfare Capitalism.* London: Routledge & Kegan Paul.

Korpi, W. 1981. *The Democratic Class Struggle.* London: Routledge & Kegan Paul.

Korpi, W. 1985. Power Resources vs. Action and Conflict: On Causal and Intentional Explanation in the Study of Power. *Sociological theory* 3, pp. 31–45.

Korpi, W. 1989. Power, Politics and State Autonomy in the Development of Social Citizenship – Social Rights during Sickness in 18 OECD Countries since 1930, *American Sociological Review* 54, pp. 309–28.

Knudsen, R. 1990. *Familieydelser i Norden 1989.* Stockholm: Nordstedts tryckeri.

Kuhnle, S. 1986. Norway. In P. Flora, *Growth to the Limits vol 4.* Berlin: Walter de Gruyter.

Kälvemark, A. 1980. *More Children of Better Quality? Aspects on Swedish Population Policy in the 1930's.* Uppsala: Almqvist & Wicksell International.

Marklund, S. 1982. *Klass, stat och socialpolitik – en jämförande studie av socialförsäkringar i några västliga kapitalistiska länder 1930–75.* Lund: Arkiv.

Myrdal, A. & Myrdal, G. 1934. *Kris i befolkningsfrågan.* Stockholm: Bonniers.

Ohlander, A. 1989. *Det osynliga barnet? Kampen om den svenska familjepolitiken i Socialdemokratins samhälle SAP och Sverige under 100 år.* Kristianstad; Tiden.

Olson, S.E. 1986. Sweden. In P. Flora, *Growth to the Limits vol 4.* Berlin: Walter de Gruyter.

Palme, J. 1990. *Pension Rights in Welfare Capitalism. The Development of Old-Age Pensions in 18 OECD Countries, 1930 to 1985.* Stockholm: Swedish Institute for Social Research.

Pampel, F.C. & Adams, P. 1990. State, Politics, and Public Policy Response to Demographic Change: Family Allowance Expenditure in Advanced Industrial Democracies, mimeo.

Parry, R. 1986. United Kingdom. In P. Flora, *Growth to the Limits vol 2.* Berlin: Walter de Gruyter.

Questiaux, N. & Fournier, J. 1978. France. In S.B. Kamerman and A.J. Kahn, *Family Policy – Government and Families in Fourteen Countries.* New York: Columbia University Press.

Rausing, L. 1986. The Population Question: The Debate of Family Welfare Reforms in Sweden, 1930–1938. *European Journal of Political Economy* 2/4.

Rothstein, B. 1990. Marxism, Institutional Analysis, and Working-Class Power – The Swedish Case. *Politics and Society* 3, pp. 317–46.

Seip, A. & Ibsen, H. 1989. Morsokonomi, familieokonomi og samfunnsokonomi. Barnetrygden i ett historiskt perspektiv. *Norsk historisk tidskrift* No. 4, pp. 413–33.

Shalev, M. 1983. The Social Democratic Model and Beyond: Two Generations of Comparative Social Research on the Welfare State. *Comparative Social Research* 6.

Skocpol, T. 1985. Bringing the State Back in: Strategies of Analysis in Current Research. In P.B. Evans, D. Rueschemeyer, T. Skocpol, *Bringing the State Back In.* New York: Cambridge University Press.

Skocpol. T. & Ritter, G. 1991. Gender and the Origins of Modern Social Policies in Britain and the United States. *Studies in American Political Development* 5 (Spring), pp. 36–93.

SOU. 1946. *Barnkostnadernas fördelning* No. 5.

Swedish Institute for Social Research [SSIB – Svensk Socialpolitik i International Belynsning] Data base.

Therborn, G. 1987. Welfare States and Capitalist Markets. *Acta Sociologica* 3/4, pp. 237–54.

Therborn, G. 1989. Social Steering and Household Strategics. Exploring Encounters between the Macropolitics and the Microsociology of Welfare States. *Journal of Public Policy* 9, pp. 371–97.

Titmuss, R.M. 1974. Social Policy – An Introduction. London: Allen & Unwin.

Tobin, J. 1968. Raising the Incomes of the Poor. In K. Gordon, *Agenda for the Nations.* Washington, DC: Brookings Institution.

US Department of Health, Education and Welfare. 1949. *Social Security Legislation Throughout the World.*

US Department of Health, Education and Welfare. 1958, 1961, 1964, 1967, 1971, 1975, 1979, 1981, 1985. *Social Security Programs Throughout the World.*

US Social Security Administration. Various years. *Social Security Programs Throughout the World.* Washington, DC: US Government Printing Office.

Vedel-Petersen, J. 1978. Denmark. In S.B. Kamerman and A.J. Kahn, *Family Policy – Government and Families in Fourteen Countries.* New York: Columbia University Press.

Wennemo, I. 1991. Arbetarrörelsen och befolkningsfrågan Knut Wicksells och makarna Myrdals befolkningsteorier. *Arkiv för arbetarrörelsens historia* No. 50, pp. 61–73.

Wilensky, H.L. 1976. *The Welfare State and Equality: Structural and Ideological Roots of Public Expenditures.* Berkeley, Calif.: University of California Press.

Wilensky, H.L. & Lebeaux, C.N. 1965. *Industrial Society and Social Welfare.* New York: Russell Sage Foundation.

Wilensky, H.L. 1981. Leftism, Catholicism, and Democratic Corporatism: The Role of Political Parties in Recent Welfare State Development. In P. Flora and A.J. Heidenheimer, *The Development of Welfare States in Europe and America.* New Brunswick, NJ: Transaction.

Väisänen, I. 1991. Socialpolitikens utveckling i konflikt- och konsensusperspektiv;
En jämförande studie av socialförsäkringar i 18 OECD-länder 1930–85.
Sociologisk forskning 2, pp. 3–26.

3

Political Parties and Public Pensions: A Quantitative Analysis

EVELYNE HUBER and JOHN D. STEPHENS

This article analyses pooled time series and cross-sections data for pension expenditure in advanced industrial democracies from 1958 to 1986, and cross-sectional data for pension quality and the distributive effect of pensions for 1980. Contrary to previous studies, it demonstrates significant effects of the party political composition of governments; both Christian democratic and social democratic incumbency are positively associated with pension expenditure. Only social democratic incumbency is associated with pension quality and less inequality and poverty among the elderly. Aspects of state structure which facilitate access of relatively small groups to the policy-making process are negatively associated with quality of pensions and their distributive effects. The article explains the discrepancies between this and earlier studies, and it explores the reasons for the differences in the determinants of pension expenditure and those of overall welfare state expenditure.

1. Introduction

There is wide agreement today in advanced industrial societies that governments should provide pensions.[1] At the rhetorical level, there is hardly any dissent from the view that governments should enable their citizens to grow old in dignity and that old age should not push people into poverty. However, in practice, there is wide variation among advanced industrial societies in the amount of resources allocated by governments for these purposes and in the ways in which these resources are allocated (table 1).

In the attempts to explain these variations, a debate has emerged similar to that concerning variations in welfare state spending in general. This debate has centered on the importance of political variables (e.g.,

TABLE 1
Public Pension Spending as a Percentage of GDP 1960 and 1980

	1960	1980
Australia	1.03	3.76
Austria	4.59	8.82
Belgium	3.13	6.48
Canada	1.15	3.27
Denmark	3.75	7.85
Finland	2.20	6.02
France	2.62	7.57
Germany	5.87	9.57
Ireland	2.30	4.87
Italy	3.30	5.49
Japan	0.22	2.55
Netherlands	3.87	11.29
Norway	2.21	7.43
New Zealand	1.66	8.24
Sweden	3.58	9.64
Switzerland	1.71	7.32
United Kingdom	1.78	5.52
United States	2.29	3.75

Data Source: ILO, Cost of Social Security (various years).

party composition of governments, labor strength, and centralization), state structure and policy legacies, and economic (e.g., level of development, openness of the economy) and demographic variables, as determinants of expenditure on and quality of welfare state programs. In a recent contribution (Huber et al., 1993) we make significant steps towards a resolution of the debate on the determinants of welfare state spending, social rights, and distributive outcomes in general. In this article, we attempt to do the same for pension spending, pension quality, and distributive outcomes in particular.

The first question to ask, then, is whether pensions should be shaped by the same determinants as welfare state programs as a whole, or whether the causal dynamics involved should be different to some extent. They certainly cannot be entirely different, as pension expenditures make up the largest single proportion of total welfare state expenditures. However, both theoretical reasons and previous empirical work suggest that pensions are in some ways different from other welfare state programs and thus can be expected to have partly different determinants. We will explore these differences below.

2. The State of the Debate

In contrast to many other areas of macrosocial research, quantitative and comparative historical research on the development of the welfare state share a common set of theoretical concerns. Though a variety of explanations for the expansion of and variations among welfare states has been offered, three dominate the literature.[2] According to the 'logic of industrialism' explanation, both the growth of the welfare state and cross-national differences in 'welfare state effort' are by-products of economic development and its demographic and social organizational consequences (Wilensky 1975). The 'power resources' or 'political class struggle' argument contends that the level of working-class mobilization and the strength of left parties are the primary determinants of the size and distributive impact of the welfare state (Korpi 1983; Stephens 1979). According to 'state-centric' explanations, the structure of the state and the policy-making activities of bureaucrats (who are seen as relatively autonomous from the pressures of social forces) are the primary sources of international differences in welfare policy and are responsible as well for the expansion of the welfare state through time (Heclo 1974; Weir et al. 1988). While it might be argued that the determinants of pensions might be different from those of overall welfare state effort, this question has received scant attention in the theoretical discussions to date.[3]

Quantitative studies of determinants of pension systems have become increasingly sophisticated methodologically, but they still arrive at apparently contradictory conclusions. The early analyses of pension expenditure were plagued by a deficiency that is troublesome for all cross-sectional analyses of advanced industrial democracies: too many variables and too few cases. The pooling of cross-sections and time series promised to break this logjam and indeed does represent a significant advance over a previous generation of research. To date, only four studies of pension expenditure using pooled data have appeared: Hicks 1990; Pampel & Williamson 1985, 1989; and Pampel et al. 1990. Unfortunately these studies yield contradictory results on key independent variables. For example, Hicks finds modest effects of centrist government on pension expenditure; Pampel et al. (1990) find strong positive effects of rightist government; and the other two studies show no party effects. Our examination of these data reveals the following sources of error in these studies: multicollinearity among key explanatory variables, failure to operationalize the party constellations properly, and poor operationalization of state structures. Above all, the omission of Catholic parties as an independent variable, which we have shown to be the single most power-ful determinant of variations in transfer payments (of which in turn pension expenditure is the most important component) seriously com-promises these studies (Huber et al. 1993).

Analyses of the social rights to pensions provided for in national legis-lation, including replacement rates, cost-of-living adjustment, degree of means testing, extent of coverage, criteria to qualify for full pensions, and the individual's share of pension financing (or pension quality, as we will term them for short), appear to yield more consistent results. Myles (1984) and Palme (1988) found that the strength of working-class unions or parties was an important determinant of public pension qual-ity. Analyses by Esping-Andersen (1990) and Palme (1990b) comparing the results of analyses with measures of pension quality as the dependent variable with pension expenditure as the dependent variable indicate that pension quality is strongly determined by political variables, particu-larly left party strength, whereas spending is not. Unfortunately, Palme and Esping-Andersen employ only a limited number of independent variables and thus do not do full justice to the analyses of the pooled data. Though we sustain their basic finding that left parties are stronger deter-minants of pension quality, we show that the determinants of the two sets of dependent variables are not as different as they indicate.

3. Hypotheses

3.1. The Distribution of Political Power

We hypothesize, first of all, that the distribution of political power mat-ters. Specifically, we expect the strength of left parties and of Christian democratic parties to have modest to strong effects on pension expendi-tures. Since pensions are transfer payments and make up the largest category of these payments, we would expect pension expenditures to have similar determinants as transfer payments overall. In other words, we expect Christian democratic incumbency to have a strong effect on pension expenditure and social democracy to have a weaker effect on pension expenditure than on the most inclusive measures of welfare state expenditure.

Pension systems shaped by social-democratic parties typically combine basic pensions, with entitlements based on citizenship, with income-related pensions, high replacement rates, and relatively lenient criteria for the degree of retirement required to receive the pension. Pension systems shaped by Christian democratic parties tend to combine heavily work-related pensions, with different programs for different occupations, with means-tested pension supplements. On the face of it, the former systems appear to require higher overall pension expenditure, and one would expect left incumbency to have a stronger effect on expenditure. However, a number of factors work in the opposite direction. In the Christian democratic pension systems, some occupational categories enjoy very high replacement rates as well. Moreover, Christian democratic parties have tolerated higher unemployment rates than social-democratic parties, and they have used early retirement on a large scale to deal with unemployment, which of course greatly increases pension expenditures. Germany and France are two cases where early retirement has assumed very large proportions. In addition, in Italy, the Christian democratic case *par excellence*, the abuse of transfer payments for clientelistic purposes is widespread. Finally, Christian democratic welfare states are very heavily oriented towards transfer payments rather than the provision of services, which would lead them to privilege pensions over other types of old-age care systems. On the basis of all these factors, one would expect a strong effect of Christian democratic incumbency on pension expenditures as well.

When it comes to the quality of pensions and their redistributive effect, we expect a strong relationship to incumbency of left parties, but not Christian democratic parties. The strength of left parties should be strongly related to program codings that tap coverage and generosity of pensions (such as Esping-Andersen's pension decommodification index or Myles' index of pension quality: high income-replacement rates, universalism, and low qualification criteria for full pensions (e.g., years of contributions). It should also be negatively related to measures of poverty and inequality among the elderly. The hypothesis about the absence of such a relationship to Christian democratic incumbency is based on the general pattern of Christian democratic welfare states: They tend to be market-conforming and thus reproduce rather than reduce inequalities stemming from position in the labor market (Huber et al. 1993).

In much of the literature, strength of social democracy is used as an indicator of the mobilization of working-class power (e.g., Korpi 1983). An alternative indicator is strength of the labor movement, conceptualized as the density, political unity, and centralization of union organization. Accordingly, we expect the effects of labor movement strength to mirror the effects of left party incumbency across the dependent variables. Some authors have also argued that working-class power mobilization results in a corporatist pattern of interest representation, in which the state and strong peak associations of labor and capital engage in tripartite negotiations (e.g., Stephens 1979; Korpi 1983). An alternative view holds that corporatism is a result of openness of the economy (Katzenstein 1985). Without entering into the debate about the social origins of corporatism, we simply note that past studies have shown that corporatism is highly correlated with strength of social-democratic parties and labor movements (Hicks & Swank 1992). Accordingly, we expect measures of corporatism also to show similar effects across our dependent variables.

3.2. State Structures

Based on recent comparative historical studies (Immergut 1992; Maioni 1992) and our own comparative historical research, we have developed a new measure to tap the effects of state structures on welfare state development. It is our hypothesis that those features of constitutions that make it difficult to reach and implement decisions based on narrow majorities – and that conversely let minority interests obstruct legislation – will impede far-reaching reforms in social policy, especially reforms that might benefit the underprivileged majority. We have shown that aspects of constitutional structure which disperse political power and offer multiple points of influence on the making and implementation of policy are negatively associated with transfer payments and overall social benefits expenditures (Huber et al. 1993). These aspects include federalism, presidential government, strong bicameralism, single-member-district electoral systems, and provisions for referenda. To some extent, this should also be the case for pension expenditures, but since pensions tend to enjoy wider support and less opposition than other welfare state programs, we would expect this effect not to be very strong. Compared to health care programs, pensions were introduced early and encountered fewer vested interests in existing systems of provision, such as doctors and other health professionals, drug companies, private insurances, etc. Compared to sickness and unemployment insurance, employers had less reason to oppose pensions, because they could not be expected to weaken labor control. Finally, a pension system – if universal – is guaranteed to have the widest impact, because virtually everybody will grow old. In contrast to pension expenditures, we would expect the more universalistic and egalitarian features of pension systems to be the target of minority opposition groups and thus to show an effect of state structure.

3.3. Policy Legacies

A number of authors have argued that the efforts of absolutist regimes to co-opt the growing working class along Bismarckian lines affected later welfare state development (Flora & Alber 1981; Esping-Andersen 1990). These countries had a wider base of social security arrangements on which expansions in the 20th century built. However, such welfare state policies introduced by absolutist regimes were corporatist and segmented; that is, they treated different occupational groups differently and thus reproduced inequalities created by the labor market. State employees in middle and higher ranks were treated best; white-collar workers were treated better than blue-collar workers; and among the blue-collar workers the most strategically located and the best organized, such as miners and metalworkers, were treated preferentially. Thus, we would expect such absolutist legacies to be positively related to expenditure but not to measures of pension quality and distributive outcomes.

3.4. Logic of Industrialism and Related Causes

The logic of industrialism thesis argues that rising affluence and the aging of the population of a society cause an expansion of welfare state expenditures. With regard to demographics, once pension and health care programs are instituted, it is obvious that a higher percentage of elderly people in the population should cause increased expenditures without increased entitlements. In addition, Pampel and Williamson (1985, 1989) claim that the aged act as an interest group, successfully pushing up or defending entitlements and thus increasing expenditures.

Where early pension programs for unemployed people exist, higher unemployment causes an increase in pension expenditures, but precisely because it increases costs in difficult times it may put a downward pressure on pension entitlements. Thus, at the same time it may be negatively related to pension quality. Because inflation triggers cost-of-living adjustments of pension benefits in many of the countries under study, we expect inflation to be positively related to pension expenditure. Military expenditure is hypothesized to be negatively related to pension expenditure due to a 'guns for butter' trade-off (Russet 1970; Wilensky 1975: 74–80).

In addition to the variables for which we have formulated clear hypotheses, we have also included in our analysis a number of variables from other studies, in order to be able to control for the effects of these variables and to comment on the findings presented in these other studies. The additional variables include economic openness, voter turnout, and strike activity. We discuss their operationalization in the section that follows.

4. The Data

The data source for the pension expenditure for 1958 to 1983 is the International Labour Office (ILO) series, *The Cost of Social Security*. The data for 1984–6 were acquired directly from ILO. With the exception of Palme (1990), all previous analyses of pension expenditure use the ILO data. Like earlier analyses, the dependent variables in our analysis are social security pensions only. Government employee pensions and other government spending benefiting the aged are not included. The ILO periodically revises this series to improve comparability. Though we consistently used the most recent figures published by ILO to maximize comparability, it is clear that the data are not fully comparable, especially for the earlier years, which is an unavoidable source of error in all the existing analyses.

We use two expenditure measures of the dependent variable in the analyses of the pooled data (see table 2): pension benefit expenditure as a percentage of GDP (PENGDP) and the same measure divided by the percent of the population over 65 (PENOLD). The latter measure controls for automatic increases in expenditure due to the increase in number of recipients. It measures pension expenditure per aged person as a ratio of GDP per capita or average pension benefits relative to the average standard of living in the country. Eighteen of the nineteen advanced industrial countries which have been democracies since World War II are included in the analysis. Luxembourg is excluded owing to missing data for some of the variables. The dates chosen (1958–86) were governed by data availability for the two dependent variables. We also list in table 2 the independent variables used in the analyses presented here. Our database includes a very large number of independent variables, virtually all causal variables – or close variants – used in previous studies of welfare state effort, including the four studies of pension systems mentioned above.[4]

Of special importance to this study are two party political variables: left party government share (LEFTCAB) and government share of all Christian democratic (primarily Catholic) parties (CDEMCAB). The full party data contained in our data set includes percentage of votes and percentage of

TABLE 2
Variables

Mnemonic	Description
PENSION	Total pension expenditure as a percentage of GDP (ILO)
PENOLD	PENSION/Percent of the population over 65 years of age
MIL	Military expenditure as a percentage of GDP
CORP	Lehmbruch's (1984) classification of countries according to degree of corporatism
LEFTCAB	Left government share, scored 1 for each year when the left is in government alone, scored as a fraction of the left's seats in parliament of all governing parties' seats for coalition government, cumulative score 1946 to date
CDEMCAB	Religious parties' government share (same coding procedure as for LEFTCAB)
UNEMP	Percentage of total labor force unemployed
UNION	Union membership as a percentage of total wage and salary earners
VTURN	Voter turnout
GDPPC	Gross domestic product per capita in US dollars
OPEN	(Imports + Export)/GDP
OLD	Percent of the population over 65 years of age
CPI	Inflation, percent increase in the consumer price index
CONSTRCT	Constitutional structure (see text)
AUTHLEG	Political regime in the late 19th century (see text)
STRIKES	Working days lost per 1000 workers
MYLES	Index of pension quality, Myles (1984)
PENDECOM	Degree of decommodification of public pension system, Esping-Andersen (1990)
GINIDISP	Gini index of disposable income among the elderly, Kangas and Palme (1990)
POVERTY	Percent of elderly in poverty, poverty defined as below 50 per cent of median income, data from Palme (1990a)

parliamentary seats of parties categorized according to seven different political tendencies. We examined all of these variables in the analysis; the two listed in table 2 proved to be the most consistent and powerful predictors of welfare state effort.

We measure 'corporatism' with Lehmbruch's (1984: 65–6) categorization of countries into four different degrees of corporatism (CORP). We use the percentage of wage and salary workers organized into unions as a measure of union strength (UNION). Working-class militance as expressed by strike rates is frequently used as an operationalization of the theoretical tradition represented by Piven and Cloward (1972) which argues that direct protest action is the most effective political tool for the lower classes. Our measures uses ILO data on working days lost per thousand workers (STRIKES). We operationalize openness of the economy as imports plus exports as a percentage of GDP, based on IMF data (OPEN).

We developed a measure of the degree to which a constitution provides entry points for minority interest groups to block social legislation (CONSTRCT). This index assesses constitutional provisions that obstruct rule by narrow majorities (or conversely give minorities the opportunity to veto legislation), and we scored countries following the information and classifications presented by Lijphart (1984). The five items which form the index are: (1) strength of federalism (high, medium, low), (2) existence of presidentialism (yes, no), (3) electoral system with single member districts versus proportional representation (single member districts, modified proportional representation, proportional representation), (4) strength of bicameralism (high, medium, low), and (5) importance of referenda (high, low).

To measure 'Bismarckian' legacies, we developed a measure of late 19th century political regimes (AUTHLEG) based on work on democracy (Rueschemeyer et al. 1992: ch 4). The countries are divided into three categories: full democracies, parliamentary governments without full working-class suffrage, and 'neo-absolutist' governments in which the principle of cabinet responsibility to the parliamentary majority had not yet been established.

The two main variables from the logic of industrialism argument, level of development and demographic structure of the population, are operationalized as in other studies as GDP per capita (GDPPC) and percent of the population over 65 (OLD), both based on OECD data. Inflation is measured by the consumer price index (CPI), based on IMF data. Unemployment (UNEM) is measured by the percentage of the total labor force that is unemployed, based on UN statistics.

In the cross-sectional analysis, we add four dependent variables: two measures of pension quality and two measures of distributive outcome. Esping-Andersen's index of pension decommodification (PENDECOM) is composed of replacement rates at two levels of income, length of qualifying period, individual's share of financing, and coverage (Esping-Andersen 1990: 50, 54). Myles' index of pension quality (MYLES) is composed of replacement rates at three income levels, indexing, degree of means testing, coverage, degree of flexibility of retirement, and retirement qualifications (Myles 1984: 63–75). Data are available for 15 of the 18 countries for Myles' index; this index refers to 1975. The measures of outcome are derived from analyses of the Luxembourg Income Surveys (LIS) by Kangas and Palme (Kangas & Palme 1990; Palme 1990), updated in personal communications with Palme. One (GINIDISP) is the Gini index of disposable income among the elderly and the other (POVERTY) is the poverty rate among the elderly with poverty defined as income below 50 per cent of median income. The LIS data are available for 10 countries only. All the other variables in the cross-sectional analysis are measured as in the pooled analysis, but for 1980. The one exception is the Myles index; in the regressions with this index, the other variables are also measured for 1975.

5. Analytic Strategy

In annual pooled data analyses, the dependent variable can be the level of expenditure or the change in expenditure from the previous date. Both strategies have advantages and disadvantages. Expressing the dependent and independent variables as change and, for some of the independent variables as lagged variables, has the advantage that it minimizes the multi-collinearity and correlated error problems characteristic of the pooled cross-sections and time series data. However, the analysis of change data assumes that the impact of the independent variables appears in the same year or in later years with a uniform lag. This is problematic in the case of welfare state expenditure in general as many programs are phased in or mature over a period of time. This is particularly true of pension expenditure. Most earnings related plans contain a provision by which entitlements are related to the number of years of contributions and thus the full impact of legislation on expenditure does not appear for one or two decades. For this reason, it seemed more advisable to use the level of expenditure as the dependent variable and then to handle the problems of multicollinearity and correlated errors with the appropriate statistical technique. A second reason to choose the level of expenditure is that it maximizes the comparability of our study with previous analyses of pooled data with the ILO measures as the dependent variable, as all of them have used the level of expenditure.

5.1. Multicollinearity

Given the problem of multicollinearity in this data, we began with an examination of the correlations among the independent variables. A key concern of the political class struggle theory is a cluster of variables: OPEN, UNION, LEFTCAB, and CORP, which Czada (1988) has shown to be related in a systematic fashion. The theoretical and comparative historical literatures argue that these are causally connected to one another. Economic openness has been hypothesized to be related to union density (Stephens 1979) and corporatism (Katzenstein 1985). High union density is favorable for incumbency of left-wing parties and vice versa (Kjellberg 1983; Stephens 1979; Wallerstein 1989b). Economic openness, strong union organization, and left government have been argued to be preconditions for corporatism (Katzenstein 1985; Stephens 1979; Wallerstein 1989a; Western 1991).

Examination of tolerance levels reveals serious multicollinearity when all variables are included in the equation. UNION exhibits the lowest tolerance level, 0.109, indicating that 89 per cent of the variation in UNION is explained by the other independent variables in the data set. Because of this multicollinearity, several variables exhibit inflated and unstable regression coefficients across different regressions when the years included or the variables included are varied. The following procedure was followed in determining which variables to delete from the equation. Our aim was to produce minimum tolerance levels of 0.25 and thereby to eliminate the inflation of regression coefficients and reduce the instability of the coefficients across equations for different time periods. Our bases for elimination rested on both statistical criteria and other empirical evidence. Statistical criteria were the level of tolerance of the variable and how its elimination from the analysis affected the tolerance levels of the remaining variables. In addition, we favored retention of variables for which there was strong comparative historical evidence that the variable in question (and not the alternative highly correlated variable) was directly related to the dependent variable. This procedure led us to delete UNION and CORP.[5]

Our analysis of the data strongly indicates that the contradictory results on the effect of politics on pension spending in previous studies was due in part to multicollinearity. All of these studies include a measure of economic openness, left government, corporatism, and union organization. We found that if we included three of these four variables in the equation and varied the dates slightly (e.g., dropping or adding two or three years at either end of the series), the left government coefficient would change from modestly positive to modestly negative while the coefficient for one of the other variables would move in the opposite direction.

5.2. Estimation Technique

We use Generalized Least Squares (GLS) error components techniques to estimate the models that follow. Pooled cross-sectional time-series models suffer from two kinds of correlated error – country specific (the same country is observed at many time points) and time specific (all countries are observed over the same span of years). Correlated errors distort computation of standard errors in Ordinary Least Squares regression, which, in turn, voids the use of confidence intervals and tests of significance (Stimson 1985). Following the analytic strategy laid out in our earlier analysis of overall welfare state expenditure (Huber et al. 1993), we (1) estimate baseline OLS models, (2) estimate GLS error components models adjusting for country-specific error, (3) estimate GLS error components models adjusting for time-specific error, and (4) estimate GLS error component models adjusting for both country-specific and time-specific error. The consequences of different kinds of error adjustment can be seen across the four different estimation techniques, ranging from no adjustment to adjustment for both types of error. Generally, we have greatest confidence in independent variables that maintain consistent effects across the four estimation techniques. When an effect is not consistent, it is useful to assess the impact of estimation techniques that eliminate or magnify the effect. Finally, we also compare the findings of the error components models with the results produced by models using Parks-Kamenta adjustment for auto-correlation and fixed country effects to provide an additional check on our conclusions.[6]

6. Results

6.1 Pension Expenditures

Contrary to previous studies of pooled data, our analysis shows strong effects of government composition on pension spending (see tables 3 and 4). The effects of Christian democracy are very strong in four of the eight regressions across the two tables. They are somewhat reduced in the equations correcting for country-specific errors and country- and time-specific errors, especially when PENOLD is the dependent variable (table 4). Social democracy has more modest effects, particularly on the PENOLD measure, but still consistently significant ones. These effects are weaker than we expected, and we will return to this finding in the next section.

TABLE 3
Pooled Time-Series Regression Analysis of Pension Benefit Expenditures as a Percentage
of GDP (ILO), 1958–1986

	OLS	GLS Country effects	GLS Time effects	GLS Both
		Estimation procedure		
Military expenditures	0.0452	–0.1387	0.0811	–0.0660
MIL	1.0117	–2.0535	1.8197	–0.9675
Population over 65	0.2947	0.3956	0.2776	0.3229
OLD	6.9026	5.6978	6.6011	4.6464
Unemployment rate	0.0191	0.0743	0.00562	0.0684
UNEMP	0.8601	3.7876	0.2392	3.3591
Consumer price index	0.0218	0.00826	0.0104	–0.000035
CPI	1.4694	0.7465	0.6018	–0.00275
Voter turnout	0.000687	–0.00418	0.00265	–0.00376
VTURN	0.0980	0.4005	0.3836	–0.3645
Strike rate	–0.2719	0.3171	–0.3004	0.2796
STRIKES	–1.2580	1.7627	–1.3881	1.5707
Christian Democratic	0.1443	0.0797	0.1405	0.0729
Cabinet CDEMCAB	13.3943	4.8820	13.2507	4.5254
Trade/GDP	0.4687	1.2805	0.5602	1.3781
OPEN	1.3743	2.4165	1.6525	2.604
Authoritarian legacy	0.1052	0.2163	0.1301	0.2283
AUTHLEG	1.0897	0.7663	1.3693	1.017
GDP per capita	0.000211	0.000130	0.000221	0.000163
GDPPC	9.5727	5.8982	8.9397	6.7945
State structure	–0.0223	0.1105	–0.0449	0.0463
CONSTRCT	–0.4484	0.9424	–0.9076	0.3926
Left party	0.0760	0.1135	0.0690	0.1056
Cabinet LEFTCAB	5.2087	6.2414	4.7615	5.9371

Unstandardized regression coefficients are reported in the first line of each row; the
second line reports associated T-statistics. The R^2 for the OLS equation is 0.804.

The strong political effects shown in our regressions but not in earlier
studies can be attributed to two improvements we have made. First, all
earlier studies of pension spending failed to include Christian democracy

TABLE 4
Pooled Time-Series Regression Analysis of Pension Benefit Expenditures per Population
over 65 as a Percentage of GDP Per Capita (ILO), 1958–1986

		Estimation procedure		
	OLS	GLS Country effects	GLS Time effects	GLS Both
Military expenditures	0.0116	–0.00646	0.0158	0.00466
MIL	2.8872	–1.0832	3.9687	0.7913
Population over 65	–0.00235	0.0148	–0.00450	0.00439
OLD	–0.6120	2.4075	–1.2006	0.7323
Unemployment rate	0.000462	0.00653	–0.000751	0.00639
UNEMP	0.2316	3.8271	–0.3519	3.6298
Consumer price index	0.00248	0.00165	0.00101	0.000464
CPI	1.8619	1.6991	0.6285	0.4176
Voter turnout	0.000346	–0.000851	0.000552	–0.000925
VTURN	0.5482	–0.9240	0.8944	–1.0454
Strike rate	–0.00472	0.0370	–0.00915	0.0296
STRIKES	–0.2430	2.3424	–0.4731	1.9553
Christian Democratic	0.0122	0.00365	0.0118	0.00246
Cabinet CDEMCAB	12.6067	2.5329	12.4527	1.7800
Trade/GDP	0.0901	0.1282	0.1003	0.1371
OPEN	2.9372	2.7400	3.3123	3.0062
Authoritarian legacy	0.00106	0.0244	0.00411	0.0361
AUTHLEG	0.1225	0.9532	0.4858	1.4316
GDP per capita	0.000018	0.000011	0.000019	0.000016
GDPPC	8.8447	5.7586	8.1338	7.3655
State structure	–0.00569	0.00212	–0.00845	–0.00758
CONSTRCT	–1.2754	0.2014	–1.9058	–0.7283
Left party	0.00419	0.00305	0.00343	0.00189
Cabinet LEFTCAB	3.1977	1.9039	2.6537	1.2457

Unstandardized regression coefficients are reported in the first line of each row; the
second line reports associated T-statistics. The R^2 for the OLS equation is 0.660.

as a political tendency. Second, multicollinearity reduced the coefficients
for social democracy, in some cases making them negative.

Our analysis also offers support for the 'logic of industrialism' explanation of welfare state development. Per capita income is strongly related to the dependent variables in all eight regressions, indicating both that pension expenditures increase with rising national incomes and that wealthy countries tend to have more generous pension plans. Percent of the population above 65 strongly affects the pension expenditure as a proportion of GDP but not average pension benefits relative to the standard of living (table 4). This indicates that pension spending under a given set of entitlements is pushed up by an increase in the aged proportion of the population but that a large aged proportion of the population does not positively affect the level of pension entitlements. Our result on this point is at variance with previous analyses of pooled data which did show an effect of the aged population on PENOLD. This difference appears to be due to their exclusion of the Christian democracy measure from the analysis: When we ran regressions with the conventional left-center-right measures, the aged proportion of the population was a significant predictor of PENOLD in some equations.

In contrast to the results of our analysis of overall welfare state benefits (Huber et al. 1993), the measure of the constitutional structure did not affect pension spending, while openness of the economy did. We suggest an interpretation of the openness finding below, and we explore the effect of constitutional structure further in the next section and suggest several reasons for the negative finding. The remaining independent variables were weakly related to the dependent variables and often inconsistent across the equations.

6.2. Pension Quality and Outcomes

As we mentioned above recent studies of 'pension quality,' that is, social rights to pensions guaranteed by legislation, have emphasized the differences between the determinants of pension quality and pension expenditure. Moreover, Palme (1990a, 1993) has argued that pension quality is more consequential for outcomes such as poverty and inequality among the aged. We have argued that a radical disjunction between the determinants of expenditure and pension quality would not appear very probable because the prototypical social democratic pension system, which provides for high income-replacement rates, universalism, and low qualification criteria for full pensions, would appear on the surface of it to be very expensive. Our analysis of pension expenditure provides support for our contention. In contrast to previous studies, it does show a social democratic effect on pension expenditures, though it also indicates that Christian democratic pension systems are yet more expensive. In this section, we further explore the relationship between pension expenditure, pension quality, and outcomes. We turn to cross-sectional data as the outcome data, all derived from LIS surveys, is only available for one time point and even then for only ten countries. The pension quality data is at present publicly available for only one time point also.[7]

Both the Esping-Andersen measure of pension decommodification (PENDECOM) and the Myles index (MYLES) of pension quality contain components which measure coverage, replacement rates, and qualifying conditions, so it is not surprising that they are highly correlated, as one can see from table 5(A). The table also confirms Palme's (1990a, 1993) analysis that measures of pension quality have a larger negative impact on poverty (POVERTY) and inequality (GINIDISP) among the aged than do the pension expenditure measures, using his poverty and inequality measures but different measures of pension quality.

Turning to the most important determinants of the pension effort,[8] the correlations between the independent variables and the pension quality variables show a clearly different pattern than in the regression on expenditure (table 5[B]). While one can attribute the lower correlation of GDP per capita and pension quality indicators at least in part to the truncated variation in the independent variable, the relationship of the two political party variables, the demographic variable, and the state structure variable to the pension quality variables is unlikely to be a product of the differences in the data sets. As predicted, social democracy is more strongly related to pension quality than to pension expenditure whereas Christian democracy shows the opposite pattern. Constitutional structure is much more strongly related to pension quality than to expenditure. Demographic structure varies across the four dependent variables but shows no consistent pattern between the quality and expenditure variables.

The correlation matrix shows a strong relationship between percent aged and the pension quality indices indicating a possible political effect of aged lobbying efforts on pension quality. To further explore the effect of the percent aged and the other political variables on the pension quality measures, we regressed LEFTCAB, CDEMCAB, CONSTRCT, and OLD on these measures.[9] We then dropped the two least significant variables (in both cases OLD and CDEMCAB) and regressed the two remaining variables on the dependent variables. Both two variable equations had higher adjusted R²s than the corresponding four variable equations, indicating a better fit with the data:

TABLE 5
Correlations

	PENOLD	PENGDP	MYLES	PENDE-COM	GINIDISP	POV-ERTY
	A. Intercorrelation of expenditure, quality, and outcome measures					
PENOLD	1.0000	0.8777**	0.3550	0.2673	−0.2151	−0.5802
PENGDP	0.8777**	1.0000	0.4744	0.5033*	−0.3823	−0.5649
MYLES	0.3550	0.4744	1.0000	0.8033**	−0.6151	−0.4612
PENDECOM	0.2673	0.5033*	0.8033**	1.0000	−0.6413*	−0.5207
GINIDISP	−0.2151	−0.3823	−0.6151	−0.6413*	1.0000	0.5639
POVERTY	−0.5802	−0.5649	−0.4612	−0.5207	0.5639	1.0000
	B. Correlation of independent variables with expenditure, quality, and outcome measures					
LEFTCAB	0.3014	0.5789*	0.5791*	0.7355**	−0.8200**	−0.4978
CDEMCAB	0.3788	0.4182	−0.0742	0.0516	0.1603	−0.3099
CONSTRCT	−0.2936	−0.3511	−0.6368*	−0.6360**	0.7487*	0.5586
OLD	0.2271	0.6615**	0.3411	0.5949**	−0.4460	−0.1227
GDPPC	0.2010	0.4705*	0.2731	0.4855*	−0.1271	−0.4671

* Signif. LE 0.05. ** Signif. LE 0.01. (2-tailed).
N = 18 except MYLES (15), GINIDISP (10), and POVERTY (10).
All data circa 1980, except MYLES, which is 1975.

PENDECOM =
    9.67 + 0.20LEFTCAB − 0.55CONSTRCT
                (t = 2.95)   (t = 1.81)
adjusted R^2 = 0.57 (significance 0.00)

MYLES =
    133.68 + 1.05LEFTCAB − 3.74CONSTRCT
                (t = 1.05)   (t = −1.23)
adjusted R^2 = 0.36 (significance 0.03)

This analysis confirms the results of our analysis of pension expenditure as a percent of GDP divided by the aged population (PENOLD): The effect of the aged population on pension systems is limited to the automatic effect of increasing expenditures in existing programs. The cross-sectional analysis also confirms the previous analyses of Palme (1990b) and Esping-Andersen (1990) that social-democratic rule is an important determinant of pension quality. Though the coefficient for LEFTCAB in the regression on the Myles index is only significant at the 0.16 level (one tailed test), it is the second strongest independent variable. More-over, the coefficient for LEFTCAB in the regression on pension decommodification is the strongest one and is highly significant. In addition, our analysis indicates that constitutional provisions that give minorities the opportunity to veto legislation are strong deterrents to the development of high pension quality.

The different impact of both the constitutional structure measure and the political party measure on pension expenditure and pension quality deserves some further comment. As we pointed out above, the typical characteristics of social-democratic pension systems would appear to make them the most expensive systems. The data analysis shows that Christian democratic pension systems bear this distinction, despite the fact that social-democratic systems appear to be 'better' by the measures of qual-ity. Why? We have suggested some hypotheses above: more extensive use of early pensions to fight unemployment in some Christian democratic countries, use of pensions for patronage purposes in others, more direct provision of services to the elderly in social-democratic countries, and high income-replacement rates among very high-income earners in Chris-tian democratic systems. With regard to the last named, it is worth point-ing out that Esping-Andersen's indicator weighs the replacement rates of lower-income earners more strongly than higher-income earners.

Constitutional structure had a very weak effect on expenditures but a consistent effect on pension quality. Our hypotheses outlined above are that pensions are very popular programs in all countries which makes it extremely difficult for even influential minorities to block their passage, and that pension programs faced fewer opponents than other welfare state programs. However, in countries with constitutions that provide many veto points, privileged minorities manage to effect changes in the distributive profile of pension legislation in return for support for the final legislation which nonetheless provides for the same level of overall expenditure as the original legislation.

7. Conclusion

One of the main findings of this analysis is the clear effects of the party composition of governments not only on pension quality but also on pension expenditures, which contrasts sharply with the findings of previ-ous analyses of pooled data sets. This is an important finding because it helps square the determinants of pension expenditure better with the determinants of general welfare state expenditures. We showed that Christian democratic incumbency, which has a particularly strong effect on overall expenditure on transfer payments, also has this effect on pension expenditure. The discrepancy between our findings and those of previous studies is due primarily to the omission in the latter of Christian democratic parties. This is confirmed by the fact that when we substituted right party for Christian democratic party, right party governance was significant and social democratic party became insignificant, as in Pampel et al.'s (1990) analysis. However, since there was a significant drop in the total variation explained, this specification did not fit the data as well. An additional reason is probably that multicollinearity depressed the effect of left incumbency, as the previous studies included union density, corporatism, and economic openness along with left incumbency in their regressions.

By the same token, our analysis suggests that previous studies may have over-estimated the discrepancy between pension expenditure and pension quality. Social-democratic pension systems, with their universalistic basic pension, the high replacement rates of earnings-related pensions, and the lenient qualification requirements are expensive, though the Christian democratic pension systems are even more so, despite their lower ranking on the indices of pension quality, i.e., on the social rights to pensions guaranteed by national legislation. We have advanced some hypotheses on why this might be so, but the precise reasons for the greater expense of the Christian democratic pension system will have to await further research.

We have also demonstrated for the first time the effects of state structure on pension systems. The existence of many access points for special interest groups to the political decision-making process does not depress pension spending, but it does affect the quality of pensions significantly. We have suggested that the difference in the effect of constitutional structure on pension expenditure compared to welfare state expenditure as a whole is due to the fact that pensions receive very wide popular support and their introduction tends to confront fewer vested interests than other welfare state programs, most prominently health care. Thus, conservative forces opposed to the introduction or expansion of pension systems may not have been able to mobilize effective coalitions to oppose their development as a whole, but were able to take advantage of multiple access points to the political decision-making process in order to modify specific provisions in the pension systems, namely those making the pension systems universalistic and redistributive. The resulting systems were not cheaper, but they were more market conforming and lacked an egalitarian thrust.

Finally, our analysis shows that the proportion of the population over 65 has an effect on total pension spending but not on pension spending per elderly person or on pension quality. This indicates that the effect of the size of the aged population on pension programs is limited to the fact that an increase in the aged population will automatically increase total pension spending. Our results directly contradict the central finding of Pampel and Williamson (1989) on the centrality of aged lobbies in explaining cross-national difference in social policy. Let us be clear: We do not dispute the fact that organized groups of elderly influence pension policy. Historical studies are replete with examples of such influence (e.g., for Sweden, see Elmér 1960, Feldt 1991; for Germany, see Hockerts 1980, for the United States, see Myles & Quadagno 1993). However, based on our own comparative historical studies, we would contest the view that the aged frequently form interest organizations independent of party politics. The United States, due to its lack of disciplined parties and the system of age-based welfare entitlements (Myles & Quadagno 1993), is perhaps the only country where independent aged lobbies, stretching from the Townsendites of the 1930s to the gray lobbies of the 1980s, have been important. Elsewhere political organizations of the aged, where they have any influence, are largely creations of political parties. Moreover, to the extent that the organization of the elderly varies through time and across countries, it is unlikely that this is measured very well by the proportion of the population that is elderly. This would be analogous to measuring working-class organization with percent of the labor force in blue-collar jobs. Just because there are a lot of elderly people does not mean that they are mobilized, and according to both pluralist and power resource theories, it is mobilization that makes groups influential in democratic politics. To properly test Pampel and Williamson's hypotheses, one would need a direct measure of organization of the aged analogous to union density as a measure for working-class organization.

What does our analysis suggest with regard to priorities for further research? A close examination of the expensive but not universalistic and not very redistributive Christian democratic welfare states is clearly of interest. Is it mostly generosity of pensions for higher-income earners that makes these systems so expensive, or high administrative costs for highly fragmented systems, or abuses of the system? International data banks are not likely to tell these stories; rather, researchers will have to examine individual pension systems in greater detail. Ultimately, though, the usefulness of analysis of expenditure data alone will be limited and researchers will have to devote more attention to qualitative aspects of pension systems.

Along these lines, it would be interesting to do a comparative historical analysis of the decision-making processes involved in shaping pension systems. Such an analysis would shed light on the ways in which aspects of state structure facilitated or obstructed the influence of forces bent upon preventing the introduction of universalistic and redistributive features as our data indicates. It would also help to answer the question about the politics of the development of Christian democratic pension plans: Is there a single Christian democratic path? Or are Christian democrats particularly likely to promote comprehensive (and expensive) pension systems only in countries where they are in competition with strong left parties that can make a credible bid for governmental power?

Notes

1 The data analyzed in the first section of this article were collected during a project in progress on 'The Welfare State in Comparative Perspective: Determinants, Program Characteristics, and Outcomes' directed by the authors and Charles Ragin. This project is supported by the Center for Urban Affairs and Policy Research at Northwestern University, the Institute for Research in the Social Sciences at the University of North Carolina, and by the National Science Foundation (Grant no. SES9108716). We thank CUAPR, IRSS, and NSF for financial support, and our research assistants William Garber, Brian Gran, Heung-Sik Kim, Wayne Krimelmeyer, Antonia Maioni, Leonard Ray, John Reynolds, Jorge Rodriguez, and Michael Trevithick for their help in assembling the data. We also thank Joakim Palme for sharing data and ideas on this topic with us, and Charles Ragin for help with the data analysis. Finally, we thank the Institute for Social Research, Stockholm University, for providing a stimulating and supportive environment for research for the month of May 1992.

2 For recent reviews of this literature, see Quadagno (1987) and Skocpol and Amenta (1986). Pescosolido (1989) provides a review of the literature and an extensive annotated bibliography.

3 See our discussion below.

4 We did not use the party competition measure used in these pension studies, because it lacks face validity. For a discussion of this, see Huber, Ragin and Stephens (1991).

120   Evelyne Huber and John D. Stephens

5 For further, more detailed information on our procedure to eliminate variables, see Huber, Ragin and Stephens (1993).
6 The results we report in this article were confirmed using this alternate technique.
7 Our research project with Charles Ragin is presently in the process of replicating the Myles index and the Esping-Andersen pension decommodification measure for five-year intervals from 1950 to 1985. These data will not be available in the near future.
8 Because of the small number of cases, we select only those independent variables which proved most important in our previous analyses.
9 In contrast to table 5, the independent variables in the regression on the Myles index are for 1975.

References

Czada, R. 1988. Bestimmungsfaktoren und Genese politischer Gewerkschaftseinbindung. In Manfred G. Schmidt (ed.), *Staatstätigkeit: International und historisch vergleichende Analysen*. Opladen: Westdeutscher Verlag.
Elmér, Å. 1960. *Folkpensioneringen i Sverige*. Lund: Gleerups.
Esping-Andersen, G. 1990. *The Three Worlds of Welfare Capitalism*. Princeton: Princeton University Press.
Feldt, K-O. 1991. *Alla Dessa Dagar ... I Regeringen, 1982–1990*. Stockholm: Norstedts.
Flora, P. Alber, J. 1981. Modernization, Democratization, and the Development of Welfare States in Western Europe. In Peter Flora and Arnold J. Heidenheimer (eds.), *The Development of Welfare States in Europe and America*. New Brunswick: Transaction Books.
Heclo, H. 1974. *Modern Social Politics in Britain and Sweden*. New Haven: Yale University Press.
Hicks, A. 1990. Social Democratic, Statist, and Pluralist Facets of the Politics of Social Policy. Paper delivered at the meetings of the American Political Science Association, Washington, DC, 11–15 August.
Hicks, A. & Swank, D. 1992. Politics, Institutions, and Welfare Spending in Industrialized Democracies, 1960–1982. *American Political Science Review* 86, 658–674.
Hockerts, H.G. 1980. *Sozialpolitische Entscheidungen im Nachkriegsdeutschland: Alliierte und deutsche Sozialversicherungspolitik 1945 bis 1957*. Stuttgart: Klett-Cotta.
Huber, E., Ragin, C. & Stephens, J.D. 1993. Social Democracy, Christian Democracy, Constitutional Structure and the Welfare State: Towards a Resolution of Quantitative Studies. *American Journal of Sociology*.

Huber, E., Ragin, C. & Stephens, J.D. 1991. Quantitative Studies of Variation among Welfare States: Towards a Resolution of the Controversy. Paper delivered at the Workshop on Comparative Studies of Welfare State Development. Helsinki, 29 Aug.–1 Sept.

Immergut, E. 1992. *The Political Construction of Interests: National Health Insurance Politics in Switzerland, France and Sweden, 1930–1970*. New York: Cambridge University Press.

International Labour Office (ILO). (various years). *The Cost of Social Security*. ILO: Geneva.

Kangas, O. & Palme, J. 1990. Statism Eroded? Labour Market Benefits and the Challenges to the Scandinavian Welfare States. Paper delivered at the World Congress of Sociology, Madrid, 9–13 July 1990.

Katzenstein, P. 1985. *Small States in World Markets: Industrial Policy in Europe*. Ithaca: Cornell University Press.

Kjellberg, A. 1983. *Facklig organisering i tolv länder*. Lund: Arkiv förlag.

Korpi, W. 1983. *The Democratic Class Struggle*. London: Routledge & Kegan Paul.

Lehmbruch, G. 1984. Concertation and the Structure of Corporatist Networks. In John H. Goldthorpe (ed.), *Order and Conflict in Contemporary Capitalism*, pp. 60–80. Oxford: Clarendon Press.

Lijphart, A. 1984. *Democracies: Patterns of Majoritarian and Consensus Government in Twenty-One Countries*. New Haven: Yale University Press.

Maioni, A. 1992. Explaining Differences in Welfare State Development: A Comparative Study of Health Insurance in Canada and the United States. PhD Dissertation, Northwestern University.

Myles, J. 1984. *Old Age and the Welfare State: The Political Economy of Public Pensions*. Boston: Little, Brown.

Myles, J. & Quadagno, J. 1993. The Politics of Income Security for the Elderly in Canada and the United States: Explaining the Difference. Working Paper Series, Pepper Institute on Aging and Public Policy.

Palme, J. 1988. Models of Pension Inequality: A Comparative Analysis. Paper delivered at a conference on the 'The Welfare State in Transition,' Bergen, 24–27 August.

Palme, J. 1990a. Pensions and Inequality: A Comparative Analysis of Nine OECD Countries. Unpublished paper, Swedish Institute for Social Research, Stockholm University.

Palme, J. 1990b. *Pension Rights in Welfare Capitalism: The Development of Old-Age Pensions in 18 OECD Countries 1930 to 1985*. Stockholm: Swedish Institute for Social Research, University of Stockholm.

Palme, J. 1993. Pensions and Income Inequality among the Elderly: 'The Welfare State and Equality' Revisited. Paper presented at Åbo Akademi 3 January 1993.

Pampel, F.C. & Williamson, J.B. 1985. Age Structure, Politics, and Cross-national Patterns of Public Pension Expenditure. *American Sociological Review* 50, 787–98.

Pampel, F.C. & Williamson, J.B. 1989. *Age, Class, Politics, and the Welfare State.* New York: Cambridge University Press.

Pampel, F.C., Williamson, J.B. & Robin Stryker, R. 1990. Class Context and Pension Response to Demographic Structure in Advanced Industrial Democracies. *Social Problems* 37, 535–50.

Pescosolido, B.A. (ed.) 1989. The Welfare State Revisited: A Review of Research, an Annotated Bibliography, and a Set of Course Syllabi. Washington, DC: American Sociological Association Teaching Resources Center.

Piven, F.F. & Cloward, R.A. 1972. *Regulating the Poor.* New York: Vintage Books.

Quadagno, J. 1987. Theories of the Welfare State. *Annual Review of Sociology* 14, 109–28.

Rueschemeyer, D., Huber Stephens, E. & Stephens, J.D. 1992. *Capitalist Development and Democracy.* Chicago: University of Chicago Press.

Russet, B.M. 1970. *What Price Vigilance?* New Haven: Yale University Press.

Skocpol, T. & Amenta, E. 1986. States and Social Policies. *Annual Review of Sociology* 12, 131–57.

Stephens, J.D. 1979. *The Transition from Capitalism to Socialism.* Urbana: University of Illinois Press.

Stimson, J.A. 1985. Regression in Time and Space: A Statistical Essay. *American Journal of Political Science* 29, 914–47.

Wallerstein, M. 1989a. Union Centralization and Trade Dependence. Unpublished paper, Department of Political Science, UCLA.

Wallerstein, M. 1989b. Union Organization in Advanced Industrial Democracies. *American Political Science Review* 83, 481–501.

Weir, M., Orloff, A.S. & Skocpol, T. 1988. Introduction: Understanding American Social Politics. In Margaret Weir, Ann Shola Orloff & Theda Skocpol (eds.), *The Politics of Social Policy in the United States*, pp. 1–37. Princeton: Princeton University Press.

Western, B. 1991. A Comparative Study of Corporatist Development. *American Sociological Review* 56, 283–94 (June).

Wilensky, H. 1975. *The Welfare State and Equality.* Berkeley: University of California Press.

4

The Three Political Economies
of the Welfare State

GØSTA ESPING-ANDERSEN

The protracted debate on the welfare state has failed to produce conclusive answers as to either the nature or the causes of welfare state development. This article has three aims: 1/ to reintegrate the debate into the intellectual tradition of political economy. This serves to put into sharper focus the principal theoretical questions involved; 2/ to specify what are the salient characteristics of welfare states. The conventional ways of measuring welfare states in terms of their expenditures will no longer do; 3/ to 'sociologize' the study of welfare states. Most studies have assumed a world of linearity: more or less power, industrialization, or spending. This article insists that we understand welfare states as clusters of regime-types, and that their development must be explained interactively.

The Legacy of Classical Political Economy

Contemporary welfare state debates have been guided by two questions. First, does social citizenship diminish the salience of class? Or, in other words, can the welfare state fundamentally transform capitalist society? Second, what are the causal forces behind welfare state development? These questions are not recent. Indeed, they were formulated by the 19th Century political economists 100 years before any welfare state can rightfully be said to have come into existence. The classical political economists – whether of liberal, conservative, or Marxist persuasion – were preoccupied with the relationship between capitalism and welfare. Their answers obviously diverged, but their analyses were unequivocally directed to the relationship between market (and property), and the state (democracy). The question they asked was largely normative: what is the optimal division of responsibility between market and state?

Contemporary neo-liberalism echoes the contributions of classical liberal political economy. To Adam Smith, the market was the superior means for the abolition of class, inequality, and privilege. Aside from a necessary minimum, state intervention would likely stifle the equalizing process of competitive exchange, creating monopolies, protectionism, and inefficiency: the state upholds class, the market can potentially undo class society (Smith, 1961: II, especially pp. 232–6).[1]

Liberal political economists were not necessarily of one mind when it came to policy advocacy. Nassau Senior and later Manchester liberals emphasized the laissez-faire element of Smith, rejecting any form of social protection outside the cash nexus. J.S. Mill and the 'reformed liberals,' in turn, were willing to let markets be regulated by a modicum of political regulation. Yet, they were all agreed that the road to equality and prosperity should be paved with a maximum of free markets and a minimum of state interference.

This enthusiastic embrace of market capitalism may now appear unjustified. But, we must take into account that the state which confronted these early political economists was tinged with legacies of absolutist privileges, merchantilist protectionisms, and pervasive corruption. They were attacking systems of governance which repressed the ideals of both freedom and enterprise. Hence, theirs was revolutionary theory, and from this vantage point, we can understand why Adam Smith sometimes reads like Karl Marx.[2]

Democracy was an Achilles heel to many liberals. Their ideals of freedom and democractic participation were grounded in a world of small property owners; not of growing property-less masses who held in their sheer numbers the possibility of seizing state power. The liberals feared the principle of universal suffrage, for it would likely politicize the distributional struggle, pervert the market, and fuel inefficiencies. Many liberals discovered that democracy would contradict the market.

Both conservative and Marxist political economists understood this contradiction, but proposed, of course, opposite solutions. The most coherent conservative critique of laissez faire came from the German historical school; in particular from Friedrich List, Adolph Wagner, and Gustav Schmoller. They refused to believe that capitalist efficiency was best assured by the pure commodity status of workers in the raw cash nexus of the market. Instead, conservative political economy believed that patriarchical neo-absolutism could provide the kind of legal, political, and social framework that would assure a capitalism without class struggle.

One prominent conservative school promoted a 'Monarchical Welfare State' that would, at once, provide for social welfare, class harmony, loyalty, and productivity. It was discipline, not competition, that would guarantee efficiency. The state (or church) was the institution best equipped to harmonize conflicting interests.[3]

Conservative political economy emerged in reaction to the French Revolution and the Paris Commune. It was avowedly nationalist and anti-revolutionary, and sought to arrest the democratic impulse. It feared social levelling, and favored a society that retained both hierarchy and class. It held that class conflicts were not natural; that democratic mass participation, and the dissolution of recognized rank and status boundaries were threats to social harmony.

The key to Marxian political economy, of course, was its rejection of the liberal claim that markets guarantee equality. Capitalist accumulation, as Dobb (1946) put it, disowns people of property, with the end-result being ever-deeper class divisions. Here, the state's role is not neutrally benevolent, nor is it a foundation of emancipation; it exists to defend property rights and the authority of capital. To Marxism this is the foundation of class dominance.

The central question, not only for Marxism but for the entire contemporary debate on the welfare state, is whether and under what conditions the class divisions and social inequalities produced by capitalism can be undone by parliamentary democracy.

The liberals feared that democracy would produce socialism and they were consequently not especially eager to extend it. The socialists, in contrast, suspected that parliamentarism would be little more than an empty shell or, as Lenin suggested, a mere 'talking shop' (Jessop, 1982). This line of analysis, echoed in much of contemporary Marxism, leads to the conclusion that social reforms emerge in response to the exigencies of capitalist reproduction, not to the emancipatory desires of the working classes.[4]

Among socialists, a more positive analysis of parliamentarism came to prevail after the extension of full political citizenship. The theoretically most sophisticated contributions came from Austro-Marxists such as Alder and Bauer, and from German social democrats, especially Eduard Heimann. Heimann's (1929) starting point was that conservative reforms may have been motivated by desires to repress labor mobilization, but that their very presence nonetheless alters the balance of class power: the social wage lessens the worker's dependence on the market and employers. The social wage is thus also a potential power resource that defines the frontier between capitalism and socialism. It introduces an alien element into the capitalist political economy. This intellectual position has enjoyed quite a renaissance in recent Marxism (Offe, 1985; Bowles and Gintis, 1986).

The social-democratic model, as outlined above, did not necessarily abandon the orthodox assumption that fundamental equality requires economic socialization. Yet, historical experience soon demonstrated that socialization was a goal that could not be pursued realistically through parliamentarism.[5]

Social democracy's embrace of parliamentary reformism as its dominant strategy for equality and socialism was premised on two arguments. The first was that workers require social resources, health, and education to participate effectively in a democratized economy. The second argument was that social policy is not only emancipatory, but also economically efficient (Mydral and Mydral, 1936). Following Marx on this point, the strategy therefore promotes the onward march of capitalist productive forces. But, the beauty of the strategy was that social policy would also assure social-democratic power mobilization. By eradicating poverty, unemployment, and complete wage dependency, the welfare state increases political capacities and diminishes the social divisions that are barriers to political unity among workers.

The social-democratic model, then, puts forward one of the leading hypotheses of contemporary welfare state debate: the argument that parliamentary class mobilization is a means for the realization of socialist ideals of equality, justice, freedom, and solidarity.

The Political Economy of the Welfare State

Our political economy forebears defined the analytic basis of much recent scholarship. They isolated the key variables of class, state, market, and democracy; and they formulated the basic propositions about citizenship and class, efficiency and equality, capitalism and socialism. Contemporary social science distinguishes itself from classical political economy on two scientifically vital fronts. First, it defines itself as a positive science and shies away from normative prescription (Robbins, 1976). Second, classical political economists had little interest in historical variability; they saw their efforts as leading towards a system of universal laws. Although contemporary political economy sometimes still clings to the belief in absolute truths, the comparative and historical method that, today, underpins almost all good political economy is one that reveals variation and permeability.

Despite these differences, most recent scholarship has as its focal point the state–economy relationship defined by 19th Century political economists. And, given its enormous growth, it is understandable that the welfare state has become a major test case for contending theories of political economy.

Below, we shall review the contributions of comparative research on the development of welfare states in advanced capitalist countries. It will be argued that most scholarship has been misdirected, mainly because it became detached from its theoretical foundations. We must therefore recast both the methodology and concepts of political economy in order to adequately study the welfare state. This will constitute the focus of the final section of this paper.

Two types of approaches have dominated in the explanation of welfare states; one, a systemic (or, structuralist) theory; the other, an institutional or actor-oriented explanations.

The Systems/Structuralist Approach

System or structuralist theory seeks to capture the logic of development holistically. It will easily focus on the functional requisites for the reproduction of society and economy; it will be inclined to emphasize cross-national similarities rather than differences.

One variant begins with a theory of the industrial society, and argues that industrialization makes social policy both necessary and possible. It makes welfare states necessary because pre-industrial modes of social reproduction, such as the family, the church, noblesse oblige, and guild solidarity, are destroyed by the forces attached to modernization – social mobility, urbanization, individualism, and market dependence. The crux of the matter is that the market is no adequate substitute because it caters only to those who are able to perform in it. Hence, the 'welfare function' is appropriated by the the nation-state. The welfare state is also made possible by the rise of modern bureaucracy as a rational, universalist, and efficient form of organization. It is a means for managing collective goods, but also a center of power in its own right, and will thus be inclined to promote its own growth.

This kind of reasoning has informed the so-called 'logic of industrialism' perspective, according to which the welfare state will emerge as the modern industrial economy destroys traditional forms of social security (Flora and Alber, 1981; Pryor, 1969). But, the thesis has difficulties explaining why government social policy only emerged 50 or even 100 years after traditional community was effectively destroyed? The basic response draws on Wagner's Law (1962; 1883) and on Marshall (1920), namely, that a certain level of economic development, and thus surplus, is needed in order to permit the diversion of scarce resources from productive use (investments) to welfare (Wilensky and Lebeaux, 1958). In this sense, the perspective follows in the footsteps of the old liberals. Social redistribution endangers efficiency, and only at a certain economic level will a negative-sum trade-off be avoidable (Okun, 1975).

The new structural Marxism offers a surprisingly parallel analysis. It breaks with its classical forebears' strongly action-centred theory. Like the industrialism thesis, its analytical starting point is not the problems of markets, but the logic of a mode of production. Capital accumulation creates contradictions that social reform can alleviate (O'Connor, 1973). This tradition of Marxism, like its 'logic of industrialism' counterpart, fails to see much relevance in actors in the promotion of welfare states. The point is that the state, as such, is positioned in such a way that it will serve the collective needs of capital. The theory is thus premised on two crucial assumptions: first, that power is structural and second, that the state is 'relatively' autonomous from class directives (Poulantzas, 1973; Block, 1977; for a recent critical assessment of this literature, see Therborn, 1986; and Skocpol and Amenta, 1986).

The 'logic of capitalism' perspective invites difficult questions. If, as Przeworski (1980) has argued, working-class consent is assured on the basis of material hegemony, that is self-willed subordination to the system, it is difficult to see why up to 40 per cent of the national product must be allocated to the legitimation activities of a welfare state. A second problem is to derive state activities from a 'mode of production' analysis. Eastern Europe may perhaps not qualify as socialist, but neither is it capitalist. Yet, there we find 'welfare states,' too. Perhaps accumulation has functional requirements in whichever way it proceeds? (Skocpol and Amenta, 1986; Bell, 1978).

The Institutional Approach

The classical political economists made it clear why democratic institutions should influence welfare state development. The liberals feared that full democracy might jeopardize markets and inaugurate socialism. Freedom, in their view, necessitate a defence of markets against political intrusion. In practice, this is what the laissez-faire state sought to accomplish. But it was this divorce of politics and economy which fuelled much of the institutionalist analyses. Best represented by Polanyi (1944), but also by a number of anti-democratic exponents of the historical school, the institutional approach insists that any effort to isolate the economy from social and political institutions will destroy human society. The economy must be embedded in social communities in order for it to survive. Thus, Polanyi sees social policy as one necessary precondition for the re-integration of the social economy.

An interesting recent variant of institutional alignment theory is the argument that welfare states emerge more readily in small, open economies that are particularly vulnerable to international markets. As Katzenstein (1985) and Cameron (1978) show, there is a greater inclination to regulate class distributional conflicts through government and interest concentration when both business and labor are captive to forces beyond domestic control.

The impact of democracy on welfare states has been argued ever since J.S. Mill and de Tocqueville. The argument is typically phrased without reference to any particular social agent or class. It is, in this sense, that it is institutional. In its classical formulation, the thesis was simply that majorities will favor social distribution to compensate for market weakness or market risks. If wage earners are likely to demand a social wage, so are capitalists (or farmers) apt to demand protection in the form of tariffs, monopoly, or subsidies. Democracy is an institution that cannot resist majoritarian demands.

In its modern formulations, the democracy thesis has many variants. One identifies stages of nationbuilding in which full citizenship incorporation requires social rights (Marshall, 1950; Bendix, 1964; Rokkan, 1970). A second variant, developed by both pluralist and public choice theory, argues that democracy will nurture intense party competition around the median voter that will, in turn, fuel rising public expenditures. Tufte (1978), for example, argues that major extensions of public intervention will occur around elections as a means of voter mobilization.

The democratic-institutionalist approach faces considerable empirical problems (Skocpol and Amenta, 1986). According to the thesis, a democratic polity is the basic precondition for welfare state emergence, and welfare states are more likely to develop the more democratic rights are extended. Yet, the thesis confronts not only the historical oddity that the first major welfare state initiatives occurred prior to democracy, but also that they were often motivated by desires to arrest its realization. This was certainly the case in France under Napoleon II, in Germany under Bismarck, and in Austria under Taaffe. Conversely, welfare state development was most retarded where democracy arrived early, such as in the United States, Australia, and Switzerland. This apparent contradiction can be explained, but only with reference to social classes and social structure: nations with early democracy were overwhelmingly agrarian and dominated by small property owners who used their electoral powers to reduce, not raise, taxes (Dich, 1973). In contrast, ruling classes in authoritarian polities are better positioned to impose high taxes on an unwilling populace.

Social Class as a Political Agent

We have noted that the case for a class mobilization thesis flows from social-democratic political economy. It differs from structuralist and institutional analyses by its emphasis on the social classes as the main agents of change, and its argument that the balance of class power determines distributional outcomes. To emphasize active class mobilization does not necessarily deny the importance of structured or hegemonic power (Korpi, 1983). But it is held that parliaments are, in principle, effective institutions for the translation of mobilized power into desired policies and reforms. Accordingly, parliamentary politics are capable of overriding hegemony, and may be made to serve interests that are antagonistic to capital. Further, the class mobilization theory assumes that welfare states do more than simply alleviate the current ills of the system; a 'social democratic' welfare state will, in its own right, establish critical power resources for wage earners and, thus, strengthen labor movements. As Heimann (1929) originally held, social rights push back the frontiers of capitalist power and prerogatives.

The question of why the welfare state itself is a power resource is vital for the theory's applicability. The answer is that wage earners in the market are inherently atomized and stratified, compelled to compete, insecure, and dependent on decisions and forces beyond their control. This limits their capacity for collective solidarity and mobilization. The social rights, income security, equalization, and eradication of poverty that a universalistic welfare state pursues are necessary preconditions for the strength and unity that collective power mobilization demands (Esping-Andersen, 1985a).

The single most difficult problem for this thesis is to specify the conditions for power mobilization. Power depends on the resources that flow from the unity of electoral numbers and from collective bargaining. Power mobilization, in turn, depends on levels of trade union organization, vote shares, and parliamentary and cabinet seats held by left, or labor, parties. But how long a period of sustained power mobilization is required in order to produce decisive effects? If power is measured over a brief time span (5–10 years), we risk the fallacy of a 'Blum'/'Mitterrand' effect: a brief spell of leftist power that proves ineffectual because the left is ousted again before having had a chance to act.

There are several valid objections to the class mobilization thesis. Three, in particular, are quite fundamental. One, is that in advanced capitalist nations, the locus of decision making and power may shift from parliaments to neo-corporatist institutions of interest intermediation (Shonfield, 1965; Schmitter and Lembruch, 1979). A second criticism is that the capacity of labor parties to influence welfare state development is circumscribed by the structure of rightist party power. Castles (1978; 1982) has argued that the degree of unity among the rightist parties is more important than is the activated power of the left. Other authors have emphasized the fact that denominational (usually social catholic) parties in countries such as Holland, Italy, and Germany mobilize large sections of the working classes and pursue welfare state programs not drastically at variance with their socialist competitors (Schmidt, 1982; Wilensky, 1981). The class mobilization thesis has, rightly, been criticized for its Swedocentrism, i.e., its inclination to define the process of power mobilization too much on the basis of the rather extraordinary Swedish experience (Shalev, 1984).

These objections address a basic fallacy in the theory's assumptions about class formation: we cannot assume that socialism is the natural basis for wage-earner mobilization. Indeed, the conditions under which workers become socialists are still not adequately documented. Historically, the natural organizational bases of worker mobilization were pre-capitalist communities, especially the guilds, but also the Church, ethnicity, or language. A ready-made reference to false consciousness will not do to explain why Dutch, Italian, or American workers continue to mobilize around non-socialist principles. The dominance of socialism in the Swedish working class is as much a puzzle as is the dominance of confessionalism in the Dutch.

The third and, perhaps, most fundamental objection has to do with the model's linear view of power. It is problematic to hold that a numerical increase in votes, unionization, or seats will translate into more welfare-statism. First, for socialist as for other parties, the magical '50 per cent' threshold for parliamentary majorities seems practically unsurmountable (Przeworski, 1985). Second, if socialist parties represent working classes in the traditional sense, it is clear that they will never succeed in their project. In very few cases has the traditional working class been numerically a majority; and its role is rapidly becoming marginal.[6]

Probably the most promising way to resolve the combined linearity and working-class minority problem lies in recent applications of Barrington Moore's path-breaking class coalition thesis to the transformation of the modern state (Weir and Skocpol, 1985; Gourevitch, 1986; Esping-Andersen, 1985a; Esping-Andersen and Friedland, 1982). Thus, the origins of the Keynsian full-employment commitment and the social-democratic welfare state edifice have been traced to the capacity of (variably) strong working-class movements to forge a political alliance with farmers' organizations; additionally, it is arguable that sustained social democracy has come to depend on the formation of a new working class–white collar coalition.

The class-coalition approach has additional virtues. Two nations, such as Austria and Sweden, may score similarly on working-class mobilization variables, and yet produce highly unequal policy results. This can be explained by differences in the two countries' historical coalition formation: the breakthrough of Swedish social-democratic hegemony stems from its capacity to forge the famous 'red-green' alliance; the comparative disadvantage of the Austrian socialists rests in the 'ghetto' status assigned to them by virtue of the rural classes being captured by a conservative coalition (Esping-Andersen and Korpi, 1984).

In sum, we have to think in terms of social relations, not just social categories. Whereas structural-functionalist explanations identify convergent welfare state outcomes, and class mobilization paradigms see large, but linearly distributed, differences, an interactive model such as the coalitions approach directs attention to distinct welfare state regimes.

What Is the Welfare State?

Every theoretical paradigm must somehow define the welfare state. How do we know when and if a welfare state responds functionally to the needs of industrialism, or to capitalist reproduction and legitimacy? And how do we identify a welfare state that corresponds to the demands that a mobilized working class might have? We cannot test contending arguments unless we have a commonly shared conception of the phenomenon to be explained.

A remarkable attribute of the entire literature is its lack of much genuine interest in the welfare state as such. Welfare state studies have been motivated by theoretical concerns with other phenomena, such as power, industrialization, or capitalist contradictions; the welfare state itself has generally received scant conceptual attention. If welfare states differ, how do they differ? And when, indeed, is a state a welfare state? This turns attention straight back to the original question: what is the welfare state?

A common textbook definition is that it involves state responsibility for securing some basic modicum of welfare for its citizens. Such a definition skirts the issue of whether social policies are emancipatory or not; whether they help system legitimization, or not; whether they contradict or aid the market process; and what, indeed, is meant by 'basic'? Would it not be more appropriate to require of a welfare state that it satisfies more than our basic or minimal welfare needs?

The first generation of comparative studies started with this type of conceptualization. They assumed, without much reflection, that the level of social expenditure adequately reflects a state's commitment to welfare. The theoretical intent was not really to arrive at an understanding of the welfare state, but rather to test the validity of contending theoretical models in political economy. By scoring nations with respect to urbanization, levels of economic growth, and the share of aged in the demographic structure, it was believed that the essential features of industrial modernization were adequately captured. Alternatively, by scoring nations on left party strength, or working-class power mobilization (with complex weighted scores of trade unionism, electoral strength, and cabinet power), others sought to identify the impact of working-class mobilization as formulated in the social-democratic model.

The findings of the first generation comparativists are extremely difficult to evaluate. No convincing case can be made for any particular theory. The shortage of nations for comparisons statistically restricts the number of variables that can be tested simultaneously. Thus, when Cutright (1965) or Wilensky (1975) finds that economic level, with its demographic and bureaucratic correlates, explains most welfare state variations in 'rich countries,' relevant measures of working-class mobilization or economic openness are not included. A conclusion in favor of a 'logic of industrialism' view is therefore in doubt. And, when Hewitt (1977), Stephens (1979), Korpi (1983), Myles (1984), and Esping-Andersen (1985b) find strong evidence in favor of a working-class mobilization thesis, or when Schmidt (1982; 1983) finds support for a neo-corporatist, and Cameron (1978) for an economic openness argument it is without fully testing against the strongest alternative explanation.[7]

Most of these studies claim to explain the welfare state. Yet, their focus on spending may be irrelevant or, at best, misleading. Expenditures are epiphenomenal to the theoretical substance of welfare states. Moreover,

134 Gøsta Esping-Andersen

the linear scoring approach (more or less power, democracy, or spending) contradicts the sociological notion that power, democracy, or welfare are relational and structured phenomena. By scoring welfare states on spending, we assume that all spending counts equally. But some welfare states, the Austrian for example, spend a large share on benefits to privileged civil servants. This is normally not what we would consider a commitment to social citizenship and solidarity. Others spend disproportionally on means-tested social assistance. Few contemporary analysts would agree that a reformed poor relief tradition qualifies as a welfare state commitment. Some nations spend enormous sums on fiscal welfare in the form of tax privileges to private insurance plans that mainly benefit the middle classes. But these tax expenditures do not show up on expenditure accounts. In Britain, total social expenditure has grown during the Thatcher period; yet, this is almost exclusively a function of very high unemployment. Low expenditures on some programs may signify a welfare state more seriously committed to full employment.

Therborn (1983) is right when he holds that we must begin with a conception of state structure. What are the criteria with which we should judge whether, and when, a state is a welfare state? There are three approaches to this question. Therborn's proposal is to begin with the historical transformation of state activities. Minimally, in a genuine welfare state the majority of its daily routine activities must be devoted to servicing the welfare needs of households. This criterion has far-reaching consequences. If we simply measure routine activity in terms of spending and personnel, the result is that no state can be regarded as a real welfare state until the 1970s! And, some that we normally label as welfare states will still not qualify because the majority of their routine activities concern defence, law and order, administration and the like (Therborn, 1983). Social scientists have been too quick to accept nations' self-proclaimed welfare state status. They have also been too quick to conclude that the presence of the battery of typical social programs signify the birth of a welfare state.

The second conceptual approach derives from Richard Titmuss' (1958) classical distinction between residual and institutional welfare states. The former assumes that state responsibility begins only when the family or the market fails; its commitment is limited to marginal groups in society. The latter model addresses the entire population, is universalistic, and implants an institutionalized commitment to welfare. It will, in principle, extend welfare commitments to all areas of distribution vital for societal welfare. This approach has fertilized a variety of new developments in comparative welfare state research (Myles, 1984; Korpi, 1980; Esping-Andersen and Korpi, 1984, 1986; Esping-Andersen, 1985b, 1987). And it has forced researchers to move away from the black box of expenditures and towards the content of welfare states: targeted versus universalistic programs, the conditions of eligibility, the quality of benefits and services, and, perhaps most importantly, the extent to which employment and working life are encompassed in the state's extension of citizens rights. This shift to welfare state typologies makes simple linear welfare state rankings difficult to sustain. We might in fact be comparing categorically different types to states.

The third approach is to select theoretically the criteria on which to judge types of welfare states. This can be done by measuring actual welfare states against some abstract model and then by scoring programs, or entire welfare states, accordingly (Day, 1978; Myles, 1984). The weakness of this approach is that it ahistorical, and does not necessarily capture the ideals or designs that historical actors sought to realize in the struggles over the welfare state. If our aim is to test causal theories that involve actors, we should begin with the demands that were actually promoted by those actors that we deem critical in the history of welfare state development. It is difficult to imagine that anyone struggled for spending per se.

A Respecification of the Welfare State[8]

Few can disagree with T.H. Marshall's (1950) proposition that social citizenship constitutes the core idea of a welfare state. What, then, are the key principles involved in social citizenship? In our view, they must involve first and foremost the granting of social rights. This mainly entails a de-commodification of the status of individuals vis-à-vis the market. Secondly, social-citizenship involves social stratification; one's status as a citizen will compete with, or even replace, one's class position. Thirdly, the welfare state must be understood in terms of the interface between the market, the family, and the state. These principles need to be fleshed out prior to any theoretical specification of the welfare state.

Rights and De-commodification

As commodities in the market, workers depend for their welfare entirely on the cash-nexus. The question of social rights is thus one of de-commodification, that is of granting alternative means of welfare to that of the market. De-commodification may refer either to the service rendered, or to the status of a person, but in both cases it signifies the degree to which distribution is detached from the market mechanism. This means that the mere presence of social assistance or insurance may not necessarily bring about significant de-commodification if they do not substantially emancipate individuals from market dependence. Means-tested poor relief will possibly offer a security blanket of last resort. But if benefits are low and attached with social stigma, the relief system will compel all but the most desperate to participate in the market. This was precisely the intent of the 19th Century poor laws. Similarly, most of the early social insurance programs were deliberately designed to maximize labor market performance (Ogus, 1979). Benefits required long contribution periods and were tailored to prior work effort. In either case, the motive was to avert work-disincentive effects.

There is no doubt that de-commodification has been a hugely contested issue in welfare state development. For labor, it has always been a priority. When workers are completely market dependent, they are difficult to mobilize for solidaristic action. Since their resources mirror market inequalities, divisions emerge between the 'ins' and the 'outs,' making labor movement formation difficult. De-commodification strengthens the worker and weakens the absolute authority of the employer. It is for exactly this reason that employers always opposed de-commodification.

De-commodified rights are differentially developed in contemporary welfare states. In social assistance dominated welfare states, rights are not so much attached to work performance as to demonstrable need. Needs-tests and typically meagre benefits, however, serve to curtail the de-commodifying effect. Thus, in nations where this model is dominant (mainly in the Anglo-Saxon countries), the result is actually to strengthen the market since all but those who fail in the market will be encouraged to contract private sector welfare.

A second dominant model espouses compulsory state social insurance with fairly strong entitlements. Yet, again, this may not automatically secure substantial de-commodification, since this hinges very much on the fabric of eligibility and benefit rules. Germany was the pioneer of social insurance, but over most of the century can hardly be said to have brought about much in the way of de-commodification through its social programs. Benefits have depended almost entirely on contributions and, thus, work and employment. In fact, before the Second World War, average pensions in the German insurance system for workers were lower than prevailing poverty assistance rates (Myles, 1984). The consequence, as with the social assistance model, was that most workers would chose to remain at work rather than retire. In other words, it is not the mere presence of a social right, but the corresponding rules and preconditions that dictate the extent to which welfare programs offer genuine alternatives to market dependence.

The third dominant model of welfare, namely, the Beveridge-type citizens benefit, may, at first glance, appear the most de-commodifying. It offers a basic, equal benefit to all irrespective of prior earnings, contributions or performance. It may indeed be a more solidaristic system, but not necessarily de-commodifying since, only rarely, have such schemes been able to offer benefits of such a standard that they provide recipients with a genuine option to that of working.

De-commodifying welfare states are, in practice, of very recent date. A minimalist definition must entail that citizens can freely, and without potential losses of job, income, or general welfare, opt out of work under conditions when they, themselves, consider it necessary for reasons of health, family, age or even educational self-improvement; when, in short, they deem it necessary for participating adequately in the social community.

With this definition in mind, we would, for example, require of a sickness insurance that individuals be secured benefits equal to normal earnings, the right to absence with minimal proof of medical impairment, and for the duration that the individual deems necessary. These conditions, it is worth noting, are those usually enjoyed by academics, civil servants and higher-echelon white-collar employees. Similar requirements would be made of pensions, maternity leave, parental leave, educational leave, and unemployment insurance.

Some nations have moved towards this level of de-commodification, but only recently and, in many cases, with significant exemptions. Thus, in almost all nations benefits were upgraded to equal normal wages in the late 1960s and early 1970s. But, in some countries, for example, prompt medical certification in case of illness is still required; in others, entitlements depend on long waiting periods of up to two weeks; and, in still others, the duration of entitlements is very short (in the United States, for example, unemployment benefit duration is maximally six months, compared to 30 in Denmark). Overall, the Scandinavian welfare states tend to be the most de-commodifying; the Anglo-Saxon the least.

The Welfare State as a System of Stratification

Despite the emphasis given to it in both classical political economy and in T.H. Marshall's pioneering work, the relationship between citizenship and social class remains severely neglected, both theoretically and empirically. Generally speaking, the issue has either been assumed away (it has been taken for granted that the welfare state creates a more egalitarian society), or it has been approached narrowly in terms of income distribution or in terms of whether education promotes upward social mobility. A more basic question, it seems, is what kind of stratification system is promoted by social policy. The welfare state is not just a mechanism that intervenes in, and possibly corrects, the structure of inequality; it is, in its own right, a system of stratification. It orders actively and directly social relations.

Comparatively and historically, we can easily identify alternative systems of stratification embedded in welfare states. The poor relief tradition, and its contemporary means-tested social assistance offshoot, was conspicuously designed for purposes of stratification. By punishing and stigmatizing recipients, it promotes severe social dualisms, especially within the ranks of the working classes. It comes as no surprise that this model of welfare has been a chief target of labor movement attacks.

The social insurance model promoted by conservatives reformers such as Bismarck and von Taaffe was also explicitly a form of class politics. It sought, in fact, to achieve two simultaneous stratification results. The first was to consolidate divisions among wage earners by legislating distinct programs for different class and status groups, each with its own conspicuously unique set of rights and privileges designed to accentuate the individual's appropriate station in life. The second objective was to tie the loyalties of the individual directly to the monarchy, or central state authority. This was Bismarck's motive when he promoted a direct state supplement to the pension benefit. This state-corporativist model was pursued mainly in nations such as Germany, Austria, Italy, and France and often resulted in a labyrinth of status-specific insurance funds (in France and Italy, for example, there exist more than 100 status-distinct pension schemes).

Of special importance in this corporatist tradition was the establishment of particularly privileged welfare provisions for the civil service ('Beamten'). In part, this was a means of rewarding loyalty to the state and in part, a way of demarcating this group's uniquely exalted social status. We should, however, be careful to note that the corporatist status-differentiated model springs mainly from the old guild tradition. The neo-absolutist autocrats, such as Bismarck, saw in this tradition a means to combat the rising labor movements.

The labor movements were as hostile to the corporatist model as they were to poor relief – in both cases for obvious reasons. Yet, the alternatives first espoused by labor were no less problematic from the point of view of uniting the workers as one solidaristic class. Almost invariably, the model that labor first pursued was that of the self-organized friendly societies or equivalent union- or party-sponsored fraternal welfare plan. This is not surprising. Workers were obviously suspicious of reforms sponsored by a hostile state, and saw their own organizations not only as bases of class mobilization, but also as embryos of an alternative world of solidarity and justice, as a microcosm of the socialist haven to come. Nonetheless, these microsocialist societies often became problematic class ghettos that divided rather than united workers. Membership was typically restricted to the strongest strata of the working class and the weakest – who needed protection most – were most likely outside. In brief, the fraternal society model contradicted the goal of working-class mobilization.

The socialist ghetto approach was an additional obstacle when socialist parties found themselves forming governments and having to pass the social reforms they so long had demanded. For reasons of political coalition building and broader solidarity, their welfare model had to be recast as welfare for the 'people.' Hence, the socialists came to espouse the principle of universalism and, borrowing from the liberals, typically designed on the lines of the democractic flat-rate, general revenue–financed, Beveridge model.

As an alternative to means-tested assistance and corporatist social insurance, the universalistic system promotes status equality. All citizens are endowed with similar rights, irrespective of class or market position. In this sense, this system is meant to cultivate cross-class solidarity, a solidarity of the nation. But, the solidarity of flat-rate universalism presumes a historically peculiar class structure; one in which the vast majority of the population are the 'little people' for whom a modest, albeit egalitarian, benefit may be considered adequate. Where this no longer obtains, as occurs with growing working-class prosperity and the rise of the new middle classes, flat-rate universalism inadvertently promotes dualism because the better off turn to private insurance and to fringe-benefit bargaining to supplement modest equality with what they have decided are accustomed standards of welfare. Where this process unfolds (as in Canada or the United Kingdom), the result is that the wonderfully egalitarian spirit of universalism turns into a dualism similar to that of the social assistance state: the poor rely on the state, and the remainder on the market.

It is not only the universalist, but in fact all historical welfare state models which have faced the dilemma of class-structural change. But, the response to prosperity and middle-class growth has been varied and so, therefore, has been the stratificational outcome. The corporatist insurance tradition was, in a sense, best equipped to manage new and loftier welfare state expectations since the existing system could technically be upgraded quite easily to distribute more adequate benefits. Adenauer's 1957 pension reform in Germany was a pioneer in this respect. Its avowed purpose was to restore status differences that had eroded due to the old insurance system's incapacity to provide benefits tailored to expectations. This it did simply by moving from contribution- to earnings-graduated benefits without altering the framework of status-distinctiveness.

In nations with either a social assistance or a universalistic Beveridge-type system, the option was whether to allow the market or the state to furnish adequacy and satisfy middle-class aspirations. Two alternative models emerged from this political choice. The one typical of Great Britain and most of the Anglo-Saxon world was to preserve an essentially modest universalism in the state and allow the market to reign for the growing social strata demanding superior welfare. Due to the political power of such groups, the dualism that emerges is not merely one between state and market, but also between forms of welfare state transfers: in these nations, one of the fastest growing components of public expenditure is tax-subsidies for so-called 'private' welfare plans. And the typical political effect is eroding middle-class support for what is less and less a universalistic public sector transfer system.

Yet another alternative has been to seek a synthesis of universalism and adequacy outside of the market. This road has been followed in the countries where, by mandating or legislation, the state includes the new middle classes by erecting a luxurious second-tier, universally inclusive, earnings related insurance scheme on top of the flat-rate egalitarian one. Notable examples are Sweden and Norway. By guaranteeing benefits tailored to expectations, this solution reintroduces benefit inequalities, but effectively blocks off the market. It thus succeeds in retaining universalism and, therefore, also the degree of political consensus required to preserve broad and solidaristic support for the high taxes that such a welfare state model demands.

Welfare State Regimes

Welfare states vary considerably with respect to their principles of rights and stratification. This results in qualitatively different arrangements between state, market, and the family. The welfare state variations, we find, are therefore not linearly distributed, but clustered by regime-types.

In one cluster, we find the 'liberal' welfare state, in which means-tested assistance, modest universal transfers, or modest social insurance plans predominate. These cater mainly to a clientele of low-income, usually working-class, state dependents. It is a model in which, implicitly or explicitly, the progress of social reform has been severely circumscribed by traditional, liberal work-ethic norms; one where the limits of welfare equal the marginal propensity to demand welfare instead of work. Entitlement rules are therefore strict and often associated with stigma; benefits are typically modest. In turn, the state encourages the market, either passively by guaranteeing only a minimum, or actively by subsidizing private welfare schemes.

The consequence is that this welfare state regime minimizes de-commodification-effects, effectively contains the realm of social rights, and erects a stratification order that blends a relative equality of poverty among state welfare recipients, market-differentiated welfare among the majorities, and a class-political dualism between the two. The archetypical examples of this model are the United States, Canada, and Australia. Nations that approximate the model are Denmark, Switzerland, and Great Britain.

A second regime-cluster is composed of nations such as Austria, France, Germany, and Italy. Here, the historical corporatist-statist legacy was up-graded to cater to the new 'post-industrial' class structure. In these 'corporatist' welfare states, the liberal obsession with market efficiency and commodification was never pre-eminent and, as such, the granting of social rights was hardly ever a seriously contested issue. What predominated was the preservation of status differentials; rights, therefore, were attached to class and status. This corporativism was subsumed under a state edifice perfectly ready to displace the market as a provider of welfare; hence, private insurance and occupational fringe benefits play a truly marginal role in this model. On the other hand, the state's emphasis on upholding status differences means that its redistributive effects are negligible.

But, the corporativist regimes are also typically shaped by the Church, and therefore influenced by a strong commitment to the preservation of traditional family patterns. Social insurance typically excludes non-working wives, and family benefits encourage motherhood. Day care, and similar family services, are conspicuously underdeveloped, and the 'subsidiarity principle' serves to emphasize that the state will only interfere when the family's capacity to service its members is exhausted. An illustrative example is German unemployment assistance. Once a person has exhausted his/her entitlement to normal unemployment insurance, eligibility for continued assistance depends on whether one's family commands the financial capacity to aid the unfortunate; this obtains for persons of any age.

The third, and clearly smallest, regime-cluster is composed of those countries in which the principles of universalism and de-commodifying social rights were extended also to the new middle classes. We may call it the 'social democratic' regime-type since, in these nations, social democracy clearly was the dominant force behind social reform. Norway and Sweden are the clearest cases, but we should also consider Denmark and Finland. Rather than tolerate a dualism between state and market, between working class and middle class, the social democrats pursued a welfare state that would promote an equality of the highest standards, rather than an equality of minimal needs as was pursued elsewhere. This implied, first, that services and benefits be upgraded to levels commensurable to even the most discriminate tastes of the new middle classes; and, secondly, that equality be furnished by guaranteeing workers full participation in the quality of rights enjoyed by the better off.

This formula translates into a mix of highly de-commodifying and universalistic programs that, nonetheless, are tailored to differentiated expectations. Thus, manual workers come to enjoy rights identical to those of salaried white-collar employees or civil servants; all strata and classes are incorporated under one universal insurance system; yet, benefits are graduated according to accustomed earnings. This model crowds out the market and, consequently, inculcates an essentially universal solidarity behind the welfare state. All benefit, all are dependent, and all will presumably feel obliged to pay.

The social democratic regime's policy of emancipation addresses both the market and the traditional family. In contrast to the corporatist-subsidiarity model, the principle is not to wait until the family's capacity to aid is exhausted, but to pre-emptively socialize the costs of familihood. The ideal is not to maximize dependence on the family, but capacities for individual independence. In this sense, the model is a peculiar fusion of liberalism and socialism. The result is a welfare state that grants transfers directly to the children, and takes direct caring responsibilities for children, the aged and the helpless. It is, accordingly, committed to a heavy social service burden, not only to service family needs, but also to permit women to chose work rather than the household.

Perhaps the most salient characteristic of the social-democratic regime is its fusion of welfare and work. It is, at once, a welfare state genuinely committed to a full employment guarantee, and a welfare state entirely dependent on its attainment. On the one side, it is a model in which the right to work has equal status to the right of income protection. On the other side, the enormous costs of maintaining a solidaristic, universalistic and de-commodifying welfare system means that it must minimize social problems and maximize revenue income. This is obviously best done with most people working, and the fewest possible living off social transfers.

While it is empirically clear that welfare states cluster, we must recognize that no single case is pure. The social-democratic regimes of Scandinavia blend crucial socialist and liberal elements. The Danish and Swedish unemployment insurance schemes, for example, are still essentially voluntarist. Denmark's labor movement has been chronically incapable of pursuing full employment policies due in part to trade union resistance to active manpower policies. And in both Denmark and Finland, the market has been allowed to play a decisive role in pensions.

Neither are the liberal regimes pure. The American social security system is redistributive, compulsory and far from actuarial. At least in its early formulation, the New Deal was a social democratic as was contemporary Scandinavian social democracy. In contrast, the Australian welfare state would appear exceedingly close to the bourgeois-liberal ideal-type, but much of its edifice has been the co-responsibility of Australian labor. And, finally, the European corporatist regimes have received both liberal and social democratic impulses. Social insurance schemes have been substantially destratified and unified in Austria, Germany, France and Italy. Their extremely corporativist character has thus been reduced.

Notwithstanding the lack of purity, if our essential criteria for defining welfare states have to do with the quality of social rights, social stratification, and the relationship between state, market and family, the World is composed of distinct regime-clusters. Comparing welfare states on scales of more or less or, indeed, better or worse, will yield highly misleading results.

The Causes of Welfare State Regimes

If welfare states cluster into three distinct regime types, we are confronted with a substantially more complex task of identifying the causes of welfare state differences. What is the explanatory power of industrialization, economic growth, capitalism, or working-class political power in accounting for regime types? A first superficial answer would be: very little. The nations we study are all more or less similar with regard to all but the working class mobilization variable. And we find very powerful labor movements and parties in each of the three clusters. A theory of welfare state developments must clearly reconsider its causal assumptions if we wish to explain clusters. The hope to find one single powerful causal motor must be abandoned; the task is to identify salient interaction effects. Based on the preceding arguments, three factors in particular should be of importance: the nature of (especially working-) class mobilization; class-political coalition structures; and the historical legacy of regime institutionalization.

As we have noted, there is absolutely no compelling reason to believe that workers will automatically and naturally forge a socialist class identity; nor is it plausible that their mobilization will look especially Swedish. The actual historical formation of working-class collectivities will diverge, and so also will their aims and political capacities. Fundamental differences appear both in trade unionism and party development. A key element in trade unionism is the mix of craft and industrial unions. The former is prone to particularism and corporativism; the latter is inclined to articulate broader, more universal objectives. This blend decisively affects the scope for labor party action and also the nature of political demands. Thus, the dominance of the AFL in pre-war United States was a major impediment to social policy development. Likewise, the heavily craft-oriented Danish labor movement, compared to its Norwegian and Swedish counterparts, blocked social democracy's aspirations for an active labor market policy for full employment. In the United States, craft unions believed that negotiating occupational benefits was a superior strategy, given their privileged market position. In Denmark, craft unions jealously guarded their monopoly on training and labor mobility. Conversely, centralized industrial unionism will tend to present a more unified and consolidated working-class clientele to the labor party, making policy consensus easier, and power mobilization more effective. It is clear that a working-class mobilization thesis must pay attention to union structure.

Equally decisive is political or denominational union fragmentation. In many nations, for example, Finland, France, and Italy, trade unions are divided between socialist and communist parties; white-collar unions are politically unaffiliated or divide their affiliation among several parties. Denominational trade unionism has been a powerful feature in Holland, Italy, and other nations. Since trade unionism is such a centrally important basis for party mobilization, such fragmentation will weaken the left and thus benefit the non-socialist parties' chances of power. In addition, fragmentation may entail that welfare state demands will be directed to many parties at once. The result may be less party conflict over social policy, but it may also mean a plurality of competing welfare state principles. For example, the subsidiarity principle of Christian workers will conflict with the socialists' concern for the emancipation of women.

The structure of trade unions may, or may not, be reflected in labor party formation. But, under what conditions are we likely to expect certain welfare state outcomes from specific party configurations? There are many factors that conspire to make it virtually impossible to assume that any labor, or left, party will ever be capable, single-handedly, of structuring a welfare state. Denominational or other divisions aside, it will be only under extraordinary historical circumstances that a labor party alone will command a parliamentary majority long enough to impose its will. We have noted that the traditional working class has, nowhere, ever been an electoral majority. It follows that a theory of class mobilization must look beyond the major leftist party. It is an historical fact that welfare state construction has depended on political coalition building. The structure of class coalitions is much more decisive than are the power resources of any single class.

The emergence of alternative class coalitions is, in part, determined by class formation. In the earlier phases of industrialization, the rural classes usually constituted the single largest electorate. If social democrats wanted political majorities, it was here that they were forced to look for allies. Therefore, it was ironically the rural economy that was decisive for the future of socialism. Where the rural economy was dominated by small, capital intensive family farmers, the potential for an alliance was greater than where it rested on large pools of cheap labor. And, where farmers were politically articulate and well organized (as in Scandinavia), the capacity to negotiate political deals was vastly superior.

The role of the farmers in coalition formation and, hence, in welfare state development is clear. In the Nordic countries, the conditions obtained for a broad red–green alliance for a full-employment welfare state in return for farm price subsidies. This was especially true in Norway and Sweden, where farming was highly precarious and dependent on state aid. In the United States, the New Deal was premised on a similar coalition (forged by the Democratic party) but with the important difference that the labor intensive South blocked a truly universalistic social security system, and opposed further welfare state developments. In contrast, the rural economy of Continental Europe was very inhospitable to red–green coalitions. Often, as in Germany and Italy, much of agriculture was labor intensive, and labor unions and left parties were seen as a threat. In addition, the conservative forces on the Continent had succeeded in incorporating farmers into 'reactionary' alliances, helping to consolidate the political isolation of labor.

Political dominance was, until after World War II, largely a question of rural class politics. The construction of welfare states in this period was, therefore, dictated by which force captured the farmers. The absence of a red–green alliance does not necessarily imply that no welfare state reforms were possible. On the contrary, it implies which political force came to dominate their design. Great Britain is an exception to this general rule, because the political significance of the rural classes eroded before the turn of the century. In this way, Britain's coalition logic showed at an early date the dilemma that faced most other nations later, namely, that the new white collar middle classes constitute the linchpin for political majorities. The consolidation of welfare states after World War II came to depend fundamentally on the political alliances of the new middle classes. For social democracy, the challenge was to synthesize working-class and white-collar demands without sacrificing the commitment to solidarity.

Since the new middle classes have, historically, enjoyed a relatively privileged position in the market, they have also been quite successful in meeting their welfare demands outside the state or, as civil servants, by privileged state welfare. Their employment security has traditionally been such that full employment has been a peripheral concern. Finally, any program for drastic income equalization is likely to be met with great hostility among a middle-class clientele. On these grounds, it would appear that the rise of the new middle classes would abort the social democratic project and strengthen a liberal welfare state formula.

The political position of the new middle classes has, indeed, been decisive for welfare state consolidation. Their role in shaping the three welfare state regimes described earlier is clear. The Scandinavian model relied almost entirely on social democracy's capacity to incorporate them in a new kind of welfare state: one that provided benefits tailored to the tastes and expectations of the middle classes, but nonetheless retained universalism of rights. Indeed, by expanding social services and public employment, the welfare state participated directly in manufacturing a middle class instrumentally devoted to social democracy.

In contrast, the Anglo-Saxon nations retained the residual welfare state model precisely because the new middle classes were not wooed from the market into the state. In class terms, the consequences is dualism.

The welfare state caters essentially to the working class, and to the poor. Private insurance and occupational fringe benefits cater to the middle classes. Given the electoral importance of the latter, it is quite logical that further extensions of welfare state activities are resisted. Indeed, the most powerful thrust in these countries is an accent on fiscal welfare; i.e., on tax expenditures and deductions for private sector welfare plans.

The third, Continental European, welfare state regime has also been patterned by the new middle classes, but in a different way. The cause is historical. Developed by conservative political forces, these regimes institutionalized a middle-class loyalty to the preservation of both occupationally segregated social insurance programs and, ultimately, to the political forces that brought them into being. Adenauer's great pension reform in 1957 was explicitly designed to resurrect middle-class loyalties.

Conclusion

We have here presented an alternative to a simple class mobilization theory of welfare state development. It is motivated by the analytical necessity of shifting from a linear to an interactive approach with regard to both welfare states and their causes. If we wish to study welfare states, we must begin with a set of criteria that define their role in society. This role is certainly not to spend or tax; nor is it necessarily that of creating equality. We have presented a framework for comparing welfare states that takes into consideration the principles for which the historical actors willingly have struggled and mobilized. And, when we focus on the principles embedded in welfare states, we discover distinct regime clusters, not merely variations of 'more' or 'less' around a common denominator.

The salient forces that explain the crystallization of regime differences are interactive. They involve, first, the pattern of working-class political formation and, second, the structuration of political coalitions with the historical shift from a rural economy to a middle-class society. The question of political coalition formation is decisive.

Third, past reforms have contributed decisively to the institutionalization of class preferences and political behavior. In the corporatist regimes, hierarchical status-distinctive social insurance cemented middle-class loyalty to a peculiar type of welfare state. In the liberal regimes, the middle classes became institutionally wedded to the market. And, in Scandinavia, the fortunes of social democracy after the war were closely tied to the establishment of a middle-class welfare state that benefits both its traditional working-class clientele and the new white-collar strata. In part, the Scandinavian social democrats were able to do so because the private welfare market was relatively undeveloped and, in part, because they were capable of building a welfare state with features of sufficient luxury to satisfy the tastes of a more discriminating public. This also explains the extraordinarily high cost of Scandinavian welfare states.

But, a theory that seeks to explain welfare state growth should also be able to understand its retrenchment or decline. It is typically believed that welfare state backlash movements, tax revolts, and roll-backs are ignited when social expenditure burdens become too heavy. Paradoxically, the opposite is true. Anti–welfare state sentiments over the past decade have generally been weakest where welfare spending has been heaviest, and vice-versa. Why?

The risks of welfare state backlash depend not on spending, but on the class character of welfare states. Middle-class welfare states, be they social democratic (as in Scandinavia) or corporatist (as in Germany), forge middle-class loyalties. In contrast, liberal, residualist welfare states found in the United States, Canada, and, increasingly, Britain depend on the loyalties of a numerically weak, and often politically residual social stratum. In this sense, the class coalitions in which the three welfare states were founded, explain not only their past evolution but also their future prospects.

Notes

This is part of an ongoing project on welfare states and labor markets, funded by the Research Council of the IUE and European Community. I wish to thank Thomas Cusack, Steven Lukes, John Mules, Fritz von Nordheim Nielsen, and the participants in my IUE seminar on Political Economy for their constructive comments and criticisms on an earlier version of this paper.

1 Adam Smith is often cited but rarely read. A closer inspection of his writings reveals a degree of nuance and a battery of reservations that substantially qualify a delirious enthusiasm for the blessings of capitalism.
2 In the *Wealth of Nations* (Smith, 1961: II: 236), he comments on states that uphold the privilege and security of the propertied as follows: '... civil government, so far as it is instituted for the security of property, in reality instituted for the defence of the rich against the poor, or of those who have some property against those who have none at all.'
3 This tradition is virtually unknown to Anglo-Saxon readers, since so little has been translated into English. A key text which greatly influenced public

debate and later social legislation was Adolph Wagner's *Rede Ueber die Soziale Frage* (1872). For an English-language overview of this tradition of political economy, see Schumpeter (1954), and especially Bower (1947).

From the Catholic tradition, the fundamental texts are the two Papal Encyclicals, *Rerum Novarum* (1891) and *Quadrogesimo Anno* (1931). The social Catholic political economy's main advocacy is a social organization where a strong family is integrated in cross-class corporations, aided by the state in terms of the subsidiarity principle. For a recent discussion, see Richter (1987).

Like the liberals, the conservative political economists also have their contemporary echoes, although substantially fewer in number. A revival occurred with Fascism's concept of the Corporative ('Standische') state of Ottmar Spann in Germany. The subsidiarity principle still guides much of German Christian Democratic politics (see Richter, 1987).

4 Chief proponents of this analysis are the German 'state derivation' school (Muller and Neususs, 1973); Offe (1972); O'Connor (1973); Gough (1979); and also the work of Poulantzas (1973). As Skocpol and Amenta (1986) note in their excellent overview, the approach is far from one-dimensional. Thus, Offe, O'Connor and Gough identify the function of social reforms as being also concessions to mass demands and as potentially contradictory.

Historically, socialist opposition to parliamentary reforms was principled less by theory than by reality. August Bebel, the great leader of German social democracy, rejected Bismarck's pioneering social legislation, not because he did not favor social protection, but because of the blatantly anti-socialist and divisionary motives behind Bismarck's reforms.

5 This realization came from two types of experiences. One, typified by Swedish socialism in the 1920s, was the discovery that not even the working-class base showed much enthusiasm for socialization. In fact, when the Swedish socialists established a special commission to prepare plans for socialization, it concluded after 10 years of exploration that it would be practically quite impossible to undertake. A second kind of experience, typified by the Norwegian socialists and Blum's Popular Front government in 1936, was the discovery that radical proposals could easily be sabotaged by the capitalists' capacity to withhold investments and export their capital abroad.

6 This is obviously not a problem for the parliamentary class hypothesis alone; structural Marxism faces that same problem of specifying the class character of the new middle classes. If such a specification fails to demonstrate that it constitutes a new working class, both varieties of Marxist theory face severe (although not identical) problems.

7 This literature has been reviewed in great detail by a number of authors. See, for example, Wilensky et al. (1985). For excellent and more critical evaluations, see Uusitalo (1984), Shalev (1983), and Skocpol and Amenta (1986).
8 This section derives much of its material from earlier writings (see, especially Esping-Andersen, 1985a, 1985b; 1987).

References

Bell, D. 1978. *The Cultural Contradictions of Capitalism.* New York: Basic Books.
Bendix R. 1964. *Nation-Building and Citizenship.* New York: John Wiley and Sons.
Block, F. 1977. 'The Ruling Class Does Not Rule.' *Socialist Review* 7 (May–June).
Bower, R.H. 1947. *German Theories of the Corporate State.* New York: Russel and Russel.
Bowles, S., and H. Gintis. 1986. *Democracy and Capitalism.* New York: Basic Books.
Brandes, S. 1970. *American Welfare Capitalism, 1880–1940.* Chicago: University of Chicago Press.
Cameron, D. 1978. 'The Expansion of the Public Economy: A Comparative Analysis.' *American Political Science Review* 4.
Castles, F. 1978. *The Social Democratic Image of Society.* London: Routledge and Kegan Paul.
Castles, F. (ed.). 1982. *The Impact of Parties.* London: Sage.
Cutright, P. 1965. 'Political Structure, Economic Development, and National Social Security Programs.' *American Journal of Sociology* 70.
Day, L. 1978. 'Government Pensions for the Aged in 19 Industrialized Countries.' In R. Tomasson (ed.), *Comparative Studies in Sociology.* Greenwich, Conn: JAI Press.
Dich, J. 1973. *Den Herskende Klasse.* Copenhagen: Borgen.
Dobb, M. 1946. *Studies in the Development of Capitalism.* London: Routledge and Kegan Paul.
Downs, A. 1957. *An Economic Theory of Democracy.* New York: Harper and Row.
Esping-Andersen, G. 1985a. *Politics against Markets.* Princeton: Princeton University Press.
– 1985b. 'Power and Distributional Regimes,' *Politics and Society* 14.
– 1987. 'Citizenship and Socialism: De-commodification and Solidarity in the Welfare State.' In G. Esping-Andersen, M. Rein, and L. Rainwater (eds.), *Stagnation and Renewal.* Armonk, NY: M.E. Sharpe.
Esping-Andersen, G., and R. Friedland. 1982. 'Class Coalitions in the Making of West European Economies.' *Political Power and Social Theory* 3.

Esping-Andersen, G., and W. Korpi. 1984. 'Social Policy as Class Politics in Postwar Capitalism.' In J. Goldthorpe (ed.), *Order and Conflict in Contemporary Capitalism*. Oxford: Oxford University Press.

– 1986. 'From Poor Relief to Institutional Welfare States.' In R. Erikson et al. (eds.), *The Scandinavian Model*. Armonk, NY: M.E. Sharpe.

Evans, E. 1978. *Social Policy, 1830–1914*. London: Routledge and Kegan Paul.

Flora, P., and J. Alber. 1981. 'Modernization, Democratization and the Development of Welfare States in Europe.' In P. Flora and A. Heidenheimer (eds.), *The Development of Welfare States in Europe and America*. London: Transaction Books.

Flora, P., and A. Heidenheimer. 1981. *The Development of Welfare States in Europe and America*. London: Transaction Books.

Gough, I. 1979. *The Political Economy of the Welfare State*. London: Macmillan.

Gourevitch, P. 1986. *Politics in Hard Times*. Ithaca, NY: Cornell University Press.

Heimann, E. 1929. *Soziale Theorie der Kapitalismus*. Frankfurt: Suhrkamp (1980 reprint).

Hewitt, C. 1977. 'The Effect of Political Democracy and Social Democracy on Equality in Industrial Societies.' *American Sociological Review* 42.

Jessop, B. 1982. *The Capitalist State*. Oxford: Martin Robertson.

Katzenstein, P. 1985. Small States in World Markets. Ithaca, NY: Cornell University Press.

Korpi, W. 1980. 'Social Policy and Distributional Conflict in the Capitalist Democracies.' *West European Politics* 3.

– 1983. *The Democratic Class Struggle*. London: Routledge and Kegan Paul.

Marshall, A. 1920. *Principles of Economics* (8th Edition). London: Macmillan.

Marshall, T.H. 1950. *Citizenship and Social Class*. Cambridge: Cambridge University Press.

Muller, W., and C. Neususs. 1973. 'The Illusion of State Socialism and the Contradiction between Wage Labor and Capital.' *Telos* 25 (Fall).

Myles, J. 1984. *Old Age in the Welfare State*. Boston: Little, Brown.

Mydral, A., and G. Mydral. 1936. *Kris i Befolkningsfraagan*. Stockholm: Tiden.

O'Connor, J. 1973. *The Fiscal Crisis of the State*. New York: St. Martin's Press.

Offe, C. 1972. 'Advanced Capitalism and the Welfare State.' *Politics and Society* 4.

– 1984. *Contradictions of the Welfare State*. London: Hutchinson.

– 1985. *Disorganized Capitalism*. Cambridge, Mass: MIT Press.

Ogus, A. 1979. 'Social Insurance, Legal Development and Legal History.' In H.F. Zacher (ed.), *Bedingungen fur die Entstehung von Socialversicherung*. Berlin: Duncker and Humboldt.

Okun, A. 1975. *Equality and Efficiency: The Big Trade-Off*. Washington, DC: Brookings Institute.

Olson, M. 1982. *The Rise and Decline of Nations.* New Haven, Conn.: Yale University Press.

Polanyi, K. 1944. *The Great Transformation.* New York: Rhinehart.

Poulantzas, N. 1973. *Political Power and Social Classes.* London: New Left Books.

Pryor, F. 1969. *Public Expenditures in Communist and Capitalist Nations.* London: Allen and Unwin.

Przeworski, A. 1980. 'Material Bases on Consent: Politics and Economics in a Hegemonic System.' *Political Power and Social Theory* 1.

– 1985. *Capitalism and Social Democracy.* Cambridge: Cambridge University Press.

Richter, E. 1987. 'Subsidiaritat und Neoconservatismus.' *Politische Vierteljahresschrift* 28.

Rimlinger, G. 1971. *Welfare and Industrialization in Europe, America and Russia.* New York: John Wiley.

Robbins, L. 1976. *Political Economy: Past and Present.* London: Macmillan.

Rokkan, S. 1970. *Citizens, Elections, Parties.* Oslo: Universitetsforlaget.

Schmidt, M. 1982. 'The Role of Parties in Shaping Macro-economic Policies.' In F. Castles (ed.), *The Impact of Parties.* London: Sage.

– 1983. 'The Welfare State and the Economy in Periods of Economic Crisis.' *European Journal of Political Research* 11.

Schmitter, P., and G. Lemruch. 1979. *Trends toward Corporatist Intermediation.* London: Sage.

Schumpeter, J. 1944. *Capitalism, Socialism and Democracy.* London: Allen and Unwin.

– 1954. *History of Economic Analysis.* New York: Oxford University Press.

Shalev, M. 1983. 'The Socialdemocratic Model and Beyond.' *Comparative Social Research* 6.

Shonfield, A. 1965. *Modern Capitalism.* Oxford: Oxford University Press.

Skocpol, T., and E. Amenta. 1986. 'States and Social Policies.' *Annual Review of Sociology* 12.

Skocpol, T., and J. Ikenberry. 1983. 'The Political Formation of the American Welfare State in Historical and Comparative Perspective.' *Comparative Social Research* 6.

Smith, A. 1961. *The Wealth of Nations.* Edited by E. Cannan. London: Methuen.

Stephens, J. 1979. *The Transition from Capitalism to Socialism.* London: Macmillan.

Therborn, G. 1983. 'When, How and Why Does a Welfare State Become a Welfare State?' Paper presented at the ECPR Workshops, Freiburg (March).

– 1986. 'Karl Marx Returning. The Welfare State and Neo-Marxist, Corporatist and Statist Theories.' *International Political Science Review* 7.

Titmuss, R. 1958. *Essays on the Welfare State.* London: Allen and Unwin.

Tufte, E. 1978. *Political Control of the Economy.* Princeton: Princeton University Press.

Uusitalo, H. 1984. 'Comparative Research on the Determinants of the Welfare State: The State of the Art.' *European Journal of Political Research* 12.

Wagner, A. 1872. *Rede Ueber die Soziale Frage.* Berlin: Wiegandt und Grieben.

– 1962. 'Finanzwissenschaft' (1883), reproduced partly in R.A. Musgrave and A. Peacock (eds.), *Classics in the Theory of Public Finance.* London: Macmillan.

Weir, M., and T. Skocpol. 1985. 'State Structures and the Possibilities for "Keynesean" Responses to the Great Depression in Sweden, Britain, and the United States.' In P. Evans et al. (eds.), *Bringing the State Back In.* New York: Cambridge University Press.

Wilensky, H. 1975. *The Welfare State and Equality.* Berkeley, California: University of California Press.

– 1981. 'Leftism, Catholicism, and Democratic Corporatism.' In P. Flora and A. Heidenheimer (eds.), op. cit.

Wilensky, H., and C. Lebeaux. 1958. *Industrial Society and Social Welfare.* New York: Russell Sage.

Wilensky, H. et al. 1985. *Comparative Social Policy: Theory, Methods, Findings.* Berkeley: International Studies. Research Series, 62.

5

Welfare Expenditure and Policy Orientation in Canada, 1960–1990, in Comparative Perspective

JULIA S. O'CONNOR

The focus of this paper is the character of Canadian public welfare effort and the changes it has undergone since 1960. I consider this issue within the context of contributions to the comparative analysis of welfare states in OECD countries (for example, see Castles, 1982; Korpi, 1983; Schmidt, 1984; Esping-Andersen, 1985b; Swank and Hicks, 1985), including analyses of Canadian public welfare effort (Cameron, 1986; Banting, 1987).

In the following section, I outline briefly some of the key theoretical issues arising in comparative analysis of welfare effort. Then I discuss various approaches to the operationalization of welfare effort. In the third section, I consider welfare effort in Canada in the 1960–90 period in the context of cross-national patterns. In the final section, I discuss the theoretical implications of this analysis.[1]

Theoretical Issues

There has been considerable interest in the comparative analysis of welfare effort over the past two decades. It is noteworthy, however, that this growth has been primarily among scholars adopting an approach to understanding public policy differences which focuses on the mobilization of power resources at the parliamentary and extra-parliamentary levels. The concern of these studies is with differences in welfare effort between countries at broadly similar levels of economic development rather than with *the* welfare state as a characteristic of advanced capitalism. The central argument is that the welfare state is the essential element of the compromise with labour on the part of the capitalist class (Korpi, 1983; Stephens, 1979). In contrast to the perspective adopted by mainstream sociological approaches, the welfare state is viewed as a class issue and its development is interpreted as the outcome of political processes which reflect the balance of class forces at the political and economic levels. Similarly, variation between welfare states is, to a considerable extent, but not exclusively, explained by variation in the balance of class forces.

While the primary emphasis is on the role of working-class mobilization, it is recognized in most studies, at least at a theoretical level, that this must be considered within the context of the total structure of power, since the relationship between the strength of the working class and welfare effort is not linear. The unity and strength of the right can be a barrier to the exercise of working-class strength (Esping-Andersen, 1985b), and the absence of such unity may facilitate reform by social-democratic movements, as Castles has argued in relation to the Scandinavian countries (Castles, 1978). Further, the institutional characteristics established over long periods set constraints on, or act as resources for, the exercise of power by different social forces, and consequently for welfare achievements.

In addition to class mobilization, a variety of factors have been linked to the welfare effort and its expansion in the postwar period. These include economic growth, demographic change (in particular, increase in the size of the pension-age population), openness of the economy, percentage of the labour force unemployed, state structure, and corporatism.

'Openness of the economy' refers to the dependence of individual economies on the world economy as reflected in the average of imports and exports as a percentage of GDP or exports as a percentage of GDP. Openness of the economy is extensively used in the analysis of public policy. However, there is no agreement on how this aspect of the economy influences welfare effort (Cameron, 1978; Castles, 1982; Martin, 1986; O'Connor, 1988). While Cameron links the impact of openness of the economy to the development of 'the social infra-structure upon which Social Democratic and Labour Party electoral support rests' (Cameron, 1978: 1257), support for this position is generally not evident in analysis of welfare effort (Castles, 1982). In a recent analysis, Cameron argues that the association of openness of the economy and public expenditure reflects attempts to insulate open economies from the international economy (Cameron, 1986). I return to this issue below.

In terms of welfare effort, the percentage of the labour force unemployed can be considered both a dependent and an independent variable.

It is an independent variable in the sense that one would expect levels and increases in unemployment to be associated with social transfer payments because of the growth in demand for unemployment benefits. It is a dependent variable in the sense that it is an outcome of public social and economic policy. I point out below that level of employment is an important indicator of the success of welfare state regimes. Moreover, in the post–World War II period, full employment was the central axis of the compromise with labour represented by the welfare state package, although the level of commitment to this objective then and subsequently has varied considerably across countries (Apple, 1980; Muszynski, 1985; Therborn, 1986).

In addition to the influence of political and economic factors, the influence of state structure, as reflected in a federal or unitary structure, has been considered in many studies of welfare effort. Federalism is generally found to be negatively associated with welfare effort (Cameron, 1978, 1986; Castles, 1982). The explanation proposed is that centralized states are in a better position than federal states to gain agreement on the introduction of new programs or to increase spending. This difference arises because of the absence of friction associated with different levels of government. While this reflects the dominant perspective on federalism, the contrary argument has also been made, that is, that decentralization facilitates bureaucratic momentum, and consequently the growth of public expenditure (Swank and Hicks, 1985: 129).

The concept of corporatism permeates much of the discussion of welfare effort and public expenditure. Indicators of corporatism are generally found to be strongly associated with welfare effort (Wilensky, 1976; Korpi, 1983; Schmidt, 1984; O'Connor and Brym, 1988). However, despite the pervasiveness of usage, there is no consistency in the definition and operationalization of corporatism. Three important points are evident from a review of studies. First, corporatism usually denotes tripartite bargaining, in the sense of the institutionalization of economy-wide bargaining on incomes and social policy involving centralized trade union and employer federations and the state. However, not all contributors to this debate regard participation by labour as necessary. Second, when one moves beyond the structural attributes of the labour movement, there is no agreement on what constitutes corporatism. Third, there is no agreement on what the relevant attributes of the labour movement are. Consequently, the classification of countries is almost as varied as the number of studies reviewed (O'Connor, 1986: 289–92). The only countries on which there is unanimity are, at one extreme, Austria, Sweden, and Norway, reflecting a high level of institutionalization of tripartite representation and decision making in the post–World War II period and, at the other extreme, the United States and Canada.

Before considering the relevance of these factors for the Canadian situation, it is necessary to consider what the welfare state refers to in comparative work and how welfare effort is defined.

Welfare Effort and Welfare State Regimes

The welfare state is sometimes considered a by-product of social democracy, yet it is obvious when global measures of welfare expenditure, such as civil public expenditure or the ILO measure of social security expenditure, are used that the Netherlands, Belgium, and France rank as high as some of those countries which have been characterized by extensive periods of social-democratic power, such as Sweden, Norway, and Denmark. This points to the fact that identical levels of welfare expenditure do not necessarily reflect similar policy orientation. Different welfare state regimes may have identical levels of expenditure, but the deployment of this expenditure may differ. Further, higher levels of expenditure, do not necessarily represent higher levels of societal welfare or equality. Consequently, not only must welfare expenditure be disaggregated, but it must be considered in the context of other indicators of welfare effort.

A variety of measures of welfare effort are used in comparative studies, and this in part explains differences in findings (O'Connor and Brym, 1988; Uusitalo, 1984). The ILO measure of social security expenditure is one of the most widely used indicators of welfare effort.[2] Studies using this measure demonstrate little or no impact of working-class mobilization on welfare effort. The reason for this non-association relates to the composition of the measure – it is skewed towards social transfer payments and includes only a very limited amount of government civil consumption expenditure.[3] The rationale for considering both elements is that they reflect different approaches to social policy (Kohl, 1981). The essential difference between public civil consumption expenditure and social transfer payments is that the former covers direct government expenditure on the provision of social services, such as health and education; consequently much of the expenditure relates to public service employment. In contrast, social transfer payments redistribute income on the market, for example, through income maintenance payments such as unemployment insurance and pensions.

As a consequence of its composition, the social transfer measure of welfare effort excludes certain types of expenditure which serve either to meet welfare needs or to prevent these needs arising. Noteworthy among these are subsidies for housing and other basic necessities, and spending for the protection of employment, both of which are included in government civil consumption expenditure. Thus, while high government civil consumption expenditure may reflect action to limit the need for social transfer expenditure, for example, through employment and training programs, high social transfer expenditure may reflect a reactive as opposed to a preventive approach to welfare service need – for example, through unemployment insurance payments. As a consequence of the differences in expenditure composition, the ranking of countries on government consumption expenditure differs from the ranking on social transfer expenditure (table 1).

The disaggregation of public social expenditure into consumption and social transfer elements is increasingly being made in comparative studies (Kohl, 1981; Castles, 1982; Cameron, 1986; O'Connor, 1986; 1988). These studies invariably demonstrate different influences on the two types of expenditure. Specifically, indicators of working-class mobilization (union density, the organizational strength of the labour movement, and long-term left party cabinet control) are positively and strongly associated with government civil consumption expenditure but only weakly associated with social transfer payments. In contrast, the strongest influences on social transfer payments expenditure are openness of the economy and need, as reflected in percentage of the labour force unemployed and pension-age population.

Despite the advantages associated with the use of social transfer and civil consumption expenditure elements over global measures of welfare effort, there are still limitations with an exclusive focus on expenditure measures. Expenditure captures only one aspect of welfare state regimes, namely, level of decommodification. 'Commodification of labour' refers to the situation where the individual's ability to sell her or his labour solely determines her or his access to resources. In contrast, a high level of decommodification reflects a high level of insulation from the pressures of the labour market and contributes to the ability of workers to resist these pressures. In other words, the citizenship entitlements reflected in social security payments and public services, which to varying degrees in different countries, and at different time periods in individual countries, are independent of class, facilitate resistance to the pressures of the market. Consequently, the level of decommodification is central to the welfare state project. However, as Esping-Andersen (1985b) points out, the social-democratization of capitalism envisaged in this project involves not only 1/ decommodification, but also 2/ redistribution along solidaristic lines, that is, a stress on universalism in the scope and coverage of programs; 3/ redistribution of income and resources; and 4/ institutionalization of full employment. These four dimensions provide a useful basis for examining Canadian welfare effort, although the comparative information is considerably more limited on the second and third aspect than on expenditure and unemployment. Most comparative studies focus exclusively on one of these latter aspects. The issue of redistribution along solidaristic lines is rarely discussed in comparative studies. Comparisons of income distribution figures are notoriously difficult, and few studies were available until the mid-1970s (Sawyer, 1976: 4). The Luxembourg Income Study, which brings together comparable cross-national micro-data on income distribution, now allows for more extensive comparisons of income distribution (Atkinson, Rainwater, and Smeeding, 1995).

Canadian Welfare Effort in Comparative Perspective

Much of the analysis of the welfare state in Canada has concentrated on the Canadian situation in isolation, focusing on the origins of the welfare state and usually on the introduction of particular programs (for example, Swartz, 1977; Cuneo, 1979; Walters, 1982; Struthers, 1983). Comparative studies with Canada as a central focus are few, and in these the issue of similarities with the United States is a dominant theme. A few studies focus exclusively on comparisons with the United States (Leman, 1980) or with the United States and one or a few European countries (Myles and Forcese, 1981; Kudrle and Marmor, 1981). While all of these studies acknowledge differences from the United States, they emphasize that the similarities between Canada and the United states are greater than are those between Canada and any other OECD country. In an analysis of the welfare state and inequality in Canada in the 1980s against the background of the growth of social expenditure in eighteen other OECD countries, Banting (1987) points out that, while differences between the United States and Canada are often stressed, the two countries are quite similar in terms of social expenditure – both have fairly low levels of expenditure. However, as I will illustrate below, this conclusion depends on the element of social expenditure considered.

Although Canada is included in most of the relatively large-scale comparative studies of welfare effort in OECD countries, the specifics of the Canadian welfare state are rarely discussed. In so far as Canada is

TABLE 1

Measure of Public Welfare Effort for Eighteen OECD Countries, 1990

	Category of Public Expenditure				
	Total civil consumption %	Social transfer %	Public health %	Education %	General and preventive civil consumption[1] %
Sweden	24.7	19.7	6.9	6.5	12.3
Denmark	23.1	18.4	5.2	6.1	11.8
Finland	19.2	10.0	6.3	6.1	6.8
Norway	17.8	19.0	7.1	6.8	3.9
Canada	17.8	12.6	6.9	6.7	4.2
Austria	16.9	19.9	5.6	5.4	6.9
United Kingdom	15.9	12.2	5.2	5.3	5.4
Germany	15.6	15.3	6.0	4.0	5.6
Australia	15.2	8.7	5.6	5.5	4.1
Italy	14.9	18.0	6.3	n/a	n/a
New Zealand	14.8	8.9	6.0	n/a	n/a
France	14.3	21.4	6.6	5.4	4.3
Ireland	14.3	14.1	5.2	5.5	3.6
United States	12.3	10.8	5.2	5.5	n/a
Netherlands	11.9	26.3	5.7	5.6	n/a
Belgium	11.8	22.7	6,8	5.4	n/a
Switzerland	11.7	13.4	5.3	5.4	n/a
Japan	8.1	11.5	4.8	3.7	n/a

[1] This refers to government civil consumption expenditure less consumption expenditure on health and education. It includes expenditure on general government services but also may include expenditure on employment creation and training, housing, and community amenities.

Sources: OECD, *Economic Outlook Historical Statistics, 1960–1990* (Paris: OECD, 1992); OECD, *Education at a Glance* (Paris: OECD, 1993), Table P1, 66; OECD, *New Orientations for Social Policy* (Paris: OECD, 1994), Table 2, 70–3.

referred to, it is invariably put in the same category as the United States as a late developer of services and/or as an exemplar of the liberal welfare state. In a few of these studies there is some focus on the Canadian situation, through concern either with specific policies or with specific aspects of welfare expenditure (Myles, 1984; Cameron, 1986). For example, Myles provides an analysis of pension quality in Canada in the context of fifteen OECD countries and demonstrates that, in terms of pension quality, Canada ranks midway among these countries (Myles,

1984: 69 and 73–5). This is not surprising, given his conclusion that the key influences on pension quality are the mobilization of the working class and its representation in Parliament (Myles, 1984: 98).[4]

Cameron (1986) provides a comparative analysis of the growth of government consumption expenditure and social transfer payments in twenty OECD countries, including Canada, in the 1964–5 to 1980–1 period. Consistent with the findings of recent cross-national studies, focusing on somewhat different time spans within the 1960–80 period, he finds different influences on government consumption and social transfer expenditure (see above). He also provides a longitudinal analysis of change in public expenditure in Canada in the post–World War II period, but does not consider growth in the elements of this expenditure.

The findings of Cameron's (1986) and other cross-national studies would lead one to expect that government consumption expenditure in Canada would be low by cross-national standards and that social transfer expenditure would be relatively higher. After all, Canada does not have a high score on any of the characteristics that are associated with high government consumption expenditure in cross-national analyses: high levels of working-class mobilization as reflected in union density and parliamentary representation, a union movement with a high level of organizational strength or tripartite bargaining. In contrast, it does have some of the characteristics associated with social transfer expenditure, specifically, consistently high levels of unemployment but a relatively low pension-age population and a federal structure. The first of these characteristics would be expected to increase social transfer expenditure, while the second and third would be expected to have a negative effect on social transfer expenditure by cross-national standards.

When one examines Canada's relative position among eighteen OECD countries in 1990, it is evident that its government *civil* consumption expenditure, at 17.8 per cent of GDP, is above both the mean and median levels and ranks fourth, after Sweden, with Norway, Denmark and Finland.[5] Moreover, this pattern has been evident since 1970 (O'Connor, 1986: 183), although Canada's relative position has disimproved from the early 1980s, when it ranked third. In contrast, Canada's social transfer expenditure, at 12.6 per cent, is below both the mean and the median levels and ranks twelfth, just above the United Kingdom, the United States, and Japan (table 1). The position is not improved when dependency, as reflected in pension-age population and percentage of the population unemployed, is taken into account. This relatively low level of social transfer expenditure is noteworthy when put in the context of the stress on the openness of the Canadian economy by Cameron (1986) and Canada's persistently high level of unemployment. However, I will illustrate below that what is exceptional by international standards in the social transfer/openness of the economy relationship is not Canada's expenditure level but the *character* of the openness of its economy.

Canadian Government Civil Consumption Expenditure

The high government civil consumption expenditure in Canada can be explained by considering the composition of the expenditure and the period when the most marked increase took place. Government civil consumption expenditure can be disaggregated into health, education, and a category which includes expenditure on general government services but also may include expenditure on such items as job creation and training, housing, and community amenities.[6] In other words, it may include expenditure which can be categorized as preventive of welfare needs. It is noteworthy that it is in terms of the latter category that the most marked variation between countries is evident.

In 1960, Canada's government civil consumption expenditure was average for the eighteen OECD countries included in table 1. The marked increase in level of government consumption expenditure occurred almost exclusively during the 1960s – an increase from 9.3 per cent of GDP in 1960 to 16.8 per cent of GDP in 1970. That is one of the highest increases among the eighteen countries. In contrast, the increase from 1970 to 1990 was only one percentage point. Further, the increase in the 1960s relates almost exclusively to education and health. Canada's expenditure on education rose from 4.6 per cent in 1960 to 7.8 per cent in 1970, and remained at about this level throughout the 1970s and 1980s. This 1960s increase was the highest in the OECD countries. Canadian public expenditure on health increased from 2.4 per cent in 1960 to 5.8 per cent in 1970, and was maintained at about this level throughout the 1970s – it was 6.9 per cent in 1990, that is, second, with Sweden, among the countries listed in table 1. In contrast to the increase in educational expenditure, the 1960s increase in health expenditure was not exceptionally high by OECD standards. This increase can be accounted for by the extension of hospital insurance to all provinces and territories and by the introduction of medical care insurance (Taylor, 1978).

The introduction of hospital and medical insurance in Canada was late by OECD standards (Flora and Heidenheimer, 1981: 83), yet, when introduced, the program was comprehensive. Explanations of this development vary widely in theoretical orientation and in the importance attributed to structural and political factors. Walters has emphasized the recognition of 'structural tensions within the health sector' by the state and the absence of strong capitalist opposition to the introduction of national medical care insurance, and argues that the role of working-class pressure was secondary (Walters, 1982: 169). In contrast, Swartz emphasizes long-term class conflict but argues that 'the state viewed health insurance as an economic concession to the working class in order to realize better the long-run political and economic interests of the capital-ist class' (Swartz, 1977: 335).

A variety of explanations which are relevant to this issue derive from attempts to explain the differences in social policy in Canada and the United States. Based on the differentiating factors stressed, these expla-nation fall into three categories: 1 / ideological differences between the two countries; 2 / differences in the party and electoral systems; and 3 / differences in power sharing between federal and local levels of govern-ment (Kudrle and Marmor, 1981; Leman, 1980). In their comparative study of a range of social policy initiatives in Canada and the United States, Kudrle and Marmor argue that ideological commitment had a positive role in Canadian social policy developments. They question Lipset's (1976) argument that the greater degree of 'leftism' in Canada relative to the United States can be attributed to the electoral system. They conclude that 'the success of public hospital insurance in Saskat-chewan developed by the NDP government there undoubtedly hastened federal health initiatives, although it seems as fitting to attribute this development to ideology as to the party system' (Kudrle and Marmor, 1981: 112).[7] This interpretations is consistent with that of other studies of hospital and medical insurance (for example, Taylor, 1978). In addi-tion to provincial party influence, there is evidence in relation to health insurance of trade union pressure mediated through some provincial representatives (Swartz, 1977: 323). Thus, while the federal structure may operate as a delaying factor in the implementation of certain social policy initiatives, for example, unemployment insurance (Kudrle and Marmor, 1981) and pension reform (Banting, 1985), it can also operate as a mechanism for the exercise of provincial party influence through pres-sure for federal support of provincial initiatives in the social policy area.

Progressive legislation during the 1960s and early 1970s was not con-fined to the health area. A relatively large number of reforms were intro-duced during this period, for example, the Canada Pension Plan in 1965, the Canada Assistance Plan in 1966, and the 1971 Unemployment

Insurance Act (Guest, 1986: 150–85). In contrast, since 1973 there has been little progress in welfare legislation, and many programs have been subject to restriction. This difference reflects in part a change in the balance of class forces from the 1960s to the 1970s (Doern, 1985; Muszynski, 1985). For example, Muszynski argues in relation to labour market policies that 'the greater leverage enjoyed by an expanding labour movement in the 1960s, in the context of minority governments in which the NDP also had greater leverage, helps account for the greater commitment to equity-oriented labour market policies during this period' (Muszynski, 1985: 299).

Finally, while acknowledging the socially progressive nature of health insurance in terms of access to services, it is important to recognize that health insurance is a relatively limited reform in terms of the spectrum of ill health and its causation in Western capitalist societies. Studies have repeatedly demonstrated the association between ill health and adverse social conditions, reflected in inequalities of income and housing, poor working conditions and environmental pollution, and unemployment (Brenner and Mooney, 1988; Sclar, 1980). With the exception of inequalities of income, the effects of none of these are influenced by the introduction of health insurance, and the effects of income inequalities are not eradicated (Manga and Weller, 1980). Health insurance reflects a concern with the payment for medical services rather than a focus on the structural causation of disease. Consequently, it is not surprising that opposition, apart from that of the medical profession, was not intense.

Turning to educational expenditure, the second component of Canada's increased expenditure during the 1960s, the increase over the ten-year period was 67 per cent, that is, 3.2 per cent of GDP. Public educational expenditure grew in all OECD countries during the 1960s and early 1970s – the average increase in the eighteen countries included in table 1 was 46 per cent. This increase can be accounted for in part by trends common to most of these countries, specifically, growth in enrolment, lengthening of the compulsory attendance period, and an increase in the quality of education provided (OECD, 1985: 41–2). Canada differs from other OECD countries in the size of the increase in enrolments – the increase of 4 per cent in the student body as a percentage of the total population in Canada from the early 1960s to the early 1970s was twice the average increase in the eighteen OECD countries included in table 1 (OECD, 1976: 10). In view of this, the increase in expenditure of 67 per cent, which is less than one and a half times the average increase in expenditure in OECD countries, is not large by cross-national standards.

As with several other OECD countries, Canada's public expenditure on education has decreased slightly as a percentage of GDP since 1970. This is not surprising in view of the decrease in enrolments at the elementary and secondary levels since 1970. Despite the decrease, Canada's public expenditure on education is among the highest in the OECD – in 1990 it was second to Norway in public expenditure (table 1), and, at 7.4 per cent, its total educational expenditure was highest among OECD countries, being slightly higher than that of the United States. In contrast, the United States ranks seventh in terms of public expenditure. Canada is more like European countries than the United States in its public/private split in educational expenditure. In Canada just over 90 per cent of educational expenditure was borne by the public sector in the early 1990s, compared with 79 per cent in the United States. In most European countries, the public sector is responsible for about 95 per cent of educational expenditure (OECD, 1976, 1993).

Educational expenditure is often not included in discussions of welfare effort. The rationale for exclusion relates to its focus on equality of opportunity and emphasis on merit. A further difference from social security expenditure is the postulated link between educational expenditure and the growth of productivity, and consequently economic growth (Wilkinson, 1986: 544–6). Each of these would lead to different pressures for the increase of educational expenditure or the maintenance of high levels of such expenditure than are associated with other types of social expenditure. Flora and Heidenheimer point out that, in its emphasis on merit, 'equality of opportunity inherently legitimizes inequality, mainly in the form of income and status differences' (Flora and Heidenheimer, 1981: 25).[8] Castles (1978: 61–4) provides a somewhat different interpretation of public educational expenditure in arguing that, despite its meritocratic character, equality of educational opportunity does provide to working-class children the right of access to a mobility route that is absent without such equality.

Canada's general and preventive civil consumption expenditure is low by OECD standards (table 1). This reflects the low expenditure on housing and employment creation. Public expenditure on housing has been consistently low in Canada and has decreased sharply, from a peak of over 1 per cent of GDP in 1975 to less than 0.5 per cent of GDP in 1985 (*Canadian Housing Statistics,* various years).[9] This low level of expenditure is not surprising, given the absence of a comprehensive housing policy. Moreover, public housing expenditure has been, and is increasingly, largely devoted to an assisted market approach rather than a commitment to social housing, as reflected in funding for public housing, federal-provincial housing, non-profit housing, and co-operative housing (Bacher, 1986; Moscovitch, 1986).

Federal expenditure on job creation reached a peak in 1972–3, when unemployment was 5–6 per cent. In 1982–3, expenditure in real terms was only 32 per cent of this level, despite unemployment of 11 per cent. The sharp increase in job creation expenditure in 1983–4 brought it to 41 per cent over the 1972–3 level, but this was in the context of an unemployment rate of 11.9 per cent, that is, 91 per cent above the 1972–3 level (Muszynski, 1985: Table 5–5). These figures reflect the fact that, with the exception of the 1960s and early 1970s, there has not been a commitment to an active labour market policy in Canada (Muszynski, 1985). While changes during the 1980s in employment and training policies reflect a more active approach, the emphasis is on efficiency rather than equity. Specifically, the focus shifted to meeting skill shortages and upgrading of skills, and funding this through the Unemployment Insurance Fund, the money being made available through more stringent conditions of access to unemployment insurance and a reduction in the duration of benefits (O'Connor, 1993: 78–80). This is a supply-side strategy, with the focus on job readiness skills and the assumption that the market will create the jobs (Yates, 1995).

A number of reasons can be suggested for the very different levels of commitment to health and education, on the one hand, and the general and preventive category of consumption expenditure, on the other. Expenditure on employment creation and training and housing and community amenities is 'discretionary' expenditure in a sense that education and health expenditure are not. None of these activities relates directly to generally taken-for-granted citizenship rights *in Canada*, although they do in many European welfare states (see McGuire, 1981, and Esping-Andersen, 1985a: 179–90, re housing, and Therborn, 1985, and Esping-Andersen, 1985a: 191–243, re employment). In other words the perceived scope of the welfare state in Canada is relatively narrow. Furthermore, government action on both housing and employment relates more closely to the economy, and is more likely to be contested than is action in the more narrowly defined domain of social policy. The historical pattern relating to both areas in Canada indicates that opposition to government action that would limit market activity has been strong and effective

(Bacher, 1986; Muszynski, 1985). Another factor that is likely to influence government action is the level of political strength of the beneficiary groups and the levels of popular support they enjoy (Banting, 1987; Coughlin, 1980). Additionally, the political strength of provider groups and the support they enjoy are relevant. On all of these counts, the general and preventive category of consumption expenditure is likely to enjoy a less favourable position than the other aspects of government civil consumption expenditure.

Canadian Social Transfer Expenditure and Openness of the Economy

As already pointed out, there is no agreement on how openness of the economy influences welfare effort. However, it is important to recognize that the most open economies are the smaller European countries which have high levels of need and/or high levels of working-class mobilization (table 2). High levels of welfare need are indicated by high unemployment and/or a high percentage of the population aged 65 and over, both of which are positively associated with social transfer payments expenditure. The three most open economies – Belgium, Ireland, and the Netherlands – are among those countries with the highest levels of unemployment in 1990 (table 2) and throughout the 1980s. Norway, Austria, Denmark, and Sweden, which are also above the median in terms of openness of the economy, have the highest levels of working-class mobilization among the OECD countries. They also have above-average pension-age populations, and Denmark has a high level of unemployment. These patterns indicate that the association between openness of the economy and social transfer payments can be explained to a considerable extent by high levels of need. In some countries this reflects high unemployment, but in others it reflects a high level of pension-age population and/or high levels of benefits.

Both in the interpretation of his cross-national analysis of welfare expenditure growth and in his longitudinal analysis of Canadian public expenditure, Cameron stresses the openness of the Canadian economy as a factor influencing government spending (Cameron, 1986: 31, 42–3). In the cross-national analysis, openness of the economy, as reflected in exports as a percentage of GDP, is strongly associated with change in social security and social assistance grants and only weakly associated with government final consumption expenditure. This suggests that the action taken to insulate most open economies from the international economy is of a reactive nature, as reflected in social security payments,

TABLE 2
Opennness of the Economy, Unemployment, and Left Strength in Eighteen OECD Countries, 1990

	Economic openness[1] %	Dependence on largest trading partner[2] %	Unem- ployment[3] %	Union density[4] %	Long- term left cabinet strength[5] %	Medium- term left cabinet strength[6] %
Belgium	73	22	10.4	51	30	19
Ireland	58	37	15.9	50	11	16
Netherlands	54	27	9.5	26	21	16
Austria	41	40	3.3	46	62	95
Norway	40	13	3.0	56	73	58
Switzerland	37	27	0.6	27	21	29
Denmark	33	21	8.1	71	60	63
Sweden	30	17	2.4	83	79	40
Germany	29	12	5.8	33	30	44
New Zealand	28	19	5.7	45[7]	19	15
United Kingdom	26	15	9.7	39	44	35
Canada	25	71	9.2	35	–	–
France	23	18	9.0	10	22	45
Finland	23	14	4.7	72	–	43
Italy	21	20	9.5	39	10	13
Australia	17	18	7.5	40	23	34
United States	12	21	7.0	16	–	–
Japan	11	28	2.5	25	–	–

[1] The average of imports and exports as percentage of GDP.
[2] Measured by the average of imports and exports to the largest trading partner.
[3] Standardized unemployment averaged over 1980–90. Standardized figures are not available for Ireland, Austria, New Zealand, and Switzerland.
[4] Trade union members as a percentage of all wage earners. Source: *OECD Employment Outlook*, 1994, chap. 5.
[5] Left party cabinet participation since 1945.
[6] Left party cabinet participation 1981–90.
[7] 1991.

rather than of a preventive nature, as would be reflected in government civil consumption expenditure. This appears to be borne out in the Canadian situation, where the sharp increase (from 7.5 to 11.2 per cent) in unemployment in the 1981-to-1984 period was accompanied by a 24 per cent increase in social transfer payments (Banting, 1987: 330).

In his longitudinal analysis of the growth of Canadian public expenditure from 1946 to 1982, Cameron concludes that the findings allow 'one to infer with confidence that a consistent and strong relationship has existed between unemployment and change in spending over the postwar era' (Cameron, 1986: 42). He links the deterioration of the Canadian economy and the growth of unemployment to the 'close relationship with, and vulnerability to, the volatile American economy that Canada, as an open economy, cannot avoid' (Cameron, 1986: 47). However, despite the strong correlations between unemployment and changes in unemployment in the two countries in the postwar period (r = 0.83 and 0.73, respectively), one cannot assume a unique causal relationship between openness of the economy and unemployment. Also it is noteworthy that, since 1981, unemployment rates in Canada and the United States have increasingly diverged – both countries had a rate of 7.6 per cent in 1981, but by 1984 the Canadian rate was 11.3 per cent and the U.S. rate was 7.5 per cent; in 1990 the Canadian rate was 8.1 per cent and the U.S. rate was 5.4 per cent (OECD, 1992, Table 2.15, p. 43). In a study published in the mid-1980s, Ashenfelter and Card concluded that the 'historical link between unemployment rates in the two countries seems to have ended in 1982' (Ashenfelter and Card, 1986: s171). Since then the divergence has continued.

Two points are important in considering the openness of the Canadian economy. First, comparative analysis indicates that an open economy is not necessarily associated with high unemployment. Second, Canada's economy is open in a different sense from that implied in the use of this concept in cross-national analysis. Canada does not have an open economy in the sense that the smaller European countries do (table 2). For example, in 1990, openness of the Canadian economy, as reflected in the average of the percentages of GDP accounted for by imports and exports, was 25 per cent, which is very close to that of France and Finland, higher than Italy (21 per cent), and substantially higher than only Australia (17 per cent), the United States (12 per cent), and Japan (11 per cent). What is distinctive about Canada is not openness of its economy in the sense of high dependence on foreign markets in general, but openness in the sense of heavy dependence on one trading partner – the United States. Taking the average of each country's percentage of exports to, and imports from, its largest trading partner, Canada's dependence on the United States, at 71 per cent, is clearly exceptional. The next-highest level of dependence is that of Austria on Germany, at 40 per cent, while the median is 20.5 per cent (table 2).

Recent cross-national analyses of unemployment consistently indicate that high unemployment is a political and strategic choice, not an economic inevitability (Schmidt, 1984; Scharpf, 1984; Therborn, 1986). This

is not to deny that the location of a country in the international economic order and/or high levels of foreign ownership constrain the policy
options and outlook for the *achievement* of economic and welfare goals.
Martin (1986) makes a distinction between the pursuit of employment
and welfare policies and their attainment. He argues that the former is
related strongly to the strength of labour movements, while the latter is
constrained by individual countries' weights in the international economy.[10]
However, as Therborn (1986) illustrates, not all low-unemployment countries are favoured economically. What distinguishes the full-employment
and high-unemployment countries is not the openness of their economies,
though this is a constraint, but the extent to which full-employment
policies are consistently pursued and institutionalized (Therborn, 1986:
23).[11] Moreover, cross-national studies consistently indicate that a commitment to full, or at least high, employment is not the prerogative of
countries with high levels of working-class mobilization, nor of countries
with centralized systems of government. Switzerland does not have either
of these characteristics, and Japan does not have the former, yet both are
among the countries with the lowest unemployment in the OECD.[12] In
contrast, while Denmark has both characteristics, it is among the high-
unemployment countries (Schmidt, 1984; Therborn, 1986).

While the emphases of cross-national studies vary, all conclude that
unemployment is amenable to government action and that low unemployment may be achieved by a variety of policies and within conditions
of either high or low constraints and/or pressures.[13] Further, while an
exceptionally high level of openness of the economy characterizes some
of those countries with the highest levels of unemployment – the Netherlands, Belgium, Ireland, and Denmark – four of the five countries with
the lowest unemployment rates throughout the 1980s – Sweden, Norway,
Austria, and Switzerland – also have relatively high levels of openness
(table 2). In contrast, Canada, which has a relatively low degree of openness in the sense of overall dependence on foreign markets, but concentrated dependence on the United States, and the United States, which
has the least open economy, have consistently high levels of unemployment. However, it is noteworthy that unemployment in the United States
has been declining slowly but consistently since 1983 in line with the
creation of low-wage jobs and the cutbacks in protection for workers,
such as minimum-wage rates and the criteria for access to unemployment
insurance and welfare (OECD, 1992, Table 2.15, p. 43).[14] In view of the
findings of cross-national studies on unemployment, it is noteworthy that
studies of unemployment in both the United States and Canada indicate

that there has not been a commitment in either country to full employment in the postwar period, and further that the definition of the 'full
employment' unemployment rate has been adjusted upwards over time
(Apple, 1980; Gottschalk, 1984; Muszynski, 1985).

In conclusion, two important points are evident from an examination
of social transfer expenditure and openness of the economy in Canada.
First, Canada has relatively low social transfer expenditure despite its
high unemployment. Second, in view of both the cross-national evidence
that high unemployment is a political choice and the absence of a consistent commitment to low unemployment in the postwar period in Canada,
there is little support for the conclusion that high unemployment can be
largely explained by the openness of the Canadian economy, although
the latter is a major constraint on the achievement of full employment.

Social Transfer Payments – Retrenchment in the 1980s

Banting's (1987) review of the various programs included in social transfer payments expenditure indicates a pattern of benefit-level erosion or
stagnation and an increased emphasis on income-tested programs since
the late 1970s. The pattern varies for the different programs, with pensions being the most favoured and unemployment insurance and the
Canada Assistance Plan being the least favoured. The trend towards
income-tested programs is evident even in pensions with the more
favourable treatment of the income-tested supplements – Guaranteed
Income Supplement and the Spouse's Allowance – relative to the universal Old Age Security payment. A similar targeting is evident in family
benefits, with resources being transferred throughout the 1980s from
Family Allowances and child tax deductions to the Child Tax Credit
system, which is targeted to lower-income families. This process culminated in 1993 with the abolition of family allowances. In the case of
unemployment insurance, a series of changes introduced since 1976
resulted in not only a cutback in benefits, but also an increase in eligibility conditions. In addition, there has been an increased labour market
orientation in the management of the program, and work incentives
have been reinforced (Banting, 1987: 324; Muszynski, 1986: 273–4).
Retrenchment was not confined to the social security programs, but was
also evident for the Canada Assistance Plan. It continued up to 1995,
when this plan was incorporated into a block grant to cover health,
postsecondary education, and welfare, but with reduced overall resources
(National Council of Welfare, 1987; O'Connor, 1998).

This restructuring of the benefit package points to two important issues associated with welfare effort. First, the relative privilege of some programs in terms of public perception and electoral attractiveness ensures less likelihood of cutbacks; second, there is a tension between the redistributive and solidarity objectives of the welfare state. Differences in the public perception of pensions and other social programs have been demonstrated in surveys of public opinion in various countries. These indicate that pensions are more likely to be seen as deserved and legitimate rewards than are other social security benefits (Coughlin, 1980; Tomasson, 1984). Consequently, mobilization of support for pension programs is easier than is the mobilization of support for programs such as family allowances or unemployment insurance. The broad range of support for pensions was evident in the composition of the opposition to the proposed de-indexing of the universal aspect of the Canadian pension program in the 1985 budget (O'Connor, 1987).

The tension between redistribution and solidarity is evident in regard to both pensions and family benefits. Universal programs foster solidarity, but, in so doing, benefits are not targeted to those most in need. When benefits are relatively low, targeting can make a contribution to redistribution. This is evident in relation to the increased targeting of low-income groups through the pension system; this targeting had the positive effect of contributing to a lessening of poverty among the elderly poor (National Council of Welfare, 1988: 1). Similarly, the targeting of low-income families through the changes in the family benefits package has had positive redistributive effects. However, while targeting may increase redistribution, it is also likely to increase the stigma associated with means testing.

Despite the relatively low level of social transfer payments in Canada by OECD standards, this expenditure contributes to the reduction in the inequality of primary income distribution and consistently plays a considerably more important role in equalizing the distribution of income than does the tax system. The first point is supported by Banting's conclusion, based on his examination of the role of the income security system in Canada in the early 1980s, that this element of social policy has 'continued to offset substantially the greater income inequality generated by the recession' (Banting, 1987: 330). The importance of social transfers in mitigating the impact of inequality in the market distribution of income, that is, income from wages, profits, and rents, is even more obvious in 1991 than in the early 1980s. In 1991 the top quintile of families had almost fifteen times the share of market income of the bottom quintile;

after the addition of transfer payments such as unemployment insurance, pensions, and social assistance, the difference in shares was reduced to just over six times (O'Connor, 1998). The second point is supported by the analysis of Gini coefficients. A comparison of these coefficients for 1981 indicates that the reduction in inequality due to social transfer payments is almost two and a half times as large as the reduction due to direct taxes (Vaillancourt, 1985: 11); by 1985 social transfers were almost four times as effective as direct taxes in reducing inequality (National Council of Welfare, 1988: 112); and by 1991 they were six times as effective (O'Connor, 1998). Despite this trend it is important to note, first, that social transfer payments in Canada play a relatively modest role in redistribution relative to many European countries (O'Connor, 1986: 315–16) and, second, that taxes and transfers have a relatively limited redistributive impact:

Even after paying income tax, families in the highest quintile receive five times the share of those in the bottom group, while upper-income unattached Canadians enjoy seven times the share of those in the lower income category. (National Council of Welfare, 1988: 111)

This conclusion still holds (O'Connor, 1998). This pattern is not unique to Canada. It illustrates one of the fundamental limitations of the welfare state – the inability to equalize the primary distribution of income. It also illustrates the twofold aspect of distribution in liberal-democratic capitalist societies, that is, distribution according to class and distribution according to citizenship.

Discussion and Conclusions

Canadian welfare effort presents a mixed picture in terms of the four dimensions of the welfare state previously outlined – decommodification, solidarity, redistribution, and full employment. In terms of these dimensions, Canada's expenditures on education and health are the best aspects of its welfare effort: both are universal programs, and consequently foster solidarity. However, they are universal in the sense of equality of opportunity rather than equality of outcome. In addition, the payment of premiums and the consequent means-tested subsidization of low-income groups, as well as the introduction of user fees in some provinces, lessens the universal character of the health program. In terms of the full-employment objective, Canada is one of the least successful welfare states within the OECD, and this is reflected in its very low general and preventive civil consumption expenditure. Its social transfer payments are low and are increasingly means-tested but also increasingly redistributive for certain groups, in particular, the elderly. Despite this, the overall level of redistribution achieved by the social transfer payments system in Canada is relatively low by OECD standards.

While the uniqueness of the Canadian situation has been stressed in the previous section, this should not be taken to imply that the general propositions relating to power mobilization have no relevance to the Canadian situation. The pattern of welfare effort outlined is consistent with the low level of working-class mobilization and the weak organizational strength of the labour movement. Despite this, studies of the development of the Canadian welfare state indicate that working-class mobilization, or fear of it, played some part in the development of all of the major programs (Swartz, 1977; Struthers, 1983; Guest, 1985: 74–9). On the other hand, the low level of mobilization and the weak organizational strength of the labour movement is reflected in the type of welfare state that Canada has and, in particular, in its limited preventive and redistributive orientation. The configuration of expenditure and policy orientation in Canada clearly fits within the framework of a liberal welfare state rather than that of a social-democratic welfare state. The liberal welfare state is characterized by state intervention 'designed to compensate for market imperfections while remaining compatible with the basic principles of market organization' (Ruggie, 1984: 13). It is characterized by a marginalist as opposed to an institutional approach, and while there is a commitment to universalism, it is universalism with an equal-opportunity focus (Esping-Andersen, 1985b: 232–4).[15] What is unique to the social-democratic welfare state is the integration of social and economic policy and the primacy of full employment for both men and women as a public policy objective (Korpi, 1983; Ruggie, 1984; Esping-Andersen, 1985a). This has implications not only for employment, but also for training programs, and for the structuring of the supports, most importantly child care services, that are essential for the participation of many women in the labour force (Ruggie, 1984).

Much of the analysis of the welfare state in Canada has focused on the similarities with the United States or the compatibility of reforms with the needs of the capitalist system. While both interpretations have some validity, neither provides an adequate explanation of the Canadian welfare state. If we compare Canada with the United States and Sweden, there is no doubt that Canada will be on the U.S. side of the continuum in terms of most aspects of welfare effort. Yet, this does not tell us very much about the Canadian welfare state except that it is not a social-democratic welfare state regime; but then, only Norway and Sweden clearly qualify for this designation. Despite similarities in social transfer and residual consumption expenditure and the low level of commitment to active labour market policies, there are some significant differences between the Canadian and U.S. systems. The free trade debates brought some of these differences into sharper focus (see, for example, Economic Council of Canada, 1987: 48–53). In addition to the marked differences in the health systems and in public educational expenditure, unemployment insurance eligibility conditions and benefit levels, despite consistent erosion since the mid-1970s, are still superior in Canada (Card and Riddell, 1993).

Studies of the welfare state which point to the limitations of reforms emphasize the logic of capitalism, and this is clearly relevant to understanding the welfare state as a phenomenon of advanced capitalism. However, an exclusive emphasis on this aspect fails to take into account the twofold nature of Western capitalist societies, that is, their democratic and capitalist characteristics and the interrelationship of these two sets of features. What differentiates the power mobilization approach is its dual focus on the democratic and capitalist aspects of Western capitalist societies. This entails recognition of the class and citizenship bases of distribution of societal resources. Important implications are associated with the dual elements of liberal democratic capitalist societies, in particular, with the non-independence of the two elements: first, an increase in citizenship rights is likely to have implications for power relations in the labour market, for example, entitlement to sickness benefit, unemployment insurance, or pensions as citizenship rights increase the bargaining power of workers in the labour market. Second, the dual focus points to the fact that welfare expenditure is essentially an element of the societal distribution of resources. Thus, in considering measures of inequality cross-nationally, both market and non-market distribution must be considered. Third, welfare states can be distinguished on the basis of the mix between class and citizenship, a principle of inequality and a principle of equality, as bases for welfare entitlements.

In conclusion, Canadian welfare effort illustrates well the twofold nature of the welfare state. At one level, it provides citizenship benefits which mitigate the impact of class, and consequently strengthen the working class. At another level, there is a strong class influence on entitlement to benefits, reflected in the income-testing approach, and this is increasing. This increase not only enhances the class character of the range of services, but may also have implications for the level of services. Despite the likelihood of being less redistributive, universal programs have a major advantage over selective programs in that they contribute to solidarity and facilitate the cross-class alliances that are necessary for the protection of programs against cutbacks. The pattern of development in Canadian welfare effort over the past decade indicates that programs directed to the entire population, such as health, education, and pensions, have fared better than those directed to specific target groups, such as the unemployed and low-income groups. Thus, while the Canadian welfare package still mitigates the inequality of the primary distribution of income, it is increasingly being restructured towards a distribution of benefits on the basis of class rather than citizenship.

Notes

I wish to thank Robert J. Brym and John Myles for comments on an earlier draft of this paper.

1 This is a slightly revised version of 'Welfare Expenditure and Policy Orientation in Canada in Comparative Perspective,' published in the *Canadian Review of Sociology and Anthropology* 26(1) 1989: 127–60. That paper was based on data from 1960–83.
2 The ILO classification of social security expenditure includes the following programs: Social Insurance and Assimilated Schemes, Family Allowances, Public Employees Pension, Social Security and Health Services, Public Health Services, Public Assistance, and Assimilated Schemes and Benefits for War Victims.
3 Social security transfers as compiled by the OECD consist of social security benefits, social assistance grants, and unfunded employee welfare benefits paid by government.
4 In 1980 Canada ranked seventeenth out of the eighteen countries listed in table 1 on pension expenditure. When expenditure is standardized for percentage of the population aged 65 and over, its rank is sixteenth (O'Connor, 1987).
5 In contrast to Cameron (1986) and Castles (1982), I refer to *civil* government consumption expenditure rather than total government consumption expenditure. The distinction is important since the total expenditure figure includes military expenditure, which varies from 1 to 7 per cent of GDP in

1983 for the countries listed in table 1. In that year, military expenditure
was 2 per cent of GDP in Canada, compared with 6.7 per cent in the United
States.

6 Public expenditure on both health and education includes a transfer
element, but the direct government expenditure is by far the largest in most
countries. The exceptions are France, Belgium, and the Netherlands.

7 Since the subject is the 1946 Hospitalization Act, the statement should refer
to the CCF government.

8 The extent to which this focus legitimizes inequality will depend to a
considerable extent on the degree of income inequality in the society. Post-
tax and social security inequality, as indicated by the Gini index, is greater in
the United States than in Canada, and considerably greater in both than in
Sweden and Denmark (O'Connor, 1986: 309–17).

9 Tables on Public Funds Authorized under the National Housing Act.

10 Martin (1986: 229) identifies two ways in which the impact of countries
with greater weight operates: 1/ They influence 'the norms and facilities
governing and supporting international financial and trade transactions and
thereby the kinds of economic strategies that are rendered permissible and
feasible'; 2/ Their economic strategies influence 'the magnitude, composition and terms of the transactions that take place within the structure of
interdependence, that is the levels of demand, inflation, interest rates and
exchange rates.'

11 'An institutionalization of the commitment to full employment involves:
a/ an explicit commitment to maintaining/achieving full employment; b/
the existence and use of countercyclical mechanisms and policies; c/ the
existence and use of specific mechanisms to adjust supply and demand in
the labour market to the goal of full employment; d/ a conscious decision
not to use high unemployment as a means to secure other policy objectives'
(Therborn, 1986: 23).

12 Schmidt (1984) argues that the achievement of full employment in Japan is
due to the pattern of paternalistic capitalism which facilitates conflict
regulation, and that such regulation is facilitated in Switzerland by the social
partnership ethos.

13 Therborn's examination of policies in low-unemployment countries indicates that almost all pursued Keynesian-type expansive policies but that,
while these were necessary, they were not sufficient to achieve low unemployment. These were accompanied by a consistently complementary
monetary policy and nationally specific direct intervention in the market.
The latter took a variety of forms: active labour market policy focusing on
public works and vocational training in Sweden, public subsidies of private

employment in Norway, expansion of public investment and publicly coordinated private labour market policy in Japan, direct public enterprise investment, cheap credit and tax incentives for private investment, and tight incomes policy in Austria. Switzerland is the exception among the low-unemployment countries, with its strong monetary policy and repatriation of foreign workers, though Austria also adopted a restrictive immigration policy with the onset of the economic recession (Therborn, 1985: 26–30). All of these countries, with the exception of Japan and Switzerland, suffered either high labour force growth – 2 to 2.5 per cent growth *per annum* in the 1975–83 period – and/or the constraint of a relatively large percentage deficit (ibid.: 135–6); in these respects they are not advantaged relative to the high unemployment countries. They all had the advantage of independence from the constraints on economic policy associated with membership of the EEC and also had low levels of foreign ownership (ibid.: 29).

14 This is associated with an increase in the working poor, that is, those who are employed but whose earnings are below the poverty line.

15 The classification of welfare states as marginal or institutional is widely used. The distinction was originally made by Titmus, who identified marginal, institutional, and economic growth type social policies (Titmus, 1974: 30–1). Korpi (1980) has identified ten subdimensions implied by the marginal/ institutional polar types. Apart from quantitative differences in terms of the proportion of GNP devoted to welfare expenditure, the principal areas of difference relate to: 1/ the scope of programs (universal/selective); 2/ the orientation of programs (preventive/ameliorative); 3/ the type of financing (progressive/regressive); 4/ private/public provision; 5/ social control emphasis (means testing, aid in kind emphasis/social rights emphasis).

References

Apple, N. 1980. 'The Rise and Fall of Full Employment Capitalism.' *Studies in Political Economy* 4: 5–39.
Ashenfelter, O., and D. Card. 1986. 'Why Have Unemployment Rates in Canada and the United States Diverged?' *Economica* 53: S171–S195
Atkinson, A., Rainwater, L., and Smeeding, T.M. 1995. *Income Distribution in OECD Countries.* Paris: OECD.
Bacher, J.C. 1986. 'Canadian Housing "Policy" in Perspective.' *Urban History Review* SV(1): 3–17.
Banting, K.G. 1985. 'Institutional Conservatism: Federalism and Pension Reform.' In *Canadian Social Welfare Policy,* ed. J. Ismael, 48–74. Kingston and Montreal: McGill-Queen's University Press.

- 1987. 'The Welfare State and Inequality in the 1980s.' *The Canadian Review of Sociology and Anthropology* 24(3): 311–38.
Brenner, M.H., and A. Mooney. 1983. 'Unemployment and Health in the Context of Economic Change.' *Social Science and Medicine* 17: 1125–38.
Cameron, D.R. 1978. 'The Expansion of the Public Economy: A Comparative Analysis.' *American Political Science Review* 72: 1243–61.
- 1986. 'The Growth of Government Spending: The Canadian Experience in Comparative Perspective.' In *State and Society: Canada in Comparative Perspective*, ed. K. Banting, 21–51. Toronto: University of Toronto Press.
Card, D., and W. Craig Riddell, 1993. 'A Comparative Analysis of Unemployment in Canada and the United States.' In *Small Differences That Matter*, ed. D. Card, and R.B. Freeman, 149–89. Chicago: University of Chicago Press.
Castles, F.G. 1978. *The Social Democratic Image of Society*. London: Routledge and Kegan Paul.
- 1982. 'The Impact of Parties on Public Expenditure.' In *The Impact of Parties*. London: Sage.
Coughlin, R.M. 1980. *Ideology, Public Opinion and Welfare Policy*. Berkeley: Institute of International Studies, University of California.
Cuneo, C. 1979. 'State, Class and Reserve Labour: The Case of the 1941 Canadian Unemployment Insurance Act.' *The Canadian Review of Sociology and Anthropology* 16(2): 147–70.
Doern, G.B. 1985. 'The Politics of Canadian Economic Policy: An Overview.' In *The Politics of Economic Policy*, ed. G.B. Doern, 1–95. Toronto: University of Toronto Press.
Economic Council of Canada. 1987. *Twenty-Fourth Annual Review*.
Esping-Andersen, G. 1985a. *Politics against Markets*. Princeton, N.J.: Princeton University Press.
- 1985b. 'Power and Distributional Regimes.' *Politics and Society* 14(2): 223–56.
Flora, P., and A.J. Heidenheimer. 1981. 'The Historical Core and Changing Boundaries of the Welfare State.' In *The Development of Welfare States in Europe and America.*, ed. P. Flora and A.J. Heidenheimer, 17–34. New Brunswick, N.J.: Transaction.
Gottschalk, P. 1984. 'United States of America: US Labour Market Policies Since the 1960s – A Survey of Programs and their Effectiveness.' In *Public Policies to Combat Unemployment in a Period of Economic Stagnation*, ed. K. Gerlach, W. Peters, and W. Sengenberger, 116–39. Frankfurt/New York: Campus Verlag.
Guest, D. 1985. *The Emergence of Social Security in Canada*. Vancouver: University of British Columbia Press.
Kohl, J. 1981. 'Trends and Problems in Postwar Public Expenditure Development in Western Europe and North America.' In *The Development of Welfare*

States in Europe and North America, ed. P. Flora and A.J. Heidenheimer, 307–44. London: Transaction.

Korpi, W. 1980. 'Social Policy and Distributional Conflict in Capitalist Democracies: A Preliminary Comparative Framework.' *West European Politics* 3: 296–316.

– 1983. *The Democratic Class Struggle.* London: Routledge and Keagan Paul.

Kudrle, R.T., and T.R. Marmor. 1981. 'The Development of Welfare States in North America.' In *The Development of Welfare States in Europe and North America.,* ed. P. Flora and A.J. Heidenheimer, 81–121. London: Transaction.

Leman, C. 1980. *The Collapse of Welfare Reform Political Institutions, Policy and the Poor in Canada and the United States.* Cambridge, Mass.: MIT Press.

Lipset, S.M. 1976. 'Radicalism in North America: A Comparative View of the Party System in Canada and the United States.' *Transactions of the Royal Society of Canada,* Ser. 4, vol. 14.

Manga, P., and G.R. Weller. 1980. 'The Failure of the Equity Objective in Health: A Comparative Analysis of Canada, Britain, and the United States.' *Comparative Social Research* 3: 229–67.

Martin, A. 1986. 'The Politics of Employment and Welfare: National Policies and International Interdependence.' In *The State and Economic Interests.,* ed. K. Banting, 157–241. Toronto: University of Toronto Press.

McGuire, C.C. 1981. *International Housing Policies.* Toronto: Lexington.

Moscovitch, A. 1986. 'The Welfare State since 1975.' *Journal of Canadian Studies* 21(2): 77–94.

Muszynski, L. 1985. 'The Politics of Labour Market Policy.' In *The Politics of Economic Policy,* ed. G.B. Doern, 251–304. Toronto: University of Toronto Press.

Myles, J.F. 1984. *Old Age and the Welfare State: The Political Economy of Public Pensions.* Toronto: Little, Brown.

Myles, J.F., and D. Forcese. 1981. 'Voting and Class Politics in Canada and the United States.' *Comparative Social Research* 4: 3–31.

National Council of Welfare. 1987. *Welfare in Canada: The Tangled Safety Net.* Ottawa: Ministry of Supply and Services.

– 1988. *Poverty Profile 1988.* Ottawa: Ministry of Supply and Services.

O'Connor, J.S. 1986. 'Public Welfare Effort and Policy Orientation in OECD Countries 1960–80.' Unpublished PhD dissertation. Toronto: Department of Sociology, University of Toronto.

– 1987. 'Age Structure, Class and Patterns of Public Pension Expenditure and Quality – A Cross-National Analysis for 1970 to 1980.' Paper presented at the 22nd Annual Meeting of the Canadian Anthropology and Sociology Association, McMaster University, June 3, 1987.

– 1988. 'Convergence or Divergence? Change in Welfare Effort in OECD Countries, 1960–80.' *European Journal of Political Research* 16: 277–99.

- 1993. 'Ownership, Class and Public Policy.' In *Social Inequality in Canada: Patterns, Problems, Policies*, ed. J. Curtis, E. Grabb, and N. Guppy, 75–88. Scarborough, Ont.: Prentice-Hall.
- 1998. 'Inequality, Social Justice, Social Citizenship and the Welfare State, 1965–1995 – Canada in Comparative Context.' In *The Vertical Mosaic Revisited*, ed. R. Helmes-Hayes and J. Curtis, 180–231. Toronto: University of Toronto Press.
O'Connor, J.S., and R.J. Brym. 1988. 'Public Welfare Expenditure in OECD Countries: Towards a Reconciliation of Inconsistent Findings.' *British Journal of Sociology* 39 (1): 47–68.
OECD. 1976. *Public Expenditure on Education*. Paris: OECD.
- 1985. *Social Expenditure 1960–80: Problems of Growth and Control*. Paris: OECD.
- 1992. *Employment Outlook Historical Statistics*. Paris: OECD.
Ruggie, M. 1984. *The State and Working Women.*. Princeton, N.J.: Princeton University Press.
Sawyer, M. 1976. 'Income Distribution in OECD Countries.' *OECD Economic Outlook Occasional Studies* July: 3–36.
Scharpf, F. W. 1984. 'Economic and Institutional Constraints of Full-Employment Strategies: Sweden, Austria and West Germany, 1973–82.' In *Order and Conflict in Contemporary Capitalism*, ed. J. Goldthorpe, 257–89. Oxford: The Clarendon Press.
Schmidt, M.G. 1984. 'The Politics of Unemployment: Rates of Unemployment and Labour Market Policy.' *West European Politics* 7(3): 5–23.
Sclar, E.D. 1980. 'Community Economic Structure and Individual Well-Being: A Look behind the Statistics.' *International Journal of Health Services* 10(4): 563–79.
Stephens, J.D. 1979. *The Transition from Capitalism to Socialism*. London: Macmillan.
Struthers, J. 1983. *No Fault of Their Own: Unemployment and the Canadian Welfare State, 1914–1941*. Toronto: University of Toronto Press.
Swank, D.H., and A. Hicks. 1985. 'The Determinants and Redistributive Impacts of State Welfare Spending in the Advanced Capitalist Democracies, 1969–80.' In *Political Economy in Western Democracies*, ed. N.J. Vig and S.E. Schier, 115–39. New York: Holmes and Meier.
Swartz, D. 1977. 'The Politics of Reform: Conflict and Accommodation in Canadian Health Policy.' In *The Canadian State Political Economy and Political Power*, ed. L. Panitch, 311–42. Toronto: University of Toronto Press.
Taylor, M.G. 1978. *Health Insurance and Canadian Public Policy*. Montreal: McGill-Queen's University Press.
Therborn, G. 1986. *Why Some Peoples Are More Unemployed Than Others*. London: Verso.

Titmus, R.M. 1974. *Social Policy.* London: Allen and Unwin.

Tomasson, R.F. 1984. 'Government Old Age Pensions under Affluence and Austerity: West Germany, Sweden, the Netherlands, and the United States.' *Research in Social Problems and Public Policy* 3: 217–72.

Uusitalo, H. 1984. 'Comparative Research on the Determinants of the Welfare State: The State of the Art.' *European Journal of Political Research* 12: 403–42.

Vaillancourt, F. 1985. 'Income Distribution and Economic Security in Canada: An Overview.' In *Income Distribution and Economic Security in Canada,* ed. F. Vaillancourt, 1–75. Toronto: University of Toronto Press.

Walters, V. 1982. 'State, Capital and Labour: The Introduction of Federal-Provincial Insurance for Physician Care in Canada.' *The Canadian Review of Sociology and Anthropology* 19(2): 157–72.

Wilensky, H. 1976. *The 'New Corporatism,' Centralization, and the Welfare State.* Beverly Hills: Sage.

Wilkinson, B.W. 1986. 'Elementary and Secondary Education Policy in Canada: A Survey.' *Canadian Public Policy – Analyse de Politiques* 12(4): 535–72.

Yates, C. 1995. '"Job Ready," I Ready": Job Creation and Labour Market Reform in Canada.' In *How Ottawa Spends, 1995–96,* ed. S. Phillips, 83–106. Ottawa: Carleton University Press.

6

Locating the Canadian Welfare State: Family Policy and Health Care in Canada, Sweden, and the United States

GREGG M. OLSEN

It is commonplace to note that the American and Swedish welfare states exemplify antipodal forms of public provision. While the latter is identi-fied by 'cradle-to-grave' coverage, the former is widely recognized for its fragmented and meagre support. Portrayals of the Canadian welfare state suggest that it may be somewhat more difficult to situate. Few students of comparative social policy would seriously contend that the Canadian welfare state approximates Sweden's in terms of generosity, comprehen-siveness, or efficacy. John Myles and Dennis Forcese (1981: 24), for example, note 'a clear division between the two North American coun-tries on the one hand and Sweden on the other.'[1] Others, however, such as Seymour Martin Lipset (1990: 136; 1986), have clearly distinguished Canada from the United States on the basis of its 'communitarianism,' by which Lipset means 'the public mobilization of resources to fulfill group objectives.' As well, most Canadians believe that their welfare sys-tem is, generally speaking, much more developed than its American counterpart.[2]

The conclusions reached regarding the nature of the welfare state in Canada have largely depended upon the particular types of social policy under scrutiny. While social security programs have received a great deal of attention, social services often have not been included in comparative studies of the Canadian welfare state. In the present paper, an attempt will be made to redress this deficiency and locate the Canadian welfare state by contrasting it with its American and Swedish counterparts in two broad social policy areas – family policy and health care – with a particu-lar emphasis upon the latter. It will be demonstrated that an accurate characterization of the Canadian welfare state must be based upon an examination of both social security and social service programs. This

comparative examination of Canadian social policies will be preceded by
a critical review of the most commonly used approaches to classify or
categorize modern welfare states.

From Social Spending to 'Welfare Worlds'

Comparative analyses of welfare states have, until fairly recently, evaluated and ranked them along a simple leader-laggard continuum based
upon the size, scope, and precocity of national welfare efforts. Accordingly, a number of European nations, which had already emplanted several major social security (income maintenance/social transfer) programs
by the outset of the First World War or earlier and routinely spent a
significant proportion of their GDP on such measures by the early 1980s,
tended to cluster at one end. Situated at the other extreme was, of
course, the American welfare state – its celebrated 'exceptionality' signi-
fying the absence, inadequacy, or belated and reluctant introduction of
these programs and relatively low levels of social expenditure. Canada
was also identified as a welfare laggard. In contrast with nations such as
the Netherlands, Belgium, and Sweden, which, as a percentage of their
GDP, spent 27.8, 23.0, and 17.9 per cent, respectively, on social security
in 1983, expenditures in Canada and the United States were quite similar, at only 12.9 and 11.0 per cent of GDP, respectively, during the same
year (Gordon, 1990).

   While useful, such categorizations on the basis of social security spending paid insufficient attention to the policy instruments used and their
impact, and were thus often misleading. The creation of a variety of
proactive and preventive social services and policies allowed the Scandinavian nations, for example, to achieve their goals while spending considerably less on reactive and redistributive social transfer payments. It is
widely known that Sweden has maintained low levels of unemployment
largely through the creation of an elaborate array of active labour-
market policies, while other countries, such as Canada and the United
States, have *responded* to rising unemployment levels, primarily through
unemployment insurance programs (Olsen, 1988). When such proactive
measures are examined, it becomes evident that Sweden was the undisputed spending leader in 1983 (25.3 per cent of GDP) while Canada
(18.6 per cent) and the United States (11.7 per cent), the welfare 'laggards,' appeared more dissimilar than they had when only social security
measures were considered (O'Connor, 1989).

Gøsta Esping-Andersen's (1990) threefold typology of 'welfare worlds' represents a significant advance over these earlier leader-laggard models and has rapidly become the predominant approach in the field of social welfare research. In this approach, the welfare states of various nations are categorized as 'Social Democratic,' 'Liberal,' or 'Conservative' on basis of the general nature of their income security and employment policies.[3] Social Democratic welfare regimes are characterized by benefits with particular features. First, they are provided mainly through the public sector and are relatively generous. Second, they provide universal coverage as a right of citizenship. Third, they tend to stress prevention, rather than simply responding to need. Social policies based on these interrelated traits serve to weaken workers' dependence upon the labour market and to foster support for the welfare state and social solidarity among the citizenry. Moreover, these policies – best typified in Sweden – tend to form a coherent package of compatible programs and policies.

Social policy in the Liberal world virtually mirrors Social Democratic policy. Here, the private production and provision of benefits plays a leading role, supplemented by modest, means-tested public assistance programs.[4] Welfare provision in the private market may be obtained through direct payment for goods and services (for example, day care), private insurance plans (for old-age, health, etc.), employment-based welfare (a wide variety of occupational or 'fringe' benefits), or voluntary, charitable organizations. However, all of these forms imply a much greater dependence upon the employer and/or the market generally than that seen in the Social Democratic world. Coverage is not universally provided but is, rather, highly dependent upon place of employment, ability to purchase, or, in the case of public provision, need, and is thus subject to means- or needs-testing. Finally, social welfare measures are largely reactive, not proactive or preventive, and often contradict one another. The United States provides the purest example of this type of welfare regime.

Despite its strengths, this reconceptualization of welfare states into ideal types conceals significant differences between Canada and the United States Although they are both viewed as belonging to the Liberal 'world,' the Canadian and American welfare states are, in some ways, notably distinct. For example, while private employment-based welfare plays an important role in both countries, it is somewhat more prominent in the United States than in Canada.[5] In a recent study it was noted that employer contributions to three major 'occupational' welfare programs (public and private health insurance, private pensions plans, and legislated income maintenance plans) in 1984 were approximately 50 per cent higher in the United States, where benefits are usually purchased privately, than in Canada, where a greater proportion of the cost is borne by the government (DuBroy, 1986). Employee benefit costs as a percentage of gross payroll were almost six points higher in the United States than in Canada in 1989 (Courchene, 1989).

In addition, the Canadian welfare state has greater scope than its American counterpart. It is commonly noted that welfare state development in the United States has been 'episodic,' the first 'big bang' occurring in 1935 with the creation of the Social Security Act (SSA). This first step into the field of welfare reform was to be the biggest step taken and, apart from some important amendments to the SSA, little subsequent development took place until the next episode in the 1960s.[6] In contrast, the Canadian welfare state developed in a more steady and deliberate manner and introduced a number of important universal social programs which still do not exist in the United States.[7]

The welfare-worlds approach has also led to two other important problems with regard to the placement of the Canadian welfare state because it categorizes nations primarily on the basis of the *general* trends and tendencies of *certain types* of policies and programs. First, the model obscures the fact that the various social policies and programs which exist in Canada may differ widely from one another. Some, for example, clearly belong to the Liberal world, while others are more properly classified as Social Democratic. This will be demonstrated through an examination of two different components of the Canadian welfare state – family policy (Liberal) and the health care system (Social Democratic) – from a comparative perspective. Second, the welfare-worlds model fails to acknowledge that any one particular social welfare policy or program may exhibit concurrently some 'Liberal World' tendencies (private provision, selective benefit distribution, or a reactive or curative orientation) *and* some 'Social Democratic World' tendencies (public provision, universal distribution, or a preventive orientation). This oversight is due in part to the almost exclusive emphasis on 'social security' by researchers in this school. While the model has been applied primarily to old-age pensions (Deviney, 1984; Palme, 1990) and the major income security programs – sickness insurance, accident insurance ('compensation'), and unemployment insurance (Kangas, 1991; Korpi, 1989) – other important areas such as education, housing, health care, and family policy/day care have not yet been included. By ignoring the central 'social service' components of the welfare state, nations like Canada may be too readily misclassified. This problem will be demonstrated here through a detailed examination of the Canadian health care system from a comparative perspective.[8] It will be argued that, while Sweden and the United States constitute the definitive Social Democratic and Liberal worlds, respectively, Canada can be only uneasily categorized into either of these two ideal types. The development of an alternative approach which builds upon the strengths of both the leader-laggard and welfare-world models is therefore suggested.

Family Policy in the 1980s

Family policy comprises two major types of benefits. The more familiar of these is the family allowance, which is an income transfer to families with children that may be provided by the state or by an employer.[9] The other major type of family support measure is the tax benefit, or what has been referred to as 'fiscal welfare.'[10] Since 1950, Sweden has relied exclusively upon income transfers, while the United States has provided only tax reductions as the means of family support. Canada has implemented both types of family support measures. Nevertheless, upon closer scrutiny, it becomes clear that family policy in Canada shares many more similarities with the United States than with Sweden in this regard and fits easily into the Liberal sphere.

Universal, publicly provided family allowances were introduced in Canada in 1944 with the Family Allowances Act, three years before they were created in Sweden. However, by 1985 Sweden provided family allowances that were almost 13 per cent of net family income. This was among the most generous of the allowances provided by the sixteen advanced capitalist countries with family allowance programs.[11] In contrast, Canada provided less than 4 per cent of net family income – the lowest level of cash benefits provided by the same sixteen nations (Wennemo, 1992). Because of its Family Allowance program, Canada appears to differ from the United States, where the absence of such a plan makes it almost unique among the advanced capitalist nations. However, the meagre amount of financial support provided by the Family Allowance program in Canada clearly qualifies it for membership in the Liberal world.[12] Moreover, by 1985 Canada had begun to rely more upon a variety of tax allowances and tax deductions than cash benefits as a means of family support.[13]

In terms of the social services aspect of family policy – the provision of day care – Canada shares few similarities with Sweden and is virtually identical to the United States. The influx of women, and especially mothers, into the workforce over the past two decades has intensified the need for day care in all three nations. This is particularly true in Sweden, where women comprised 50 per cent of the workforce, and 80 per cent of all Swedish women worked outside the home by the mid-1980s.[14] The corresponding employment figures for female workers in Canada and the United States were 44.0 and 44.8 per cent, respectively (Anderson, 1991).

While Sweden has not yet achieved its goal of universal public day care provision, public sector day care was available in all of the large- and medium-sized cities (thirty-five municipalities) for 75 per cent of pre-school children whose parents were employed or studying by the late 1980s (Hwang and Broberg, 1992). There also exist more market-oriented forms of day care such as organized child-minding schemes (in which municipalities pay childminders directly and are reimbursed by parents) and private care in the home, although these forms do not predominate. In addition to family allowances and public day care, Sweden provides its widely admired 'parental insurance' scheme.[15]

Day care in Canada and the United States is woefully inadequate and is provided primarily in the private sphere. The most widespread form of day care provision in these countries involves care by relatives; private, informal, and unregulated day care centres; or employer-sponsored work-place centres (Goelman, 1992; Lamb et al., 1992; Mayfield, 1990). Both countries are characterized by a shortage of spaces in licensed or regu-lated day care homes. These tendencies were confirmed in a recent Canadian task force report which examined day care provision in the advanced capitalist nations in the 1980s (Cook, 1986).

In Canada and the United States, the state's role is linked to a variety of funding mechanisms which parents may use to help pay for day care costs on the market. Such mechanisms, like the Canada Assistance Plan or Title XX of the Social Security Act in the United States, are not available universally as a right, but are aimed only at low-income families and are thus means-tested. Moreover, the benefits they have provided are quite modest. In addition, neither country provides 'parental insur-ance.' However, Canada provided mothers with fifteen weeks of 'mater-nity' leave benefits in the late 1980s at 60 per cent of their earnings (up to a maximum) through the unemployment insurance program, while there have been no statutory requirements in the United States (Bronfenbrenner, 1992; National Council of Welfare, 1988).[16] These characteristics of Canadian family policy bear the hallmarks of the Lib-eral world. The Canadian health care system, in striking contrast, is much more Social Democratic in orientation while remaining somewhat Lib-eral according to some policy dimensions.

The Health Care System in the 1980s

Expenditures and Outcomes

It is common knowledge today that health care expenditure in the United States is astronomically high – the highest in the world in both absolute and relative terms. At 11.2 per cent, *total* expenditure on health in the United States, as a proportion of GDP, was significantly higher than Canadian (8.6 per cent), Swedish (9.0 per cent), or average OECD (7.3 per cent) spending levels by 1987.[17] However, as would be expected, *public* spending on health, as a proportion of GDP, was almost twice as high in Social Democratic Sweden (8.2 per cent) as it was in the Liberal United States (4.6 per cent). Public health spending in Canada, at 6.5 per cent, fell approximately midway between these two extreme expenditure cases and was somewhat higher than the OECD average of 5.6 per cent. As a proportion of total health spending, public health expenditures in Sweden, Canada, and the United States were 90.6 per cent, 74.8, and 41.4 per cent, respectively, the same year (OECD, 1990; Schieber and Poullier, 1989). Moreover, despite record-high expenditures in the United States, 'output' measures, while somewhat crude, suggest that the American health care system is among the least effective. As illustrated in table 1, Canada has been more successful than the United States with respect to infant mortality rates, life expectancy at birth, and mortality rates from chronic conditions, but has not performed as well as Sweden.

The three nations under consideration here also differ markedly regarding their delivery of health care. The United States and Sweden represent two almost entirely dissimilar approaches to health care. While the former emphasizes plurality and provision in the private market, the latter is sometimes characterized as 'socialized medicine.' As will become apparent from the following overview, health care delivery in Canada shares some features with both, but has more in common with the Swedish health system, despite Canada's common designation as a member of the Liberal world.

Organization: Public Sector/Private Sector

The delivery of health care in Sweden has much in common with Britain's more familiar National Health Service (NHS).[18] Like Britain, Sweden has allowed administrative coordination and public planning to supplant the market to a great extent. Hospitals are publicly owned and administered and, apart from some nursing homes, there exist few private alternatives

TABLE 1
Health Care Output in the United States, Canada, and Sweden, 1982

Health Care	United States	Canada	Sweden
Infant mortality rates[a]	11.5	9.1	6.8
Life expectancy at birth (in years)	74.7	75.5	76.6
Mortality rates from chronic conditions[b]	842.4	761.8	757.5

[a] Death of infants per 1,000 live births.
[b] Age-standardized death rates per 100,000. These data must be interpreted cautiously
since they apply to different periods (1982 for the United States, 1984 for Canada and
Sweden), they may be subject to yearly fluctuations (e.g., epidemics), categories are
highly aggregated, and death may result from multiple causes.
Source: OECD (1987).

for in-patient care. Ninety-seven per cent of hospital admissions, for example, are public, and more than 90 per cent of Sweden's physicians
(and 50 per cent of its dentists) are salaried public employees. While the
pharmaceutical industry itself remains largely privately owned, the Swedish government nationalized one company (Kabi) in the late 1960s, and
in 1971 organized the retail drug industry (pharmacies) into a single
corporation (Apoteksbolaget), two-thirds of which is owned by the state
and one-third by the pharmacists' association (Kurian, 1990; OECD,
1990). This has made it easier for the government to control the price of
drugs in Sweden.

   Unlike the NHS, however, the Swedish health care system is surprisingly decentralized, a feature that has characterized it since its inception.
As Odin Anderson (1972) points out, health care has been 'informally
regionalized' since the 1800s, when the counties and municipalities took
over responsibility for the financing and operation of hospitals from the
local parishes. Today, hospitals are still owned and administered
subnationally, rather than by the central government, and provide their
services to all, largely free of charge. The central government, however,
does assume the financial responsibility for their operation, and Sweden's
health system, like the NHS, relies heavily on tax-financing.

   Given its mix of private- and public-sector ownership, variety of organizational forms, numerous sources of funding, and decidedly market orientation, the American health care system could not be much more
dissimilar from Sweden's. A network of private hospitals, owned largely
by non-profit corporations sponsored by private citizens and sectarian

groups, and public hospitals, run jointly by various levels of government, are complemented by a throng of private health insurance providers and public health agencies and clinics. Most physicians (and dentists) practise privately in their own offices, using their own equipment. The pharmaceutical industry (manufacturers and retailers) also operates almost exclusively in the private sphere. The combination of uninformed consumers and multimillion-dollar advertising campaigns by drug companies contributes to the high medical costs seen in the United States.[19]

Sometimes described as 'socialized medicine' by organizations and individuals with an interest in maintaining the status quo in the United States, the health economy in Canada actually closely resembles its American counterpart.[20] As in the United States, health care is provided largely in the private sector. While some government-owned and -administered hospitals exist, the great majority of hospitals in Canada (90 per cent) are private non-profit corporations, although their global operating budgets are provided largely by provincial governments. Ninety-five per cent of all physicians maintain private practices and earn their income on a fee-for-service basis. As in the United States, doctors are paid by a third party – although, in Canada, the third party is the government, rather than a plethora of private insurance companies (General Accounting Office, 1991). Finally, as would be expected, given the central role of foreign (especially American) branch plants in Canada, the pharmaceutical industry operates almost entirely in the private sector, under relatively little public control.[21] Therefore, with respect to the organization of its health economy, Canada, like the United States, is situated in the Liberal world.

Coverage: Universal/Selective

Low-cost health care is available for the entire population in Sweden through a compulsory health insurance plan which operates largely at the regional (county/municipal) level. In 1955, Sweden created its mandatory National Health Insurance plan by converting existing voluntary, state-subsidized sickness funds and employer-financed schemes into public funds, which became part of the existing social security insurance system in 1963 (Serner, 1980). Regional councils, originally established in the 1860s to operate the hospitals, administer the existing twenty-six regional (twenty-three county and three municipal) funds today. Financed primarily by employer payroll fees and, to a lesser extent, the state, these funds largely subsidize the provision of outpatient medical services in

Sweden. Patients pay only a standard nominal fee to the regional council for each visit to a public clinic regardless of the amount of treatment or number of tests provided, and are partially reimbursed for their travel costs. Compensation is also received for a portion of the costs of drugs and dental care (Olsson, 1988). Despite decentralization in the Swedish system, regional hospitals and councils are monitored closely by the Ministry of Health and Social Affairs through the National Board of Health and Welfare to ensure uniformity in the quality of health care, if not in its delivery (Borgenhammar, 1984).

The United States is commonly known as the only industrial country without a national health insurance system. This, of course, does not mean that a majority of Americans are not covered by insurance. In fact, 85 per cent of the American population have some form of health insurance protection. However, 35 to 37 million Americans are without health insurance. Although it includes the unemployed, the majority of this uninsured group comprises the working poor and their families – that is, those who are not old enough or poor enough to qualify for existing public programs. Many millions more have only partial coverage. Fifty million Americans have such poor coverage that a serious illness would mean financial devastation (Bernard, 1992).

Only about 20 per cent of Americans are covered by one of the two major public programs created in 1965 or by the military and veterans' programs. Medicare, a federal health insurance program for the elderly and disabled, covers about 12 per cent of the population, while Medicaid, a state- and federally funded program for the indigent, provides benefits to another 7 per cent. These programs illustrate the tendency toward decentralization and fragmentation in the United States and the conviction, held at least among policy-makers, that health care is not a right of citizenship, as it is in Sweden and elsewhere, but a benefit of group membership (Klass, 1985). Also, they ensure that it is the state, not the employer, that takes on the high cost of caring for those segments of the population with the greatest need.

Most American citizens obtain health protection in the private sphere. By the early 1980s, private insurance handled 81 per cent of private consumer hospital expenditures and approximately 62 per cent of physicians' charges (Gordon, 1990). Today, about 57 per cent of Americans are covered through occupational health insurance programs purchased for them by their employers from 'third parties' as part of their benefits package. Another 8 per cent of the American population purchase health insurance directly from the commercial insurance industry on an individual basis. Contrary to popular belief, it is thus collective rather than individual purchases which predominate in the United States. Today more than 1,500 companies are involved in health insurance. However, the major private non-profit agencies, Blue Cross (for hospital insurance) and Blue Shield (for medical expenses), and the approximately 300 companies which comprise the Health Insurance Association of America are the major providers.[22]

Employment-based health insurance programs first began to spread in the 1930s and multiplied rapidly during the 1940s. Wartime wage-controls and favourable tax legislation encouraged employers to offer a variety of 'fringe benefit' programs as an alternative to wage increases. This expansion was given further impetus when the American Federation of Labor, thwarted in its attempts to expand public welfare protection, concentrated its efforts on the attainment of workplace welfare (Stevens, 1990). But, while they are widespread today, employers are under no legal obligation to provide health insurance. More importantly, private occupational welfare serves to increase a worker's dependence upon the employer and the market. Workers seeking to change jobs may risk losing their benefits. Those individuals who must purchase their own insurance are, of course, even more dependent upon the market. Even those who can afford insurance are sometimes hesitant to risk increasing their premiums by using it. Facing soaring medical costs, insurance companies have recently become much less willing to continue to cover or take on those in poor health.

The Canadian approach to health care delivery diverged sharply from the American over two decades ago. With the passage of the Medical Care Insurance Act in 1966, and Ontario's entry into the federal scheme in 1972, Canada established a national, compulsory, health insurance system which is, in its essentials, very similar to the Swedish plan. While privately provided, health care in Canada is publicly funded, with costs shared by the provincial and federal governments, and administered by the provincial and territorial governments rather than the federal.[23] The passage of the Canada Health Act in 1984 ensured that Canada's health care system remained affordable by outlawing the 'extra billing' of patients above and beyond insurance coverage.[24] Most important, Canada's health insurance system is both compulsory and comprehensive. It includes all Canadians as a right of citizenship and covers most types of medical care (with a few exceptions such as eyeglasses, outpatient medications for those under 65 years of age, and cosmetic surgery). On the basis of these aspects of its health care system, Canada, like Sweden, falls within the Social Democratic world.

Orientation: Intervention/Prevention

One of the most definitive characteristics of Social Democratic regime policies is the emphasis placed on preventive measures. With regard to health care, this involves a recognition that ill-health is closely tied to a variety of interrelated 'environmental' conditions such as poverty, unemployment, homelessness, and poor education which must be addressed before individual intervention can be effective. Sweden's social and economic policies and its elaborate welfare state are part of a coherent program which has been remarkably successful in altering those conditions by virtually eliminating poverty and unemployment. Specific problems, such as drug abuse and childhood disorders, are targeted through a variety of public preventive educational programs provided for students and parents (Nikelly, 1987). By allowing parents to care for their sick children, the public provision of 'parental insurance' discourages the development of minor ailments into more serious illnesses.[25]

In addition to the benefits and preventive measures described above, Sweden's national health insurance plan provides compensation for income lost due to disability or illness. Indeed, when the national health insurance plan was introduced, 'cash sickness benefits' were easily the most important and expensive component. Today, these earnings-related sickness insurance benefits cover over 90 per cent of economically active Swedes between the ages of 15 and 64. Stay-at-home spouses and unmarried parents of children under 16 years of age are also eligible for a flat-rate cash benefit which can be 'topped up' with voluntary insurance. A recent study demonstrated that, of those nations offering such coverage, Sweden was among the most generous in terms of replacement levels (90 per cent of gross income up to a ceiling), length of compensation period (no maximum), length of waiting period before benefits can be collected (0 days), and other qualifying conditions (Kangas, 1991).[26] In keeping with the public orientation of health care, the private provision of such sickness benefits plays only a very minor role in Sweden (Kangas and Palme, 1991).

Health and other programs in the United States are highly fragmented and largely geared toward intervention. There is a much greater tendency to hold individuals, rather than their environments, responsible for their plight. Americans are, for the most part, expected to manage their own health care and seek treatment when they become ill. However, preventive programs, designed to reduce many companies' rapidly increasing health care expenditures, have recently begun to proliferate in the private sphere.[27] Two out of three firms in the United States employing more than fifty workers now provide some type of 'wellness' plan which may provide prenatal/nutritional courses, fitness centres, or rebates for those individuals who manage to stay well (Schwartz and Padgett, 1989). Finally, given the absence of a national public-sector income maintenance insurance program, most Americans must rely on their employers for sick leave, although a few states (California, Hawaii, New Jersey, New York, and Rhode Island) do offer compulsory temporary disability insurance (Gordon, 1990).

By virtue of its health insurance program alone, health care in Canada is oriented somewhat more strongly toward prevention than is that in the United States. The existence of 'free' universal care allows those Canadians most vulnerable to illness, such as the poor and the unemployed, to make precautionary visits to their physicians and to take other prophylactic measures. Indeed, the numbers of checkups and pre-natal consultations carried out among low-income Canadians increased dramatically with the introduction of medicare. Although there is, strictly-speaking, no sickness insurance in Canada, provisions for time-limited sickness benefits have been in place since 1971 through the Unemployment Insurance Act. Nevertheless, compared to its Swedish counterpart, the Canadian health care system, like its welfare state generally, is geared more toward cure than care. Canada clearly falls between Sweden and the United States on this measure of health care provision.

Conclusion

The Canadian welfare state has been viewed by some as 'advanced,' while others have depicted it as stunted. An attempt has been made here to reconcile such disparate judgements and locate Canada's welfare state. The conclusions reached regarding the nature of social policy in Canada have much to do with the particular model used and the types of policies and dimensions (e.g., expenditures) emphasized. The most popular of these, the welfare-worlds approach, has focused primarily upon social security and suggests that Canada and the United States are much more similar than different. However, despite Canada's increasingly common designation as a Liberal welfare regime, certain social service programs, such as the Canadian health care system, are not so easily categorized. While it closely resembles the Liberal regime along one dimension (organization of the health economy), it is much closer to the Social Democratic regime in terms of the second (coverage), and falls somewhere between the two models on the third dimension (orientation). It is also positioned midway between Sweden and the United States in terms of expenditures and outcomes.

The comparative overview of health care systems here suggests that the welfare-worlds approach has not adequately represented the various dimensions of particular social policies, ignoring social services in favour of examining income transfer programs. In order to adequately represent various national welfare states, the welfare-worlds approach must include this central element. While the focus here has been on health care, studies comparing other social service elements of the welfare state, such as education and housing, must also be conducted if the model is to reflect adequately the nature of welfare states. In addition, it has been suggested here that studies of welfare programs can more accurately classify them if they more closely examine the various dimensions of particular social policies. It may be useful, therefore, to re-introduce into such analyses the concept of multiple continua. As demonstrated in the present paper, a particular policy may be classified as Liberal on one dimension but as Social Democratic on another. A multidimensional conceptualization not only permits a more precise evaluation of social policies and welfare states, but also makes it easier to track abrupt or incremental changes in the direction of particular social policies and the gradual restructuring of the welfare state currently under way in most capitalist nations, reflecting significant changes in the balance of power in each.[28]

It would be entirely premature to suggest that we are witnessing a gradual 'convergence' of the three welfare states under consideration here toward a more 'mixed' approach. However, significant developments are taking place that cannot be ignored. In Sweden, where a strong labour movement and decades of Social Democratic rule have served to entrench the welfare state, changes to the health system have been, so far, much less dramatic than those seen in other European nations or in North America during the recent period of retrenchment and welfare 'crisis.' Yet even Sweden has not been totally immune to change. A privatization campaign organized by powerful business interests in the 1980s bore fruit beginning with the creation of new private health insurance schemes by companies such as Skandia, and the takeover of a hospital in Stockholm (Sophiahemmet) by the Wallenberg

Empire in 1987. With the election of the 'bourgeois coalition' govern-ment in September 1991, employer demands for changes to the public sickness insurance plan are beginning to be realized as well. Even more recently, a variety of market-oriented reforms have been introduced or proposed for health care delivery in Stockholm county through the so-called 'Stockholm Model' (Diderichsen, 1993). In the United States, as numerous companies cut back contributions to their private health care programs and increasingly stringent eligibility rules ensured that ever-fewer Americans were covered by public insurance, many of the leaders of the large corporations (such as Bethlehem Steel, Chrysler, and Gen-eral Motors) expressed a strong desire for the creation of some type of public insurance system which would shift the financial burden from their shoulders onto the state. However, the Clinton government failed in its attempt to increase coverage through health care reform. The Canadian health care system has been beset by federal and provincial cutbacks, and calls for user-fees are now the order of the day. The dis-tinction between the Canadian and American welfare systems outlined here soon may be only academic if the current trends continue.

Notes

The author would like to thank Bob Brym, Joan Durrant, Julia O'Connor, and the anonymous reviewers for the *Canadian Journal of Sociology* for their helpful comments.

1 The gradual unstringing of the safety net since the mid-1980s through a series of cutbacks and 'clawbacks' (family allowances and Old-Age Security), the elimination of federal contributions to Unemployment Insurance and the eventual 'replacement' of the Family Allowance program, has further 'Americanized' the welfare state in Canada. For an overview of some of these developments see Gray 1990 and Mishra 1990.
2 According to a recent Environics poll, Canadians ranked health care 'first out of 15 items that made Canada superior to the U.S.' (quoted in Armstrong and Armstrong, 1991: 3-4). Another survey indicated that, while 61 per cent of Americans would prefer the Canadian health care system to their own, only 3 per cent of Canadians would prefer the American health care system to their own (Blendon, 1989; Blendon and Taylor, 1989).
3 Given the nations under scrutiny here, the Conservative social policy regime will not be examined. In this 'corporatist' regime-type, the concern with market efficiency and commodification that characterizes Liberal regimes is

not salient. Occupational welfare and private insurance thus play a minimal role. Instead, welfare provision occurs largely through the state. However, benefits are provided in a manner that serves to maintain status differences within the population, rather than to redistribute wealth. Austria, France, Germany, and Italy would be considered Conservative welfare regimes.

4 However, a high level of private welfare does not necessarily imply a low level of public welfare. For example, the growth of public welfare may trigger further development of occupational welfare, rather than replace or curtail it. Or, as is presently the case in many capitalist societies, public and private welfare may be pared back simultaneously as the state and private enterprises attempt to cut costs.

5 Occupational pensions, for example, covered approximately 37 per cent of the total labour force in Canada in 1984 and almost 42 per cent in the United States in 1985 (Deaton, 1989).

6 The Social Security Act of 1935 established three main programs: (1) federally subsidized, state-administered public assistance programs for the elderly poor (replaced by Supplemental Security Income [SSI] in 1971), dependent children (Aid to Families with Dependent Children [AFDC] or 'welfare') and the blind; (2) federal unemployment insurance based on employer taxes set by the states; and (3) national, contributory old-age insurance (OAS or 'social security'). Survivors' benefits for widows and children of the insured were added to the latter in 1939 (OASI), as was Disability Insurance (OASDI) for severely disabled workers in 1956.

7 The Canadian welfare state 'evolved' through the gradual establishment of major social programs – old-age assistance (1927), industrial accident insurance (1930), unemployment insurance (1940), family allowances (1944), old-age security (1951), hospitalization insurance (1961), sickness insurance (1971), and health insurance (1972) – as in Europe, if at a somewhat slower pace and later date. The United States, in contrast, has no public, universal family allowance, old-age pensions, or sickness and health insurance (Kudrle and Marmor, 1984; Lemen, 1977).

8 Following public pensions, public health care is the second most expensive element of the welfare state (OECD, 1987, 1988). Although the health care information introduced here may not be new to those with an interest in social policy and health care, the purpose of the comparative presentation of the various 'traits' of social welfare is to help characterize and situate the Canadian welfare state.

9 These were formerly called 'children's allowances' because the amount of income they provided depended upon the number of children in the family (Gordon, 1990).

10 In his widely cited work on the welfare state, Richard M. Titmuss (1963) distinguished between 'social welfare,' 'occupational welfare,' and 'fiscal welfare.' These labels are still quite useful as a means of distinguishing between types of welfare measures.

11 Only Austria and France paid out higher levels of cash benefits.

12 There is a parallel here with the pension system. Old-age security in Canada is provided through a Swedish style three-tier system (universal public pensions, earnings-related pensions, occupational pensions), but public pension payments are grossly inadequate, as they are in the United States (Myles, 1989).

13 As a result of their partial 'de-indexation,' the value of the Family Allowances provided in Canada was eroding through inflation, and many families were losing most of their benefits in a 'clawback' when they filed their annual income tax returns. As of January 1993, Canada's universal family allowance system ('baby bonus') was eliminated altogether and replaced by tax credits, a change that ended a long-standing universal program in Canada.

14 While women have a relatively high rate of labour force participation in Sweden, it should be noted that, during the late 1980s, approximately 43.5 per cent of these women worked part-time. However, almost all of these female part-time workers worked 'long' part-time hours (between 20 and 34 hours per week) (Persson, 1990).

15 Introduced in 1973, it included the following entitlements by the latter part of the 1980s: (1) ten days' leave of absence at 90 per cent of pay for new fathers upon the birth of a child to allow them to care for their partners and newborns; (2) a total of twelve months' parental leave (taken by either parent or shared) at 90 per cent of salary and an additional three months at the national flat-rate pay level; and (3) two paid 'contact days' per child per year off work to enable parents to spend time with their children, to get acquainted with day care facilities, and to make contact with the staff. As discussed below, it also provides 'sick leave' for parents when their children are sick (Hwang and Broberg, 1992; Persson, 1990). For a critique of the parental insurance program from a feminist perspective see Widerberg 1991.

16 A new law implemented by the Clinton administration now provides women with twelve weeks of *unpaid* maternity leave. However, it does not cover women employed in small businesses (i.e., those with fewer than fifty employees).

17 Newhouse (1977) and others (OECD, 1990) maintain that health care expenditure is positively associated with per capita income. This would appear contrary to arguments by Sombart (1976 [1906]) and Anderson (1978), among others, which suggest that high income levels were partly responsible for the relative underdevelopment of the American welfare state.

18 Founded in 1948 by the Labour government, the National Health Service
   was created to provide free, quality medical treatment financed through
   taxation.

19 A recent examination of the pharmaceutical industry in the United States
   described it as the most profitable business in America. Moreover, Drake
   and Uhlman (1993: 4) note that 'prescription drug prices rose three times
   faster than inflation in the last decade, and [that] the industry has circum-
   vented every effort by the government to contain prices.' The American
   government has, however, had some success in regulating the delivery of
   health care in the United States more directly since 1983, when it introduced diagnostic related groups (DRG). The DRG system provides the
   government with some control over physicians and hospitals by setting fixed
   prices for the treatment of certain categories of illnesses (see Ruggie 1992).

20 For many years, lobbying efforts by the American Medical Association and
   the pharmaceutical and insurance industries as well as numerous government officials were highly successful in short-circuiting any discussion of the
   Canadian health care system by equating it with 'socialism' (Kudrle and
   Marmor, 1984).

21 However, while Canada has not been as successful as Scandinavia or other
   European countries in keeping down the costs of drugs, wholesale prices in
   Canada are, on average, 30 per cent lower than those in the United States
   largely as result of government efforts (Drake and Uhlman, 1993). This may
   change with the introduction of a new bill (C-91) which dramatically and
   retroactively extends the patent period on prescription drugs to twenty
   years.

22 The existence of myriad insurance providers and the administrative costs
   implied by the attendant multitude of fee schedules and variations in
   eligibility, deductibles, and co-payments is one reason commonly cited for
   exorbitant health care expenditures in the United States. Woolhandler and
   Himmelstein (1991), for example, not that the proportion of health care
   costs consumed by administration in 1983 was 60 per cent higher in the
   United States than in Canada. By 1987, administrative costs amounted to
   19.3 to 24.1 per cent of total health costs in the United States but only 8.4
   to 11.0 per cent of the same in Canada. In addition to the rising health costs
   associated with expensive new technologies, high-income physicians, and the
   increasing numbers of aged that affected most industrial societies, other
   important factors which are more specific to the United States include the
   duplication of services and technology utilized by competing medical
   institutions, and the malpractice system (the number of suits filed each year

and the consequent need for malpractice insurance) (Public Agenda Foundation, 1992).

23 Critics of public sector health care systems maintain that they stifle innovation, are technologically less well equipped, and result in longer waiting periods for treatment (OECD, 1990). Supporters of such systems point out in response that waiting lists may exist for elective, cosmetic, and diagnostic surgery, but not for life-saving procedures. Moreover, they maintain that public health care systems have adequate levels of technological support (Rublee, 1989). See Diderichsen and Lindberg 1989 and Ingemar Ståhl 1981 for a critical evaluation of health care delivery in Sweden.

24 Critics charge that this only encourages doctors, who are paid on a fee-for-service, or 'piecework,' basis, to further increase the numbers of patients seen, tests administered, etc.

25 In the 1980s, parental insurance in Sweden allowed either parent to take up to 60 days per year off work to care for their sick children and receive 90 per cent of their pay. This was gradually increased to 90 days (and up to 120 days per year if the child was unable to stay in the place where care was normally provided) (Hwang and Broberg, 1992; Persson, 1990). However, these benefits recently have been reduced.

26 Critics of Sweden's cash sickness program charge that its overly generous provisions are primarily responsible for the internationally high levels of absenteeism there; at 23.4 sick days for the average worker, the absentee rate in 1989 was almost three times as high as it was in North America. However, supporters of the plan suggest that, unlike workers in North America, workers in Sweden are not economically constrained from staying home when they are sick. As a result, workers are less likely to develop more serious illnesses and are less of a fundamental burden on the welfare state.

27 In 1990, General Motors, for example, spent more on health care benefits ($3.2 billion) than it spent on steel.

28 Accounts of policy-making in capitalist society have become increasingly sophisticated, taking a variety of social and political factors into consideration. Approaches examining the balance of power between capital and labour have contributed significantly to our understanding of the origins and development of welfare states. On this approach see Esping-Andersen 1985, Korpi 1983, O'Connor 1989, and Stephens 1980. For constructive critiques of this model, see Baldwin 1989, Kelman 1990, and Olsen 1990, 1991, 1992.

29 The prime minister and Conservative party leader of the new four-party Right-wing coalition from 1991 to 1994 (Carl Bildt) introduced a one-day

waiting period for cash sickness benefits and made employers responsible for compensation during the first fourteen days of a period of illness. Forcing employees to apply to their employer for benefits during this period, they maintain, will cut down on 'abuse' of the benefit program and lower rates of absenteeism. In addition, cash sickness benefits have been reduced from 90 per cent replacement level to 80 per cent, while fees for visits to the doctor and charges for prescriptions were increased.

References

Andersen, Odin. 1972. *Health Care: Can There Be Equity? The United States, Sweden, and England.* New York: John Wiley and Sons.

Anderson, Doris. 1991. *The Unfinished Revolution: The Status of Women in Twelve Countries.* Toronto: Doubleday Canada.

Anderson, Martin. 1978. *Welfare: The Political Economy of Welfare Reform in the US.* Stanford: Hoover Institute Press.

Armstrong, Pat, and Hugh Armstrong. 1991. *Health Care as a Business: The Legacy of Free Trade.* Ottawa: Canadian Centre for Policy Alternatives.

Baldwin, Peter. 1989.'The Scandinavian Origins of the Social Interpretation of the Welfare State.' *Comparative Studies in Society and History* 31(1): 3–24.

Blendon, Robert J. 1989. 'Three Systems: A Comparative Survey.' *Health Management Quarterly* 11(2): 2–10.

Blendon, Robert J. and Humphrey Taylor. 1989. 'Views on Health Care: Public Opinion in Three Nations.' *Health Affairs* 8(1): 149–57.

Bernard, Elaine. 1992. 'The Politics of Canada's Health Care System.' *New Politics* 3(4): 101–8.

Borgenhammar, Edgar. 1984. 'Sweden.' In M. Raffel ed., *Comparative Health Systems.* University Park: Pennsylvania State University Press.

Bronfenbrenner, Urie. 1992. 'Child Care in the Anglo-Saxon Mode.' In Michael E. Lamb et al., eds., *Child Care in Context: Cross-cultural Perspectives.* Hillsdale: Lawrence Erlbaum Associates, Publishers.

Cook, Katie. 1986. *Report of the Task Force on Child Care.* Ottawa: Ministry for the Status of Women.

Courchene, Melanie. 1989. *The Current Industrial Relations Scene in Canada: Wages, Productivity and Labour Costs Reference Tables.* Kingston: Industrial Relations Centre, Queen's University.

Deaton, Richard L. 1989. *The Political Economy of Pensions: Power, Politics and Social Change in Britain, Canada and the United States.* Vancouver: University of British Columbia Press.

Deviney, Stanley. 1984. 'The Political Economy of Public Pensions: A Cross-National Analysis.' *Journal of Political and Military Sociology* 12 (Fall): 295–310.

Diderichsen Finn. 1993. 'Market Reforms in Swedish Health Care: A Threat or Salvation for the Universalistic Welfare State?' *International Journal of Health Services* 23(1): 185–7.

Diderichsen Finn, and Gudrun Lindberg. 1989. 'Better Health – But Not for All: The Swedish Public Health Report.' *International Journal of Health Services* 19(2): 221–55.

Drake, Donald, and Marian Uhlman. 1993. *Making Medicine, Making Money.* Kansas City: Andrews and McMeel.

DuBroy, Robert. 1986. *A Comparison of Compensation in Canada and the United States: Report 08-86.* Ottawa: Conference Board of Canada.

Esping-Andersen, Gøsta. 1990. *The Three Worlds of Welfare Capitalism.* Princeton: Princeton University Press.

– 1985. *Politics against Markets.* Princeton: Princeton University Press.

General Accounting Office. 1991. *Canadian Health Insurance: Lessons for the United States.* Washington: General Accounting Office.

Goelman, Hillel. 1992. 'Day Care in Canada.' In Michael E. Lamb et al., eds., *Child Care in Context: Cross-Cultural Perspectives.* Hillsdale: Lawrence Erlbaum Associates, Publishers.

Gordon, Margaret S. 1990. *Social Security Policies in Industrial Countries: A Comparative Analysis.* Cambridge: Cambridge University Press.

Gray, Gratton. 1990. 'Social Policy by Stealth.' *Policy Options* March: 17–29.

Hwang, C. Phillip, and Anders G. Broberg. 1992. 'The Historical and Social Context of Child Care in Sweden.' In Michael E. Lamb et al., eds., *Child Care in Context: Cross-Cultural Perspectives.* Hillsdale: Lawrence Erlbaum Associates, Publishers.

Kangas, Olli. 1991. *The Politics of Social Rights.* Stockholm: Swedish Institute for Social Research.

Kangas, Olli, and Joakim Palme. 1991. 'Statism Eroded? Labour Market Benefits and Challenges to the Scandinavian Welfare States.' In Erik Jorgen Hansen, Stein Ringen, Hannu Uusitalo and Robert Erikson, eds., *Welfare Trends.* New York: Sharpe.

Kelman, Hans. 1990. 'Social Democracy and the Politics of Welfare Statism.' *The Netherlands' Journal of Social Sciences* 26(1): 17–34.

Klass, Gary M. 1985. 'Explaining America and the Welfare State: An Alternative Theory.' *British Journal of Political Science* 15: 427–50.

Korpi, Walter. 1983. *The Democratic Class Struggle.* London: Routledge and Kegan Paul.

– 1989. 'Power, Politics and State Autonomy in the Development of Social Citizenship: Social Rights during Sickness in 18 OECD Countries since 1930.' *American Sociological Review* 54(3): 309–28.

Kudrle, Robert T., and Theodore R. Marmor. 1984. 'The Development of Welfare States in North America.' In Peter Flora and Arnold J. Heidenheimer, eds., *The Development of Welfare States in North America.* London: Transaction Books.

Kurian, George T. 1990. *Facts on File National Profiles: Scandinavia.* Oxford: Facts on File Ltd.

Lamb, Michael E., Katherine Sternberg, C. Phillip Hwang, and Anders G. Broberg.
– 1992. 'The Child Care in the United State: The Modern Era.' In Michael E. Lamb et al., eds., *Child Care in Context: Cross-Cultural Perspectives.* Hillsdale: Lawrence Erlbaum Associates, Publishers.

Lemen, Christopher. 1977. 'Patterns of Policy Development: Social Security in the United States and Canada.' *Public Policy* 25(2): 261–91.

Lipset, Seymour Martin. 1990. *Continental Divide: The Values and Institutions of the United States and Canada.* New York: Routledge.
– 1986. 'Historical Traditions and National Characteristics: A Comparative Analysis of Canada and the United States.' *Canadian Journal of Sociology* 11(2): 113–55.

Mayfield, Margie. 1990. *Work-Related Child Care in Canada.* Ottawa: Labour Canada.

Mishra, Ramesh. 1990. *The Welfare State in Capitalist Society: Policies of Retrenchment in Europe, North America and Australia.* Toronto: University of Toronto Press.

Myles, John. 1989. *Old Age in the Welfare State: The Political Economy of Public Pensions.* Lawrence: University of Kansas Press.

Myles John, and Dennis Forcese. 1981. 'Voting and Class Politics in Canada and the United States.' *Comparative Social Research* 4: 3–31.

National Council of Welfare. 1988. *Child Care: A Better Alternative.* Ottawa: Minister of Supply and Services.

Newhouse, Joseph P. 1977. 'Medical Expenditure: A Cross-National Survey.' *Journal of Human Resources* 12(1): 115–25.

Nikelly, Arthur G. 1987. 'Prevention in Sweden and Cuba: Implications for Policy Research.' *Journal of Primary Prevention* 7(3): 117–31.

O'Connor, Julia S. 1989. 'Welfare Expenditure and Policy Orientation in Canada in Comparative Perspective.' *Canadian Review of Sociology and Anthropology* 26(1): 127–50.

OECD. 1987. *Financing and Delivery of Health Care: A Comparative Analysis of OECD Countries.* Paris: OECD.
– 1988. *Reforming Public Pensions.* Paris: OECD.
– 1990. *Health Care Systems in Transition: The Search for Efficiency.* Paris: OECD.

Olsen, Gregg M. Ed. 1988. *Industrial Change and Labour Adjustment in Sweden and Canada.* Toronto: Garamond Press.

Olsen, Gregg M. 1990. 'Swedish Social Democracy and Beyond: Internal Obstacles to Economic Democracy.' In Larry Haiven, Stephen McBride, and John Shields, eds., *Regulating Labour: The State, Neo-Conservatism and Industrial Relations.* Toronto: Garamond Press.

– 1991. 'Labour Mobilization and the Strength of Capital: The Rise and Stall of Economic Democracy in Sweden.' *Studies in Political Economy* 34: 109–45.

– 1992. *The Struggle for Economic Democracy in Sweden.* Aldershot: Avebury.

Olsen, Gregg M., and Robert J. Brym. 1996. 'Between American Exceptionalism and Social Democracy: Public and Private Pensions in Canada.' In Michael Shalev, ed., *The Privatization of Social Policy: Occupational Welfare and the Welfare State in America, Scandinavia and Japan.* London: Macmillan.

Olsson, Sven. 1988. 'Social Welfare in Economically Advanced Countries: Social Services and Social Security in Sweden.' In J. Dixon and R. Scheurell, eds., *Social Welfare in Developed Market Countries.* London: Croom Helm.

– 1990. *Social Policy and the Welfare State in Sweden.* Lund: Arkiv.

Persson, Inga. 1990. 'The Third Dimension – Equal Status Between Men and Women.' In Inga Persson, ed., *Generating Equality in the Welfare State: The Swedish Experience.* Oslo: Norwegian University Press.

Public Agenda Foundation. 1992. *The Health Care Crisis: Containing Costs, Expanding Coverage.* New York: McGraw-Hill.

Rublee, Dale A. 1989. 'Medical Technology in Canada, Germany and The United States.' *Health Affairs* 8(3): 178–81.

Ruggie, Mary. 1992. 'The Paradox of Liberal Intervention: Health Policy and the American Welfare State.' *American Journal of Sociology* 97(4): 919–44.

Schieber George J., and Jean-Pierre Poullier. 1989. 'International Health Care Expenditure Trends: 1987.' *Health Affairs* 8(3): 169–77.

Schwartz, John and Tim Padgett. 1989. 'Wellness Plans: An Ounce of Prevention.' *Newsweek,* January 30.

Serner, Uncas. 1980. 'Swedish Health Legislation: Milestones in Reorganization Since 1945.' In Arnold J. Heidenheimer and Nils Elvander, eds., *The Shaping of the Swedish Health System.* New York: St. Martin's Press.

Sombart, Werner. 1976. *Why Is There No Socialism in the United States?* New York: M.E. Sharpe Inc.

Ståhl, Ingemar. 1981. 'Can Equality and Efficiency be Combined? The Experience of the Planned Health Care System.' In Mancur Olsen, ed., *A New Approach to the Economics of Health Care.* Washington: American Institute for Public Policy Research.

Stephens, John D. 1980. *The Transition from Capitalism to Socialism*. London: Macmillan.

Stevens, Beth. 1990. 'Labor Unions, Employee Benefits, and the Privatization of the American Welfare State.' *Journal of Policy History* 2(3): 233–60.

Titmuss, Richard M. 1963. *Essays on the Welfare State*. London: Allen and Unwin.

Widerberg, Karin. 1991. 'Reforms for Women – On Male Terms – The Example of the Swedish Legislation on Parental Leave.' *International Journal of the Sociology of Law* 19: 27–44.

Wennemo, Irene. 1992. 'The Development of Family Policy: A Comparison of Family Benefits and Tax Reductions for Families in 18 OECD Countries.' *Acta Sociologica* 35: 201–17.

Woolhandler, Steffie and David U. Himmelstein. 1991. 'The Deteriorating Administrative Efficiency of the U.S. Health Care System.' *New England Journal of Medicine* 324(18): 1253–58.

PART II
POWER RESOURCES THEORY:
A CRITICAL APPROACH

7

Gender, Class, and Citizenship in the Comparative Analysis of Welfare State Regimes: Theoretical and Methodological Issues

JULIA S. O'CONNOR

This paper focuses on theoretical and methodological issues associated with the incorporation of gender into the comparative analysis of welfare states. The impetus for this project arises from a number of concerns related to welfare state research: First, there is an absence of gender analysis in almost all comparative research, while most studies that focus on gender are not comparative. Second, while change in the principle of distribution from class to citizenship is analysed in much comparative research, it is not self-evident that citizenship rights are gender-neutral. Consequently, the incorporation of gender into the analysis raises questions concerning taken-for-granted assumptions about the meaning of citizenship and, in particular, concerning the relationship between formal citizenship status and the exercise of citizenship rights. The premise on which this paper is based is that we cannot hive off 'gender and the welfare state' as a women's issue. Gender is integral to the understanding of the welfare state, and its importance is increasing due to changes in the structure of the labour market and welfare state restructuring associated with resource constraints.[1] Similar comments are applicable to structuring around race, which is particularly salient in some welfare states.[2] These comments are not meant to imply that gender, race, and class are independent structuring mechanisms. On the contrary, analysis must focus on their interaction in the structuring of welfare state regimes.

Welfare state regimes refer to clusters of more or less distinct welfare state types in terms of the principles of stratification and the basis of social rights on which social policy is built. These principles, which result in qualitatively different arrangements among state, market, and family, are reflected in the configuration of policies relating to 'targeted versus universalistic programs, the conditions of eligibility, the quality of benefits and services and, perhaps most importantly, the extent to which employment and working life are encompassed in the state's extension of citizen rights.'[3] Esping-Andersen has identified three regime types: social democratic, as exemplified by Sweden and Norway; liberal, as exemplified by the United States, Canada, and Australia; and conservative-corporatist or status-based, as exemplified by Germany, France, and Italy. The social-democratic regime is unique in its emphasis on universalism, its strong role for the state, its integration of social and economic policy, and its emphasis on the primacy of full employment. The liberal regime is characterized by state intervention which is clearly subordinate to the market. It has a relatively strong emphasis on income and/or means-tested programs, and, while there may be a commitment to universalism, it is universalism, with an equal-opportunity focus. The key characteristic of the conservative-corporatist welfare state regime is the linkage of rights to class and status through a variety of social insurance schemes. There is a strong commitment to the maintenance of the traditional family, and social services tend to be provided only when the family's ability to cope is exhausted.[4]

Recent comparative studies of welfare states – in particular, those concerned with the relationship between the mobilization of power resources by social classes and the modification of market inequities – have focused on differences among welfare state regimes rather than differences in expenditure, which was the focus of most earlier comparative studies. However, analysis continues to be concentrated on the class-citizenship dimension of the stratification system, with little or no attention to gender and/or race. In contrast, most feminist analyses of welfare states are not comparative. While there is a common concern with women's relationship to the welfare state in these analyses, significant differences in emphasis are evident among them. Single-country studies based on British, U.S., Canadian, and Australian experience tend to emphasize the oppressive characteristics of the welfare state for women. In contrast, the few comparative studies available and those based on Scandinavian experience, while recognizing the subordination of women, emphasize the possibilities for empowerment of women through the welfare state.[5] This difference in focus is not surprising when put in the context of the variation in welfare state regimes and points to the importance of a comparative approach.

The objective of this paper is to develop a comparative analytical approach incorporating class, citizenship, and gender. To this end I outline some of the key issues arising in three sets of literature: (i) classical and contemporary literature on citizenship and social class; (ii) recent literature on gender and citizenship; and (iii) feminist analyses of issues associated with gender, citizenship, and labour market participation in social-democratic welfare state regimes. Finally, drawing on these literatures and related studies, I discuss some of the key theoretical and methodological issues associated with the incorporation of gender into the comparative analysis of welfare state regimes.

Citizenship and Social Class

Most contemporary discussions of citizenship take as their source the essay 'On Citizenship and Social Class' presented by T.H.Marshall in 1949.[6] On the basis of British history, Marshall divided the development of citizenship into three stages: civil citizenship, relating to liberty of the person and property rights, is dated from the eighteenth century with the development of the judicial system. Political citizenship, relating primarily to the right to vote and to organize, is dated from the nineteenth century. Social citizenship, which relates to rights to economic welfare and security, is dated from the twentieth century with the extension of the educational system and the development of the welfare state. Marshall saw the extension of social citizenship rights as a process, aimed not just at class abatement, as was the extension of civil and political rights, but directed towards the modification of 'the whole pattern of social inequality' within capitalist society.[7] This is achieved through the extension of social services – a means of distribution which operates outside the labour and capital markets.

Marshall's periodization is neither universal nor evolutionary. What is clear from his and subsequent analyses is that the development of citizenship rights is a process of expansion of the rights of membership and participation in societal institutions within capitalist societies.[8] This process of expansion is achieved through collective struggle. The actors in this struggle are identified by Marshall, and most recent analysts, as representatives of social classes.[9]

The contemporary analysts of the welfare state who accord the strongest niche to citizenship and its juxtaposition with class are those who focus on the mobilization of power resources by the working class and its allies. These analysts focus on the possibilities within the political system for the modification of market inequities.[10] In a later part of this paper I discuss the implication of incorporating gender into this analysis.

Citizenship and Gender

Despite references to the distinct treatment of married women in the development of citizenship rights, Marshall implies that citizenship, which is 'bestowed on those who are full members of a community,' is an undifferentiated status.[11] Two problems can be identified with this perspective. The first problem is that not all of those who possess citizenship status 'are equal with respect to the rights and duties with which the status is endowed.'[12] Indeed, Marshall recognized barriers to the exercise of civil rights.[13] A cursory review of the exercise of political citizenship rights indicates that several groups, including women, are still grossly underrepresented in the formal political system and at the decision-making level in public policy bodies in all countries. Even in the Scandinavian countries, where they are relatively well represented in the parliamentary system, women have been greatly underrepresented in the corporatist decision-making bodies, which were until recently very influential. In other words, participatory citizenship rights have a gender dimension. In addition, gender differences in social citizenship rights can be identified in all OECD countries, though the extent of the difference varies considerably. A tiered system of access to social rights has been identified in several countries and is particularly marked in liberal welfare state regimes.[14] This comprises, at one extreme, a predominantly female stratum of welfare or social assistance clients who are granted service on the basis of need, generally household need, and, at the other extreme, a stratum with individual benefit entitlements based on paid work–related social insurance contributions, in which men are concentrated. There is a third category of beneficiary, namely, those family members whose eligibility is dependent on the social insurance contributions of a family member in the paid labour force – in other words, those with indirect social rights, for the most part women and children.

These differences indicate that formal citizenship status does not always accord with actual status, in other words formal citizenship does not always imply full social membership.[15] As Barbalet has pointed out, civil and political rights may be universal in principle but have a class bias in practice.[16] Social rights may also fall into this category, and a gender and/or race bias may exist singly, or in interaction with one another, or with a class bias, in relation to all elements of citizenship. The exercise of citizenship rights is not independent of class position; rather, it is often dependent on economic and/or educational resources and such resources as time and energy.Similarly, while the achievement of formal citizenship rights was significant for women, gender neutrality in the realization of these rights cannot be assumed.

The second and more fundamental problem associated with Marshall's perspective is that the creation of 'an image of an ideal citizenship against which achievements can be measured and towards which aspiration can be directed' evolved when women were still denied or had only just achieved political citizenship and were not participants in the political decision-making process.[17]

This raises the issue of the conceptualization of citizenship and what constitutes taken-for-granted citizenship activities. The image of the ideal citizen which is evident in Marshall and which emerges in power resources analysis is that of the paid worker, generally the organized paid worker, in the public sphere. Indeed, as Pateman points out, the history 'of the welfare state and citizenship (and the manner in which they have been theorized) is bound up with the history of the development of "employment societies." '[18]

The dominant conception of citizenship implies the subordination of particular identities, not only of class, but also of gender and race. Citizenship as a principle of equality is readily contrasted with class, as a principle of inequality, with the implied assumption that the two principles of distribution vary inversely. In contrast to class, gender is based on the recognition of difference, a principle that is not necessarily inconsistent with equality. However, differences associated with biological, social, and/or economicconditions may interfere with the translation of formal equality into equality in practice.[19]

The issue of difference is a key thread within feminist critiques of citizenship analysis; for example, Kathleen, B. Jones identifies issues related to difference as one of three dimensions relevant to the development of a theory of citizenship. First, she points out that feminist political discourse recognizes the body as a significant dimension in the definition of citizenship.[20] This calls attention to the traditional linkage of citizenship with the ability to take part in armed struggle for national defence, the equation of this ability with maleness, and the equation of femaleness with weakness and the need for male protection.[21] Several feminist analysts have proposed a conceptual shift from armed defence to empowerment as a key criterion for the exercise of citizenship rights. Such a shift 'unsettles the connection between male bodies and citizenship.'[22] Jones argues that this acknowledgment of the body as a basis of political difference has implications for the application of the concept of equality as traditionally conceived: 'In a democratic polity, citizens are meant to enjoy equal individual rights. Still, biological, social, and discursively defined differences make the granting of the same rights to different persons more likely to sustain a hierarchy of rights than uniformity of status.'[23] This raises the issue of equality of opportunity in the context of inequality of condition. In this regard it is important to recognize the distinction between the achievement of equality in civil rights and its achievement in human or social rights: In the former case equality entails treating everyone the same, since 'every individual has the same presumptive right as every other individual to individual autonomy subject only to those limitations the state can justify as reasonable'; in contrast, equality in human rights entails treating people as equals, which implies recognizing their differences, since here we are talking of 'individuals in their capacity as members of groups which are disadvantaged for arbitrary reasons.'[24]

The second thread identified by Jones relates to the conception of political space and the implications for the definition of this space of the recognition that 'the personal is political.' A major consequence of the traditional institutional focus of political analysis has been that women were largely excluded. The recognition of this exclusion, and the associated focus on women's political behaviour, implies a broadening of the concept of political action to include the ways in which political space and political alliances are structured. This has implications for the spatial dimension of citizenship which up to now has been largely institutional and has ignored those political processes associated with movements to transform public consciousness on issues such as sexual harassment, rape, and pornography, which 'are examples of a definition of participation that is focused not on government action but on the reclamation of public space itself.'[25]

A third theme in feminist political analysis relates to the conception of political participation. Defining participation purely in terms of active participation, and/or interest, in parliamentary politics is likely to under-represent the participation of women, particularly in some countries. These indicators do not include participation in the informal political system of social movements or participation as client representatives 'in negotiating the content and forms of delivery of their entitlements.'[26] Birte Siim has identified these informal political activities as 'power from below' in contrast to participation in formal politics, or 'power from above.'[27] The incorporation of women into the analysis implies a broadening of what constitutes formally recognized political space and action in order to take into account this power from below.

The recognition of differences in condition associated with gender does not imply a focus on difference in any metaphysical sense or the construction of gender-based norms of citizenship. It does imply a rethinking of the concept of citizenship with the objective of reconciling the achievement of equality with difference in condition associated with structural inequalities. Specifically, it implies an examination of the conception of the ideal citizen and recognition of the possible disjunction of formal and de facto citizenship rights associated with this conception. I consider the implications for political analysis in a later section.

Gender and Citizenship in the Social-Democratic Welfare State

Feminist analyses of the social-democratic welfare state are instructive since they are concerned with the most developed welfare state regime in terms of social rights based on citizenship as opposed to class. Despite this, and the advantaged position of women, there are still significant gender differences in welfare state experience and in the exercise of citizenship rights. This is not meant to imply that the Scandinavian welfare states are identical; what is distinctive about these countries is that women's social and economic position is considerably better than in other OECD countries. My focus is on issues related to labour market participation since this participation is crucial to gender equality and illustrates well the intersection of women's multiple statuses as clients and consumers of welfare services, as employees, and as political citizens, and signals both opportunity and dependence associated with welfare state developments.

Labour Market Participation, Gender, and Citizenship

High rates of female labour force participation is one of the criteria on which welfare state success is measured. Despite this, experience in the Scandinavian countries indicates that high levels of participation may mask some serious problems, namely, a very high level of part-time work and a highly gender-segregated labour force. The latter is associated with the same problems as occupational segregation in other countries: Women are concentrated in low-wage, low-status occupations with relatively few opportunities for training.[28] The high level of part-time work reflects the high level of demands on women associated with caring work, primarily child care responsibilities, and notwithstanding clear superiority in OECD terms, the less-than-adequate levels of child care services.[29] Despite wage solidarity and a commitment to equal pay, gender differentials in pay still persist. These are considerably less than those in other OECD countries and are associated largely with the horizontal and vertical gender segregation of the labour force. The high level of part-time work by women also ensures overall lower earnings. Furthermore, in so far as economic poverty exists in Scandinavia, it is concentrated among women as heads of households, and the main reasons are part-time work and gender segregation of the labour force.[30]

These facts point to some important problems in relation to the image of the ideal worker/citizen and, in particular, in relation to how general interests are defined. The positive consequences for Swedish women associated with the privileged position of workers as a whole in the policy-formation process has been identified by Mary Ruggie, yet she argues that 'whenever women's interests could not be articulated in terms of their roles as workers in general or wives/mothers in general, those interests have remained unexpressed and unrealized.'[31] Similar conclusions have been reached by other analysts.[32] For example, while identifying the superior position of women in the social-democratic welfare states, Borchorst and Siim argue that state policies for gender equality fail to take seriously the problem of combining paid and unpaid work.[33] Notwithstanding the fact that the division of labour within households is relatively unchanged and the transfer of most care services to the public sector is partial, paid work is still predicated on the assumption of an ideal worker who has no domestic or care-work responsibilities. In addition, the sexual-equality strategy of integrating women into 'non-traditional jobs' has been unsuccessful due to the failure to deal effectively with transforming male-dominated workplaces to the extent of making them hospitable environments for women.[34]

The problems identified in relation to labour market participation in social-democratic welfare states have implications for the analysis of public policies in all welfare state regimes. The development of a large welfare state is associated with considerable opportunities but also some contradictions for women. The availability of benefits and services facilitates the employment of people with care-giving responsibilities, and a large welfare state creates employment directly in the public sector. Yet, this increased labour force participation is achieved at the cost of an increase in the double day of work and possible dependence on state agencies, and is associated with increased gender segregation of the labour force. On the positive side, there is considerable evidence to indicate that a large welfare state facilitates the political mobilization of women and the possibilities for combating through public policies the negative aspects of current labour force participation patterns.

Helga Hernes argues that 'women's lives are more dependent on and determined by state policies than men's' because of women's greater involvement in reproduction not only in the family, which affects their client status, but as employees in the public sector. In addition, women's lesser incorporation into political organizations, especially trade unions, means that they do not have the 'same organizational buffer as men between themselves and the authorities that can articulate and defend their interests. This affects their citizen status.'[35] Despite the validity of Hernes' argument, it must be recognized that reliance on public policy and state agencies is not necessarily associated with public dependence, as is often suggested in analyses of liberal welfare states. The impact of reliance on state agencies in terms of dependency is likely to be influenced by the criteria for access to benefits and services, the general configuration of policies relating to labour market participation and to social and sexual rights, and the level of access to decision-making positions. In addition, dependence on state agencies may be sowing the seeds of its own destruction. Several analysts of the social-democratic welfare states have argued that the political mobilization of women is facilitated by their ties to the state, whereas the mobilization of men was effected through their ties to the market.[36] Frances Fox Piven has made a similar argument relating to the political mobilization potential of the much less developed U.S. welfare state.[37]

Scandinavian experience points to the fact that policies must be examined not only in terms of formal equality, but also in terms of their outcome. This means that the possible impact on the exercise of citizenship rights of differences in material and social conditions must be recognized. This implies that gender must be an integral element of welfare state analysis.

Class, Citizenship, Gender, and Welfare State Regimes

Welfare state regimes are structured by, and in turn structure, both class and gender. Consequently, both dimensions must be incorporated into a comprehensive analysis of welfare states. How these dimensions are articulated will vary cross-nationally, historically, and depending on past institutional developments. A gender-sensitive comparative analysis will not be achieved by focusing exclusively on gender or by adding gender to the power resources framework of analysis. Some key concepts must

be re-examined and a broader focus adopted in terms of both independent and dependent variables. The mobilization of power resources is
the key independent variable, and the welfare state regime concept is the
key dependent variable in comparative power resources research. I will
discuss each with reference to class, citizenship, and gender.

Mobilization of Power Resources, Class, Citizenship, and Gender

In considering influences on the development of welfare state regimes,
the primary focus of most power resources research is on working-class
political mobilization, in particular, the mobilization of workers through
trade unions and the associated labour and social-democratic party
strength. Increasingly, there is an emphasis on the pattern of coalition
building and 'the institutionalization of class preferences and political
behavior' that has emerged from past reforms.[38] In so far as the pattern
of coalition building has been considered, the focus has been on coalitions between the working class and farmers in the transition from a
rural to an urban society, and between the working class and parties
supported strongly by the middle class in urbanized societies. The influence of non-party groups, specifically new social movements such as the
feminist movement, has generally been ignored.

An exclusive focus on the labour market and mainstream political
organizations is not inherently gender-biased, but it does largely exclude
women and/or fails to recognize the consequences for participation of
their intersecting and often contradictory statuses. The right to vote and
the right to organize for collective action, which are the principal power
resources in democratic politics, are citizenship rights which apply to
men and women equally; however, the exercise of participatory rights,
both at the trade union and at the political party level, is constrained by
historical precedent and by the individual's statuses within the economy
and the family, and her or his resources of time and money. There is
considerable evidence that these attributes and resources vary by gender.

The feminist critique of citizenship outlined earlier implies the need
for a rethinking of conventional political analysis in order to achieve
gender balance. A broadening of what constitutes formally recognized
political space and action allows for the fact that participation in the
political system occurs not only through traditional loci of power, but
also through bureaucracies, client representative groups, and social movements. In relation to public bureaucracies, it must be recognized that
certain policy developments may be crucial in the creation of possibili-

ties for incorporation of women into the political system. Some feminist analysts have suggested that gender conflict is being institutionalized through public agencies such as equal opportunity commissions, whereas class conflict was institutionalized through trade unions, political parties, and corporatist institutions.[39] This points to the importance of considering institutional structures and legacies and the cross-national and historical variation in the relative importance of different institutional structures.

A comprehensive indicator of women's possible impact on the policy process must include not only a measure of control over power positions, but also a measure of influence over the policy agenda through women's caucuses within political parties and trade unions and by the organized feminist movement. There are no easy measures on which to make comparative assessments of the political effectiveness of women's movements; however, qualitative differences relating to the strength, unity in terms of issues, and lobbying activity and coalition potential of the movement in various countries can be identified.[40] In terms of the unity of the feminist movement on issues, the most important are those that come within the broad heading of sexual politics – abortion, violence against women, incest, pornography – and those related to the 'organization of daily life' – the length of the working day, child care, pay and employment equity.[41]

In summary, the incorporation of gender into the analysis of the mobilization of power resources has several implications: In addition to recognizing the gender composition of mainstream political organizations, the institutional legacy must be evaluated in terms of its conduciveness to facilitating or hindering the incorporation of women into the political system and to effecting change through corporatist institutions, policy bodies such as Pay or Employment Equity agencies, and client-representative associations.

Furthermore, the organizational structure and actions of new social movements, such as the feminist movement, must be assessed in terms of their ability to influence the policy agenda and form coalitions with mainstream political organizations.

Welfare State Regimes, Class, Citizenship, and Gender

Numerous studies within the comparative analysis framework have demonstrated the value of the welfare state regime concept, but, with the exception of Mary Ruggie's analysis of policies relating to working women in Britain and Sweden, none has incorporated gender into its analysis.[42]

The concern of this section is with how the welfare state regime concept can be modified to incorporate gender within a comparative analysis framework. From this point of view, four questions are important: First, are social rights, as reflected in the criteria governing access to benefits and services, gender-linked and do these criteria contribute to the stratification of the population by gender? Second, are the social and sexual rights of individuals protected and enhanced by public policy? Third, since labour force participation is central to gender equality, is it facilitated by public policy? Fourth, does the policy process facilitate the exercise of participatory rights through equal access to decision-making positions? These questions relate essentially to personal autonomy. Just as the level of de-commodification is a key to understanding differences among welfare states, so is the level of personal autonomy.

The extent of de-commodification depends on the range of services which insulate individuals from dependence on the labour market and the extent to which these services are accessible as citizenship rights. Similarly, the level of personal autonomy depends on the range of services which insulate individuals from involuntary personal economic dependence on family members and/or public dependence on state agencies. The absence of involuntary economic dependence does not imply the absence of interdependence. Whereas interdependence implies choice, equality, and reciprocity, dependence implies an unequal power relationship, inequality, and the absence of choice. As Ruth Lister has argued, full interdependence is possible only when involuntary economic dependence is absent.[43]

A central element of this insulation from dependence is the extent to which public services are available as citizenship rights as opposed to a dependence-enhancing income and/or means-tested basis. Several recent studies have pointed to the gender component in access-to-benefits criteria. In particular, there is considerable evidence that, irrespective of welfare state regime, women constitute the vast majority of social assistance recipients and make claims on the basis of need, usually family need, rather than as individuals with citizenship- and/or employment-related entitlements. In contrast, men are concentrated in the employment-related social insurance benefits category. The dependents of social insurance beneficiaries, who are mostly women and children, have an indirect right to services, the continuity of which is dependent on their link to an insured labour force participant. While women's representation in the category of direct social insurance rights is growing with the increase in female labour force participation, their concentration in lower-level jobs is associated with lower-level benefits and, consequently, greater exposure to economic dependence. In theory the citizenship-based access criterion is the most egalitarian and least stratifying; yet, it may also have a gender-stratification impact if the level of benefits is low: Since women are less likely to have access to the resources necessary for additional private coverage, they may be forced into private dependent relationships or into reliance on supplementary social assistance. One implication of these patterns is that the quality of social rights may be associated with the maintenance or lessening of dependence and that a benefit structure may secure de-commodification for some while perpetuating dependence for others.

Rights not directly linked to the labour market have been relatively neglected in comparative analyses of welfare state regimes. The analysis by Pippa Norris of the position of women in Western democracies is an exception, since she does consider the social position of women and its relationship to their economic position.[44] Specifically, she examines influences on, and cross-national variation in, abortion, family planning, maternity services, child care, and higher education. These issues and others related to social and sexual rights, such as violence against women, incest, and pornography, have been central to feminist campaigns for gender equality. This focus is based on the recognition that personal autonomy, especially within families, can be achieved only when social and sexual rights are legally guaranteed and can be exercised in practice. Furthermore, changes in productive relations are severely limited in terms of gender equality if not accompanied by changes in the conditions of reproduction.

De-commodification is associated with a focus on entitlements and social rights which protect individuals, irrespective of gender, from total dependence on the labour market for survival. This protection from forced participation, irrespective of age, health conditions, family status, and availability of suitable employment, is obviously of major importance to both men and women. However, before de-commodification becomes an issue for individuals a crucial first step is access to the labour market. The de-commodification concept does not take into account the fact that not all demographic groups are equally commodified and that this may be a source of inequality. Limitation of access to the labour market may be the result of systemic discrimination or inequality of condition, such as that associated with caring responsibilities. Since both labour force participation and quality of employment are gender-linked and constrained by caring responsibilities, which are in turn gender-linked, those entitlements which facilitate labour force participation are of crucial importance to the economic and social rights of women and in the mitigation and/or prevention of dependence. Services related to 'the organization of daily life' may facilitate or hinder labour force participation.[45] Policies relating to the length and flexibility of the working day, availability of child care and facilities for caring for other dependents, employment and pay equity, maternity and parental leave, training and retraining services facilitate, or make difficult, the articulation of production and reproduction or labour market and family. Public policies in these areas illustrate clearly the intersection of state, market, and family. There is considerable evidence that the state is of particular importance for women's employment; its action or inaction may facilitate, hinder, or be neutral in regard to the level and quality of labour market participation.[46]

In considering the quality of labour market participation it is important to note the distinction made by Helga Hernes between women's policy and gender-equality policy. The former 'is concerned with the redistribution of goods, services and transfers' and refers to traditional social policy aimed at the improvement of the situation of women and children. In contrast, gender-equality policy is concerned with 'the redistribution of status and social power'.[47] These policies relate essentially to access to employment and decision making at senior levels. This implies, for example, that the focus of policy is not just labour market participation, but the quality and conditions of that participation. This approach to public policy implies that both inequality of condition and systemic discrimination are recognized in the policy-formation process. The objective is not just equality of opportunity, but the change of institutional structures which give rise to, and sustain, structured gender inequalities. Since policies with a gender-equality focus are directed to making women the subjects, not just the objects, of social policy, the realization of participatory citizenship rights becomes an objective of social policy. This is, of course, crucial to the lessening of dependence and the achievement of autonomy.

In summary, de-commodification is a central concept in the analysis of welfare state regimes, and its extent is dependent on the quality of social rights, which, in turn, through the criteria for access to benefits, is an active force in the stratification of societies not only in class, but in gender terms. However, the gender dimension of de-commodification does not exhaust the stratification of social relations by gender associated with welfare state activities or their absence. A gender-sensitive analysis of welfare state regimes entails not only an examination of benefits and services in terms of their gender-stratification effects, but a focus on the way in which productive and reproductive activities are articulated, and on the range and quality of social and sexual rights. In other words, the concept of de-commodification must be supplemented by the concept of personal autonomy or insulation from dependence, both involuntary personal economic dependence on family members and/or public dependence on state agencies.

Conclusions

Major contributions to our understanding of the welfare state have been made by both the power resources and the feminist research traditions. However, neither is adequate to achieve a comprehensive analysis of welfare state regimes. Key insights of the mobilization of power resources analysis relate to the possibilities inherent in the political system for modification of market inequities. These possibilities are realized through the mobilization of power resources by the working class and through the formation of political coalitions around the objective of shifting the principle of stratification and the basis of social rights from class to citizenship. In this analysis citizenship as a principle of equality is juxtaposed against class as a principle of inequality with the implied assumption that the two principles vary inversely and to the same extent for all citizens. One of the key insights arising from feminist analysis is that citizenship rights may have different implications for men and women because of structured gender inequalities. This is true in terms of social rights and also in terms of participatory rights. The recognition of difference in condition associated with gender does not imply a need for gender-based norms of citizenship; it does imply a rethinking of the concept of citizenship with the objective of reconciling the achievement of equality with difference in condition. This highlights the distinction between equality in civil rights, which entails treating everyone the same, and equality in social rights, which entails treating people as equals and consequently recognizing differences in condition due to structural inequalities.

The incorporation of gender into the analysis has implications for the key concepts of power resources research, in particular, the mobilization of power resources and the welfare state regime concepts. Mobilization of power resources research has traditionally focused on class and mainstream political organizations. A comprehensive analysis of political processes necessitates the incorporation of gender into this analysis and a broadening of the concept of the political to take into account the exercise of power through bureaucratic organizations and the influence of social movements and client representative groups.

De-commodification is a central concept in the analysis of welfare state regimes; it refers to insulation from the pressures of the labour market. I argue that this must be supplemented by the concept of personal autonomy. This refers to insulation from involuntary personal economic dependence on family members and/or public dependence on state agencies and is central to unravelling the complexity of the relationships among state, market, and family. It is noteworthy that power resources research has concentrated on the relationship between the labour market and the state with little attention to the family aspect of this tripartite relationship. The concept of personal autonomy remedies this imbalance since it relates directly to the articulation of relations of reproduction and production. This is the area where the contradictions associated with welfare state development, namely, the simultaneous increase in opportunity and dependence, are likely to be most evident.

The concern with the incorporation of gender in this paper is not meant to downplay the importance of class or of race; it is based on a recognition that capitalist societies and welfare state regimes are structured by both class and gender, and in some cases by race, in historically specific interacting ways, and that the restructuring of the welfare state is largely a restructuring around gender. However, an exclusive focus on gender is not adequate. A comparative approach across regime types which incorporates both class and gender and their historically specific interaction is necessary. Such an approach implies that, in comparing welfare states, the status of individuals as providers and consumers of welfare services, as employees and political citizens must be considered in addition to their client status. It must be asked how the relative dominance of the different statuses varies for both men and women across welfare states, and over time within particular welfare states.

The focus on the Scandinavian countries has indicated that, notwithstanding considerable lessening of the pervasiveness of class as a basis for social rights in the social democratic welfare states, gender differences are still evident – they are probably more easily identifiable because of the lessening of class differences. However, the potential for challenging these differences exists. This potential has been developed largely through the mobilization of women through the welfare state and is likely to be realized through an increase in their participatory rights. According to

Hernes, the challenge for the welfare state is 'to design a gender equality policy that allows for pluralism and gender difference while guaranteeing equality.'[48] The challenge for comparative analysts is to identify the determinants of such policies and the reasons for differences among welfare state regimes.

Notes

An earlier version of this paper was presented at the International Sociological Association Meetings, Madrid, Spain, 9–13 July 1990, Research Committee 19. I thank John Myles, as chair, Robin Stryker, as discussant, and other participants for comments.

1 M. Rein, 'Women, Employment and Social Welfare,' in R. Klein and M. O'Higgins, eds., *The Future of Welfare* (Oxford: Basil Blackwell, 1985), 37–58.
2 J. Quadagno, 'Race, Class, and Gender in the U.S. Welfare State: Nixon's Failed Family Assistance Plan,' *American Sociological Review* 55 (1990): 11–28.
3 G. Esping-Andersen, 'The Three Political Economies of the Welfare State,' *Canadian Review of Sociology and Anthropology* 26/1 (1989): 20.
4 G. Esping-Andersen, *The Three Worlds of Welfare Capitalism* (Princeton, NJ: Princeton University Press, 1990), 26-9.
5 Studies of liberal welfare state regimes include C. Andrew, 'Women and the Welfare State,' *Canadian Journal of Political Science* 17/4 (1984): 667–83; C.V. Baldock and B. Cass, eds., *Women, Social Welfare and the State in Australia* (Sydney: George Allen and Unwin, 1983); N. Fraser, 'Women, Welfare and the Politics of Need,' in *Unruly Practices* (Minneapolis: University of Minnesota Press, 1989), 144–6; E. Wilson, *Women and the Welfare State* (London: Tavistock, 1977). Comparative studies include P. Norris, *Politics and Sexual Equality: The Comparative Position of Women in Western Democracies* (Boulder, CO: Rienner, 1987), and M. Ruggie, *The State and Working Women: A Comparative Study of Britain and Sweden* (Princeton, NJ: Princeton University Press, 1984). Several Scandinavian studies are discussed throughout this paper.
6 T.H. Marshall, 'Citizenship and Social Class,' in *Class, Citizenship and Social Development* (Westport, CT: Greenwood Press, 1964), 65–122.
7 Ibid., 96.
8 J.M. Barbalet, *Citizenship Rights, Struggles and Class Inequality* (Minneapolis: University of Minnesota Press, 1988); B.S. Turner, *Citizenship and Capitalism* (London: Allen and Unwin, 1986).

226 Julia S. O'Connor

9 Turner (*Citizenship and Capitalism*, 85–100) is a rare exception to the social-class emphasis in that he recognizes the role of new social movements, especially the feminist movement, in the expansion of citizenship rights.

10 W. Korpi, *The Democratic Class Struggle* (London: Routledge and Kegan Paul, 1983); G. Esping-Andersen, *Politics against Markets* (Princeton, NJ: Princeton University Press, 1985).

11 Marshall, 'Citizenship and Social Class,' 78–81, 84.

12 Ibid.

13 Ibid., 91.

14 B. Nelson, 'Women's Poverty and Women's Citizenship,' in B. Gelpi, N. Hartsock, C. Novak and M.H. Strober, eds., *Women and Poverty* (Chicago: University of Chicago Press, 1984), 209–31; Fraser, 'Women, Welfare and the Politics of Need.'

15 Carole Pateman cites the example of black people in the United States: 'The Patriarchal Welfare State,' in A. Gutmann, ed., *Democracy and the Welfare State* (Princeton, NJ: Princeton University Press, 1988), 238.

16 Barbalet, *Citizenship Rights, Struggles and Class Inequality*.

17 Marshall, 'Citizenship and Social Class,' 84.

18 Pateman, 'The Patriarchal Welfare State,' 237.

19 The relationship between equality and difference has been the subject of considerable debate among feminists over the past decade. See J.W. Scott, 'Deconstructing Equality-Versus-Difference: Or, the Uses of Poststructuralist Theory for Feminism,' in M. Hirsch and E. Fox Keller, eds., *Conflicts in Feminism* (New York: Routledge, 1990), 134–48. Also see C.L. Bacchi, *Same Difference* (London: Allen and Unwin, 1990).

20 K.B. Jones, 'Citizenship in a Woman-Friendly Polity,' *Signs* 15/4 (1990): 786.

21 Pateman, 'The Patriarchal Welfare State'; Jones, 'Citizenship in a Woman-Friendly Polity.'

22 Jones, 'Citizenship in a Woman-Friendly Polity,' 787.

23 Ibid., 798.

24 R. Abella, 'Equality and Human Rights in Canada: Coping with the New Isms,' *University Affairs* June/July (1991): 22.

25 Jones, 'Citizenship in a Woman-Friendly Polity,' 803.

26 H. Hernes, 'The Welfare State Citizenship of Scandinavian Women,' in K.B. Jones and A.G. Jonasdottir, eds., *The Political Interests of Gender* (London: Sage, 1988), 198.

27 B. Siim, 'Towards a Feminist Rethinking of the Welfare State,' in Jones and Jonasdottir, eds., *The Political Interests of Gender*, 176.

28 T. Skard and E. Haavio-Mannila, 'Equality between the Sexes – Myth or Reality in Norden?' in S.R. Graubard, ed., *Norden – The Passion for Equality* (Oslo: Norwegian University Press, 1986), 176–99.

29 Ibid.
30 H. Hernes, *Welfare State and Woman Power: Essays in State Feminism* (Oslo: Norwegian University Press, 1987), 32.
31 M. Ruggie, 'Gender, Work and Social Progress,' in J. Jenson, E. Hagen, and C. Reddy, eds., *Feminization of the Labor Force* (New York: Oxford University Press, 1989), 186.
32 Skard and Haavio-Manilla, 'Equality between the Sexes'; A. Borchorst and B. Siim, 'Women and the Advanced Welfare State – A New Kind of Patriarchal Power?' in A. Showstack Sassoon, ed., *Women and the State: The Shifting Boundaries of Public and Private* (London: Hutchinson, 1987).
33 Borchorst and Siim, 'Women and the Advanced Welfare State – A New Kind of Patriarchal Power,' 131.
34 Ibid., 143.
35 Hernes, *Welfare State and Women Power*, 37–8.
36 Ibid., 160.
37 F. Fox Piven, 'Ideology and the State: Women, Power and the Welfare State,' in L. Gordon, ed., *Women, the State and Welfare* (Madison: University of Wisconsin Press, 1990), 250–64.
38 Esping-Andersen, *Three Worlds of Welfare Capitalism,* 32.
39 D. Dahlerup, 'Confusing Concepts – Confusing Reality: A Theoretical Discussion of the Patriarchal State,' in Showstack Sassoon, ed., *Women and the State,* 110.
40 See, for example, M.F. Katzenstein and K. McClurg Mueller, *The Women's Movement's of the United States and Western Europe* (Philadelphia: Temple University Press, 1987), and D. Dahlerup, *The New Women's Movement* (London: Sage, 1986).
41 Hernes, *Welfare State and Woman Power,* 47.
42 Mary Ruggie does not use the term 'welfare state regime,' but she characterizes the British and Swedish welfare states as the liberal and corporatist welfare models, respectively, 'in terms of their frames of reference for state intervention' (Ruggie, 'Gender, Work and Social Progress,' 13). See note 5, above, for references to analyses using a mobilization of power resources approach. In an analysis of Australian social policy, Sheila Shaver has extended the social policy regime concept to include gender. Shaver identifies three key dimensions of state/gender relations: (i) the gender basis of legal personhood, (ii) labour and the relations between state and economy, and (iii) family and reproduction. While the framework adopted in this paper is different, issues related to the first of Shaver's categories are discussed in 'Gender and Citizenship'; issues related to her second and third categories are discussed in this and the previous section. S. Shaver, 'Gender, Social Policy Regimes and the Welfare State,' presented at Annual

Meetings of the American Sociological Association, Washington, DC, 11–15 August 1990.

43 R. Lister, 'Women, Economic Dependency and Citizenship,' *Journal of Social Policy* 19/4, (1990): 446–7.

44 Norris, *Politics and Sexual Equality*.

45 Hernes, *Welfare State and Woman Power*, 47.

46 M. Ruggie, 'Gender, Work and Social Progress'; C. O'Donnell and P. Hall, *Getting Equal* (London: Allen and Unwin, 1988).

47 Hernes, *Welfare State and Woman Power*, 26.

48 Ibid., 163.

8

Gender and the Development of Welfare Regimes

JANE LEWIS

This paper builds on the idea that any further development of the concept of 'welfare regime' must incorporate the relationship between unpaid as well as paid work and welfare. Consideration of the private/domestic is crucial to a gendered understanding of welfare because historically women have typically gained entitlements by virtue of their dependent status within the family as wives and mothers. The paper suggests that the idea of the male-breadwinner family model has served historically to cut across established typologies of welfare regimes, and further that the model has been modified in different ways and to different degrees in particular countries.

It is suggested that Ireland and Britain are examples of historically 'strong' male-breadwinner states and that this helps to account for the level and, more importantly, the nature of women's (part-time) labour market participation; the lack of child care services and maternity rights; and the long-lived inequality between husbands and wives in regard to social security. Strong male breadwinner states have tended to draw a firm dividing line between public and private responsibility. The picture is different in France, which is taken as an example of a 'modified' male-breadwinner country. The nature of French women's labour market participation has historically been stronger in that it has been predominantly full-time, and women have benefited, albeit indirectly, from a social security system that has prioritized horizontal redistribution via the wage system between families with and without children. Patriarchal control has been located within the family rather than in collective institutions, and unlike Britain and Ireland, France recognized women's claims as both wives and mothers and paid workers. Sweden is taken as an example of a 'weak' male-breadwinner country. During the late 1960s and 1970s successive Social Democratic governments consciously decided to move towards a dual-breadwinner society, pulling women into paid employment by the introduction of separate taxation and parental leaves, and by increasing child care provision.

While both the French and Swedish models would seem to offer women more than the British, the paper concludes with a cautionary note. In neither France nor Sweden did women's own demands play a significant role in determining their treatment. Paradoxically, the feminist movement has been historically stronger in Britain. This must raise issues as to what can be expected of the state and as to the possible fragility of the gains.

Gender and the Development of Welfare Regimes[1]

Recent comparative work on modern welfare states has emphasized the importance of the relationship between state and economy, and in particular between work and welfare (especially Esping-Andersen 1990). Work is defined as paid work, and welfare as policies that permit, encourage or discourage the decommodification of labour. While this is a substantial advance on the older literature which focused only on the comparative development of policies of social amelioration, it misses one of the central issues in the structuring of welfare regimes: the problem of valuing the unpaid work that is done primarily by women in providing welfare, mainly within the family, and in securing those providers social entitlements. The crucial relationship is not just between paid work and welfare, but as Peter Taylor Gooby (1991) recently signalled in this journal, between paid work and unpaid work and welfare.

The latter set of relationships is gendered, because while it is possible to argue that the divisions in paid work have substantially diminished to the extent that greater numbers of women have entered the labour market (although not with regard to pay, status and hours) all the evidence suggests that the division of unpaid work remains substantially the same (see, for example, Morris 1990). Thus concepts such as 'decommodification' or 'dependency' have a gendered meaning that is rarely acknowledged. While Esping-Andersen (1990) writes of decommodification as a necessary prerequisite for workers' political mobilization, the worker he has in mind is male and his mobilization may depend as much on unpaid female household labour as state policies. Decommodification for women is likely to result in their carrying out unpaid caring work; in other words 'welfare dependency' on the part of adult women is likely to result in the greater independence of another person, young or old. The unequal division of unpaid work thus blurs the dichotomous divisions between dependent and independent, commodified and decommodified.

As Kolberg (1991) has noted, the interface between the private in the sense of the informal provision of welfare, the market and the state has not been subjected to close analysis. Indeed, informal care was absent from Titmuss's (1963) classic threefold division of welfare into state, fiscal and occupational provision, and as Langan and Ostner (1991) comment, it is just as absent from more recent categorizations. In the work of Esping-Andersen or of Leibfried (1991), women disappear from the analysis when they disappear from labour markets. Yet consideration of the private/domestic is crucial to any understanding of women's position because historically women have typically gained welfare entitlements by virtue of their dependent status within the family as wives, the justification being a division of labour perceived to follow 'naturally' on their capacity for motherhood. Women have thus tended to make contributions and draw benefits via their husbands in accordance with assumptions regarding the existence of a male-breadwinner family model (Land 1980). Furthermore, in welfare regimes where the social security system operates a dual insurance/assistance model, this in and of itself tends to be gendered, with first-class (insurance) benefits going mainly to men and second-class (welfare/assistance) benefits to women (Gordon 1990). In Britain 2.5 million working women are excluded from the contributory social security system because they fall below the lower earning limit.

The development of modern welfare states in the late nineteenth and early twentieth centuries coincided with the period when the boundary between the public world of paid work and political participation and the private domain of the family was strongest in both the prescriptive literature and in reality, at least for middle-class women. In its ideal form, the male-breadwinner model prescribed breadwinning for men and caring/ homemaking for women. It was part of a much larger gendered division between public and private that informed the work of political philosophers after Locke, and was taken as one of the measures of a civilized society by late-nineteenth-century social scientists such as Herbert Spencer. Working within an evolutionary framework, Spencer argued that society was 'progressing' towards a position whereby all women would be able to stay home in their 'natural' sphere. While it may be argued that his was a shared ideal – between men and women, employees and employers and the state (Lewis 1986) – it is important to note that it was never completely achieved. The male-breadwinner model operated most fully for late-nineteenth-century middle-class women in a few industrialized countries. Working-class women have always engaged in paid labour to some degree.

In reality, as Sokoloff (1980) and Pateman (1989) have insisted, the two spheres have been and are intimately interrelated rather than separated. Not least as a provider of welfare, the family has been central to civil society, rather than separate from it. Over time, the boundary between public and private has been redrawn at the level of prescription. For example, in English the phrase 'working mother' entered the language during and after World War II, but wage earning was always deemed a secondary activity for women. Given that in modern societies independence derives primarily from wage earning (Pateman 1988), the assumption that women were located mainly in the private sphere supported by a male breadwinner also meant that women have only been partially individualized. In regard to social policies, the liberal dilemma first described by Okin (1979), whereby individuals in fact meant male heads of families, has persisted.

Modern welfare regimes have all subscribed to some degree to the idea of a male-breadwinner model. Indeed, its persistence, to varying extents, cuts across established typologies of welfare regimes. Leira (1989), for example, has shown that Esping-Andersen's identification of a Scandinavian welfare regime breaks down as soon as gender is given serious consideration. The Norwegian system, which has continued to treat women primarily as wives and mothers, is closer in many respects to that of Britain than it is to Sweden. But just as the male-breadwinner model has not existed in its pure form, so the model has been modified in different ways and to different degrees in particular countries. In its pure form we would expect to find married women excluded from the labour market, firmly subordinated to their husbands for the purposes of social security entitlements and tax, and expected to undertake the work of caring (for children and other dependants) at home without public support. No country has ever matched the model completely, but some have come much closer than others. This paper looks at the way in which twentieth-century welfare states have treated women as wives and mothers and as paid workers, comparing Britain (with reference also to Ireland) as historically strong male-breadwinner states with, first, France, where it is argued that the male-breadwinner model remained implicit in social policies because of the focus on children rather than on women and where women's historically stronger position in the labour market also modified the operation of the model; and second, Sweden, where it is suggested that there has been a shift away from a strong male-breadwinner model towards something very different: a dual-breadwinner model. It is suggested that the strength or weakness of the male-breadwinner model serves as an indicator of the way in which women have been treated in social security systems, of the level of social service provision, particularly in regard to child care; and of the nature of married women's position in the labour market.

The paper is intended as an exploratory charting exercise; very little attempt has been made so far to gender welfare regimes.[2]   While it is impossible to come to any definitive conclusion as to where women 'do best,' both France and Sweden would seem to offer women more than Britain. However, the paper concludes with a cautionary note. In neither France nor Sweden did women's own demands play a significant role in determining their treatment. Paradoxically, the feminist movement has historically been stronger in Britain. This must raise issues as to what can be expected of the state and as to the possible fragility of the gains.

Strong Male-Breadwinner States – Ireland and Britain

Ireland has been historically, and more unusually, has remained well into the late twentieth century an extremely strong male-breadwinner state. Despite the choice of export-led development during the 1960s and 1970s, the labour market participation of women remained virtually the same, at just under 30 per cent. Incoming electronics firms that employed 80 per cent female workers elsewhere in the world employed 51 per cent in Ireland; in manufacturing more generally, 30 per cent of the labour force was female. Pyle (1990) has argued convincingly that government policy, particularly that of the Industrial Development Authority, played a decisive role in ensuring that men had priority in the labour market. In the civil service, a marriage bar prevented married women from working until 1977. Those married women determined to enter the labour market faced exceptionally harsh treatment under the tax system, with high marginal rates and a very low tax-free allowance, and the lowest levels of child care provision in Europe. Married women's treatment under the social security system has also exhibited the kind of features that might be hypothesized for a strong male-breadwinner country until very recently, when reform was prompted in large part by EC law. Until 1984 married women received lower rates of benefit, shorter length of payment of benefit, and were not eligible for unemployment assistance. Indeed, Ireland has been the only European country to pay dependents benefits regardless of whether the wife is in paid work (Callender 1988).

Britain has also shared a historical commitment to the male-breadwinner model, which, while it has been substantially modified in the late twentieth century, makes more explicable some of the differences in the position of British women, especially *vis-à-vis* the labour market.

In line with the dominant turn-of-the-century view of gender roles in the family and their link to social stability and welfare (Lewis 1991), one cabinet minister tried to ban the work of married women during the 1900s, and during the inter-war years a marriage bar operated in the professions. A parallel effort was put into the education of working-class wives and mothers in household management and infant welfare, using the small army of female visitors attached to charities and, increasingly by World War I, health visitors employed by local authorities (Lewis 1980).

This pattern of thinking about the family meant that policymakers faced a number of contradictory pulls. While women's welfare as wives and mothers was paramount, social policies were not permitted to undermine the man's responsibility to provide for dependants. Thus, national health and unemployment insurance introduced in Britain in 1911 did not cover women and children unless the woman was in full-time insurable employment (only 10 per cent were so placed). Nor was much protection offered the married woman as worker; Britain failed to implement paid maternity leave and never ratified the ILO Washington Convention provision for six weeks' paid leave (Lewis and Davies 1991). Again the argument was that the father must support his family and that women's waged work was detrimental to the welfare of children and to the stability of the family. In Britain, protective labour legislation was, as Mary Poovey (1989) has commented, the obverse of control. The concern was not so much to maximize the welfare of working women as mothers, but to minimize their labour market participation, a position that was shared by male and female trade unionists and by middle-class women social reformers. The position of women workers was more complicated in that, while there is evidence that they supported the family wage ideal, their material circumstances dictated their need to earn.

Under the post-war Beveridgean settlement, women continued to be treated as dependants for the purposes of social security entitlements. Beveridge (PP. 1942) wrote at length of the importance of women's role as wives and mothers in ensuring the continuance of the British race (at a time of fears about population decline) and insisted on marriage as a 'partnership' rather than a patriarchal relationship (Wilson 1977; Lewis 1983). It was, however, a partnership in which the parties were to be equal but different. Hence women were defined as wives and mothers, and therefore as dependent on a male wage. Married women were accordingly invited to take the 'married women's option,' paying less by way of contributions and collecting less in benefits. The married women's option was not abandoned until the middle of the 1970s, with the passing of equal opportunities legislation. From the mid-1970s, Britain offered an allowance for the unpaid work of caring for infirm dependents (the invalid care allowance) within the social security system, but, at the very same time that legislation was being passed to provide women with the means of legal redress on an individual basis against sex discrimination in pay, promotion, hiring and other mainly workplace related issues, the invalid care allowance was denied to married women on the grounds that caring was part of the 'normal' duties of such women.

The strong male-breadwinner model also predicts relatively low levels of female labour market participation and of social services such as child care. All northern European countries (except Ireland) have experienced a significant increase in women's labour market participation rates, particularly for married women. In Britain, married women's participation increased from 10 per cent in 1931 to 26 per cent in 1951, 49 per cent in 1971 and 62 per cent in 1981. On the face of it, British married women's labour participation rates have much in common with those of France. Dex and Walters' (1989) analysis of two samples of French and British women with dependent children drawn during the early 1980s found identical participation rates of 51 per cent. However, it is important that virtually the whole of the post-war expansion in married women's work in Britain is accounted for by part-time employment (44.5 per cent worked part-time in 1987, compared to 22.5 per cent in France). Sweden also has high levels of part-time work (43 per cent in 1989), but here again it is important to distinguish the meaning of 'part-time.' In Britain part-time work tends to be 'precarious' (following the OECD definition), with short hours and few benefits. While, in 1979, 29.8 per cent of women in part-time manual jobs and 23 per cent in non-manual jobs worked less than sixteen hours, by 1990 these figures had become 43.7 percent and 31.8 per cent (Lister 1992). In Sweden most women working part-time are in fact in full-time jobs (with full benefits), but are exercising their right to work a three-quarter time day while their children are small. In Britain, the inheritance of the male-breadwinner model is reflected in the nature rather than the level of women's labour market participation.

In particular, Britain has large numbers of non-working mothers of below-school-age children. This is related to the low level of child care provision, which is especially striking compared to France, where some

95 per cent of 3–5-year-olds are in publicly funded child care and 25 per cent of 0–2-year-olds. The figures for Britain are 44 per cent and 2 per cent, respectively (Phillips and Moss 1988). It is also significant that Britain tends to make less provision (thereby arguably giving less encouragement) to women workers who become mothers. Women with two years' continuous service have the right to 11 weeks leave before the birth of a child and 29 weeks afterwards at 90 per cent replacement income for 6 of those weeks, and the right to reinstatement, but, given the precarious labour market position of British women, only 60 per cent qualify.

Strong male-breadwinner states have tended to draw a firm dividing line between public and private responsibility. If women enter the public sphere as workers, they must do so on terms very similar to men. It is assumed that the family (that is, women) will provide child care and minimal provision is made for maternity leaves, pay and the right to reinstatement. During the 1980s in Britain, the public/private divide has been drawn more tightly. Thus eligibility for unemployment benefit has been linked much more firmly to recent employment and to availability for work, with attendant problems for women who interrupt paid work to care or who need to find child care. The maternity rights women won under the equal opportunities legislation of the mid-1970s have also been significantly weakened. Indeed, Britain is the only European Community member state in which maternity rights diminished during the 1980s. While no effort is now made to stop women working, the assumption is that women will be secondary wage earners and, despite the large numbers of women in paid employment, they tend to be in short part-time, low-status work. Davies and Joshi's (1990) econometric analysis of gross cash earnings forgone by a woman bearing one, two or three children shows the costs in Britain (and Germany) to be similar and high at 50 per cent of income. In France and Sweden the costs are similar and low at 10 per cent or less.

Modified Male-Breadwinner Countries – France

The picture is different in France, where the nature of women's labour market participation has historically been stronger in that it has been predominantly full-time, and where women have benefited, albeit indirectly, from a social security system that has prioritized horizontal redistribution between families with and without children, rather than vertical redistribution between rich and poor. In 1945 twice as much flowed out in family allowances as in social insurance. The allowances enabled a French family of four to double its income, whereas in Britain it received 15 shillings from family allowances when the average male wage was 121 shillings (Pedersen 1991: 447). In 1971 the French three- and four-child family on median earnings received four times as much in family benefits as its British counterpart (Dawson 1979: 203).

Family policy has been dominant within the French social security system and, in contrast to Britain, its goals have been clear (on the conflicting goals of British policy, see Brown 1987). The primary aim of French social security has been to compensate parents for the costs of children, and to this extent the system has been gender-neutral; Pedersen (1991) has described the early-twentieth-century development of French family policy as following a 'parental,' as opposed to a male-breadwinner, model. Historically, family benefits have been financed in large measure by employers and must therefore be seen as part of the wage system. The family allowances paid by employers during the 1930s were in some regions used as a means of controlling the labour force. Allowances were forfeited if work was missed for any reason, including strikes, and were also used as a means of attaching other family members, including women, to a particular firm. In other occupations the aim was less labour force control and more straightforwardly wage control during the Depression (Pedersen 1991; Thibault 1986). While rewarding women for the un-paid work of caring for children therefore had nothing to do with the introduction of family benefits in France, the nature of the redistribution from wage earners to non-wage earners did benefit women as well as children, especially given that some benefits were increasingly paid directly to women. Unlike Britain, there was no debate about this; family allowances had never been viewed as a feminist demand as they were in Britain during the 1920s (Land 1975; Lewis 1980; Pedersen 1991) and, given French family law, which vested complete parental authority in the husband (until reform in 1970), it was assumed that the interests of husband and wife would be as one. In fact, all the research on the division of resources within the household during the last decade (e.g., Pahl 1990) has revealed the existence of substantial inequalities between family members and in so far as family allowances, the most substantial of the many family benefits (which have included pre- and post-natal allowances, family supplements, payments to single-earner families, and payments in respect of child care) have been linked firmly to wages, and thus to the wage earner, it is of course impossible to be sure how far they actually benefited women and children in practice.

The case for generous family benefits was legitimated in France by pronatalist concerns. This resulted in substantial emphasis on the importance of good mothering and the pioneering French efforts to improve maternal and child welfare in the early twentieth century by, for example, the *Gouttes de Lait* were exported to Britain. Nevertheless, the percentage of women in full-time paid work increased during the late nineteenth and early twentieth centuries in France (from 30 per cent in 1866 to 37 per cent in 1911), in contrast to Britain, where the percentage fell. This was in large measure attributable to the different occupational structure in France and the large number of women employed in family businesses; as late as 1968, 20 per cent of French women were employed in the rural sector (Silver 1977). While in Britain it became part of the badge of working-class male respectability to keep a wife, enforced by a strong trade union movement as well as by the discourse of social reform, so in the French context this was neither so possible nor desirable. Patriarchal control was firmly located within the family rather than in collective institutions, and for a significant number of husbands it was not in their self-interest to exercise their legal right (which they held until 1965) to prevent their wives working. Thus, in France, there were no early-twentieth-century attempts to push women out of the labour market, and paid maternity leave was introduced in 1913.

During the 1930s, pronatalist concern deepened and gave rise to increased pressure for an allowance for *la mère au foyer* (women at home raising children). Such an allowance was introduced in the 1930s, although under the 1939 *Code de la Famille* it was paid only to urban families, the reasoning being that in rural areas women could both engage in farm work and mind children (Laroque 1985). The allowance was thus conceptualized more as a compensation for earnings forgone and, as Pedersen has argued, stood in stark contrast to the British treatment of married women workers under the 1931 Anomalies Act, which effectively deprived them of the right to unemployment insurance (see also Deacon 1976). Only during the Vichy regime were efforts made actively to prevent married women's employment, and the *mère au foyer* allowance was extended and uprated.

Thus the French model recognized the reality of women's claims as both mothers and workers. In this sense it was, as Douglas Ashford (1982) has argued more generally in regard to French politics, more pragmatic than the British. As the labour force participation rate of married women increased, from 34 per cent in 1968 to 40 per cent in 1975 (Hantrais 1990), so French policy documents addressed the reality of changes in women's labour market behaviour and their implications for family policy. As Rodgers (1975) noted, this approach stands in marked contrast to the tendency of British policymakers to ignore changes in family roles and structures (see, for example, Land and Ward's [1986] comments on the Fowler Review of British social security system). In 1972 the *frais de garde* was introduced specifically for families with working mothers and a number of articles began to question the social justice of paying benefits to women staying at home when they might be better off than women in the workforce. One of the most forceful contributions came from Rolande Cuvillier in an article republished in the *Journal of Social Policy* in 1979. This line of argument played, in the manner of many Anglo-Saxon contributions of the 1980s (e.g., Murray 1984 and Mead 1986) on the rhetoric of equality in the sense of treating women the same as men, but also within the French context reflected the increasing preoccupation of the 1970s and 1980s with achieving vertical as opposed to horizontal redistribution. This was promoted by means testing and by reducing the importance of family benefits – by 50 per cent between 1955 and 1985 (Questiaux, 1985) – within the social security system. Prost (1984) has suggested that the French family policy had lost its coherence by the 1980s.

French governments stated their explicit commitment to policy-neutrality regarding women's role, but the outcomes of the shifts in both family and labour market policy during the late 1970s and 1980s have been mixed for women. In 1977 the *frais de garde* was rolled up with the allowance for single wage earners (the extended *mere au foyer* allowance) into the *complément familial*. During the course of the Senate debate on this measure, the minister, Simone Weil stated firmly: 'Le complément familial serait versait aussi bien aux mères restant a leur foyer qu'a celles qui exercent une activité professionelle. Cette neutralité nous a semblé également equitable' (Journel Officiel, Senat Debats, 22/4/76: 609). The commitment both to neutrality regarding women's choice to go out to work or not and explicitly to seeking policies that would help them (but not men) to combine 'la vie professionelle et la vie familiale' persisted through the 1980s (e.g., the report of the Haut Conseil de la Population et de la Famille 1985).

However, as Pierre Laroque (1985) has pointed out, the *complément familial* continued to benefit one-earner families more than two-earner families. This was in part because the benefit (like all benefits introduced after 1970) was means-tested in accordance with the new priority given vertical redistribution. Research during the 1980s (e.g., Ekert 1983) has also shown that working wives pay a disproportionate amount towards the funding of family benefits. The operation of the joint tax system also works to penalize married women's work and may account for the greater incidence of part-time work among higher-paid women (Crompton, Hantrais and Walters 1990), while the interaction of the tax system with a benefit system that gives significantly more to large families may also encourage lower-income women to stay at home (Hantrais 1993). Third children attract more family benefit via the *allocation au jeune enfant* and more tax relief; working women giving birth to a third child are entitled to longer maternity leave.

During the 1980s, while French women have done somewhat better than British women relative to men in terms of both pay and measures of vertical segregation (Hantrais 1990) and ten times as many work continuously through the childbearing and childrearing years as in Britain (Crompton, Hantrais and Walters 1990), the percentage of French women working part-time has increased significantly due to conscious efforts to restructure the labour market. Between 1982 and 1986, 13,000 women lost a full-time job, while at the same time 450,000 part-time jobs were created (Jenson and Kantrow 1990: 133). Thus Jenson (1988) and Mazur (1991) have pointed out that while the 1983 Loi Roudy represented a strong measure of 'equality' legislation that notably provided for action to counter sex discrimination and segregation at the workplace level, government action also encouraged part-time work, albeit regulating it to ensure the payment of pro-rata benefits. French women giving birth to a child get between 16 and 26 weeks' maternity leave at 84 per cent replacement income, and 90 per cent of working mothers qualify. There is a tax allowance for child care, and public child care provision is among the best in Europe. Within the EC, France was one of only three countries in 1988 where more than 50 per cent of women with children under the age of five were in employment.

Thus pronatalist-inspired social policies resulted in generous benefits to compensate for the costs of children, and the way in which they have been financed also benefited women as mothers. These benefits have been diluted by more recent moves towards giving greater priority to vertical redistribution and to means testing, and also serve to penalize women workers. Nevertheless, compared to Britain or Ireland, France's modified male-breadwinner model – in which patriarchal control has been vested in husbands more than in trade unions, employers or governments, while state policy has recognized the reality of women's roles as both mothers and paid workers – has offered real gains to women.

Weak Male-Breadwinner Countries – Sweden³

Sweden was not always a weak male-breadwinner state. Pre-World War II Swedish social democracy embraced the idea of difference in its thinking about the relationships between men and women, largely as a result of the great influence wielded by Ellen Key. Her ideas inspired the social-democratic movement as to what was 'good and rightful' in everyday life (Key 1912, 1914). The most powerful image in Swedish social democracy has been that of building the 'people's home,' which encompasses the double idea, first, of society and state as a good family home, where no one is privileged, all co-operate and no one tries to gain advantage at another's expense; and, second, of ensuring that productive capacity is used to the advantage of people and their families. Whether in the big 'people's home' of state and society, or the small people's home of individual household and family, women's contribution (and rewards) were allocated on the basis of wife and motherhood in line with the family wage model (Hirdman 1989).

During the 1930s and 1940s, the situation in Sweden changed to resemble the French, albeit that the policy logic was somewhat different. During this period, the Social Democrats' conceptualization of women's place in society was significantly influenced by the writings of Alva and Gunnar Myrdal, themselves members of the party. Picking up the common theme of national suicide in the face of falling birth rates, the Myrdals insisted on 'democratic' population planning (which differentiated them from the extremes of national socialism) and the importance of society investing in the welfare of families. But alongside this maternalist politics and policies to encourage a higher birth rate, they also insisted that state policies should aim to realize the potential of each individual. Thus while women's roles as mothers acquired 'national' significance, so it was also insisted that women had the right to develop their talents in other fields, particularly that of paid employment. The Myrdals argued that if the state wanted babies, it must also make it possible for mothers to work, albeit sequentially (Kalvemark 1980). During the late 1940s Alva Myrdal developed with Viola Klein her influential idea of 'women's two roles,' whereby women should be encouraged to enter the labour market until the birth of a first child, returning when the child left school (Myrdal and Klein 1954). The state and employers were asked to support motherhood and married women's role as workers, albeit that these would be, much more than was envisaged in France, sequential and therefore separate endeavours. It was not envisaged that workers would also be the mothers of small children. In terms of Myrdal's policy inheritance in Sweden, it was important, first, that she sought to reconcile women's claims both as workers on equal terms to men and as mothers within a single strategy; second, that her main justification for such a strategy was, not unlike the French, the nation's need for women's labour power and for more babies, rather than women's expressed needs; and, third, that she was content to change women's lives without pressing for concomitant changes in those of men.

During the 1950s and 1960s, the labour force participation rates of women over 15 remained constant at about 30 per cent, with the low participation rates for married women in the childbearing years that were consistent with the dual-roles model. But during the late 1960s and early 1970s, Swedish Social Democratic governments took conscious steps to bring all adult women into the workforce and to make 'the *two-bread-winner family* the norm' (Hirdman 1989, my emphasis). As a result, the basis for women's social entitlements was transformed from that of dependent wife to worker. Since the mid-1970s women have been treated as workers and have been compensated for their unpaid work as mothers at rates they could command as members of the labour force.

The most important changes designed to promote women's market work were, first, the introduction of separate taxation in 1971. This, together with high marginal tax rates, has meant that it has been generally favourable for family income if a woman goes out to work rather than the man adding extra overtime hours (Gustafsson and Stafford 1988). In Britain, where separate taxation was introduced in 1989, the labour market effects are not the same because of low progressivity in the tax system. The second major change was the increase in the number of places in public day care: in 1968, 10 per cent of all children under school age had places; in 1979, 27 per cent; and in 1987, 47 per cent. Finally, in 1974 a scheme of parental insurance was introduced; rather than women being given flat-rate maternity benefits, they were offered compensation for loss of market earnings. Men were also offered the same 90 per cent replacement of earnings if they chose to care for children. The 1974 legislation gave a parental leave of six months to be taken before the child reached four years, together with a ten-day-per-year child sick leave. The leave was extended again in 1975 and again in 1980 to twelve months' parental leave and 60 days child sick leave.

Not surprisingly the labour market participation rate of women in Sweden increased dramatically. Participation rates in the 1950s and 1960s were lower than in many other Western countries, but, by 1986, 89.8 per

cent of women aged 25–54 (only 5 per cent less than men of comparable age) were in the labour market and 85.6 per cent of women with
children under 7 worked, compared with 28 per cent in Britain. By
1984, only 7 per cent of Swedish women between 25 and 54 were classified as 'housewives.' Thus Sweden may be seen as having moved away
from the male-breadwinner model towards treating women as well as
men as citizen workers, and then grafting on women's claims as mothers
through parental leave schemes and the like. This dual-breadwinner model
which makes social entitlements for all adults dependent on their labour
market status would seem to offer more in terms of benefit levels (paid
at market rates) and the level of social service provision, particularly in
respect of childcare, than strong family-breadwinner models. It is easier
to combine paid and unpaid work in Sweden, but this is not to say that it
is easier for women to 'choose' to engage in paid work. Women have
been 'forced' into the labour market, but they have retained their responsibility for the unpaid work of caring; men's behaviour has not been
changed. In terms of their labour market position, Swedish women are
better off in the sense of finding themselves in less precarious employment than British women, for example. But is has been argued that the
reorganization of women's labour together with policies such as parental
leaves, which are taken by women rather than by men, have served to
reinforce the sexual segregation of paid labour, which is among the
worst in the Western world (Jonung 1984). In this sense, the Swedish
model has less to offer than that of strong male-breadwinner states and
considerably less to offer than France, which provides almost as much for
the working mother (parental leave is unpaid, but child care provision is
better) and has also taken equal-opportunities legislation further than
either Sweden or the strong male-breadwinner countries.

The various ways in which modern welfare states have treated women
as unpaid carers and as paid workers have thus been complicated and no
one policy logic can be said to have the undisputed advantage. The
outcomes for lone-mother families provide a useful summary illustration
of this point. Women with children and without men have historically
posed a particularly difficult problem for governments. In Britain, policies have tended to oscillate over time between treating these women
primarily as workers (under the nineteenth-century poor law) or primarily as mothers (under post-war welfare state legislation). Predicting the
treatment of lone mothers in strong male-breadwinner countries is virtually impossible because their position defies the logic of the system, but
governments have tended historically to categorize lone mothers firmly

as either mothers or workers. In late-twentieth-century Britain no lone mother with a child under 16 who is claiming income support is obliged to register for work, and they have the lowest labour market participation in the European Community. While 47 per cent of lone mothers were in paid work during the period 1977–9, this figure actually dropped to 39 per cent for the period 1986–8 (Millar 1989). Indeed, Britain is the only EC country where lone mothers have a lower employment rate than mothers in two-parent families. In France, as Baker (1991) has pointed out, lone mothers reap the advantage of generous family benefits paid to all families with children, and while they have the highest labour force participation rate in the EC next to Denmark and Luxembourg, France is unusual in that the incomes of employed and unemployed lone-mother families are very similar (Millar 1989). In Sweden, as might be expected, 87 per cent of lone mothers are in the labour force and for the most part work full-time. In material terms they are the best off, but at the price of being particularly time poor.

What Can Be Hoped For from the State?

The position of women within different welfare regimes revolves around two related issues, the valuing of unpaid work and the sharing of it. Nowhere have these issues been addressed directly. In moving from the male-breadwinner to a dual-breadwinner model, Sweden may be judged to have gone a long way towards solving the first issue (because women get compensated at market rates for caring work), but not to have touched the second. France has also provided women with substantial, albeit indirect, rewards for mothering as a by-product of the priority it has accorded family policy, and arguably women have greater choice than in Sweden as to whether to work at home or in the labour market.

Many English-speaking feminists have remained at best ambivalent as to their expectations as to what state policy can deliver. While recognizing that the outcomes of social policies have changed familial and other structures in society such that male power has been challenged, they have argued that the state has also served to perpetuate patriarchal structures (Pateman 1988; Siim 1987). On the other hand, Scandinavian feminists have insisted on the possibility of a 'woman-friendly' state (Hernes 1987). Kolberg (1991: 144) has gone one step further and dismissed any idea that the Scandinavian welfare state might be patriarchal, insisting that it has increased women's 'independence, empowerment and emancipation.'

Yet it is noteworthy that in both France and Sweden women played little part in securing such advantages as accrued to them from the respective welfare regimes. In pre-war France feminists were forced to couch their claims in pronatalist terms. Pedersen (1991) suggests that paradoxically it was in large part the strength of British feminism compared to the French in putting forward a claim to family allowances as a means of both paying women as mothers (as well as providing for children) and securing equal pay for women at work (by abolishing the grounds for men's claim to a family wage) that resulted in such a weak measure. In France, family allowances were never conceptualized as a gender issue, and the matter of redistribution between men and women was never articulated.

In Sweden, the Social Democratic Women's League was an active campaigning force in the late 1960s and 1970s, but one of its most important original demands for the six-hour day was not met by the body of legislation that transformed women's labour market participation because of opposition from the trade union movement. Such a measure may well have served to redistribute unpaid and paid work between men and women. On the other hand, the Swedish case may lend support to Balbo's (1987) argument that modern welfare states call forth greater female public participation. All Nordic parliaments with the exception of Iceland have reached a critical mass (30–40 per cent) of women members and it is in part this that has led to Scandinavian women's optimism about the role of the state. (In Sweden the percentage fell from 38 to 28 as a result of the 1991 election, although the number of women ministers has remained the same at eight.) What is secured as a by-product of other concerns, for example, pronatalism in France, or the desire to increase the size of the labour force as in Sweden, can be reversed. Political and institutional power is crucial not so much for securing material well-being, as for putting issues that are central to enlarging women's choices, like the division and valuing of unpaid work, onto the political agenda.

Notes

1 I am indebted to Ilona Ostner for her ideas about the concepts developed in this paper.
2 The most significant attempts to date are by Langan and Ostner (1991) and by Shaver (1990).

3 The material in this section is drawn from a larger piece of work carried out in co-operation with Gertrude Astrom.

References

Ashford, D. (1982) *British Dogmatism and French Pragmatism: Central-Local Relations in the Welfare State*. London: Allen and Unwin.

Baker, J. (1991) Family policy as an anti-poverty measure, in M. Hardey and G. Crow (eds) *Lone Parenthood*. Brighton: Harvester Wheatsheaf.

Balbo, L. (1987) Family, women and the state: notes toward a typology of family roles and public intervention, in C.S. Maier (ed.) *Changing Boundaries of the Political: Essays on the Evolving Balance Between the State and Society, Public and Private in Europe*. Cambridge: Cambridge University Press.

Brown, J.C. (1987) *The Future of Family Income Support*. London: Policy Studies Institute Studies of the Social Security System, No. 15.

Callender, R. (1988) Ireland and the implementation of Directive 79/7/EEC, in Gerry Whyte (ed.) *Sex Equality, Community Rights and Irish Social Welfare Law*. Dublin: Irish Centre for European Law.

Crompton, R., Hantrais, L. and Walters, P. (1990) Gender relations and employment, *British Journal of Sociology*, 41(3): 329–49.

Cuvillier, R. (1979) The housewife: an unjustified financial burden on the community, *Journal of Social Policy* 8(3): 1–26.

Davies, H. and Joshi, H. (1990) The Foregone Earnings of Europe's Mothers, Discussion Papers in Economics, 24/90. Birbeck College, University of London, London.

Dawson, P.E. (1979) Family benefits and income redistribution in France and the UK, 1891–1971, unpublished PhD thesis, York, York University.

Deacon, A. (1976) *In Search of the Scrounger. The Administration of Unemployment Insurance in Britain, 1920–1931*, Occasional Papers in Social Administration, No. 60. London: London School of Economics.

Dex, S. and Walters, P. (1989) Women's occupational status in Britain, France and the USA: explaining the difference. *Industrial Relations Journal.* 20(3): 203–12.

Ekert, O. (1983) Activité féminine, prestations familiales et redistribution. *Population* 38(3): 503–26.

Esping Andersen, G. (1990) *The Three Worlds of Welfare Capitalism*. Cambridge: Polity.

Gordon, L. (ed.) (1990) *Women, The State and Welfare*. Madison, Wisconsin: University of Wisconsin Press.

Gustafsson, S. and Stafford, F. (1988) *Daycare Subsidies and Labour Supply in Sweden.* Centre for Economic Policy Research Discussion Papers, No. 279, London.

Hantrais, L. (1990) *Managing Professional and Family Life. A Comparative Study of British and French Women.* Aldershot: Dartmouth Publishing Company.

Hantrais, L. (1993) Women, work and welfare in France, in J. Lewis (ed) *Women, Work and Social Policies in Europe.* Aldershot: Edward Elgar.

Haut Conseil de la Population de la Famille (1985) Vie Professionelle et Vie Familiale, de Nouveaux Equilibres a Construire, La Documentation Français. Paris: Ministére des Affaires Sociales et de l'Emploi.

Hernes, H. (1987) *Welfare State and Woman Power: Essays in State Feminism.* Oslo: Norwegian University Press.

Hirdman, Y. (1989) The Swedish Welfare State and the gender system: a theoretical and empirical sketch. *The Study of Power and Democracy in Sweden, English Series.* Report No. 7. Stockholm.

Jenson, J. (1988) The limits of 'and the' discourse: French women as marginal workers, in J. Jenson, E. Hagen, and C. Reddy (eds) *The Feminization of the Labour Force: Paradoxes and Promises.* New York: Oxford University Press.

Jenson, J. and Kantrow, R. (1990) Labour market and family policy in France: an intersecting complex for dealing with poverty, in G. Schaffner Goldberg and Eleanor Kremen (eds) *The Feminization of Poverty. Only in America?* New York: Praeger Publications.

Jonung, C. (1984) Patterns of occupational segregation in the labour market, in Gunther Schmid and Renate Weitzel (eds) *Sex Discrimination and Equal Opportunities.* Aldershot: Gower.

Kalvemark, A.S. (1980) *More Children of Better Quality? Aspects in* [sic] *Swedish Population Policy in the 1930s.* Stockholm: Alqvist and Wiksell.

Key, E. (1912) *The Woman Movement.* New York: G.P. Putnam's Sons.

Key, E. (1914) *The Renaissance of Motherhood.* New York: G.P. Putnam's Sons.

Kolberg, J.E. (1991) The gender dimension of the welfare state. *International Journal of Sociology* 21(2): 119–48.

Land, H. (1975) The introduction of family allowances: an act of historic justice?, in P. Hall et al. (eds) *Change, Choice and Conflict in Social Policy.* London: Heineman.

Land, H. (1980) The family wage. *Feminist Review* 6: 55–78.

Land, H. and Ward, S. (1986) *Women Won't Benefit.* London: National Council for Civil Liberties.

Langan, M. and Ostner, I. (1991) Gender and welfare, in Graham Room (ed.) *Towards a European Welfare State.* Bristol: School of Advanced Urban Studies.

Laroque, P. (1985) *La politique familiale en France depuis 1945.* Documents
   Affaires Sociales, Paris, Ministére des Affaires Sociales et de la Solidarité
   Nationale.

Leibfried, S. (1991) *Towards a European Welfare State? On the Integration Potentials
   of Poverty Regimes in the EC.* TS, Bremen, Bremen University.

Leira, A. (1989) *Models of Motherhood, Welfare State Policies and Everyday Practices:
   The Scandinavian Experience.* Oslo: Institute for Social Research.

Lewis, J. (1980) *The Politics of Motherhood.* London: Croom Helm.

Lewis, J. (1983) Dealing with dependency: state practices and social realities,
   1870–1945, in J. Lewis (ed.) *Women's Welfare/Women's Rights.* London: Croom
   Helm.

Lewis, J. (1986) The working class wife and mother and state intervention,
   1870–1918, in J. Lewis (ed.) *Women's Experience of Home and Family, 1850–
   1940.* Oxford: Blackwell.

Lewis, J. (1991) *Women and Social Action in Victorian and Edwardian England.*
   Aldershot: Edward Elgar Publishers.

Lewis, J. and Davies, C. (1991) Protective legislation in Britain, 1870–1990:
   equality, difference and their implications for women. *Policy and Politics,*
   19(1): 13–25.

Lister, R. (1992) *Women's Economic Dependency and Social Security.* Manchester:
   Equal Opportunities Commission.

Mazur, A. (1991) Agendas and égalité professionelle: symbolic policy at work in
   France, in E. Meehan and S. Sevenhuijsen (eds) *Equality, Politics and Gender.*
   London: Sage.

Mead, L. (1986) *Beyond Entitlement. The Social Obligations of Citizenship.* New York:
   The Free Press.

Millar, J. (1989) *Poverty and the Lone Parent Family. The Challenge to Social Policy.*
   Aldershot: Avebury.

Morris, L. (1990) *The Workings of the Household. A US–UK Comparison.* Cambridge:
   Polity Press.

Murray, C. (1984) *Losing Ground. American Social Policy, 1950–1980.* New York:
   Basic Books.

Myrdal, A. and Klein, V. (1954) *Women's Two Roles.* London: Routledge and
   Kegan Paul.

Okin, S.M. (1979) *Women in Western Political Thought.* Princeton: Princeton
   University Press.

Pahl, J. (1990) *Money and Marriage.* London: Macmillan.

Pateman, C. (1988) The Patriarchal Welfare State, in A. Gutman (ed.) *Democracy
   and the Welfare State.* Princeton: Princeton University Press.

Pateman, C. (1989) Feminist Critiques of the Public/Private Dichotomy, in C. Pateman (ed) *The Disorder of Women*. Stanford: Stanford University Press.

Pedersen, S. (1991) Social policy and the reconstruction of the family in Britain and France, 1900–1945, unpublished PhD thesis, Cambridge, Mass., Harvard University.

Philips, A. and Moss, P. (1988) *Who Cares for Europe's Children? The Short Report of the European Childcare Network*. Brussels: EC.

Poovey, M. (1989) *Uneven Developments. The Ideological Work of Gender in Mid-Victorian England*. London: Virago.

PP. (1942) Cmd. 6404, Report of the Committee on Social Insurance and Allied Services. HMSO: London.

Prost, A. (1984) L'évolution de la politique familiale en France de 1938 à 1981. *Le Mouvement Social* no. 129 Oct–Dec: 7–28.

Pyle, J.L. (1990) *The State and Women in the Economy. Lessons from Sex Discrimination in the Republic of Ireland*. Albany: SUNY Press.

Questiaux, N. (1985) Family policy in France, in S.N. Eisenstadt and Ora Ahimeir (eds) *The Welfare State and its Aftermath*. London: Croom Helm.

Rodgers, B.N. (1975) Family policy in France. *Journal of Social Policy* 4(2): 113–28.

Shaver, S. (1990) *Gender, social policy regimes and the welfare state*, Social Policy Research Centre Discussion Papers, no. 26. Sydney: University of New South Wales.

Silver, C.B. (1977) France: contrasts in familial and societal roles, in J. Zollinger Giele and A. Chapman Smock (eds) *Women, Roles and Status in Eight Countries*. New York: John Wiley.

Siim, B. (1987) The Scandinavian welfare states – towards sexual equality or a new kind of male domination? *Acta Sociologica* 30(3/4): 255–70.

Sokoloff, N. (1980) *Between Money and Love. The Dialectics of Women's Home and Market Work*. New York: Praeger.

Taylor Gooby, P. (1991) Welfare state regimes and welfare citizenship. *Journal of European Social Policy* 1(2): 93–105.

Thibault, M.-N. (1986) Politiques familiales, politiques d'emploi. *Nouvelles Questions Feministes* 14–15, Winter: 147–61.

Titmuss, R.M. (1963) The Social Division of Welfare, in R.M. Titmuss, *Essays on the Welfare State*. London: Allen and Unwin.

Wilson, E. (1977) *Women and the Welfare State*. London: Tavistock.

9

Race, Class, and Gender in the U.S. Welfare State: Nixon's Failed Family Assistance Plan

JILL QUADAGNO

The central arguments about the formation of the U.S. welfare state view it as a product of class struggle driven by conflicts between labor and capital over problems of production. The emphasis on class struggle as the central dynamic has led class analyses to ignore a defining feature of social provision: its organization around race and gender. This historical case study of Richard Nixon's proposal for a Family Assistance Plan (FAP) to provide a guaranteed annual income to the working poor demonstrates that welfare programs mediate relations not only between classes but between politically dominant and politically repressed groups. By subsidizing the low-wage labor of black males and the childbearing role of black females, the FAP would reinstate male dominance over women in the household and retain white dominance over blacks in the labor market. The analysis suggests that while social policy may be used to increase female dependence, under certain historical conditions (in this case, those that existed in the South) social policy may enhance gender and racial equality. If economic power gained through redistributive measures from the state creates political opportunities for the excluded, then social policy becomes a liberating force.

In 1969, President Richard Nixon proposed abolishing Aid to Families with Dependent Children (AFDC), a means-tested welfare program for poor women and children, and replacing it with a guaranteed annual income for poor working families with children under 18. The unique feature of Nixon's Family Assistance Plan (FAP) was that it was designed to stimulate work through market incentives, rather than through compulsory work requirements. The guaranteed income took the form of a negative income tax (NIT), wherein a recipient could increase family income through additional work effort. Under FAP, the family benefit level was to be determined according to a formula: $500 each for the first two members of the family, $300 for each additional member, a $720 annual earnings exemption, and a 50 percent marginal tax on nonexempt earnings. The marginal tax meant that as family earnings moved above $720, the benefit would be reduced 50 cents for each dollar of nonexempt earnings until benefits reached zero and earnings were carrying the full load of family support. A family of four with no working members, i.e., a welfare family, would be guaranteed a minimum income of $1,600 a year, whereas a family of four with an employed household head could receive federal benefits until its income reached $3,920.[1] On April 16, 1970, the FAP (H.R. 16311) passed the House by a margin of 243 to 155 and passage in the more liberal Senate seemed guaranteed. Yet the bill was never reported out of the Senate Finance Committee, and the Senate defeated a substantially revised proposal on October 4, 1972, by a vote of 52 to 34.

The FAP's defeat poses an intriguing historical puzzle. Explanations of reform efforts in the American welfare state have variously emphasized the critical roles played by leading fractions of capital, state officials responding to civil disorder, and organized labor. In a context of mass turmoil, the FAP was designed and recommended by leading officials in the state bureaucracy, it had the support of big business and the endorsement of the labor movement, and yet it failed. Its failure suggests that existing explanations of U.S. social policymaking require modification.

I argue that the inability of existing theories of social policy to explain satisfactorily this counterfactual case rests on two problems. First is the shared assumption that social policy is shaped in a context of class struggle between capital and labor. The FAP's failure illustrates how conflicts based on gender and race also have a significant impact on the social policy agenda. A second problem is that the focus on successful social policies implies an historical inevitability that narrows the evaluation of causal factors. The analysis of social programs that become forgotten historical alternatives widens the range of explanatory potential. In a counterfactual case such as the FAP, the reasons why certain factions came to oppose the policy and what their opposition meant to its final outcome not only provide explanatory power lost in analyses of policy successes but also help to define policymaking limits.

Class Struggle Models of the Welfare State

The three dominant arguments about the formation of the U.S. welfare state have viewed it as a product of class struggle driven by conflict between labor and capital.

The Mass Turmoil Thesis

In Piven and Cloward's (1971, p. 3) classic formulation of the mass turmoil thesis, 'when mass unemployment leads to outbreaks of turmoil,
relief programs are ordinarily initiated or expanded to absorb and control enough of the unemployed to restore order; then as turbulence
subsides, the relief system contracts, expelling those who are needed to
populate the labour market.'

In the mass turmoil thesis, the state is linked to the capitalist social
order through welfare institutions, which serve two broad functions for
capital – accumulation and legitimation. When a threat to the legitimacy
of the state occurs, the state expands welfare institutions to restore order
and allow accumulation to continue (Isaac and Kelly 1981, pp. 1356–7).
The implicit view of the policy formation process is that strong state
managers with relative autonomy to shape social policy respond to pressures from otherwise powerless groups only when they threaten societal
and state legitimacy. Thus, 'the dynamic that periodically pushes the
expansion of the state forward' is 'class struggle between the agents of
capital and labor, capital and the state, and labor and the state' (Isaac
and Kelly 1982, p. 214).

The need to legitimate the existing social order may at times require
ignoring the interests of some fraction of business, so that 'some capitalist interests may be forgone or harmed in the short run' (Isaac and Kelly
1981, p. 1357). In the long run, however, the capitalist social order is
preserved.

Elite Dominance

The elite dominance thesis represents a variant of what has come to be
called instrumentalism. This view is rooted in statements by Marx charac-
terizing the state as an instrument in the hands of capital. The state acts
because it is directed to do so by representatives of the ruling class.

The elite dominance perspective has been modified along several
themes. Block (1977, p. 10) suggests that capitalists are generally not
aware of what is necessary to reproduce the social order. Because the
continued power of state managers rests on the maintenance of political
and economic order, they are forced to concern themselves with this
function. In this sense, the state has a degree of autonomy from capital
that is constrained primarily by the need of state managers to monitor
'business confidence,' which falls during political turmoil and rises when

there is a restoration of order (Block 1977, p. 10, 16). Dependent upon the investment accumulation process, state managers will use whatever resources they possess to aid that process.

The class fraction argument represents a further specification of the elite dominance model. This thesis suggests that fractions within the capitalist class may have a different stake in any given policy proposal and that 'the primary mediating function of the state takes place between divergent groups within the capitalist class' (Quadagno 1984, p. 646). For example, large monopoly corporations operating in international markets are often unconcerned with the labor supply issues that concern smaller businesses operating in highly competitive local markets (Quadagno 1984, p. 645). Because various fractions of capital have competing interests, the state is neither autonomous from capital nor a tool of it. Rather, the 'state functions as a mediating body, weighing the priorities of various power blocs within it' and designing policies that reconstitute traditional power relations between classes (Quadagno 1984, p. 646).

The elite dominance perspective and the mass turmoil thesis share a view that power moves from the top down, with the working classes or masses the passive recipients of elite decisions. In both views, social programs are a product of class struggle and these programs invariably sustain the interests of a ruling elite.

Power Resources Theory

In contrast to the mass turmoil and elite dominance arguments, power resources theorists believe that under certain conditions the working classes can use the state as a vehicle to counteract the inequities of the market. Power mobilization occurs when collectivities that are relatively weak in terms of market resources use political resources to affect the outcome of market conflicts (Korpi 1989, p. 312). The ability of wage earners to initiate social programs that modify market forces depends on the degree to which working-class parties make effective use of the franchise.

When wage earners are successful in organizing labor parties to represent their interests, they create 'social democratic' welfare states. Social-democratic welfare states are characterized by universal benefits that are granted as civil rights earned through worklife participation (Korpi 1989, p. 310). They emerge from strong labor movements, which create welfare states that decommodify wage workers by endowing 'individuals with a relative independence of the cash nexus and work compulsion' (Esping-

Andersen 1985, p. 224). The outcome is a more egalitarian society in which resources are redistributed more equitably and individuals gain the strength for communal action (Esping-Andersen 1985, p. 228).

When wage earners are unable effectively to mobilize political resources (generally because they fail to create a labor party), a 'liberal' welfare state results (Stephens 1979, p. 148). Liberal welfare states are dominated by 'social assistance' policies characterized by strict entitlement rules, social stigma, and modest benefits. Social assistance supports the market by decreasing the security of the poor and forcing them to rely on their labor power (Esping-Andersen 1989, p. 25). The outcome is a class-political dualism with stratification based on the fragmentation of workers into universal and nonuniversal benefit recipients (Esping-Andersen 1989, p. 25).

Power resources theory's emphasis on the balance of power between capital and labor, usually used in comparative welfare state analysis, helps explain why the U.S. never achieved the advanced welfare state status of, say, Sweden. At first glance, this 'negative' approach (it explains what didn't happen) appears less useful for understanding the evolution of welfare state development in liberal welfare states because it 'defines things negatively and begs the question of what workers and other classes were doing ... and with what consequences' (Myles 1989, p. 4). But power resources theorists also argue that the coalitions that wage earners form within and between classes are the key to understanding differences in the creation of welfare states, an insight that moves theorizing beyond the weak labor/strong labor impasse. If successful political mobilization depends on the ability of wage earners to forge coalitions, then one impediment to class political mobilization may be the failure to form such alliances (Esping-Andersen and Friedland 1982, p. 38; Esping-Andersen 1989, p. 18).

What impedes or facilitates alliance formation? According to Hicks, Friedland, and Johnson (1978, p. 302–3), unionized and nonunionized fractions of the working class in the U.S. share similar class interests for three reasons. First, organized labor depends on the Democratic party, which requires the political mobilization of the nonunionized. Second, labor unions are interested in protecting the incomes of the nonunionized to raise the floor under the union wage. Finally, many of the nonunionized are ex-union members who are retired, disabled, or laid-off. The check on organized labor's ability to mobilize cross-class coalitions is either corporate power, which can exert a negative impact on redistributive measures, or conflict between the two segments of unionized workers – skilled and unskilled labor (Esping-Andersen 1989, p. 28).

The split labor market perspective suggests that inherent conflict exists between three distinct groups: business or employers, high-paid labor, and cheap labor. The main goal of employers is to maintain a cheap labor force. Unionized labor is antagonistic toward low-wage workers because they pose a competitive threat. High-paid labor protects itself from cheap labor by monopolizing skilled positions, by preventing cheap labor from developing the skills necessary to compete with high-paid labor, and by denying it political resources (Bonacich 1972). Thus, unionized and nonunionized workers cannot form alliances, because they are in a competitive market position.

In spite of their different views on how policy is formed and what policy outcomes are possible, all of the above arguments presume that the welfare state is a product of class struggle centering around problems of production.

Gender and Race in Welfare State Dynamics

The emphasis on class struggle as the central dynamic of welfare state development has blinded class analyses to a defining feature of social provision: its organization around gender. The means-tested social assistance programs in the U.S. welfare state such as AFDC primarily support women, while the more generous, nonmeans-tested entitlement programs such as old age insurance allow men greater access to benefits and reward men more generously.[2] The differential distribution of the rewards received from entitlement programs reflects their eligibility rules. Although these rules are technically gender-neutral, they are modeled on male patterns of labor force participation. By rewarding continuous attachment to the labor force, long years of service, and high wages, these rules disadvantage women whose shorter and more irregular work histories make it more difficult for them to obtain full benefits (Quadagno 1988b, p. 542). In this sense, social insurance benefits merely replicate market inequities.

In contrast to social insurance programs, social assistance benefits are not earned but are based on both market and nonmarket factors. Social assistance programs have a means-test (a labor control factor) and a family status requirement. Women are eligible for benefits as wives or widows, or as caretakers of children when they do not have a man who is able to provide support (Acker 1988, p. 491; Shaver 1983). Unlike 'earned rights' guaranteed through worklife participation, benefits based on family status provide no guarantee of future income security – when family status changes, benefits are lost. Class-based theories of the welfare state cannot explain why women receive fewer benefits than men, nor can they explain why family status criteria govern access to social assistance.

Feminist theorists argue that welfare programs constitute a mechanism furthering women's subordination in the way they link income security with family structure and dependency relations. Eligibility rules for income support 'reflect and reconstruct relations between men and women in terms of sexuality, marriage, fertility, parenthood and kinship' (Shaver 1989, p. 4). Welfare programs reinforce male dominance over women by maintaining the economic subordination of women (Shaver 1983, p. 146).

The mechanism through which male dominance is maintained is the 'family wage,' which is embodied in eligibility rules for benefits (Pascal 1986, p. 3). The family wage requirement presumes that 'the nuclear family is the norm, that married and cohabiting women are supported financially by a male breadwinner, and that they are available to act as unpaid carers of those who are physically dependent' (Dale and Foster 1986, p. 105). Men receive benefits earned through their own market labor and any nonmarket labor performed by the dependent spouse. Women primarily receive benefits through their relationship to a male breadwinner and their benefits represent the lesser value of their nonmarket labor.

The problem with the family wage argument is that it is not at all apparent that welfare programs invariably reconstruct the male bread-winner/female caregiver family type. As Jenson (1986, p. 12) argues, 'any analysis which is dependent upon assumptions about who does the housework, about family forms, and even about the characteristics of women's waged work can be no more than historically contingent.' Assumptions about the family that are built into social programs are neither constant nor universal and thus require historical and comparative analysis.

Another problem is that while social benefits may maintain male dominance, they do not invariably increase women's dependence. They may also empower women by providing economic independence, 'opening for women areas of autonomy, free from direct subordination to a man' (Acker 1988, p. 493). The question then becomes one of explaining the conditions under which female empowerment will occur. According to Ruggie (1984, p. 298), the extent to which social policies support women is a function of the relative power of organized labor and its relation to the state. When labor is able to implement an agenda of solidaristic social and economic policies, women benefit indirectly by becoming incorporated into the category of worker. Hernes (1987, pp. 21–3) contends, however, that gender-equal policies depend on the political empowerment of women and that public policies formulated and implemented by political bodies dominated by men are likely to ignore the consequences of political decisions for women. Because gender-equal policies involve the redistribution of status and social power, enactment depends on women becoming actors in the political process, not objects of policies made by men.

In the U.S., the distribution of social benefits is not only biased by gender, but also by race. This may reflect the inferior labor market status of blacks, a status that has been maintained both by the use of black workers to undercut high-paid labor and by organized labor's exclusion of blacks (Bonacich 1972, p. 554). Because of their concentration in low-wage, less secure industries, blacks are overrepresented in social assistance programs, particularly AFDC, where 40 percent of the beneficiaries are black women (Rodgers 1982, p. 74). Average old age insurance benefits are lower for blacks than for whites because benefits are tied to previous market earnings (Quadagno 1988a, p. 12).

While the overrepresentation of blacks in social assistance programs reflects their position in the economy, it also is a product of their political suppression by whites. Historically, the Southern planter class's control over welfare helped them maintain economic and political dominance over a primarily black labor force of tenant farmers (Quadagno 1988a).

The disfranchisement of blacks allowed Southern Congressmen to impede and later to shape national welfare programs to confine blacks to locally controlled public assistance programs (Quadagno 1988a, p. 116). For example, the Social Security Act of 1935 excluded from coverage more than three-fifths of black workers (Quadagno 1984, p. 263). As a result, most blacks were eligible to receive old age benefits only from the means-tested, locally controlled old age assistance program. Like gender equality, racial equality depends on blacks becoming actors in the political process, not objects of policy designed by whites.

Turning points in welfare history highlight the forces shaping social policy developments. This paper uses the FAP as an historical case study to examine prevailing theories of the welfare state. The next section evaluates how well the evidence supports a mass turmoil thesis, which predicts that urban riots provoke plans for welfare expansion from state managers.

Mass Turmoil and the Crisis of the Black Family

When Richard Nixon sent his Family Assistance Plan to Congress, he stressed the plan's ability both to resolve a social crisis and to increase the labor supply: 'We face an urban crisis, a social crisis – and at the same time, a crisis of confidence in the capacity of government to do its job.' The FAP would open job training for those on welfare and expand day care facilities to 'make it possible for mothers to take jobs by which they (could) support themselves and their children' (Nixon 1969, p. 674–6). In Nixon's view, AFDC had to be abolished because 'any system which makes it more profitable for a man not to work than to work, or which encourages a man to desert his family rather than stay with his family is wrong and indefensible' (Nixon 1968, p. 675). Thus, the FAP was sold to the American public as a program to calm social unrest, increase the labor force participation of poor women, and discourage family breakup.

The Impact of Mass Turmoil

Nixon's proposal for welfare reform emerged during a period that could be considered a legitimation crisis for the state and for capital. Between 1964 and 1968, major riots causing destruction of property and deaths and injuries to rioters and police occurred in New York, Newark, Los Angeles, Philadelphia, Detroit, and numerous other cities. The summer of 1967 was particularly tumultuous, with 64 disorders in the first nine months of that year. Newspaper estimates of damage (which later turned out to be greatly exaggerated) ranged from $200 million to $500 million (National Advisory Commission on Civil Disorders 1968, p. 6).

Nearly all the riots centered around race – of the 31 cities where the proportion of blacks had doubled in the past twenty years, 20 had serious disorders (Piven and Cloward 1971, p. 259). The causes were 'bitterness and resentment against society in general and white society in particular,' as exclusion from employment and education had created 'economic inequality reflected in the deprivation of ghetto life' (National Advisory Commission on Civil Disorders 1968, p. 203–4).

During this period, welfare rolls skyrocketed – the number of families receiving AFDC increases by 214 percent between 1960 and 1970 (Piven and Cloward 1979, p. 264). An important influence in welfare expansion was a short-lived but highly visible women's liberation movement, the National Welfare Rights Organization (NWRO). The NWRO was an organization of AFDC mothers whose activities were directed at class and gender issues. They demanded increased benefits, jobs, and sexual freedom including the elimination of 'man in the house' rules. Although the NWRO was virtually defunct by 1970, at its peak it staged hundreds of sit-ins and confrontations at welfare offices (Piven and Cloward 1979, p. 303) and the percentage of eligible families applying for aid increased from about 33 percent in 1960 to more than 90 percent in some regions by 1971. Poor women came to view welfare as a right rather than a privilege (Patterson 1986, p. 179).

Political class-struggle theorists argue that state managers use welfare policy to 'insure capitalist accumulation ... to placate or encourage competing class groups ... and to rebuff demands of mass insurgents' (Griffin, Devine, and Wallace 1983, pp. 355–6). A number of analyses linking the riots to welfare expansion support the 'legitimation crisis' argument (Hicks and Swank 1983, p. 711; Isaac and Kelly 1981, p. 1371). Since the FAP, by some estimates, would more than double the welfare population, it could be viewed as an effort by the state to contain insurgency by expanding welfare. The planning of the proposal also supports this contention.

In March, 1967, New York Governor Nelson Rockefeller convened the Arden House Conference to evaluate the American welfare system. Invited to the meeting were heads of large corporations whose concern over urban rioting predisposed them to consider social issues. Taking income maintenance as their subject, conference members evaluated the relative merits of family allowances over a negative income tax and concluded that they favored the latter. Thereafter, they constituted an ongoing lobby to replace the existing welfare system with a program of automatic income maintenance (Moynihan 1973, p. 57).

The following year, in response to a National Advisory Commission Report on Civil Disorders (1968) calling for action to end poverty and racial discrimination, President Lyndon Johnson established a Commission on Income-Maintenance to consider welfare reform (Piven and Cloward 1979, p. 273). The group was headed by Ben W. Heineman, head of Northwest Industries, an industrial conglomerate, and included representatives from business, organized labor, and academia. The Heineman Commission also adopted and recommended to President Nixon a negative income tax with a $2,400 cash floor for a family of four and abolition of food stamps (Burke and Burke 1974, p. 170).

If the urban riots represented a legitimation crisis for the state, then the solution proposed by both capitalists and the state, welfare expansion through the inclusion of the working poor in AFDC, seems to confirm the mass turmoil thesis. But according to the National Advisory Commission report (pp. 129–30), the rioters were primarily young, black males. Survey data from Detroit, for example, indicated that 61.3 percent of the self-reported rioters were between the ages of 15 and 24, and 86.3 percent were under 35. Nearly 90 percent of those arrested for rioting in Detroit were male and more than half were single. Since the beneficiaries of a negative income tax would be employed household heads, how could such a plan stop single young men from rioting? The answer lies in an analysis of policymakers' views, which were focused more on the state of the black family than on the state of the economy.

The Crisis of the Black Family

By accepting the idea that the legitimation crisis was caused by riots and civil disorder, mass turmoil theorists failed to delve further into policymakers' interpretations of its source. The result is a superficial connection between insurgency and welfare expansion that misses the concerns about the black family that policymakers believed were linked to the crisis.

While policymakers believed that black unemployment and inequality of opportunity in the labor market prompted the crisis, they believed that the disintegration of the black family was the ultimate cause. This thesis first appeared in a report by Daniel Patrick Moynihan, then Assistant Secretary of Labor, which said 'the breakdown of the Negro family led to a startling increase in welfare dependency' (Moynihan 1965, pp. 12–13). The problem was rooted in the failure of the wage system to provide a family wage for black males, resulting in a 'tendency for black women to fare better interpersonally and economically than men and thereby to dominate family life' (Rainwater and Yancey 1967, p. 6). As Moynihan (1965, p. 25, 29) explained, 'Ours is a society which presumes male leadership in private and public affairs,' but in the Negro family 'the dependence on the mother's income undermines the position of the father.' He called for 'a national effort to strengthen the Negro family,' which could not be accomplished until the government guaranteed that 'every able-bodied Negro man was working, *even if this meant that some jobs had to be redesigned to enable men to fulfill them*' (Moynihan 1965, p. 93; Rainwater and Yancey 1967, p. 29). Moynihan proposed that government policy support black males in the labor market so that they could be reinstated as household heads, a goal that could be accomplished by reducing the labor force participation of black women. In his view, social policy could reestablish male dominance in the black family, a prerequisite for social stability.

The National Advisory Commission on Civil Disorders (1968, pp. 13–14) reached a similar conclusion. 'The condition of Negroes in the central city [was] in a state of crisis' because of chronic unemployment among males and because of the concentration of black males at the lowest end of the occupational scale. The employment problems of black males made them 'unable or unwilling to remain with their families.' Because Negro males had less secure and low-paying jobs, mothers were forced to work to provide support. Black family structure was directly related to the riots, as 'children growing up under such conditions [were] likely participants in civil disorder.'

A central cause, according to the Commission (p. 457), was the welfare system, which 'contributed materially to the tensions and social disorganization that [has] led to civil disorders.' The solution the Commission proposed (p. 466) was a system of income supplements to subsidize those who worked at low-paying jobs and 'to provide for mothers who decide to remain with their children.'

Reconstructing the Family Wage

By subsidizing the low wages of black males, the FAP would indirectly resolve the turmoil in urban ghettos by providing incentives for black males to become family breadwinners and allowing black women to return to the household to take care of their children.

Although Nixon attempted to sell the FAP as a program to increase AFDC mothers' labor force participation, it contained no programs to accomplish this goal. When the Senate Finance Committee queried Robert Finch, Secretary of Health, Education and Welfare (HEW), on how the FAP might ensure jobs for program recipients, he responded that that was an issue which 'more appropriately comes under Labor' (U.S. Congress, p. 321). Further, HEW had not studied the labor market to determine where and how jobs might be obtained and how many jobs were presently available (U.S. Congress, p. 384).

Under the FAP, the federal government would pay the costs of day care and would allow parents in training or employment to exclude this payment from their reported income, a revolutionary innovation (U.S. Congress, p. 305). But numerous gaps in day care planning rendered it ineffective. One problem was inadequate funding. Although HEW estimates placed the costs of adequate day care at $2,000 per child per year, the FAP allowed only $858 a year. A second problem was that day care was not available and the FAP left provision of day care to a market that wasn't meeting existing demand, let alone low-income demand (U.S. Congress, pp. 242, 305, 1742). Further, day care planning was weak, with HEW officials complaining that regulations were 'unclear' about who was eligible and what agency was responsible for day care.[3]

The FAP ignored the labor force participation of welfare women because the employment component of the bill was directed at men. As Finch explained, 'In no state is any federally-assisted welfare available to families headed by full-time working men who earn poverty wages – the working poor ... We have backed ourselves into a situation in which we will help men who don't work [under AFDC-UI], but we cannot help those who do work.'[4] Similarly, another HEW employee explained to the Senate Finance Committee, 'I would remind the committee that the term "working poor" in this case is a term of art. It means families headed by fathers who are working full time at the present time and who are not covered by the present law' (U.S. Congress, p. 190). This definition was maintained throughout the various revisions of the FAP. In preparing an evaluation of the FAP for the Senate Finance Committee, the new HEW Secretary, Elliot Richardson, explained that 'taken together these proposals do assure that the family of a working man will always be better off than a family of the same size headed by a man who is not working.'[5]

The original version of the FAP called for 150,000 new training slots 'to train people for jobs at decent wages whenever we find that they cannot get good jobs with their present skills' (Schultz 1970, p. 6). In discussing the training programs, Frank Carlucci, Director of the Office of Economic Opportunity (OEO), suggested ranking employment and training opportunities for the various categories of beneficiaries to be created by the FAP:

We believe that priorities for manpower services should be explicitly structured to provide for the maximum improvement in employability and earning potential, at minimum federal cost. We have already suggested that a high priority be assigned to AFDC-UI fathers. In general, we would support giving higher priority to the training and employment of men than women. Given the greater employment opportunities for men generally available, they are more likely to achieve self-sufficiency. Moreover, training and employment will often be much more expensive for women, if child care must be provided.[6]

To the program bureaucrats, the working poor targeted by the FAP were male, and the challenge was to train the unemployed and to reward low-income breadwinners by guaranteeing male household heads sufficient income to support a family.

The FAP was structured to separate responsibility for welfare mothers and poor, working men. Administrators within HEW agreed that the manpower services under the FAP were 'clearly the responsibility of the Department of Labor alone.'[7] The problem, however, was which agency, HEW or the Department of Labor, should administer benefits to the working poor when they were in the marginal status or registering for training or seeking work. HEW claimed responsibility 'for female headed families in which no member is required to register for work or training' but agreed to transfer jurisdiction to the Department of Labor when 'a family member actually enters a training program or public service job.'[8] Since training and employment were to be oriented toward male household heads, such an arrangement would create a dichotomy in welfare administration, with welfare mothers under the jurisdiction of HEW and men in training or in employment under the jurisdiction of the Department of Labor. Assumptions about family structure and the differential labor force participation of men and women were built into every component of the program.

A policy of supporting the poor male in his role as breadwinner was directed at black families, who constituted one-third of the working poor. Although Secretary of Labor George Schultz proclaimed that the FAP's goal was to place breadwinners in good jobs at good wages, the economy was generating low-wage jobs, and Schultz (1970, pp. 6–8) admitted that 'we are not going to be remaking the economy in this program. We can only put people in the jobs that exist.' Thus, the FAP channeled poor men, particularly poor black men, into the low-wage sector of the economy.

The FAP would have done nothing to improve the circumstances of AFDC beneficiaries, 85 percent of whom were in female-headed households, for they were not the working poor. Among AFDC recipients, less than 25 percent had some earnings (U.S. Congress, p. 1940). Nixon's only guarantee to AFDC women (a promise he could not keep) was that 'in no case would anyone's present level of benefits be lowered' (Nixon 1969, p. 675).[9] Implicit in the program planners' strategy was the notion that a family wage for low-income males would resolve the income deficit of poor women by relocating them within a male breadwinner/female dependent family.

This analysis highlights the limitations of the mass turmoil thesis for explaining the expansion of social assistance. Although welfare expansion may be a response to a legitimation crisis for the state, it cannot explain the form of the state's response: reconstituting the working-poor family. The legitimation crisis was rooted in what policymakers defined as a crisis of black family structure. The replacement of a social program that paid benefits to single women by one that supported intact families with an employed male demonstrates how policy can be influenced by male dominance. Designed by male bureaucrats, the FAP would have maintained the dependence of some poor single women on the state while transferring the dependence of others to a male breadwinner. Since benefits would be tied to the primary breadwinner's wages and to family size, it would reduce the importance of the wife's economic contribution to the household and subsidize childbearing, thereby encouraging her to leave the labor force. Neither welfare mothers nor women in working-poor households would have gained autonomy. Designed by white males, the FAP also would sustain a racially segregated labor force and do nothing to increase the occupational mobility of black males.

The Elite Agenda

According to the elite dominance perspective, state managers play a mediating role in program formation by selecting a fraction of capital as an ally. The most likely fraction is large-scale capital, which should support welfare expansion at the national level. Small business, by contrast, should work against any expansion 'because of its direct need for labor and its anti-state bureaucratic orientation' (Isaac and Kelly 1982, p. 218).

The reaction of the business community, represented primarily by the National Association of Manufacturers (NAM) and the Chamber of Commerce, appears to sustain an elite dominance argument. State managers sought the cooperation of corporate capital while working to minimize the objections of small employers.

The NAM was dominated by large corporations (Burch 1973, p. 108). The Government Operations/Expenditures Committee of the NAM began studying AFDC reform in 1967 and agreed with the Nixon administration that welfare reform ranked 'very high on the nation's domestic agenda' (Bolton 1971, p. 12).

HEW policymakers recruited Roy Bolton, chairman of the NAM committee, to sell the FAP to the NAM members. Bolton 'was directly instrumental in mustering the support of the NAM's 20,000 membership' and 'also testified ... on behalf of H.R. 16311 in the Senate.'[10]

Although the NAM supported the FAP, its support was contingent on a number of revisions, including phasing out the food stamp program over a five-year period, eliminating the eligibility of anyone involved in a labor dispute, and removing the requirement that recipients be allowed to reject employment if the wage level was below that prevailing for similar work (Bolton 1971, p. 13). These revisions represented the traditional concerns of capital, as reflected in class-based theories – reducing income redistribution and controlling labor. The NAM's concerns were not expressed in political action, however, and its support was a negligible factor. The NAM represented core employers in capital-intensive rather than labor-intensive industries, and the labor supply issues that the FAP generated were of little interest to its members. Thus, the NAM was able to take a broad perspective on welfare reform and saw the FAP as a mechanism for calming urban ghettos and encouraging work, particularly among black males.

The Chamber of Commerce, by contrast, was vehemently opposed to the FAP and undertook an extensive lobbying campaign against the proposal.[11] With 3,800 trade associations and local chambers and a direct membership of more than 35,000 business firms, Chamber influence was extensive.

According to Chamber analysts, the U.S. economy was troubled because the welfare state pushed the economy toward chronic budget deficits, because excessive cost-push by unions in an economy pledged to full employment had lessened the resistance of employers to wage demands, and because the shift in employment from goods to services had reduced productivity. The FAP would expand the welfare rolls enormously, reduce the amount of work performed, and raise taxes (Davis 1971, pp. 766–7).

The key issue in Chamber opposition was the threat the FAP represented to its members' labor supply. Dominated by small service sector firms, many in the South, Chamber members were aware of the feminization of the labor force, in regard to both present needs and future expansion.[12] Since Chamber analyses indicated that most AFDC families were on welfare because of the loss of the primary breadwinner, the solution was 'to make the remaining family adult – the mother – a regular breadwinner' (U.S. Congress, p. 1895). Local Chambers were advised to tackle the 'manpower-welfare' problem by hiring women on welfare. A Chamber newsletter proposed an appropriate slogan: 'If you won't hire her, don't complain about supporting her.'[13]

Although policymakers portrayed the FAP as a program designed to increase work among welfare recipients, it contained no real work requirement. If the household head refused work or training, other family members were eligible for benefits. Not surprisingly, the Chamber, which had studied welfare reform for more than a decade, focused on the lack of a work requirement. Although revisions in AFDC were necessary, the FAP would only further reduce work incentives (U.S. Congress, p. 1886). In the Chamber's view, the FAP was simply a guaranteed income that would eventually put 50 percent of the population on welfare.

The Chamber's efforts to defeat the FAP demonstrate the importance of class conflict among elites. It also shows that the labor supply issue was not merely a conflict between labor and capital, for it centered around a sex-differentiated labor force. Small service sector firms were interested in maintaining the advantages offered by a sex-segregated labor force and feared that expanding the welfare population would discourage welfare mothers and other low-income women from working. Chamber members were not interested in empowering women through worklife participation but in preserving a supply of low-wage female labor.

Impediments to Working-Class Alliance

Power resources theorists believe that universalistic social programs are most likely to be legislated when wage earners form alliances within and between class fractions. One argument suggests that the main impediment to class alliance is the power of the business elite, while a second emphasizes conflicts between unionized and nonunionized workers, which may be organized around race or gender as well as class.

In 1970, organized labor was entrenched in national politics. It was still closely linked to the Democratic party, and the Democratic majority in the Senate relied on labor's support for the passage of legislation. In spite of the relative political strength of organized labor, the U.S. working class was highly fragmented. Within organized labor, the powerful and progressive United Auto Workers union withdrew from the AFL-CIO over such issues as civil rights and organizing service sector workers and formed an unlikely alliance with the International Brotherhood of Teamsters (Barnard 1983, p. 197). During the 1968 presidential election, trade unionists bolted from the Democratic party to support the segregationist ticket of George Wallace (Converse, Miller, Rusk, and Wolfe 1969, p. 1102). Furthermore, 'the emergence of demands for power-sharing and positive discrimination for blacks, Hispanics and women directly threatened the exclusivist operation of ethnic patronage politics and craft union apprenticeships' (Davis 1986, p. 223).

The welfare explosion of the 1960s added to working-class fragmentation. State and local governments contributed at least 45 percent of the costs of AFDC, leading to racially motivated resentment between the working and non-working poor (National Advisory Commission on Civil Disorders 1968, p. 461). As Finch explained to the Senate Finance Committee, the present law generated discontent among those who see others no worse off receiving welfare. Further, this discontent carried 'ominous racial overtones ... since current AFDC recipients ... are about 50 percent nonwhite, while the working poor ... are about 70 percent white.'[14] Unionists shared this resentment, as Clinton Fair, Legislative Director of the AFL-CIO, explained to the Senate, 'One of the most frustrating and discouraging features of all is that a male worker, employed full time, may be worse off than his neighbor, working only part time, but receiving welfare' (U.S. Congress, p. 1728).

Yet when the FAP, an apparent solution to the AFDC mess, was first unveiled, organized labor opposed it because it violated 'principles the labor movement ha[d] long espoused, including opposition to wage subsidies and minimum reliance on means-tested programs.'[15] The bill's quick passage in the House caught labor off guard, but by the time the FAP reached the Senate, labor was prepared to extract two major changes as the price of its support. Labor's bitterest opposition was directed at a provision specifying that a family head receiving FAP benefits be required, under penalty of benefit reduction, to work at a job not covered by the minimum wage so long as the job paid the prevailing wage for that work (U.S. Congress, pp. 1729, 1747). Labor wanted to protect the minimum wage so that wages would not be frozen at poverty levels, undermining union wage levels (U.S. Congress, p. 1736).

A second issue for labor was the possibility that the FAP would flood the market with low-wage workers. Increased numbers of employable welfare recipients would be induced to work at the same time that the working poor would increase their work efforts. The result would be intensified competition for a fixed number of jobs and a proliferation of low-wage employment. In the long run, low wage rates in the subsidized sector would have a negative impact on wage rates in the non-subsidized sector. Burt Seidman, Director of the AFL-CIO Social Security Department, explained 'there is no reason why the government through subsidies or tax credits, should "buy" low-level jobs for welfare recipients' (U.S. Congress, p. 1730). Further, the proposed training programs threatened to undermine the union's autonomy over skilled craft jobs, allowing workers to enter the protected segments of manufacturing and skilled trades. According to Seidman, 'FAP legislation should imply no authority for' ... 'training programs in the lower wage industries where prior skill or training is typically not a prerequisite to hiring and where labor turn-over is high' (U.S. Congress, p. 1730). Instead, unionists demanded federal financing and administration of a separate tier of public sector jobs that would reduce this threat. Because the administration recognized that the FAP could not pass the Senate over AFL-CIO opposition, it incorporated labor's two demands (Burke and Burke 1974, p. 144) and organized labor withdrew its opposition to the bill.

The FAP represented a fundamentally different vision of a welfare state than that of organized labor. The FAP's poverty prevention agenda centered around increasing the supply of low-wage labor by reducing work disincentives in existing welfare programs and increasing labor flexibility at the bottom of the income distribution. Organized labor wanted manpower training under labor's control, a higher minimum wage, and improved social insurance.[16]

Why, then, did organized labor accept two minor concessions as a trade-off for withdrawing its opposition? The answer lies in the impediments to class solidarity that the FAP would have reinforced. The major impediment was the segmentation of the working class by race and gender, which created further conditions for class fragmentation.

In 1970, the U.S. labor force was highly stratified on the basis of sex and race. Women were relegated primarily to peripheral service industries or to less secure, low-paying positions in the core sector of the economy (Form 1985, p. 45). Among males, whites held the predominant share of high-wage jobs, and union contracts granted them job security and fringe benefits that provided protection over the life course.

Unionists had little concern for the nonunionized black and female low-wage service industry workers for they did not compete in the same labor market, and they took action to ensure that gender and racial barriers to class fragmentation remained. During the 1960s, the AFL-CIO launched a campaign against the Equal Rights Amendment for women and fought vehemently against government attempts to desegregate the construction industry in Philadelphia.[17] Organized labor's actions support the view that a split labor market is partially maintained by privileged workers seeking to keep cheap labor non-competitive. When cheap labor comprises women and blacks, the bases of exclusion are clearly defined.

Not only was organized labor's agenda for the FAP directed toward its own maintenance, but unionists paid only lip service to the problem of the welfare poor. The concern over placing the working poor in jobs at minimum wage did not extend to nonworkers, 'the unemployable or mothers with children in their care,' whom labor was willing to leave at benefit levels below minimum wage (U.S. Congress, p. 1735). Although labor proposed increasing AFDC benefits up to the poverty level, this was not necessary for labor's support of the bill.

A second impediment to alliance formation between organized labor, the working poor, and the welfare poor was social policy. Those involved in social protest wanted access to high-wage employment and higher welfare benefits, placing them in direct confrontation with organized labor. Unionists feared both the high costs of welfare expansion and the erosion of market privilege.[18]

Once its self-protective concerns about the minimum wage and public service employment were addressed, organized labor was willing to lend its support to the FAP because skilled craft jobs remained reserved for white males. Organized labor did not perceive the FAP as a significant threat because the split labor market meant its impact would not be felt by its constituents. As one AFL-CIO position paper explained, the union's strategy on the FAP could be to 'disavow (not necessarily publicly) any responsibility for the labor movement to "solve" this problem. Instead, keep to our basic position as expressed in our Convention resolution and keep our options open as to solutions proposed by others. This means criticizing such proposals in their context but based on our overall principles.'[19]

A final impediment to alliance formation was the avenue of political expression pursued by each class fraction. Power resource theorists emphasize institutional power and pay little attention to the noninstitutional avenues through which class struggle may take place. Institutional power, the formal mechanisms of political participation such as electoral and interest group politics, is most likely to be used by groups like organized labor with recognized authority to act in the political arena. The politically powerless poor, who have no formal opportunities to present their grievances, are often forced to rely on noninstitutional sources of power (Griffin, Devine, and Wallace 1983, p. 343). Disfranchised blacks used riots and welfare mothers used demonstrations and sit-ins to access a power structure that excluded them. The varying avenues of political expression prevented the different class fractions from forming an alliance because their demands challenged the very basis of the system (McAdam 1982, p. 38).

Although organized labor and big business supported the FAP, the only push for the proposal came from state bureaucrats who mediated among class factions to resolve a legitimation crisis. Their failure to get this legislation through Congress suggests that the FAP's opponents were more powerful. Among these, Southern Congressmen were a formidable force.

FAP's Impact on the Political Economy of the South

Among the problems that the FAP would eliminate, according to Nixon (1969, p. 274), was 'regional inequities in the distribution of benefits.' Regional differences in potential program impact were a major factor in FAP's defeat.

The interest in welfare reform generated by urban unrest and the fiscal problems of Northern cities did not exist in the South. According to HEW estimates, more than 30 percent of all FAP funds would go to California, another 38 percent to five Northeastern states, and the other 44 states would receive the remaining 32 percent (U.S. Congress, p. 292). Southern states would receive little or no fiscal relief because their existing benefit levels were low (U.S. Congress, p. 340). But the FAP would have an enormous impact on the Southern economy where per-capita income was only 66 percent of that of the North or West.[20] The FAP funds would raise the entire Southern wage base and revolutionize its economy. By empowering blacks economically, the FAP would also empower them politically, undermining the structures that maintained caste relations in the South. How could the FAP accomplish such substantial changes when critics charged it was nothing more than a subsidy to low-wage labor? The answer lies in the tremendous political and economic differences between the South and the rest of the nation, a dualism that is seldom recognized as a significant factor in American Welfare state development.

FAP's Impact on the Southern Labor Supply

Although administration estimates varied from proposal to proposal, there is no doubt that the FAP would increase the number of welfare recipients enormously. At the time of the Senate hearings, approximately 10 million persons were AFDC recipients. The FAP would increase the number eligible to 28 million (U.S. Congress, p. 254).[21] What was significant, however, was the regional distribution of new beneficiaries. By HEW estimates, the number of welfare recipients in high-benefit states like New York would increase by 30 to 50 percent, whereas welfare rolls in the low-benefit states of the South would rise by 250 percent to 400 percent (U.S. Congress 1970, pp. 981–4).

According to the original proposal, a family of four earning less than $3,000 would qualify for a FAP supplement (Moynihan 1973, p. 137). Slightly more than 53 percent of black male household heads, 82.5 percent of black female household heads with children under 18, and 37.7 percent of white female household heads with children under 18 had incomes below the poverty level ($2,970) in 1970 (U.S. Bureau of the Census 1970, Table 209).[22] Furthermore, none of the Southern states had AFDC-UI, so the FAP would not only extend welfare payments, it would have to grant them to males of working age. HEW estimates that 35 percent of the Mississippi population would be on welfare if FAP were implemented were modest at best (U.S. Congress, Chart 2). Overall, it was estimated that 52 percent of those covered by the FAP would be Southerners and that two-thirds of poor blacks in the South would receive some payment (Armstrong 1970, p. 67).

Not only did the FAP have the potential of raising wages of blacks in the South, it could totally undermine local labor markets. A black male head of a family of four in the urban Deep South working at minimum wage in factory work or manual labor would gain only $296 a year in income from the FAP plus $360 in food stamps, a modest improvement. A large share of the Southern black urban labor force was not working at minimum-wage jobs, but was only marginally employed. Two out of three black women workers in the South were employed in service jobs, mostly as maids at a median of $40 per week. Under the FAP, a service station attendant or a maid earning $40 a week as the head of a family of four would earn $3,408 a year, almost as much as a man working in a factory at minimum wage ($3,984) (Armstrong 1970, p. 152). Thus, the FAP would equalize earnings at the bottom of the wage scale between men and women, blacks and whites, and minimum- and nonminimum-wage workers (Herman 1970, p. 4).

Since the greatest determinant of benefits was family size, the FAP would double or triple household incomes. A family of four would receive a minimum of $2,350 through the FAP plus food stamps. The implications for rural blacks were even greater, for most rural blacks lived in large households.

The FAP undoubtedly would reduce the supply of low-wage labor in the South, particularly women. The FAP exempted any woman who had a preschool child, was over the age of 65, or had an unemployed husband, from the work registration requirement. According to an estimate of one Mississippi town, only two out of 18 maids would have to register to work in order to receive the full FAP payments (Armstrong 1970, p. 154). A number of small business associations in the South such as the

Restaurant Association registered their opposition to the FAP (Armstrong 1970, p. 152). As Georgia Representative Philip Landrum, who cast one of the three negative votes in the House Ways and Means Committee, declared, 'There's not going to be anybody left to roll these wheel-barrows and press these shirts' (Armstrong 1970, p. 68).

A steady stream of migrants from Southern farms kept wage levels low in Southern cities. Because of the high cost of living in urban areas, the FAP would provide a financial disincentive to leave a farm job for a city job at minimum wage. According to U.S. Department of Agriculture statistics, the typical Southern farm laborer in 1969 earned a median wage of $1,034. The FAP would triple his income with an additional $1,443 in FAP payments and $624 in food stamps.

The Empowerment of Southern Blacks

For more than a century, blacks had been excluded from welfare in the South because the welfare system was an instrument of social control, a part of the local racial caste system. Welfare caseloads in the Deep South averaged only 50 per 1,000 inhabitants compared to 125 in New York City, with blacks disproportionately excluded from welfare (Armstrong 1970, pp. 66, 151). In Mississippi, for example, 55 percent of the state's population was below the poverty level, but only 14 percent of those received any kind of assistance; less than 10 percent of Mississippians participated in the federal free lunch program (U.S. Congress, p. 1510). According to a U.S. Department of Agriculture estimate, 929,000 Alabamians in 1970 lacked the income necessary for a marginal diet, yet only 277,000 benefitted from USDA's food assistance programs (Salamon 1971, p. 18). As Robert Clark, the first black elected to the Mississippi legislature in almost 100 years, explained, 'Should you be able to walk or crawl, then you do not qualify for such programs' (U.S. Congress, p. 1510).

Evidence from HEW records demonstrates that the Southern welfare system was manipulated to provide planters with farm labor by support-ing field hands at federal expense during the winter and forcing them into the fields at low wages in the spring and summer (Salamon 1971, p. 18). Under the Work Incentive Program, 'welfare recipients are made to serve as maids or to do day yard work in white homes to keep their checks. During the cotton-picking season no one is accepted on welfare because plantations need cheap labor to do cottonpicking behind the cottonpicking machines' (U.S. Congress, p. 1511).

Although the Voting Rights Act of 1965 eliminated political barriers to voting by Southern blacks, economic barriers to political participation remained. By 1970, few blacks held political office. In only one of the 29 Mississippi black-majority counties did more than 50 percent of eligible black voters vote in county-wide elections between 1965 and 1970 (Salamon 1971, p. 17). Voting patterns in these counties show that the key to black voter turnout was not the amount of income but the source – counties with high black voter turnouts were those in which blacks were least directly dependent on whites for their livelihood. No other variables were 'as strongly or as consistently related to the differences between black and white voter registration rates as were the combined effects of the concentration of white farm owners and the black farm tenants and laborers who typically worked for white farm owners' (James 1988, p. 205). As the U.S. Commission on Civil Rights concluded in 1968, barriers to black political participation in the South could only be eliminated 'by eliminating the economic dependence of Southern Negroes upon white landlords, white employers, and white sources of credit-dependence which deters Negroes from voting freely and seeking political office' (Salamon 1971, p. 18).

Engaging in political activity threatened the welfare benefits received by black men and women. In the Deep South, blacks were systematically excluded from welfare for engaging in civil rights activities or registering to vote. County officials cut blacks off the welfare rolls, suspended commodity distributions, and warned that benefits would be restored only when blacks 'surrendered their uppity ideas about changing the local balance of power' (Salamon 1971, p. 18; U.S. Congress, p. 1512; Armstrong 1970, p. 66).

Redistributing income also redistributes political power. By reducing economic dependence on whites, the FAP would empower blacks and undermine the local economy. Southern blacks, both men and women, were the one class fraction that would benefit from the FAP because it would free them from the necessity to accept the lowest wage work.

The Defeat of the Family Assistance Plan

The Southern power elite was unwilling to relinquish existing political and economic arrangements. The most determined opponents of the FAP were Southern Democrats. In the Ways and Means Committee, five of the six Southern Congressmen opposed the FAP (Moynihan 1973, p. 257). Although the House passed the bill by an overwhelming majority,

79 of the 155 negative votes came from the 11 Southern states comprising the Deep South. Only 17 Southern Congressman voted for the FAP
(*Congressional Record* 1970, pp. 12105–6).

The South alone could not defeat the bill. Another source of opposition emerged from liberal Senators on the Senate Finance Committee
who were influenced by the vehement opposition of the National Welfare Rights Organization, which complained the FAP failed to address
their problems of inadequate income and exclusion from higher-paying
jobs. At the urging of the NWRO, liberal Senator Eugene McCarthy
(D-Minn.) scheduled an unofficial hearing on the FAP in the Senate
Office Building in November, 1970. At these hearings, NWRO members
testified against the FAP, which they feared would reduce their present
benefit levels (Burke and Burke 1974, p. 163), and demanded that minimum AFDC benefits be raised to $5,500, the average benefit in New
York. Their opposition helped coalesce the liberal position. In the Senate Finance Committee, three of the six 'liberal' Senators voted against
the original proposal, while a fourth abstained. The voiceless poor women
on welfare had mobilized their political resources to protest a program
that would reduce their economic security.

By 1972, the FAP had alienated a number of powerful constituents
whose support was necessary for welfare reform. Southern conservatives
and Northern liberals, urban welfare mothers and the Chamber of Commerce, all objective to the proposal. According to several interpretations,
Nixon withdrew his support, deciding 'that he would be wiser politically
to have an issue than an enacted plan' (Burke and Burke 1974, p. 185).

This analysis demonstrates the importance of considering the potential impact of social policy as a factor in the policy-formation process.
In the case of the FAP, those who believed the proposal was against
their interests lined up against it. Their combined opposition was more
powerful than the coalition of big business, organized labor, and state
bureaucrats who supported it. Coalition formation is not a unidimensional phenomenon, and the tendency of power resource theorists to
examine positive instances of political action ignores the potential of
coalition formation for policy defeats.

Conclusion

The defeat of Richard Nixon's proposal for a Family Assistance Plan
appears to contradict the predictions of three class-based arguments about
welfare state formation. All of the actors that the theories predict would

be required for a successful policy initiative – organized labor, big business, and state bureaucrats – supported a proposal for a guaranteed annual income for the working poor. Yet the debates surrounding the FAP and the events leading to its defeat were not framed primarily by issues of class struggle. Instead they were dominated by conflicts of race and gender within the context of such 'class' issues as labor force participation and social control.

While some evidence supports a mass turmoil thesis, this argument ignores the fact that the FAP was a response to policymakers' perceptions that the disintegration of the black family was responsible for the civil disorders of the 1960s. The result was not merely welfare expansion, as mass turmoil theory would predict, but welfare expansion centered around the reconstruction of the family.

Feminist theorists argue that welfare programs – initiated in a male-dominated state – maintain male dominance. Several features built into the FAP's operation confirm this view. First, the FAP attempted to eliminate the disincentives to family formation in the existing AFDC program (which in many states disallowed payments if a man resided in the house) by subsidizing the low-wage labor of black males and paying benefits to working-poor households. Second, because FAP benefits were based on family size, they promoted childbearing and encouraged women to leave the labor market and remain in the household to care for their children. Finally, benefits were calculated on family rather than individual income so that a woman's right to benefits depended on her husband's income. Beyond a certain point, additional earnings to the household (and most likely the woman's would be seen as supplementary, given the higher earning power of men) would reduce the family payment. In a variety of ways, then (except in the South), the FAP would increase the dependence of women on men.

According to power resources theory, civil rights are earned through worklife participation. The link between citizenship and worklife participation depends on the ability of social policy 'to modify the play of market forces' and free individuals from the cash nexus (Korpi 1989, p. 312; Esping-Andersen 1985, p. 228). Outside the South, the FAP had contradictory but non-empowering implications for black men and black women. It would have locked them into jobs with the greatest market pressure and the fewest opportunities for occupational mobility. Black men might gain authority in the household, increasing their gender power, but they would remain subservient to white males in the labor market.

The impact of the FAP in the South compared to the rest of the nation demonstrates the need for historically specific analyses rather than universal generalizations. As the plantation economy declined, the South developed around a low-wage industry and service economy that relied heavily on black labor. While the FAP might operate like a negative income tax in the North, it would have enormous consequences for the local labor supply in the South. The FAP benefits would have been so high relative to existing wage levels that they would reduce the power of the market over Southern blacks and allow them to refuse low-wage work. By empowering blacks economically, the FAP would empower them politically. Direct federal funds would expand the limited citizenship rights of Southern blacks and undermine the Southern racial state.

What happens to class solidarity in a liberal welfare state? Power resource theorists suggest that dualism in social benefits is both a cause and a consequence of class fragmentation. Fragmentation stems partly from the resistance of actors in favorable market positions to attempts to redistribute resources to those in weak market positions. In the U.S., protected workers are white males, whereas women and blacks are in weak market positions. These lines of cleavage are a powerful disincentive to alliance formation. By highlighting the identity of challengers to the polity, a labor force divided by race and sex reinforces the exclusionary tendencies of unionized workers.

Varying definitions of the social policy agenda also reduce possibilities for class solidarity. The agenda of those involved in social protest – access to high wage employment, demands for higher welfare benefits – placed them in direct confrontation with organized labor, which wanted to preserve market privilege and prevent the drift of low-wage workers into the skilled trades through benefits that subsidized low wages.

Finally, the political resources available to each class fraction formed an impediment to class solidarity. Power resources theorists emphasize institutional routes to power (for organized labor) but have paid little attention to the noninstitutional avenues of power (in this case, for poor women and blacks). State managers, large employers, and organized labor, who have greatest access to the polity, addressed the FAP through the formal mechanisms of political participation. The black underclass was outside of the political system of electoral politics – insurgency and protest were its main political resources. The different avenues of political expression of each class fraction prevented an alliance, not only because there was no common meeting ground, but because the tactics (and costs) of insurgency alienated organized workers.

The dominant arguments regarding the development of the welfare state stem from a political class struggle perspective in which the primary actors are labor and capital. Within this paradigm, welfare states arise in response to differing historical problems of production. Welfare programs mediate relations not only between classes but between politically dominant and politically repressed groups, as demonstrated by the failure of these theories to explain the defeat of the Family Assistance Plan. Because gender- and race-neutral policy involves the redistribution of status and social power, its enactment depends on women and blacks becoming actors in the political process, not objects of policies made by white males.

The analysis sustains feminist arguments that social policy may be used to increase female dependence, but it also suggests that under certain historical conditions (those that existed in the South, for example) social policy may enhance gender and racial equality. If economic power gained through redistributive measures from the state creates political opportunities for the excluded, then social policy becomes a liberating force.

Notes

Support for this research was provided by a grant from the National Science Foundation. I would like to thank John Goldthorpe, Gunhild Hagestad, Larry Isaac, Fred Pampel, Richard Rubinson, Charles Tolbert, Theda Skocpol, Frances Fox Piven, John Myles, Mustafa Embirbayer, Katherine Ragsdale, Leland Neuberg and numerous ASR reviewers for comments on this paper. I also appreciate both the comments and the extensive library work of Madonna Harrington Meyer.

This paper was presented at the annual meeting of the American Sociological Association, San Francisco, August, 1989, and the conference on 'The Welfare State in Transition,' Bergen, Norway, August 1989.

1 Mildred and Claude Pepper Library, RG 309B, Box 56, File 7. 'The Bill to Revamp the Welfare System,' Legislative Analysis, American Enterprise Institute, April 6, 1970, Analysis No. 4.

2 Women's average old age insurance benefits are about two-thirds of the male average (Estes, Gerard, and Clarke 1986, p. 546). Because of their lower wages, women who do receive unemployment benefits get less than men (Pearce 1986, p. 158).

3 Federal Archives and Records Center, Dept. of Health, Education and Welfare, Secretary's Correspondence Files, (hereafter FARC), RG 235, Box

3, 'Periods of Eligibility for Day Care,' HEW memo, Dec. 29, 1970; 'Day Care Planners,' HEW memo, April 2, 1970.

4 FARC, RG 235, Box 2. Prepared testimony of the Secretary of Health, Education and Welfare Before the Committee on Finance, July 21, 1970, p. 4. AFDC-UI paid benefits to unemployed fathers.

5 FARC, RG 235, Box. 2, Letter from Elliot Richardson to Tom Vail, July 8, 1970, p. 3.

6 FARC, RG 235, Box 1, 'Suggested Modification in H.R. 1. 'Paper prepared by the Office of Equal Opportunity for HEW Secretary Elliot Richardson, August 6, 1971. Tables prepared by HEW on the estimated impact of the FAP also emphasized male employment. See 'What a Working Man Must Earn to Be as Well Off as a Welfare Family.'

7 FARC, RG 235, Box 1, Internal HEW Memo from Jim Edwards to John Montogmery, Sept. 22, 1971.

8 FARC, RG 235, Box 2, 'Issue Memo Re Departmental Jurisdiction for Payment of FAP Benefits to Families,' March 18, 1971, p. 3.

9 Despite Nixon's promise in his speech on welfare reform, when the FAP was revised to meet Senate Finance Committee objections, a loss in welfare benefits to those residing in high-payment states would have occurred (U.S. Congress, p. 340).

10 FARC, RG 236, Box 2. Memo from Director of Welfare Reform Planning, Letter of Commendation to Mr. A.L. Roy Bolton, Nov. 19, 1971.

11 FARC, RG 235, Box 1, Internal Memo, Dept. of HEW, August 18, 1971: Report of our efforts to determine the positions of state and local Chambers of Commerce on proposed welfare reform legislation. See also 'The Great Welfare Debate,' Nation's Business, April, 1970, pp. 56–9.

12 See 'Here Come the Girls,' Nation's Business, December, 1969, pp. 38–41.

13 FARC, RG 235, Box 2. Excerpt from Washington Report newsletter, p. 5.

14 FARC, RG 235, Box 2. Testimony of Robert Finch before the Committee on Finance, U.S. Senate, July 21, 1970, reprint, p. 5.

15 George Meany Memorial Archives, Silver Spring Maryland, Legislative Reference Files (LRF), Box 25, File 62, 'The Negative Income Tax Dilemma, Welfare Reform and Possible Alternatives,' p. 2.

16 Meany Archives, LRF, Box 25, File 62, 'The Negative Income Tax Dilemma,' p. 4.

17 Meany Archives, LRF, Box 55, Files 22–26; Box 6, Files 19–20.

18 Meany Archives, LRF, Box 25, Files 62, 'The Negative Income Tax Dilemma,' p. 2. High cost was mentioned as one of the program dilemmas.

19 Meany Archives, LRF, Box 25, File 62, 'The Negative Income Tax Dilemma,' p. 7.

20 FARC, RG 235, Box 2, John F. Kain and Robert Schafer, 'Regional Impacts
    of the Family Assistance Plan.' Office of Economic Research, Department of
    Commerce, 1971, p. 24.
21 Estimates of the cost and coverage of the FAP were continually revised as
    changes were made in the bill or better data became available.
22 For white male household heads in Mississippi, the poverty rate was 8.1
    percent (U.S. Census 1970, Table 209).

References

Acker, Joan. 1988 'Class, Gender, and the Relations of Distribution,' *Signs*
    13: 473–97.
Armstrong, Richard. 1970. 'The Looming Money Revolution Down South.'
    Fortune, 66–9, 151–9.
Barnard, John. 1983. *Walter Reuther and the Rise of the Auto Workers.* Boston:
    Little, Brown.
Block, Fred. 1977. 'The Ruling Class Does Not Rule: Notes on the Marxist
    Theory of the State.' *Socialist Revolution* 33: 6–28.
Bolton, A.L. Jr. 1971. 'Plain Talk on Welfare Reform.' *NAM Reports* 23: 12–13.
Bonacich, Edna. 1972. 'A Theory of Ethnic Antagonism: The Split Labor
    Market.' *American Sociological Review* 37: 547–59.
Burch, Phil. 1973. 'The NAM as an Interest Group.' *Politics and Society*
    4: 97–130.
Burke, Vincent J. and Vee Burke. 1974. *Nixon's Good Deed.* New York: Columbia
    University Press.
Congressional Record. 1970. April 16, House. Washington, D.C.: U.S. Government
    Printing Office.
Converse, Philip, Warren Miller, Jerrold Rusk, and Arthur Wolfe. 1969.
    'Continuity and Change in American Politics: Parties and Issues in the 1968
    Election.' *American Political Science Review* 63: 1083–1105.
Dale, Jennifer and Peggy Foster. 1986. *Feminists and State Welfare.* London:
    Routledge and Kegan Paul.
Davis, Archie K. 1971. 'Welfare Reform, Time to Do It Right.' *Vital Speeches of the
    Day* 37: 765–8.
Davis, Mike. 1986. *Prisoners of the American Dream.* London: New Left Books.
Esping-Andersen, Gøsta. 1985. 'Power and Distributional Regimes.' *Politics and
    Society* 14: 223–56.
– 1989. 'The Three Political Economies of the Welfare State.' *Canadian Review
    of Sociology and Anthropology* 26: 10–36.

Esping-Andersen, Gøsta, and Roger Friedland. 1982. 'Class Coalitions in the Making of West European Economies.' *Political Power and Social Theory* 3: 1–52.

Estes, Carroll, Lenore Gerard, and Adele Clarke. 1986. 'Women and the Economics of Aging.' Pp. 546–62 in *Growing Old in America*, edited by Beth Hess. New Brunswick, N.J.: Transaction Books.

Federal Archives and Records Center, Dept. of Health, Education and Welfare, RG 235, Secretary's Correspondence Files, Boxes 1–3. Suitland, Maryland.

Form, William. 1985. *Divided We Stand.* Urbana, IL: University of Illinois Press.

Griffin, Larry, Joel Devine, and Michael Wallace. 1983. 'On the Economic and Political Determinants of Welfare Spending in the Post-World War II Era.' *Politics and Society* 12: 331–72.

Herman, Tom. 1970. 'Welfare Reform: The Southern View.' *Wall Street Journal,* December 15, p. 4.

Hernes, Helga. 1987. *Welfare State and Women Power.* Oslo: Norwegian University Press.

Hicks, Alexander, Roger Friedland, and Edwin Johnson. 1978. 'Class Power and State Policy: The Case of Large Business Corporation, Labor Unions and Governmental Redistribution in the American States.' *American Sociological Review* 43: 302–17.

Hicks, Alexander, and Duane Swank. 1983. 'Civil Disorder, Relief Mobilization, and AFDC Caseloads: A Re-examination of the Piven and Cloward Thesis.' *American Journal of Sociology* 27: 695–716.

Isaac, Larry, and William Kelly. 1981. 'Racial Insurgency, the State and Welfare Expansion: Local and National Level Evidence from the Postwar United States.' *American Journal of Sociology* 86: 1348–86.

– 1982. 'Developmental/Modernization and Political Class Struggle Theories of Welfare Expansion: The Case of the AFDC "Explosion" in the States, 1960–1970.' *Journal of Political and Military Sociology* 10: 201–35.

James, David. 1988. 'The Transformation of the Southern Racial State: Class and Race Determinants of Local-State Structures.' *American Sociological Review* 53: 191–208.

Jenson, Jane. 1986. 'Gender and Reproduction: Or, Babies and the State.' *Studies in Political Economy* 20: 9–46.

Korpi, Walter. 1989. 'Power, Politics and State Autonomy in the Development of Social Citizenship: Social Rights during Sickness in Eighteen OECD Countries since 1930.' *American Sociological Review* 54: 309–28.

McAdam, Douglas. 1982. *Political Process and the Development of Black Insurgency, 1930–1970.* Chicago: University of Chicago Press.

Meany, George. Memorial Archives. Silver Spring, Maryland. Legislative Reference Files, Boxes 25, 65.

Moynihan, Daniel Patrick. 1965. *The Negro Family: The Case for National Action.*
  United States Department of Labor: Office of Policy Planning and Research.
– 1973. *The Politics of a Guaranteed Income: The Nixon Administration and the Family
  Assistance Plan.* New York: Random House.
Myles, John. 1989. 'Introduction: Understanding Canada: Comparative Political
  Economy.' *Canadian Review of Sociology and Anthropology* 26: 1–9.
National Advisory Commission on Civil Disorders. 1968. *Report.* New York:
  E. P. Dutton.
Nixon, Richard M. 1969. 'Welfare Reform, Shared Responsibility.' *Vital Speeches
  of the Day* 35: 674–8.
Pascal, Gillian. 1986. *Social Policy, A Feminist Analysis.* London: Tavistock.
Patterson, James. 1986. *American's Struggle against Poverty, 1900–1986.* Cambridge,
  MA: Harvard University Press.
Pearce, Diana. 1986. 'Toil and Trouble: Women Workers and Unemployment
  Compensation.' Pp. 141–62 in *Women and Poverty,* edited by Barbara Gelpi,
  Nancy Hartsock, Clare Novak, and Myra Strober. Chicago: University of
  Chicago Press.
Pepper, Mildred and Claude Library. Ways and Means Committee. RG 309B,
  Florida State University, Tallahassee, Florida.
Piven, Frances Fox, and Richard Cloward. 1971. *Regulation the Poor: The Functions
  of Public Welfare.* New York: Random House.
– 1979. *Poor People's Movements: Why They Succeed, How They Fail.* New York:
  Random House.
Quadagno, Jill. 1984. 'Welfare Capitalism and the Social Security Act of 1935.'
  American Sociological Review 49: 632–47.
– 1988a. *The Transformation of Old Age Security: Class and Politics in the American
  Welfare State.* Chicago: University of Chicago Press.
– 1988b. 'Women's Access to Pensions and the Structure of Eligibility
  Rules: Systems of Production and Reproduction.' *Sociological Quarterly* 29:
  541–58.
Rainwater, Lee, and William Yancey. 1967. *The Moynihan Report and the Politics
  of Controversy.* Cambridge, MA.: The Massachusetts Institute of Technology
  Press.
Rodgers, Harrell R. Jr. 1982. *The Cost of Human Neglect, America's Welfare Failure.*
  Armonk, NY: M.E. Sharpe.
Ruggie, Mary. 1984. *The State and Working Women.* Princeton, N.J.: Princeton
  University Press.
Salamon, Lester M. 1971. 'The Stakes in the Rural South,' *The New Republic:*
  17–18.
Schultz, George P. 1970. 'The Nixon Welfare Plan.' *New Generation,* 3–9.

Shaver, Sheila. 1983. 'Sex and Money in the Welfare State.' Pp. 146–63 in *Women, Social Welfare and the State in Australia*, edited by C.V. Baldcock and B. Cass. Sydney: Allen and Unwin.

– 1989. 'Social Policy Regimes: Gender, Race and the Welfare State.' Paper presented at the conference on 'Women and the Welfare State,' University of Wisconsin, Madison.

Stephens, John D. 1979. *The Transition from Capitalism to Socialism.* Urbana: University of Illinois Press.

U.S. Bureau of the Census. 1970. *Census of Population.* Washington, D.C.: U.S. Government Printing Office.

U.S. Congress, Senate, Committee on Finance. 1970. *Hearings on H.R. 16311.* Washington, D.C.: U.S. Government Printing Office.

10

Labour-Market Institutions
and Working-Class Strength

BO ROTHSTEIN

The central question in this essay is simple yet important: Why are some working classes more organized that others? This phenomenon has since World War II shown increased variation among Western capitalist countries (von Beyme 1980; Wallerstein 1989). The latest figures show that unionization among these countries ranges from below 15 per cent in France to 8 per cent in Sweden (see table 1). Among industrialized Western states hardly any other political variables of this kind vary to such an extent. In this essay I will equate degree of unionization with working-class strength. It can of course be argued that working-class strength is also dependent on other variables such as party organization and cultural homogeneity. But following Marxist theory, unionization may be seen as the primary organization form of the working class and can thus be considered a basis for other forms of working-class strength, such as political and cultural organization (Olofsson 1979; Offe and Wiesenthal 1980).[1]

The importance of the level of working-class organizational strength stems, inter alia, from the established positive correlation between union strength and the development of welfare-state policies. One can say that, with few exceptions, the stronger is the organization of the working class, the more developed the welfare state (Korpi 1983; Shalev 1983a, b; Amenta and Skocpol 1986; Noble 1988). But, critically, this correlation does not in itself show how the causal link between social policies and working-class formation operates. It does not show, that is, which of the two variables explains the other or in what way they are interconnected (Esping-Andersen 1985; Przeworski 1985; Skocpol 1988).

How can this great variation in workers' inclination to join unions be explained? A traditional interpretation of Marxist theory (such as that of

Cohen 1978) would explain it as due to differences in the development of the productive forces. But it is obvious that this cannot explain why Swedish workers are almost six times more organized than their French colleagues. Even if Sweden technologically is a well-developed country, France, and for that matter Japan and the United States, are not such laggards. A traditional interpretation of Marxist theory that seeks to reduce political factors to the level of economic development obviously cannot help us here (von Beyme 1980: 73–84). Nor can the timing and pace of industrialization – that is, the formation of the working class *an sich* – explain the variation in unionization. Nor does it seems convincing to point to such variables as cultural factors or social norms (Elster 1989). If union membership reflects the norm – for example, of solidarity among workers – then we still need to know why some working classes are more inclined to the norm of collective action than others. For instance, two countries that may be said, without any deeper analysis, to be culturally and socially rather similar, such as Belgium and the Netherlands, differ dramatically in degree of unionization (74 per cent and 29 per cent, respectively). The same, albeit to a lesser degree, goes for such very similar countries as Sweden and Norway (86 per cent and 58 per cent respectively). Obviously, we have to look for some kind of independent variable(s) *between* socioeconomic structure and social norms.

The following section discusses theoretically the kinds of variables that can be expected to explain differences in the degree of unionization – that is, working-class strength – among Western capitalist countries. A comparative quantitative description and statistical analysis of these variables follows. Then, in order to illuminate the causal logic of the statistical analysis, a brief historical comparative overview is presented. Finally, for reasons that will be obvious, a more detailed analysis of the Swedish case is undertaken.

Institutional Factors and Working-Class Organizational Strength

The theoretical point of departure here is that differences in unionization can to a large extent be explained by historical variation in national *political institutions*. Arguing that political institutions are important is of course not new; indeed it has been a commonplace theme in political science from Aristotle through Tocqueville and beyond (see March and Olsen 1984; Steinmo 1989). Yet there is a fresh insight in what has been called 'new institutionalism,' namely, the treatment of political institutions as important *independent* variables in explaining political behavior and social change (Douglas 1987; Thelen and Steinmo, 1992). As against social and economic structures (such as the productive forces), political institutions are entities that might once have been deliberately created by rational, goal-oriented, political agents (Levi 1990; Tsebelis 1990: 9–11, 96f). While political institutions may be understood as setting limits on, as well as enabling, agents in the pursuit of their objectives (Giddens 1979), they can, because of their general 'stickiness,' be seen also as political and administrative *structures* (Shepsle 1989). This takes us right into one of the basic questions in social science and history, namely, whether agency or structure is primary in causing social change (Mouzelis 1988; Cerny 1990). If institutions set limits on what some agents can do, and enable other agents to do things they otherwise would not have been able to do, then we need to know under what circumstances these institutions were created. For if political agents can design or construct institutions, they may then construe an advantage in future political battles (Knight 1988: 25; Levi 1990).

If we can empirically identify such moments of institutional creation in history, then we will have moved much closer to understanding the agency – structure, micro–macro problem in social science. The analysis of the creation and destruction of political institutions might thus serve as a bridge between the 'men who make history' and the 'circumstances' under which they are able to do so. Thus my theoretical object in this essay is not restricted to showing that institutions are important in shaping political behavior but that, at certain *formative moments* in history, these institutions are created with the object of giving the agent (or the interests the agent wants to further) an advantage in the future game of power. I agree with Tsebelis's argument (1990: 96–100) that the choice of institutions is the sophisticated equivalent of selecting policies. I am, however, less confident than he or other rational choice theorists that their approach can be used to explain why some actors are better suited than others in choosing institutions that maximize their future goals, or for that matter why some actors have goals different from others.

Pointing to the relation between public policies or institutions and working-class formation (or deformation) is not of course unique (see Esping-Andersen 1985; Korpi 1985: 38; Przeworski 1985; Skocpol 1988). However, two problems are left unsolved in the literature relating public policy and institutions to class formation. First, as the number of political institutions and public policies is very great, one needs some sort of theory distinguishing the political institutions that are more decisive then others in influencing working-class formation. To point to public policy or government institutions in general is not very helpful. In other words, we need a theory that explains why some games (or their structuring) are more important than others. Second, one needs to show exactly how differences in the operation of these government institutions affect workers' inclination to join in collective action. By 'exactly' I mean that one must specify the way in which the operational logic of a government institution changes the rationality (or ordering of preferences) of agents when deciding how to act. This is thus a *methologocial* request for a 'microfoundation' of institutional or structural analysis but without any hard-nosed *theoretical* restriction to methodological individualism (Callinicos 1989). Such an approach might bridge the gap between rational choice and historical approaches to institutional analysis (see Thelen and Steinmo 1992).

As a solution to the problem of deciding which political institutions are important to study in this matter, I will argue that the organizational strength of a social class is based in its position in the *relations of production*. The latter are, however, not to be seen as a mere reflection of the productive forces but as having an explanatory force of their own (Callinicos 1989). By this I mean that while in every capitalist society, the relations of production contain capitalists and wage-workers involved in a special sort of uneven economic exchange, this is nonetheless not the whole story. It is not the whole story because the power of workers and capatalists, respectively, in the relations of production differs greatly between different capitalist societies operating more or less at the same stage of the development of the productive forces (Korpi 1983; Wright 1985: 123f). In some capitalist democracies workers have been able to organize themselves to a large extent and thus confront the capitalists on a more intense and equal level than in other such countries.

Logically, if we wish to explain these differences from a Marxist standpoint, we should concentrate on *political institutions directly affecting the relations of production*. In common language this means labor-market institutions or policy taken in a broad sense, including such things as rules governing the right of labor to organize and take collective action against capitalists, unemployment policies, training programs. The argument is that of all the games to be played, this is the most important one in the explanation of working-class organizational strength. This also involves a shift of focus for Marxist social analysis from the economic to the political and organizational spheres, which implies that we should be looking at how organized class interests invest power resources when shaping and creating political institutions on the labor market (Korpi 1983: 19). Marxists have sometimes argued that the only social structures that matter are the purely economic ones. Because such structures by definition are not deliberately created, but rather result from the evolutionary logic of economic and technological development (Cohen 1978), focusing solely on such structures has imparted to Marxist social science a flaw of structural determinism (Elster 1985). The rational choice variant of this involves seeing institutions solely as resulting from evolutionary processes rather than deliberate creation. Following Nicos Mouzelis (1984, 1988) I argue here that political institutions, such as bureaucracies, armies, and the complex of legal regulations, can be as constraining for agents as economic structures. If it can be shown that more or less *deliberately created* political institutions exist on the labor market that affect class formation and class organization, then we can escape the structural-determinist trap in Marxist (and other kinds of) social science (Callinicos 1989; Cernyy 1990).

Explaining Unionization

According to Mancur Olson (1965), workers would not join unions if acting out of individual rationality, because the benefits unions provide are collective goods. Rationally acting workers would choose to become 'free-riders' – that is, to collect the benefits from the organization without contributing to the costs of reproducing it. The fact that workers historically have joined unions, sometimes on a rather large scale, Olson explains by showing that unions have been able to create *selective incentives* that lie outside their main purpose of collective bargaining. If Olson's theory is correct, then we need to know two things. First, why are unions in some countries more successful than others in creating these selective incentives? Since the degree of unionization differs to a very great extent between similar countries, it would seem that the creation of such selective incentives must be done on a nationwide scale. Second, if it is in their rational interest to create such incentives, and if the theory of rational choice is all that is needed to explain political behavior, then why are some working classes more rational than others?

Many objections have been made to Olson's famous theory about collective action, but it is fair to say that it is still at the center of efforts to explain problems of collective action. One telling criticism of Olson's theory, however, is that he neglects the uniqueness of labor power as a commodity in that it is inseparable from its individual bearer. Unions, therefore, unlike organizations of capitalists, have good reason to take the *individual* well-being of their members into account (Offe and Wiesenthal 1980). Thus, when there is no further demand for an individual worker's labor power on the labor market, there is a cost to the union if it simply abandons him or her. This is so because the main power resource unions possess is their control over the supply of labor power. If unions abandon workers when the demand for their labor power declines, the workers, now deprived of their means of existence, will be liable to start underbidding the union-set price for labor power. This leads to a situation in which capitalists are able to get labor power at a price below that which the unions have decided upon, which is to say the unions no longer control the supply of labor power. There is simply no greater threat to union strength or working-class mobilization, than this (Unga 1986; Åmark 1986; Wallerstein 1989: 484f).

If the preceding line of reasoning is correct, the searchlight in our quest for important institutions should be directed at government institutions and policies influencing unions' prospects of maintaining their control over the supply of labor power. This can be done in several ways, such as by a 'closed shop,' but one of the most common is the institutionalization of public unemployment-insurance systems. Public unemployment insurance is a direct way for governments to intervene in the labor market by supporting that portion of the labor power for which there is presently no demand. Unemployment insurance is more important in this matter than are other government social policies such as sickness, disability, and old-age insurance, because workers in any of these latter three circumstances do not usually have the possibility to start underbidding wages. Thus, in contrast to the direct link between unemployment policy and the power situation in the relations of production, social policy in general has only indirect effects, if any, on the relations of production (see Przeworski 1985).

Many analysts of labor relations have hitherto tried to explain variations in unionization (von Beyme 1980; Kjellberg 1983). Strange as it may seem, differences in government labor-market institutions have usually not been taken into account. It has recently been shown that neither the traditional business-cycle thesis, nor theories based on differences in dependency on international trade, can explain variations in unionization (Wallerstein 1989). Instead, a structural factor, the size of the national labor force, is reported to be strongly but negatively correlated to degree of unionization. The argument behind this is that the larger the number of potentially recruitable wage-earners, the more difficult and expensive the process of recruitment (Wallerstein 1989).

There are, however, a few problems with treating this correlation as an explanation. One is that it is not the national central union organization, if it exists at all, that recruits members, but rather the local, more or less branch-specific, union. Why costs for recruitment should increase with the size of the *national* labor force is thus not clear. The other problem is why there could be no such thing as a diminishing marginal cost in organizing workers. Size is certainly statistically significant, but, as will be shown subsequently, there are countries with practically the same number of wage-earners in the labor market that differ considerably in unionization (for example, Belgium and the Netherlands). The evident conclusion is that, however important, the size of the labor force can be overcome as an organizational problem by some working classes.

Second, it has been shown that the political color of governments is important in explaining national differences in the degree of unionization (Kjellberg 1983; Wallerstein 1989). The more frequent and the longer the periods of left-party government, the higher the degree of unionization. The problem with this explanation is that it is not clear which of these two variables explains the other. Having a large number of workers organized in unions is evidently an important resource for labor parties competing in national elections, and that once in government, labor parties can launch labor-market laws that facilitate unionization. But one might also claim that union strength is sometimes detrimental to the stability of labor governments, as in the British 'winter of discontent' 1978–9.

It is however, reasonable to think of the relation between level of unionization and degree of left-party government as dialectical. Theda Skocpol, for example, has argued against the existence of any unidimensional causality between working-class strength and left-party government or the development of social policies. Instead, she argues that the social policies launched in some European countries during the 1930s, such as Sweden, furthered working-class strength and that the causal link between the two variables is to be understood as a continuous 'positive loop' (Skocpol 1988:9; compare Weir and Skocpol 1985). But even if we accept the hypothesis that these two variables are interdependent, we need to know how this relationship works; that is, we need a microfoundation of how, exactly, left-party government promotes unionization. In what ways can, for example, government labor-market institutions change workers' preferences as to whether or not to join unions? It has been argued that, compared to other countries, labor-market legislation in the United States imposes comparatively high costs for unions in their efforts to organize labor (Goldfield 1987). Another example is former West Germany, where the Supreme Court ruled out the legal possibility of the Budestag passing any law that gives privileges to workers on account of their being union members (Streeck 1981). Another example is of course the fate of the British trade unions during the 1980s.

In Sweden, on the other hand, almost all legal entitlements that wage-earners possess concerning their position in the relations of production (and they are many) have been granted them in their capacity as union members – have been granted, that is, to their unions (Schmidt 1977). I would argue that, while the choice of whether or not to join a union is a free choice, the rationality in the decision can be severely affected by the operation of government labor-market institutions. If this is so, then we cannot understand national differences in unionization solely by using some sort of rational-choice or game-theoretic approach, because we need to know how preferences were established in the first place, and in what way and by whom the game of collective action has been structured. When we know all this, rational choice and game theory can be used as an analytical tool to understand the outcome (Berger and Offe 1982; Grafstein 1988; compare Bianco and Bates 1990; Tsebelis 1990).

Walter Korpi has argued that the high degree of unionization in Sweden should not be attributed to that country's having developed some form of corporatist political system, which essentially forces wage-earners to join unions, but rather arises from workers' self-interest in collective action (Korpi 1983: 7–25). But why then do workers in capitalist countries have such different interests in furthering their own interests by collective action? Obviously, this problem cannot be solved without discussing what causes this variation in the formation of workers' preferences as to whether or not to join unions. This is where institutionalist analysis comes in because, contrary to rational choice and game theory, institutions to a large extent explain preference formation, the ordering of preferences, and the number as well as the resources of the player (March and Olsen 1984: 739; Douglas 1987). I contend that the explanation of the variation in degree of unionization to a great extent lies in the variation of the operational logic of the national public unemployment schemes.

Comparing Public Unemployment Schemes

All major industrialized Western countries introduced some form of public or publicly supported unemployment-insurance system before World War II. These schemes took two different institutional forms: (1) as a compulsory system administered by government agencies and, (2) as a voluntary but publicly supported scheme administered by unions or union-dominated funds. The latter system is also called the Ghent system, after the Belgium town in which it was established in 1901.

In order to understand the difference in operational logic between these systems, it is necessary to examine briefly the *mode of administration* of insurance against such a thing as unemployment. One of the major problems in designing an unemployment scheme is how to identify that part of the nonworking population that should be entitled to support. This cannot be done in a simple way using precise rules defined in laws such as those regarding pensions or child allowances. First of all, people not belonging to the labor force must be excluded. It is always difficult to decide if a person really is part of the supply to the labor market. Second, workers are not just unemployed in general, they are *as individuals* unable to find work at a certain place and time, within a certain trade, and at a certain level of payment. It is thus often the case that an unemployed worker can find a job if he or she is willing to move, to take a job outside his or her trade or below his or her qualifications, or to accept a job at a lower level of payment. Therefore, the paramount question in the implementation of an unemployment-insurance scheme is to decide what kind of job an unemployed worker cannot refuse without losing the insurance benefit. In the literature about unemployment insurance, this is known as the problem of defining 'the suitable job' (Lester 1965; Erici and Roth 1981). In contrast to the case with capital, there is no such thing as labor power in general, as each and every unit of labor power is physically attached to an individual human being with unique characteristics (Rothstein 1990).

This means that what constitutes a suitable job must be decided for each and every individual seeking support from the insurance scheme. This can be done only by granting a considerable measure of discretion to the 'street-level bureaucrats' that are necessary to manage the scheme (see Lipsky 1980). As can easily be imagined, these questions are very delicate, and who has the power to decide them is a matter of paramount importance for both unions and workers. The unemployed worker does not wish to be forced to take a job that he or she, for some reason, finds unsuitable. This need not of course be due to idleness. Indeed both the society's and the individual's interest may require that the un- employed worker resist accepting any job immediately available, if for instance it would cause serious damage to his or her skills or impose large social costs (if moving is necessary, for example). To wait for a suitable job instead of taking any available job is thus in many cases perfectly rational from both an individual and a social standpoint. On the other hand, if suitable jobs are available, unemployed workers are expected to leave the dole queue and accept them.

From a union perspective, the critical task is to ensure that workers are not forced to accept jobs at wages below the union-set level, because unions then lose control of the supply of labor power (Unga 1976). When unions started setting up their own unemployment funds in the nineteenth century, benefits were primarily seen as a way to prevent unemployed workers from underbidding the union wage rates; relieving distress came second (Harris 1972: 297; Edebalk 1975).

Given our concern with institutional power, the paramount question is: Who shall be given the power to decide the question of suitable jobs in general, as well as in individual cases? It is obviously not enough for the union movement to influence the enactment of the general rules governing the scheme, because the critical issues are necessarily decided in the course of applying rules to each specific case (see Lipsky 1980).

In the case of the Ghent system, the unemployment insurance is ad- ministered by the unions or by union-run unemployment funds; and it is thus union officials who possess institutional power in the implementa- tion of the unemployment scheme. Usually this insurance is tied to union membership – that is, all union members must also be members of the insurance system – but it is possible, de jure, to be a member of the insurance scheme without being a member of a union. In a compulsory system, it is typically government officials who have the aforementioned institutional power, and union membership has nothing to do with en- titlement to unemployment insurance.

Others have frequently argued that in order to enhance the working class's political strength, public policies should provide universal entitle- ments and avoid individual means tests and voluntary insurance schemes based on principles of 'self-help' (Esping-Andersen and Korpi 1984; Esping-Andersen 1985: 33). The Ghent system in unemployment insur- ance, however, is clearly based on these principles. We should therefore expect countries with a Ghent system to have a low degree of unioniza- tion. But as shown in table 1, the facts are exactly the opposite.

TABLE 1
Union Density, Potential Union Membership, Left-Party Participation in Government and
the Public Unemployment Insurance System

Country	Union density (%)	Potential membership (thousands)	Left government	Ghent system
Sweden	86	3,931	111.84	Yes
Denmark	83	2,225	90.24	Yes
Finland	80	2,034	59.33	Yes
Iceland	74	81	17.25	Yes
Belgium	74	3,348	43.25	Yes[a]
Ireland	68	886	0.00	No
Norway	58	1,657	83.08	No
Austria	57	2,469	48.67	No
Australia	51	5,436	33.75	No
United Kingdom	43	25,757	43.67	No
Canada	38	10,516	0.00	No
Italy	36	15,819	0.00	No
Switzerland	34	2,460	11.87	No
Germany (West)	31	23,003	35.33	No
Netherlands	29	4,509	31.50	No
Japan	28	39,903	1.92	No
USA	18	92,899	0.00	No
France	15	18,846	8.67	No

[a] Belgium has a mixed system of compulsory insurance but union participation in the
administration (Flora 1987:776).

Sources: Union density – definition in Kjellberg 1983, figures from Kjellberg 1988 (figures
for 1985 or 1986) except Australia, Iceland, and Ireland that are taken from Wallerstein
1989 (figures for 1979, 1975, and 1978, respectively). System of public unemployment
insurance – Flora 1987 and Kjellberg 1983 except Australia (Castles 1985: ch. 3) and
Iceland (Nordiska Rådets Utredningar 1984: 10: 220). Potential membership – figures
from Wallerstein 1989. The measure is the sum of the number of wage and salary earners
and the unemployed. Index of left government – Wilensky 1981 (quoted in Wallerstein
1989). The index includes all Communist, Socialist, Social Democratic, and Labor parties
except the Italian Socialist and Social Democratic parties in the period from 1919 to 1979.
Sample – all industrialized countries where unions have been free to organize since 1945,
except Luxembourg, New Zealand, excluded because it has compulsory union membership (Davidson 1989: ch. 6), and Israel, excluded because its main union is also one of the
country's largest employers.

As can be seen from table 1, the five countries with the highest degree
of unionization all have the same public unemployment-insurance scheme,
the Ghent system, while all the other countries have some type of compulsory system. Hence it seems reasonable to conclude that institutional

power in the administration of government labor-market institutions is important in determining union density, or working-class strength. This is because with a Ghent system: (1) unions can make it difficult for non-union members to obtain the insurance; (2) unions control, or greatly influence, the determination of what constitutes a suitable job; and (3) unions can, by controlling the scheme, increase their control over the supply of labor power. Table 1 also lists an index of left-party participation in government and number of potential union members, because these two variables have, as stated earlier, been shown to be strongly correlated with union density (Wallerstein 1989). In order to compare the relative strength of these three variables, a multivariate regression analysis is presented in table 2.

Table 2 shows that all three variables have an independent explanatory effect of about the same standardized size. Together they explain 82% of the variation in union density. Controlling for the variables measuring left-party participation in government and size of the labor force, the Ghent system makes a difference of about 20 percent in union density.[2] Taking the 'visual' result from table 1 into consideration, we can say that it is possible to have a fairly strong union movement without a Ghent system, but that in order to have really strong unions, such a

TABLE 2
Cross-National Differences in Union Density as a Function of Unemployment-Insurance Scheme (GHENT), Left-Party Government (LEFT), and (Natural log of) Potential Union Membership (SIZE)

Independent variable	Unstandardized coefficient	Standardized coefficient	Standard error
Constant	86.77	0.00	17.50
LEFT	0.23	0.34	0.09
SIZE	5.80	−0.41	1.90
GHENT	20.29	0.38	8.60

Number of cases: 18
r^2 .82

Note: Data from table 1, GHENT was set at 1 and NON-GHENT set at 0 with the exception of Belgium, which was set at 0.5 because the country has a mixed system. Results are significant at the .5 level.

Using the natural log of SIZE means that the percentage increase, rather than the absolute increase, is what matters for union density.

system seems necessary. It must be recalled, however, that this statistical analysis does not help us understand how the causal link operates. It might well be true that already very strong labor movements have introduced Ghent systems, rather than vice versa. In order to get a handle on this problem, we must go from static comparison to diacronic comparative analysis.

Historical Comparison

The first question here is whether a correlation existed between union strength and system of unemployment insurance at the time the schemes were established. If it did, our hypothesis about the importance of institutional power in government labor-market administration must be reconsidered. Historical data about union density is not easily available, and when available, it is of doubtful reliability. For some of the eighteen countries in the statistical analysis, figures of a reasonable reliability are available, but not for all years. As the 1930s have been said to be the crucial decade in this case (Skocpol 1988), it is fortunate that accurate figures are available for these years. Fortunately, data about when different unemployment schemes were introduced are both available and reliable.

The data in table 3 show that there is no significant correlation between union strength and type of unemployment scheme in the 1930s. The four countries with the highest level of unionization had either compulsory insurance or no public insurance at all. The mean of union density in the countries with a compulsory scheme was slightly higher than for those with a Ghent scheme (33 percent compared to 25 percent). Hence it seems fair to conclude that in general it has *not* been already especially strong labor movements that have introduced union-controlled public unemployment-insurance schemes. Moreover, the effect of the Ghent system on union density seems to be considerably delayed. In any case, the question is then who introduced what kind of scheme? Did the different labor movements have the political strength and the strategic skill necessary to institutionalize the Ghent system? Note that the political force behind the establishment of any form of social insurance is notoriously difficult to isolate. For instance, a Conservative party in government might unwillingly introduce a social policy in order to deny the opposing Labor party a political weapon. It seems rather unlikely, though, that a Labor party in government would need in this way to bow to the pressure of an opposing Conservative or Liberal party. Hence, who holds government responsibility should be of interest here.

TABLE 3

Union Density, 1930, by Type of Public Unemployment Scheme and Year of Introduction

Country	Union density (%)	Unemployment insurance scheme	Year of introduction
Germany	48	Compulsory	1927
Australia	44	Compulsory	1922[a]
Sweden	41	–	–
Austria	38	Compulsory	1920
Denmark	37	Ghent	1907
Netherlands	30	Ghent	1916
Belgium	28	Ghent	1901
Great Britain	26	Compulsory	1911
Norway	23	Ghent	1906
United States	11	Compulsory[b]	1935
France	9	Ghent	1905

[a] Queensland. [b] Ten states.

Sources: Union density (Kjellberg 1983: 36f); unemployment scheme and year of introduction (Pettersen 1982: 199).

In view of the results mentioned previously about the positive impact of a Ghent system on the organizational strength of the working class, the results in table 4 are surprising. Voluntary systems seem above all to have been favored by Liberal governments, while Labor governments have, with one exception, introduced compulsory schemes. How can this seemingly paradoxical result be understood? One possible explanation is that individual responsibility and self-help organization have strong roots in liberal ideology, while the notion of social insurance as a right of citizenship has strong support in socialist ideology. Perhaps then ideology has sometimes taken primacy over strategic calculation (cf. Lewin 1988).

Although there is no space in this essay for a detailed description of why these countries institutionalized the system they did, some important details can be mentioned. In France a Ghent system was introduced as early as in 1905, but union leaders' reluctance to collaborate with the state left the insurance system practically a dead letter. This was probably due to the strong syndicalist, and thus antistate, influence in the French labor movement. The same thing happened in Norway where a Ghent system was introduced in 1906, although the Norwegian labor movement was left-socialist and communist oriented rather than syndicalist

TABLE 4
Party in Government and Introduction of Different Public Unemployment Insurance
Schemes

Type of scheme	Party in government		
	Labor	Liberal	Conservative
Compulsory	3	2	3
	(AU, NE, NO)	(IT, UK)	(BE, FR, GE)
Voluntary	1	4	2
	(SW)	(DE, FR, NE, SZ)	(BE, FI)

Source: Alber 1984: 170.

(Pettersen 1982; Alber 1984: 153f). In Norway some union-run funds
that had been established went bankrupt, and the whole system was
discredited during the 1920s and early 1930s because the unions could
not perform the necessary economic supervision, which is to say cut
benefits and raise payments. In 1938 a Labor government introduced a
compulsory system in collaboration with the Liberal party and the Con-
servative(!) party. It seems there was no discussion about the effects this
would have on unionization (Pettersen 1982). In the Netherlands in
1949 as in Norway, a Labor government replaced a voluntary system with
a compulsory one (Albert 1984).

In Britain, on the other hand, the union movement condemned the
introduction of a compulsory scheme unless it was managed by organized labor, and argued that the insurance should be restricted to union
members. However, this was denied them when the Liberal government
introduced the world's first compulsory system in 1911 (Harris 1972:
317f). Under questioning by the president of the Board of Trade, the
Parliamentary Committee of the British Trades Unions Congress (TUC)
argued that if the insurance was not restricted to union members, 'You
will have men to support who never have been and never will be self-
supporting. They are at present parasites on their more industrious fellows and will be the first to avail themselves of the funds the Bill provides' (quoted in Harris 1972: 317f).

In Denmark the union movement argued strongly for a Ghent system,
which was introduced by a Liberal government in 1907. The Liberal
government seems simply to have miscalculated in believing that unemployment funds would be established by liberal Friendly Societies and
not by the socialist unions. Although critical of aspects of the insurance

scheme, the Danish unions were quick to establish funds or enroll existing union funds in the scheme, and hence a Ghent system was established. Afterward, the Danish labor movement fought hard to preserve the system, in contrast to their more radical Norwegian fellows (Andersen et al. 1981). Thus, as confirmed by Alber, the initial union response to differences in the structure of unemployment insurance schemes varied considerably (Alber 1984: 154, compare Harris 1972: 299f). Some labor movements were unable to introduce a Ghent system even though they wanted to, while other labor movements saw no strategic advantage in a Ghent system.

As shown in table 4, there is, nonetheless, one country in which a Labor government did manage to introduce a Ghent system: Sweden in 1934. If there is such a thing as strategic behavior in the process of designing political institutions, then Sweden deserves a closer look.

The Swedish Case

Unionization came late but rapidly to Sweden. For the reasons stated, that is, to reduce the temptation of unemployed workers to undermine union solidarity, many unions established their own unemployment funds during the late nineteenth and early twentieth centuries (Heclo 1974: 68). One of the labor movement's first demands upon the government was for the establishment of a public unemployment-insurance system. Compared to many similar countries, especially Denmark and Norway, the Swedish labor movement succeeded rather late in its efforts to introduce a public unemployment-insurance scheme (1934; see table 3). There were two major reasons for the delay. One is that, beginning in 1918, Sweden developed a unique unemployment policy, the main substance of which was to organize relief works rather than to distribute unemployment benefits. The unemployed were typically sent away to distant relief-work camps where conditions were very harsh, to put it mildly. Cash benefits were also provided, but not on a basis of entitlement to insurance; they were granted only after a series of rigorous individual means tests. Those who refused to take jobs at the relief-work camps and who could not be supported by their unions had no choice but to endure the humiliation of asking for help at the poor-relief agencies.

The problem with this system was that the wages paid at the relief works were far below the union rate. This meant that some employers, mainly the local municipalities, could buy labor power outside the unions' control. It was generally believed that the only cure for unemployment was to lower the wage level, and the relief-works system explicitly promoted this by providing labor at a lower price than the unions would (Heclo 1974; Unga 1976). This wage-deflationary policy naturally led to intense industrial disputes. The bourgeois parties, who had a majority in Parliament throughout the period between the wars, supported this deflationary policy; moreover, they decided that all workers belonging to trades in which unions were involved in industrial disputes should be cut off from any help, relief works, or cash benefits. The Unemployment Commission could even in some cases force unemployed workers to act as strikebreakers on penalty of losing any form of assistance. This unemployment policy came thus to be a paramount threat to union control over the supply of labor. Two Social Democratic minority governments actually chose to resign (in 1923 and 1926), when they could not get a parliamentary majority in favor of changing the system. It may be said that this policy, and its administration, were the most hotly contested issues between the labor movement and the bourgeois parties during the 1920s. The bourgeois parties, together with the employers' federation, saw in the operation of this unemployment policy a major weapon with which to weaken the labor movement, while for the labor movement the policy and its administration were seen as the very incarnation of the bourgeois class character of the capitalist state (Rothstein 1985a).

The demand for an unemployment-insurance scheme to replace the established system was thus the main issue for the Swedish labor movement during the 1920s, but because of the established relief-work policy and the controversies it provoked, the matter resulted in a deadlock. No fewer then four government commissions produced reports and detailed plans for the introduction of such a policy before 1934, but because of intense resistance from the Conservative and Agrarian parties, they never materialized into legislation (Heclo 1974: 99–105; Edebalk 1975). Apart from arguing for the necessity of lowering the wage level, these two parties claimed that such a system would only further the organizational strength of the unions, and thus the Social Democratic party. But the bourgeois front was split, as one of the two Liberal parties (the Prohibitionist) was generally in favor of introducing public unemployment insurance.

The two major variants of unemployment insurance discussed previously were of course also considered in the Swedish debate. The Liberals, who had been in government from 1926 to 1928 and from 1930 to 1932, found themselves in a difficult position. On the one had, they hesitated to introduce a compulsory scheme because they considered the costs too high and the administration too complicated. A Ghent system had neither of these drawbacks, but the Liberals realized such a system would strengthen the labor movement and thus be detrimental to their own political interests. (After the unions' defeat in the general strike of 1909, unions with unemployment funds managed to keep their members to a much higher degree than those without. Hence the impact of the Ghent system on union strength had at that time been 'proven' in Sweden; see Edebalk 1975). Another argument against the Ghent system was that the union-run unemployment funds would be merged with the unions' strike funds (Unga 1976: 112).

From early on, the Social Democratic party favored the introduction of a Ghent system. But when the combined effects of the relief-work system and rising unemployment hit the unions in the late 1920s, they started to press the Social Democrats to strike a deal with the Liberals in order to introduce an insurance scheme whether compulsory or attached to the unions. However, the Liberals, although in government from 1930 to 1932, never managed to introduce a bill proposing a compulsory scheme. One reason was that unemployment insurance was considered suitable only for 'normal' times of unemployment, which the early 1930s certainly were not. The other reason was that the lessons learned from the British and German compulsory schemes during the economic crisis was not particularly encouraging (Heclo 1974: 97).

After their electoral victory in 1932 the Social Democrats formed a minority government. In order to introduce unemployment insurance, therefore, they needed support from at least one of the bourgeois parties. The only prospect was the Liberals, but they were more inclined to a compulsory than a Ghent system. However, after failing in 1933, the Social Democrats managed, by striking a deal with a section of the Liberals, to introduce a Ghent system in 1934. In order to reach this compromise they had to sacrifice an important part of their original proposal concerning the rules and regulations of the scheme. First, the union unemployment funds had to be licensed and supervised by the National Board of Social Affairs. Second, workers outside the unions also were given the right to become members of the funds. Third, the level of benefits was set rather low, and the rules governing entitlement to support (e.g., gauged by the number of days in work and contributions from individual members) were very restrictive. Finally, the employers were not obliged to contribute to financing the insurance (Heclo 1974: 102–5; Edelbalk 1975). Notwithstanding these concessions, the compromise meant that the implementation of the scheme was to be managed by union-run funds, which is to say union officials were given the power of deciding the important question of a suitable job. Moreover, in practice, although not in law, workers would not be expected to take jobs at workplaces affected by industrial conflict, nor accept wages below the union rate. In sum, the Social Democrats compromised greatly about the content of the scheme (i.e., the actual policy) in order to be able to institutionalize an insurance scheme that would greatly enhance their future organizational strength. The question that has to be answered is whether this strategy was intentional – that is, whether this was a case of deliberate and (which seems to be something rare) successful institutional design in political history (Miller 1988; Tsebelis 1990).

The answer is yes, for we can, in this case, identify the specific political agent behind the strategy: the Social Democratic Minister of Social Affairs Gustav Möller. When speaking in Parliament in 1933 about accepting the demands of the Liberals, he declared that they were very difficult for him to accept, but the he nevertheless would do so because

I do not want, if I can prevent it, ... the Swedish Parliament to let this possibility slip away, which we perhaps have, to take away from the agenda the struggle about the very principle about, whether Sweden should have publicly supported unemployment insurance or not. (Parliamentary Records, Second Chamber 1933–50: 96; my translation)

He admitted the scheme to be introduced was not very impressive and would not be especially efficient in helping the unemployed masses. But, he argued, if the principle was settled, then the substance could be improved later on (Parliamentary Records, First Chamber [PRFC] 1933–47: 47f). It should be mentioned that Möller said this in 1933, when the bill in fact was rejected by Parliament because some Liberals got cold feet. When it was actually accepted a year later, Möller had to make even greater concessions to the Liberals (Edebalk 1975). Interestingly enough, the Communists, for their part, strongly opposed the bill as they preferred a compulsory state-administered system. In the debate in Parliament in 1934, Möller openly argued that one of the advantages of a voluntary system compared to a compulsory one was that it would support only those workers who 'show such an interest in the insurance system ... that they take the initiative to create or to join an unemployment insurance fund' (PRFC 1934–7: 12; my translation).

As early as 1926, in a widely distributed political pamphlet. Möller had emphasized the importance a Ghent system would have for the union movement and argued such a system was preferable to a compulsory scheme. He did not deny such a system would be rather 'union-friendly,' but according to Möller nothing was wrong, in principle, in the state supporting only those workers who had taken an interest in their own and their families' well-being. Workers who had not shown such an interest – those choosing to be 'free-riders' instead of joining the union movement – should, according to Möller, be sent away to the relief-work camps, if helped at all (Möller 1926). The central moment seems to have been a meeting with the executive committee of the trade union conference in 1930, where Möller persuaded the union leaders that the labor movement, although beset by difficulties arising from high unemployment, should press for a Ghent system because it 'would force workers into the unions' (quoted in Unga 1976:; 118; my translation).

The problem for the Social Democrats at that time (1930) was the risk that the Liberal government would propose a bill to Parliament introducing a compulsory scheme; hence proposing a voluntary system would made the the party 'look ridiculous' (Unga 1974: 118). Thus, mainly for tactical reasons (hoping that the Liberal government would not take action), the Social Democrats demanded in Parliament that an insurance system be introduced no matter what type (Edelbalk 1975). But after the Social Democrats formed the government in 1932 and Möller became minister of social affairs, there was no question about which system he preferred (Unga 1976). It should be mentioned that this was neither the first nor the last time Gustav Möller combined strategic political skill with a remarkable sense of the importance of designing the administrative institutions of the welfare state (Rothstein 1985b). In this case, in order to further his (that is, the labor movement's) long-term interest, policy substance was traded for institutional design.

Although this is not the place for a 'life and letters,' some details about Möller should be given. One important fact is that Gustav Möller was not only minister of social affairs, he was also party secretary from 1916 to 1940. In the Swedish Social Democratic party, this position is second in the hierarchy, and it carries special responsibility for the party organization. One can easily imagine that this position gave Möller a special sensitivity to the problem of free-riding. In contrast to most other European Social Democratic parties, which, when in government during this period, often made people of minor importance responsible for social affairs, Möller's position shows the importance the Swedish party at that time placed on social policy (Therborn 1989). Second Möller had been in the forefront in the fight against the Unemployment Commission and the threat its policies posed to the union's organizational strength.

The scheme established in 1934 was to be almost a complete failure as a means of helping the unemployed masses during the 1930s. But Möller did not consider the insurance system to be a method for curing unemployment during crises. For this, he relied on a massive program of job creation that was implemented during 1934–9 (Heclo 1974: 104; Rothstein 1986). One of the reasons the insurance did not work well was that very few unions actually applied to register their funds, or establish new funds, under the scheme. This issue often aroused intense debate within the unions during the second half of the 1930s. One example is the powerful metalworkers' union, where the majority of the board argued for accepting the conditions and putting the union fund under the scheme (because doing so would be economically favorable). However, at the union's conferences in 1936 and 1939, it was decided to put the question to a vote. In both cases the members voted against the proposal. The most powerful argument, made mostly by communists and left-socialists, was based on a lingering suspicion of having anything to do with government labor-market authorities (Erici and Roth 1981).

Möller's prediction in 1934, that the substantive rules in the insurance system could be changed in the future, was vindicated in 1941 when a unanimous Parliament changed the rules in favor of the unions. From that date the scheme started to grow; that is, unions started to apply to register their funds under the scheme or create new funds. Since then, the rules have been successively changed in favor of the union funds and the unemployed. To take economic contributions as an example: From an original 50–50 basis, the scheme has been changed to one in which, since the 1970s, the government pays almost all the costs of the system (Erici and Roth 1981). Although since the mid-1960s the institutional principles have been attacked by the bourgeois parties and the employers' federation, who argue that the connection between union membership and the insurance should be cut, no such institutional changes have been made (Lindkvist 1989). While it is legally possible for any wage-earner to be a member only of the insurance fund, unions make this very difficult in practice (and also more expensive). Those wage-earners who have succeeded in being members of the funds but not the unions amounted in 1986 to about 0.6 percent of the total number insured (Statens Offentliga Utredningar 1987: 56).

One of the reasons the bourgeois parties, although in government from 1976 to 1982, did not succeed in changing the system, is that not only the blue-collar unions, but also the comparatively strong white-collar unions in Sweden have forcefully defended union power in the administration of the scheme, and so, for electoral reasons, it was difficult for the bourgeois parties to resist strong demands from these unions (Hallgren 1986: 31–58). Hence an institution such as a Ghent system can be considered to some extent self-reinforcing, because it tends to strengthen the very forces that have a positive interest in preserving the institution. Thus, strange as it may seem, Sweden is today a country where the bourgeois parties, and the employers' organization, press for the introduction of a compulsory unemployment-insurance scheme, even at the price of raising public expenditure, while the labor movement successfully fights to keep it a voluntary scheme (see Hallgren 1986).

Summary and Conclusions

The theoretical aim of this chapter has been to show that institutional analysis can serve as a bridge between structural and agent-oriented analysis in political science. Since the seminal work of Mancur Olson, rational choice and game theorists have tried to find out how people solve the prisoner's dilemma. Writing from a game-theoretical perspective, Jonathan Bendor and Dilip Mookherjee have been forced to admit that such an approach can explain neither why patterns of collective action persist nor why they arise. They state that 'the emergence of cooperation is a hard problem – one that may require other methods of analysis' (Bendor and Mookherjee 1987: 146). As should be obvious, I agree. Moreover, game theorists have usually pointed at the important role of iteration (repeated play) in explaining collective action. William Bianco and Robert Bates, also writing from a game-theoretical perspective, have recently shown the limited impact of iteration, and instead pointed at the important role that 'leaders' play in initiating collective action among rational, self-interested individuals. What leaders need, according to them, is an appropriate strategy and reputation among followers. As might be expected, I agree, but I want to add that in order to find the actual leader and to identify his or her 'incentives and capabilities' used in creating the institution that makes collective action possible (solves the prisoner's dilemma), game theory seems to be of limited value (Bianco and Bates 1990: 133). The value of this approach emerges only when we have a more substantial theory from which to draw hypotheses about why some players, resources, and institutions are more important than others.

When it comes to institutional analysis, I have tried to show four things. The first is that in order to understand the importance of political institutions, institutional theory is not enough. The reason is simply that one needs a theory about *what kind* of institutions are important for *what issues*. Without generalizing, I have shown in the case of explaining working-class organizational strength that Marxism and institutional theory go together. The former has been used to identify the important agents and institutions, and the latter to explain how and why they make a difference. Second, as the statistical analysis shows, the institutionalization of government labor-market policy is important in explaining variation in working-class organizational strength among the Western industrialized countries. Third, organized class power stems not only from socioeconomic factors, but also from the power that social classes at times are able to invest in political institutions. There is thus definitely a dialectical relationship between government institutions and class formation.

Moreover, I have tried to move beyond the question of the mere importance of institutions. Even if institutions give an advantage to some social forces, there remains the question of intentionality. It has two dimensions: The first is whether the *creation* of a political institution should be considered an intentional act, or if instead it results from social evolution. If the creation is intentional, then the question arises of the outcome of the institution's operation – that is, whether the outcome is what the creative agent expected or not. My knowledge of political history tells me the latter result is the most common one. For a Swedish example, one can point to the Social Democratic party's efforts in 1907 to keep a 'winner take all' majority electoral system, which if successful would have created a Tory-like party in Sweden (instead of three different and oft-divided bourgeois parties), making the long reign of the Social Democrats very improbable (see Pontusson 1988). It was the party's sheer luck to be forced to accede to the Conservative party's demand for a proportional electoral system in 1906–7 (Lewin 1988: 69–79).

Nevertheless, two things have been shown in this case. The first is that many labor movements seem simply to have made the wrong choice in deciding what system of unemployment insurance to strive for. 'Designing social structures' (Miller 1988), or creating the right kind of 'positive loops' (Skocpol 1988), or being a rational goal maximizer when creating institutions (Tsebelis 1990) seems thus not so simple. Unions, especially, seem to have been unaware of what type of unemployment-insurance institution would be advantageous to them. This was also true in the

Swedish case in which, when under pressure, the unions seemed willing to trade long-term institutional power for short-term interests. Moreover, when the Ghent system was introduced, they hesitated to join and thereby strengthen the system. Before 1941 the Swedish Ghent system was so weak that it could easily have been changed into a compulsory scheme.

In the Swedish case it has been shown both that the establishment of the Ghent system was deliberate and that it has had the outcome expected by its creator(s). Political institutions are certainly sources for the determination of political behavior, but *homo politicus* cannot be considered a total structural-cum-institutional dope. In some, albeit probably rare, historical cases, people actually create the very institutional circumstances under which their own as well as others' future behavior will take place. It is thus possible not only to bind oneself to the mast in order to avoid being tempted by the sirens' song, but also at times to use the ropes to structure the future choices of others as well (Elster 1979).

Notes

This essay is an outcome of a research project titled Interest Organizations and the Public Interest, financed by the Swedish Central Bank's Tercentenary Fund. I would like to thank Frank Longstreth, Jonas Pontusson, Theda Skocpol, Ulla Arnell-Gustafsson, Stefan Björklund, Charles Noble, and Michael Wallerstein for their valuable comments on earlier versions. Thanks also to Anders Westholm who helped me in computing the statitics and to Peter Mayers for checking the language.

1 In a letter in March 1875 to August Bebel, the leader of the German Social Democrats, Friedrich Engels criticized the Gotha Party program for not paying due attention to the fact that the trade union is 'the real class organization of the proletariat' (quoted in Bottomore 1985: 482).

2 The unstandardized coefficient for SIZE (−5.8) shows that a doubling of the potential union membership would reduce union density by $\ln(2)(5.8) =$ (.69)<(5.8) ≈ 4.0 percentage points. The unstandardized coefficient for LEFT (0.23) indicates that three years of Social Democratic majority government (= 9 point in Wilensky's index) would increase union density by approximately 2 percentage points (cf. Wallerstein 1989: 492).

References

Alber, Jens. 1984. 'Government Responses to the Challenge of Unemployment: The Development of Unemployment Insurance in Western Europe.' In Peter Flora and Arnold J. Heidenheimer, eds., *The Development of Welfare States in Europe and America.* New Brunswick, N.J.: Transaction Books.

Åmark, Klas. 1986. *Facklig makt och fackligt medlemskap.* Lund: Arkiv.

Amenta, Edwin, and Theda Skocpol, 1986. 'States and Social Politics.' *Annual Review of Sociology* 12: 131–57.

Andersen, John, Per Jensen, Jorgen E. Larsen, and Carsten Schultz. 1981. 'Klassekamp og reformisme.' Unpublished paper, Department of Sociology, University of Copenhagen.

Bendor, Jonathan, and Dilip Mookherjee. 1987. 'Institutional Structure and the Logic of Ongoing Collective Action.' *American Journal of Political Science* 81: 129–54.

Berger, Johannes, and Claus Offe. 1982. 'Functionalism vs Rational Choice.' *Theory and Society* 11: 521–6.

Bianco, William T., and Robert H. Bates. 1990. 'Cooperation by Design: Leadership Structure and Collective Dilemmas.' *American Political Science Review* 84: 133–47.

Bottomore, Tom, ed. 1985. *A Dictionary of Marxist Thought.* London: Macmillan.

Callincos, Alex. 1989. *Making History. Agency, Structure and Change in Social Theory.* Oxford: Polity Press.

Castles, Francis. 1985. *The Working Class and Welfare.* Wellington: Allen and Unwin.

Cerny, Philip G. 1990. *The Changing Architecture of Modern Politics.* London: Sage.

Cohen, Gerald. 1978. *Karl Marx's Theory of History. A Defence.* Oxford: Oxford University Press.

Davidson, Alexander. 1989. *Two Models of Welfare.* Stockholm: Almqvist and Wiksell International.

Douglas, Mary. 1987. *How Institutions Think.* London: Routledge and Kegan Paul.

Edebalk, Per-Gunnar. 1975. *Arbetslöshetsförsäkringsdebatten.* Lund: Department of Economic History.

Elster, Jon. 1979. *Ulysses and the Sirens.* Cambridge: Cambridge University Press.

– 1985. *Making Sense of Marx.* Cambridge: Cambridge University Press.

– 1989. *The Cement of Society.* Cambridge: Cambridge University Press.

Erici, Bernt, and Nils Roth. 1981. *Arbetslöshetsförsäkringen i Sverige, 1935–1980.* Stockholm: Arbetslöshetskassornas samorganisation.

Esping-Andersen, Gøsta. 1985. *Politics against Markets*. Princeton, N.J.: Princeton University Press.

Esping-Andersen, Gøsta, and Walter Korpi. 1984. 'Social Policy as Class Politics in Post-War Capitalism: Scandinavia, Austria and Germany,' In John H. Goldthorpe, ed., *Order and Conflict in Contemporary Capitalism*. Oxford: Oxford University Press.

– 1985. 'From Poor Relief towards Institutional Welfare States: The Development of Scandinavian Social Policy.' In Robert E. Eriksson, ed., *The Scandinavian Model: Welfare States and Welfare Research*. New York: M. E. Sharpe.

Flora, Peter, ed. 1987. *Growth to Limits. The Western European Welfare States Since World War II*. *Vol 4*. Berlin: De Gruyter.

Giddens, Anthony. 1979. *Central Problems in Social Theory*. London: Macmillan.

Goldfield, Michael. 1987. *The Decline of Organized Labor in the United States*. Chicago: University of Chicago Press.

Grafstein, Robert E. 1988. 'The Problem of Institutional Constraint.' *Journal of Politics* 50: 577–9.

Hallgren, Sive. 1986. *Från allmosa till rättighet*. Stockholm: Tidens förlag.

Harris, John. 1972. *Unemployment and Politics*. Oxford: Charendon Press.

Heclo, Hugh. 1974. *Modern Social Policies in Britain and Sweden: New Haven*, Conn: Yale University Press.

Kjellberg, Anders. 1983. *Facklig organisering i tolv länder*. Lund: Arkiv.

– 1988. 'Sverige har fackligt världsrekord.' *LO-tidningen* 9: 10–11.

Knight, Jack. 1988. 'Strategic Conflict and Institutional Change.' Paper presented at the annual meeting of the American Political Science Association, Washington, D.C.

Korpi, Walter. 1983. *The Democratic Class Struggle*. London: Routledge and Kegan Paul.

– 1985. 'Power Resource Approach vs. Action and Conflict. On Causal and Intentional Explanation of Power.' *Sociological Theory* 3: 31–45.

Lester, Richard. 1965. 'Unemployment Insurance.' In *International Encyclopedia of the Social Sciences*. London: Macmillan.

Levi, Margaret. 1990. 'A Logic of Institutional Changes.' In Karen Schweers Cook and Margaret Levi, eds., *The Limits of Rationality*. Chicago: University of Chicago Press.

Lewin, Leif. 1988. *Ideology and Strategy. A Century of Swedish Politics*. Cambridge: Cambridge University Press.

Lindsvist, Ann. 1989. 'Fackföreningsrörelsen och arbetslöshetsförsäkringen.' Working Paper, Department of Government, University of Uppsala.

Lipsky, Michael. 1980. *Street-level Bureaucracy. Dilemmas of the Individual in Public Services*. New York: Russell Sage Foundation.

March, James H., and Johan P. Olsen. 1984. 'The New Institutionalism. Organizational Factors in Political Life.' *American Political Science Review* 78: 734–49.

Miller, Trudi. 1988. 'Designing Social Structures.' Paper presented at the annual meeting of the American Political Science Association, Washington, D.C.

Möller, Gustav. 1926. *Arbetslöshetsförsäkringen jämte andra sociala försäkringar.* Stockholm: Tiden.

– 1938. 'The Swedish Unemployment Policy.' *The Annals of the American Academy of Political and Social Sciences* 197.

Mouzelis, Nicos. 1984. 'On the Crises of Marxist Theory.' *British Journal of Sociology* 25: 112–21.

– 1988. 'Marxist or Post-Marxism.' *New Left Review* 167: 107–23.

Noble, Charles F. 1988. 'State or Class? Notes on Two Recent Views of the Welfare State.' Paper presented at the annual meeting of the American Political Science Association, Washington, D.C.

Nordiska Rådets Utredningar (Reports from the Nordic Council).

Offe, Claus, and Helmuth Wiesenthal. 1980. 'Two Logics of Collective Action.' In Maurice Zeitlin, ed., *Political Power and Social Theory.* Greenwich, Conn: JAI Press.

Olofsson, Gunnar. 1979. *Mellan klass och stat.* Lund: Arkiv.

Olson, Mancur. 1965. *The Logic of Collective Action: Public Goods and the Theory of Groups.* Cambridge, Mass.: Harvard University Press.

Parliamentary Records, First Chamber.

Parliamentary Records, Second Chamber.

Peretz, David. 1979. *The Governments and Politics of Israel.* Boulder, Colo.: Westview Press.

Pettersen, Per A. 1982. *Linjer i norsk sosialpolitikk.* Oslo: Universitetsforlaget.

Pontusson, Jonas. 1988. 'Swedish Social Democracy and British Labour. Essays on the Nature and Conditions of Social Democratic Hegemony.' Western Societies Program Occasional Paper no 19. New York Center of International Studies, Cornell University, Ithaca, N.Y.

Przeworski, Adam. 1985. *Capitalism and Social Democracy.* Cambridge: Cambridge University Press.

Rothstein, Bo. 1985a. 'The Success of the Swedish Labour Market Policy: The Organizational Connection to Policy.' *European Journal of Political Research* 13: 153–65.

– 1985b. 'Managing the Welfare State: Lessons from Gustav Möller.' *Scandinavian Political Studies* 13: 51–70.

– 1986. *Den socialdemokratiska staten. Reformer och förvaltning inom svensk arbetsmarknads-och skolpolitik.* Lund: Arkiv.

– 1990. 'State Capacity and Social Justice: The Labor Market Case.' Paper presented at the meeting of the American Political Science Association, Aug. 28–Sept. 2, 1990, San Francisco.

Schmidt, Folke. 1977. *Law and Industrial Relations in Sweden.* Stockholm: Almqvist and Wiksell International.

Shalev, Michael. 1983a. 'Class Politics and the Western Welfare State.' In S. E. Spiro and E. Yuchtman-Yaar, eds., *Evaluating the Welfare State.* New York: Academic Press.

– 1983b. 'The Social Democratic Model and Beyond. Two Generations of Comparative Research on the Welfare State.' *Comparative Social Research* 6: 315–52.

Shepsle, Kenneth A. 1989. 'Studying Institutions – Some Lessons from the Rational Choice Approach.' *Journal of Theoretical Politics* 1: 131–47.

Skocpol, Theda. 1988. 'Comparing National Systems of Social Provision: A Polity Centered Approach.' Paper presented at the International Political Science Association meeting, Washington, D.C.

Statens Offentliga Utredningar (Government Public Commission).

Steinmo, Sven. 1989. 'Political Institutions and Tax Policy in the United States, Sweden and Britain.' *World Politics* 41: 500–35.

Streeck, Wolfgang. 1981. *Gewerkschaftliche Organisationsprobleme in der socialstaatlichen Demokratie.* Königstein: Athenäum.

Thelen, Kathleen, and Sven Steinmo. 1992. 'Historical Institutionalism in Comparative Politics.' In Sven Steinmo, Kathleen Thelen, and Frank Longstreth, eds., *Structuring Politics: Historical Institutionalism in Historical Perspective.* New York: Cambridge University Press.

Therborn, Göran. 1989. 'Arbetarrörelsen och välfärdsstaten.' *Arkiv för studier i arbetarrörelsens historia* 41–2: 3–51.

Tsebelis, George. 1990. *Nested Games: Rational Choice in Comparative Politics.* Berkeley: University of California Press.

Unga, Nils. 1976. *Socialdemokratin och arbetslöshetsfrågan, 1912–34.* Lund: Arkiv.

von Beyme, Klaus. 1980. *Challenge to Power. Trade Unions and Industrial Relations in Capitalist Countries.* London: Sage.

Wallerstein, Michael. 1989. 'Union Growth in Advanced Industrial Democracies.' *American Political Science Review* 83: 481–501.

Weir, Margaret, and Theda Skcopol. 1985. 'State Structures and the Possibilities for "Keynesian" Responses to the Great Depression in Sweden, Britain, and the United States.' In Peter B. Evans, Dietrich Rueschemeyer, and Theda Skocpol, eds., *Bringing the State Back In.* Cambridge: Cambridge University Press.

Wilensky, Harold L. 1981. 'Leftism, Catholicism and Democratic Corporatism: The Role of Political Parties in Recent Welfare State Development.' In Peter Flora and Arnold J. Heidenheimer, eds., *The Development of Welfare States in Europe and America*. New Brunswick, N.J.: Transactions Books.

Wright, Eric O. 1985. *Classes*. London: Verso.

11

The Scandinavian Origins of the Social Interpretation of the Welfare State

PETER BALDWIN

If a question can be *mal posée*, surely an interpretation can be *mal étendue*. This has been the fate of the social interpretation of the welfare state. The cousin of social theories of bourgeois revolution, the social interpretation of the welfare state is part of a broader conception of the course of modern European history that until recently has laid claim to the status of a standard. The social interpretation sees the welfare states of certain countries as a victory for the working class and confirmation of the ability of its political representatives on the Left to use universalist, egalitarian, solidaristic measures of social policy on behalf of the least advantaged. Because the poor and the working class were groups that overlapped during the initial development of the welfare state, social policy was linked with the worker's needs.[1] Faced with the ever-present probability of immiseration, the proletariat championed the cause of all needy and developed more pronounced sentiments of solidarity than other classes.[2] Where it achieved sufficient power, the privileged classes were forced to consent to measures that apportioned the cost of risks among all, helping those buffeted by fate and social injustice at the expense of those docked in safe berths.

One of the attractions of the social interpretation of the welfare state has been its snug fit with a broader social interpretation of Western European history. In this, the bourgeois revolution paved the way for liberal capitalist democracy, which, in turn, would eventually be swept away in the proletariat's rise to power. Merely a reading of past events, the first half of this analysis was left to historians to pick over. The second contained a prediction that has proven to be inaccurate. As a result, there developed an alternative version of the social interpretation, a reformist socialist account that sought to identify significant victories won peacefully by the Left to mark a gradual transformation from the bourgeois era to that of the working class. In this scheme, certain social-policy reforms in certain countries took the place of the socialist revolution. Under the right circumstances, social policy went beyond fine-tuning the capitalist system or appeasing the laboring classes. Certain kinds of social policy restricted the rule of the market over basic conditions of existence, taking a step beyond capitalism. The social interpretation of the welfare state became part of a social-democratic variant of the traditional Marxist reading of modern history. Its outcome was social reform, not socialist revolution; a pensioned, not a dictatorial, proletariat; not the stateless society, but the welfare state.

Although simple, the social interpretation of the welfare state was not immediately obvious. It seemed to work only for some countries. It fit certain periods better than others. In liberal Britain, the working class was at best partially responsible for first forays into welfare-statism. Even worse, Bismarck's Bonapartist goals were impossible to reconcile with the social interpretation. The working class was the passive object of social policy, not its initiator. Welfare measures were meant to preserve an unjust order by improving, while not fundamentally changing it. On the other hand, William Beveridge and Labour's reforms in Britain after World War II and the success of egalitarian social policy in socialist Scandinavia, offered examples of an alternative approach to the welfare state, one that went beyond liberal tinkering, one that reflected the interests of workers, not their masters. Out of this contrast a conceptual tension developed between at least two kinds of social policy, two kinds of welfare states: the conservative and the authentically reformist. Observers of the Anglo-Scandinavian scene (especially after World War II) could, and largely did, rest content with some variant of the social interpretation.[3] Observers of other countries were left to seek explanations for why social policy there did not resemble this ideal. The result has been a curious ambivalence about the social interpretation. Often taken for granted, rarely articulated, it frequently lies implicit in discussions of social policy without informing them. The cause of this mixture of widespread assumption and rudimentary expression is a fundamental ambiguity at the heart of the welfare state as an historical concept.

The bourgeois revolution, in the manner that construct was used before its recent decline, assumed its classic form in France. Subsequent and analogous events in Germany were judged a failure in comparison to what they ought, by this account, to have been. The ideal nature of the French phenomenon was not marred by Germany's inability to emulate it. On the contrary, not the model, but the circumstances across the Rhine were pronounced an aberration. For the welfare state, the path from event to interpretation, from the classic historical example to its deviations, was reversed. At almost the same time as Bismarck tainted the bourgeois revolution in Germany by imposing it from above on the class that ought, in the traditional social interpretation, to have been its initiator, he associated the inauguration of the welfare state with the preservation of an archaic social order, the smooth functioning of the capitalist system, the political domination of conservatives.[4]

The social interpretation of the welfare state has been made possible only to the extent that social policy was freed from its tie to Bismarck and Bonaparte and associated positively with the downtrodden, particularly the workers, and their strivings for greater equality and a fairer distribution of burdens. Based on a selective reading of certain historical experiences, it was first made plausible by the world-wide push for a universalist, egalitarian social policy that culminated during the final years of World War II, spilling over into major attempts at change, of which the Beveridge Plan and Clement Attlee's legislation were the crowning achievements. The postwar wave of reform undermined the Bonapartist view of social policy that Bismarck's legislation had encouraged. Social policy could be used for reactionary purposes, but, given the right circumstances, social legislation could also be the autonomous, authentically emancipatory action of the underprivileged.

While Labour's reforms inaugurated a new conception of social policy, they were unable to sustain it alone. Illuminating the sky like a flare, brilliantly but briefly, wartime efforts permitted the discovery of a non-Bismarckian strain of social policy that both preceded and was to outlive it. Developments in the Scandinavian countries had generally passed unremarked until Beveridge.[5] With the attention devoted to reform during and after the war, it no longer escaped notice that, in the North, long traditions of socialist power coincided with social policy of an universalist, egalitarian sort. Neither social policy nor Scandinavian countries came into their own as examples of nations where enlightened, egalitarian social policy seemed to have been the independent achievement of the neediest classes. Where Scandinavia had earlier attracted the attention mainly of those interested in, say, pig farming or temperance movements, the North suddenly found itself the center of international attention. Admired by many, it was reviled only by a shrill coterie, whose use of epithets like 'the new totalitarians' for what more reasonable spirits described as 'the middle way' suggested a degree of hyperbole likely to defeat its own purposes.[6] Languishing on the periphery of European history, Scandinavia, in certain respects, suddenly became its cynosure. By extending its geographical horizons, the social interpretation seemed to have demonstrated its continued power. The ideal case of the bourgeois revolution had been French. The peaceful victory of the working class proved to be Scandinavian.[7]

Novelty and accuracy have not in this case been completely compatible bedfellows. The result of this new focus has been an anachronistic reading of the history of Nordic social policy. To the extent that Scandinavia is taken, in these respects, as the standard against which to measure other countries, this distortion has consequences for an understanding of developments south of the Eider. The long tradition of social-democratic rule in the North has encouraged a tendency to associate even reforms inherited from another age with the socialists who followed. The Nordic welfare states came, with good cause, to be hailed as the pinnacle of social-policy achievement. More important for the social interpretation, they were regarded as the antithesis of the Bismarckian approach.

Bismarck's social policy is usually considered reactionary, Bonapartist, and unsolidaristic. It reflected these characteristics in at least three ways: It focussed only on the workers, in the hope of politically defusing that dangerous class. It avoided any wide-ranging social equalization and gave expression to existing market hierarchies through benefits differentiated according to wages. It relied on unredistributive financing collected directly as premiums or through regressive consumption taxes. Conversely, Scandinavian welfare policy was the fruit of the common masses' political power, represented by the socialists. It therefore incorporated a solidarity of the entire community by including all citizens, offering them egalitarian flat-rate benefits, and relying heavily on tax financing to distribute burdens by ability to shoulder them. Socialist success in implementing measures of universalist, flat-rate, tax-financed social policy, it is claimed, qualitatively distinguishes social-democratic welfare states from liberal and conservative systems elsewhere. Scandinavian social policy is seen as most closely embodying the ideal 'institutional' model of the welfare state that fulfills the concept of social citizenship, limits the free working of market relations in important areas, and lessens inequalities.[8]

The social interpretation asserts that the Scandinavian welfare states were the autonomous achievement of the underprivileged classes, that their nature was determined by the needs of the impoverished. In other countries, where social policy reflected a fear of social upheaval, mea-

sures were restricted, divisive, and manipulative. The features that define
the exceptionalism of Nordic welfare policy were, in contrast, the result
of the Left's ability to forge a coalition of the downtrodden powerful
enough to implement the demand of the poor and unfortunate for help
from the affluent and favored.[9] This view – and there was an essential
link between the apparent solidarity, the universalism of early Scandinavian welfare policy, and the socialists – is misleading.[10] It anachronistically
reads back a misunderstanding of postwar reforms to an earlier period in
which other factors were at work.[11] The characteristic features of Scan-
dianvian social insurance were not born in the postwar period, when
socialist power reached its height, but were formed at the time the first
legislation went on the books, at the turn of the century. They were
determined at the behest of parties and social groups not associated with
the Left. Universalist, solidaristic social policy was, in this case, not the
sort of qualitative change claimed by social interpretation. Only apparently did it transcend narrow class or group interests. Only in retrospect
has it come to seem the demand of the rising working class and the Left.
When first introduced in Scandinavia, universalist, egalitarian, tax-financed
welfare measures were a goal some bourgeois groups and parties were
able to inflict in their own interests on the rest of society.

The rest of this account argues the case for these assertions by examining the origins of Scandinavian social policy's unique features. It analyzes
the reasons why measures here were universalist, covering all regardless
of social class, and why they were financed significantly through taxes,
not premiums. It takes pension policy as the most convenient gateway to
these issues. It concludes that universalism and tax financing were not
the expression in terms of welfare policy of any uniquely Nordic sense of
social solidarity and certainly not one inspired by socialists or workers.
Instead, these features were the result of narrow interest disputes fought
out between the rising rural middle class and the entrenched bureaucratic and urban elites. It follows that the social interpretation of the welfare state rests on shaky foundations even in its Scandinavian redoubt.

Farmers, Conservatives, and the Origins of Universalist Social Policy: Denmark

The first Danish social-insurance reforms were articulated in the context
of the major political dispute of the late nineteenth century. This crisis
was sparked by the unwillingness of the conservative Højre (the party of
the monarchical bureaucracy, the urban professional and manufacturing

classes and the aristocratic landowners) to grant the mainly agrarian liberal Venstre Party the political representation to which farmers' growing social and economic importance gave them a claim. Farmers sought reforms that would benefit them financially. When the constitutional conflict dragged on, social policy became part of the larger political struggle between liberals and conservatives, and eventually was an element in its resolution. Social reform was taken up as an alternative way of achieving the effects of the fiscal demands still blocked by the conservatives. Farmers used social policy tailored to their specifications to squeeze concessions from a state they did not yet control, before more direct solutions were possible. Without coverage of all, agrarians would not benefit from social measures. Without tax financing and state subsidies, farmers, as employers, would be disadvantaged by higher production costs that they, as exporters, could accept less sanguinely than the urban manufacturers among their political opponents, who aimed only at the home market. The political victory for the liberals that permitted farmers to reform the tax system and shift burdens from the countryside to the cities had to wait until the turn of the century. Universalist, tax-financed social policy was its herald.

Early discussions of social-policy reform gave farmers their first chance to demand a respite from the growing burdens of poor relief on local authorities.[12] As more of the population was granted a voice in politics during the late eighteenth and early nineteenth centuries, the contradiction was aggravated between the absolutist monarch's comparatively generous social policy, and the disinclination of farmers, who paid the lion's share of local taxes, to bear a heavier load than necessary. Especially after 1835, with widened representation in the estates, farmers lamented the growing cost of poor relief, and debated the merits of workhouses on the British model and a declassing treatment of the poor. In 1874, liberals first tried to reduce their costs through another, and ultimately more successful, approach, demanding subsidies from the state for self-help, praising the relief this would bring to tax burdens.[13] The report of the Commission on Workers' Conditions in 1878 continued the liberal farmers' interest in state subsidies.[14] They worried, lest employers bear the brunt of the social provision, especially in agriculture, where a dependence on foreign markets made it difficult to pass along expenses. If low wages in the countryside were not to be raised, costs would have to be shifted to consumers or employers. Neither possibility was attractive, so the farmers' solution for pensions was based on voluntary arrangements, with the state responsible for half of the funding.[15] The commission's conservative minority, on the other hand, saw no justification for state financing. Shifting the burdens from local governments to the state did not lessen the demoralizing effect of public subsidies as such. Farmers had long exploited poor relief as a subsidy to their laborers' inadequate wages, but it was not the public's task to supplement incomes. Since wages that were sufficient even in times of old age and disability were the employer's responsibility, contributory financing was the solution.[16]

For the time being, farmers' hopes for state-subsidized social policy failed with the sharpening of the constitutional conflict that pitted the liberal majority in the lower house against a conservative government. Once moderates in the opposing camps wearied of battle, a rapprochement, phrased in terms of social policy, became possible, and eventually it was consummated in the 1891 pension law that sent Denmark into the welfare vanguard as the bearer of a universalist, tax-financed pension system unlike that of Bismarck.[17] Among liberals, the conflict was coming to a head between radicals, who resisted cooperation with the government before settlement of the constitutional issue, and moderates, who were willing to compromise.[18] Moderates were willing to trade an end to the hostilities for conservative support of agricultural tariff reform.[19] They proposed replacing tariffs on raw sugar with a tax on the urban workingman's beer, and to distribute small garden parcels to otherwise landless agricultural labourers.[20] Cheaper sugar and land redistribution might, they hoped, stimulate a preserves industry and supplement rural incomes. Among the conservatives, estate owners were encouraged to compromise with liberals by the problems they shared in common as agrarians.

In 1890, poor relief and reform of tariffs and taxes intersected with the chance to resolve the constitutional dispute to bring forth the first pension legislation. Faced with an understanding between moderate liberals and conservatives for new taxes on the urban and laboring classes' favorite inebriants, radical liberals proposed using their income to finance noncontributory pensions for the poor of all classes.[21] Four months later, in March 1891, moderates from the parties to the future rapproachement agreed on a response. A compromise over tariffs foundered on the upper house's unwillingness to relax protectionism, but was reached instead on pensions. The moderates' move was an overbid that shifted tax burdens from sugar to beer and carved out of a previous government proposal on poor relief a bill on statutory aid for the worthy elderly.[22] Local authorities were to grant pensions to all morally upright needy over age sixty, with half their expenses reimbursed by the state.[23] What the moderate liberals and conservatives had agreed on was to begin to end the constitutional conflict and, in return, to shift a significant fraction of local poor-relief expenses from agrarians' shoulders, to the state.

Two points stand out on the socialists' attitude to this effort at social-policy reform. First, Denmark's agrarian society prevented the socialists, to the extent they entertained ambitions to power, from limiting their concern to the urban working class.[24] In social policy, this meant not restricting arrangements to any particular class. Nor could special consideration for urban areas be pressed.[25] The socialists' need to appeal to the petite bourgeoisie also introduced an ambivalence in their relations with the unskilled lowest layers of the working class, allowing them to accept the demeaning criteria of moral worth and respectability that remained a persistent characteristic of Danish social policy.[26] Second, like their British colleagues, Danish socialists rejected the contributory and self-help principles of pension policy. Members of the extensive network of voluntary sickness funds could pay premiums, but further contributions, for other forms of social policy would strain the average budget.[27] Wages were modest, the right to work was not recognized, and workers were the source of surplus value; unconditional help from the state was, therefore, their right in times of distress.[28] This derivation of the right to aid from the theory of surplus value was a common socialist position at the time, shared with the German Left.[29] The right to benefits founded on the production of surplus value remained a purely theoretical ideal among German socialists, soon replaced in practice by contractual entitlement based on contributions.[30] In Denmark, where a happy overlap of interests between socialists and liberals allowed significant public participation and a non-contributory system, reliance on the state remained both theory and practice.

Socialists, however, were not the ones who mattered in this period. Without a doubt, liberals and conservatives hoped to dampen the Left's appeal by supporting social policy and other improvements for rural laborers and smallholders. Nevertheless, the nature of social reform was determined by the agrarian liberals, for their own reasons. The constitutional conflict saw Danish politics split between the conservatives and liberals. Much has been made of earlier land reforms, the influence of popular education, and the flowering cooperative movement to explain the political liberalism of Danish farmers.[31] These were certainly factors. Their liberalism was provoked by conservative unwillingness to grant them political power proportional to their social importance. One of the peculiarities of the Danish situation, however, was the manner in which farmers reacted to the agricultural crisis, undergirding their political opposition with economic motives that prevented their division into protectionists and free-traders.

Danish farmers, who were exporters dependent on cheap foreign fodder, had obvious cause to be economic liberals. What distinguished them from their German and Swedish colleagues was their ability, once grain prices began to drop, to shift to dairy farming and livestock and continue exporting.[32] Their consistent support for free trade, even as the rest of Europe turned coats, made impossible the common ground behind high tariffs between some agriculture and some industry, that Germany achieved with the marriage of iron and rye in 1879.[33] Because Danish industrialists and manufacturers produced for the home market, political realignments – based on a common protectionist position, cutting across occupational categories – were hampered. The farmers' inability to compromise with protectionist conservatives laid the socioeconomic foundation of the constitutional conflict. The political deadlock, in turn, prevented liberal agrarians from introducing the tax reforms on their agenda, above all income and wealth taxes to lessen those on land, until after social reform had passed.[34]

Tax reform was a longstanding agrarian demand. Direct state income and wealth taxes had been on the liberal program since 1882. The large aristocratic landowners among the conservatives wished to retain land and property taxes that, though weighty, founded their claim to disproportional power. Since land taxes affected them only slightly, the conservative urban mercantile and manufacturing classes agreed. On the other side, farmers resented the old tax structure, since their debt burdens, increased during the shift to livestock and dairy farming, were ignored. Local taxes seem to have prompted the most justified reason for complaint. Unlike the income of the state, raised largely from indirect taxes, local revenues were the fruit of direct property taxes that increased during that century.[35] As agriculture gradually became more differentiated, with other professions making inroads in the countryside, the inherited local tax system was unable to adjust, prompting increasingly vociferous complaints.[36] Since poor relief was funded by local taxes, there was a direct connection between social and tax reform. State-financed pensions promised to shift the costs of maintaining the indigent elderly from local authorities' property taxes to the central state's indirect consumption levies. Farmers expected to gain most from this displacement. Because the constitutional conflict blocked more direct reforms, publicly-financed pensions became a partial substitute for tax reform.

Both state financing and premiums on the German model would have relieved the weight that instead fell on the most progressively assessed levies of the day: local cadastral taxes. While farmers' ambition to reduce their fiscal burdens could have been satisfied by either means, financing through taxes promised them several advantages. First, it eliminated the need for an employer's contribution. Far and away the largest group of employers, farmers stood to bear the brunt of costs distributed in this way. Because most farms were small or medium-sized enterprises practicing labor-intensive agriculture, they could not bear premiums with the same facility as the large protectionist industries of Germany.[37] Second, the use of tax financing avoided the higher wages needed to enable workers to pay premiums.[38] Unlike the protectionist Germans and Swedes, Danish farmers sold at prices determined on the world market and could absorb higher production costs only at the risk of decreased competitiveness. State financing held out special economic advantages to farmers to the extent they could side-step the higher taxes that would follow. Related to these considerations was a third factor born of the severity of the late nineteenth-century agricultural crisis. Funded contributory social insurance could have begun only after a lengthy transition period during which the currently needy would still be without aid. Tax-financed, noncontributory measures, on the other hand, took effect at once.[39]

Such factors determined agriculture's reluctance to assume social burdens directly. There still remained the question of where they could be placed. The inherited tax structure and antagonisms between urban and rural groups gave state financing the advantage of shifting burdens not merely away from the farmers, but from the countryside to the cities. Farmers attached great importance to the state-financed pensions' ability to reduce their local poor-relief costs by displacing the expense of providing for the elderly to state taxes.[40] The countryside contributed proportionally less to the state's revenue (raised largely from indirect taxes) than cities. The new taxes introduced to help finance pensions, they reasoned, would affect urban workers more than their rural colleagues, and, generally, economies based on cash more than in kind.[41] Finally, there was also an element of institutional inertia that tipped the balance toward tax financing. The 1891 pension law resembled the old poor-relief system, shorn of its most disagreeable aspects. Avoiding a massive new bureaucracy in the train of a Bismarckian system appealed to the liberals' penchant for administrative minimalism and their disinclination to swell the ranks of civil servants, who usually voted for conservatives.[42]

Taxes were only one of the reasons why farmers favored reform that promised to ease their burdens. Despite a successful shift in products, they faced worsening problems as the agricultural crisis deepened.[43] Agrarians were affected simultaneously by two problems. The transition to animal production was profitable because livestock and dairy prices remained stable, while feed costs declined. In the 1890s, transportation efficiencies intensified competition with the New World and pressed livestock prices. As profits were squeezed, labor problems arose. Animal and dairy farming were more labor intensive than grain, while, perversely, the new productive techniques allowed smallholders to withdraw from wage earning to cultivate their own land. Large farmers needed more labor at the same time that competition and falling prices limited their ability to improve conditions and to stem migration. How to make rural life more attractive was an important concern. Pensions were but one of the most successful measures considered that demonstrated the close connection between the agricultural crisis and social reform. Because agrarians sought to improve the lot of their laborers, and because their work force included both wage earners and smallholders, dependent only partially on outside employment, limiting social measures to wage earners, not to mention the urban working class, was out of the question.[44]

Farmers, Conservatives, and the Origins of Universalist Social Policy: Sweden

Although the political circumstances surrounding pension reform in Sweden differed from those in Denmark, the most important features were shared. Above all, universalist legislation was rooted in its agrarian social structure. Both the government administration and the socialists initially favored pensions aimed at the working class alone. The bureaucrats and the Left could do little against the wishes of farmers not to be excluded from statutory beneficence and their disinclination to pay for measures from whose enjoyment they were barred. The decision against contributory social insurance on the German model was the result of similar forces. Extending pensions to all citizens undermined financing by premiums. The self-employed, especially farmers, saw no reason to pay for their benefits alone, while workers were helped out by their employers. Tax financing proved necessary in a country where most citizens were still independents. While contributions were tolerable for large businesses, they were, for the mass of small agricultural employers, an unacceptable burden that could be transferred to the state and the tax-paying community at large. The universalist and largely tax-financed pension system, in these ways, reflected the demands of small farmers.

Attempts to solve the pension problem in Sweden at the end of the nineteenth century failed, with success reserved for a law in 1913 based on novel principles. This legislation introduced, for the first time, 'folk pensions' that gave all citizens at least token benefits, regardless of class or income. Reform came late because farmers opposed the bureaucracy's inclination to follow Bismarck's example but, for the time being, they could only obstruct government plans, not yet implement their own. At the same time, while farmers were still unable to dictate change, their desires were less clearly opposed to the conservative program than in Denmark. Previous satisfaction of agricultural demands on tax and military issues, that to the south were resolved only with or after disputes over social policy, moderated antagonisms between farmers and landed aristocrats on the one hand, and industrialists, manufacturers, urban professional classes, and the civil service on the other.

Among the issues of concern to farmers, two were closely connected: military reorganization and tax reform. Military burdens were distributed unevenly, resting with particular weight in the countryside. Taxes, too, were archaically and unfairly apportioned. The conservatives' ambitions to modernize the armed forces and the farmers' contradicting hopes of a frugal administration and their determination not to concede military reform without tax reform were reconciled by degrees over two decades. Taxes that especially burdened agricultural land were gradually reapportioned, and the army was reformed.[45] Unlike in Denmark, where social reform coincided with the political deadlock between urban and rural groups, major agrarian demands had been satisfied in Sweden by the time social reform was first put on the agenda. Tariffs were another issue over which the Swedish agrarians and conservatives fought less bitterly than across the Kattegat. Rather than following their Danish colleagues on free trade, Swedish farmers reacted much like their German counterparts.[46] Those with rye for sale, generally larger farmers in central Sweden, welcomed high tariffs. Dairy and livestock farmers, who were grain consumers, opposed them.[47] Protectionist agriculture, represented by landed aristocrats in the senate and rye-producing farmers in the lower chamber, made itself heard. Politically, the tariff dispute had far-reaching effects. The agrarians split, dividing into free-trading and protectionist wings, with other parties following suit. Large farmers in the lower chamber, and landed aristocrats and industrialists in the senate, identified common interests and inaugurated a tradition of agrarian-conservative cooperation that lasted until the 1930s. In the lower house, the traditional opposition between city and countryside was moderated by new realignments over tariffs as workers and free-trading liberals found common ground.[48]

Developments in social insurance began in Sweden at about the same time as in Denmark.[49] For pensions, the First Workers' Insurance Commission's report in 1889 unsuccessfully proposed measures covering all with flat-rate contributory benefits. Deciding whom to include, the commission defied its mandate to provide only for workers and those in comparable circumstances. Insurmountable difficulties, it concluded, would plague attempts to distinguish workers from the self-employed and to deal with the many who would cross any such line during their careers.[50] The Second Workers' Insurance Commission's proposals differed.[51] Following Bismarck's lead, measures were now limited to the working class.[52] The need for insurance varied among social groups, it concluded. Wage earners were more dependent on poor relief than independents, who enjoyed a certain protection through their property. As increasing numbers of workers relied on poor relief, burdens that were unequally distributed through local taxes increased. The workers and their employers were therefore to pay premiums. The clarity of the commission's proposal was marred, however, by the dissenting opinion of the agrarian leader, A. P. Danielson.[53] Speaking for the interests of farmers not to be barred from what otherwise threatened to become exclusively working-class legislation, he regretted the exclusion of the most rural inhabitants, classified by the law as employers. And he wanted the financing foreseen for employer contributions to be assumed by the state, in order to distribute the required sacrifices among all.

The government's bill, introduced in 1895, was able closely to follow the commission's recommendations because the farmers had not yet made their objections felt.[54] In parliament, however, the relevant committee, more influenced by Danielson, remained unpersuaded.[55] Employer contributions, even as limited in the bill, hurt small employers, while the greater reliance on tax funds spared unreasonable burdens for independents.[56] The government's next try, still unsuccessful, was a compromise bill in 1898 that took another step toward the universalist, state-financed measures that were farmers' goal.[57] The classes covered remained largely limited to workers, but employer premiums were eliminated altogether, and state subsidies increased.

With this bill's defeat, the government's efforts reached their final rest in this round. Matters lay fallow until, at the end of 1907, the Old Age Pensions Commission was appointed. Its report, five years later, surveyed the field.[58] Industrial workers now challenged agrarians as the dominant social group. Even though social insurance was related to the increased importance of wage earners as a class, it should not cover them alone. The German system was inadequate in excluding independents and reserving the blessings of state subsidies for only one group. Complete state financing of universalist pensions, on the other hand, was prohibitively expensive.[59] Were all included, contributions would have to be collected. Employer contributions played no role in a system not limited to wage earners, but state subsidies allowed higher benefits than otherwise possible. To keep residents of expensive urban areas off poor relief, means-tested local supplements to the otherwise inadequate pensions were permitted. The government's bill followed the commission.[60] Had measures been passed some decades earlier, it admitted, they would probably have been limited to wage earners. Favorable economic developments now allowed all to be included. Employer premiums had been replaced by state financing for fear that wage earners would be privileged while small employers were called on to pay both for themselves and their workers.

The socialists' approach to this reform was interesting. Unlike their Danish colleagues in the late nineteenth century, Swedish socialists focussed attention on the urban industrial working class, undistracted by the desire to appeal to agrarians. The social and economic complexions of the two countries partially explain this result. Sweden's mining and timber gave the economy an industrialized hue.[61] Denmark was still more urbanized than Sweden, but agriculture played a dominant role. Danish agriculture was characterized by comparatively large farms worked by laborers, who were riper for socialist recruitment than Sweden's generally small independent farmers.

Socialist ideology in Sweden reflected these differences. When formulating its first party program, the Swedish Left ignored the agrarian question, assuming, and therefore assuring, the futility of winning support among rural workers.[62] A Kautskain approach to agriculture squared off against a Danish-style attempt at a 'folk party' in internal debate.[63] Only after the turn of the century did the orthodox approach make way for a more reformist angle. In part, the Swedes replicated an adjustment of Marxist doctrine to political reality found across European socialist parties. In equal measure, they took account of domestic social peculiarities, the political costs of ignoring rural classes with too blindered a favoritism for workers. The advantages of appealing to agrarians became especially obvious after the electoral reforms of 1907–9 extended the franchise. In 1911, the year of the first elections with universal manhood suffrage, a major revision of the party's platform shifted its focus from the working class, narrowly defined, to all oppressed, whatever their social origin.[64]

Despite such shifts, socialist support for the 1913 pension bill, coinciding with a sharpening internal conflict between doctrinaires and reformists, was far from unanimous.[65] Early in the year, the party's parliamentary deputies had decided for an universalist approach. Later discussion revealed the presence of a minority in favor of treating various social groups differently. Several supported a contributory system.[66] Although the parliamentary group accepted the government bill, conflicts arose within the broader movement. The party executive was displeased that the deputies had abandoned employer contributions, and were seconded in their doubts by the unions.[67] Some, like Gustav Steffen, the well-known sociologist in the senate, preferred pensions on the German model that treated workers and independents separately. Imposing on all citizens a social-insurance system developed for wage earners was unfortunate, he admitted, but no worse than the government's converse choice of extending to all a system formulated in the interests of the self-employed. The productive process ought to meet the cost of old age and disability through employer premiums.[68]

On the other side, Hjalmar Branting, leader of the socialists, accepted the bill. His defense of it in parliament was a masterful summation of the pension issue and its social background. Had the Swedish working class been more powerful when legislation was first proposed, he conceded, the problem might have been resolved as in Germany. But even with measures limited to workers, changes would have followed. Contributory workers' insurance could not have been extended beyond the ranks of large industrial employers. In Sweden, small employers were powerful and able to resist contributory financing more resolutely than their counterparts across the Baltic.

The socialists had shifted their stance, he admitted. They had supported insurance limited to workers, but now favored universalist measures. This broad acceptance of all-inclusive arrangements was due to the advance of the popular classes in the countryside, whose interests had been given representation through electoral reform. Sweden was not an industrialized society like Germany or Britain, and small independents relied on poor relief as much as wage earners. Thus social insurance that focussed only on workers ignored Sweden's social structure. Conceding that universalist social policy was unavoidable, Branting went on to the difficulties of securing fair treatment for workers within a system that covered all: That harmonizing the interests of the poorest rural inhabitants, with those of urban workers, was troublesome. State subsidies should be given in proportion to the premium paid, more to urban than rural groups. Eliminating urban municipal supplements that would have given workers larger pensions than farmers had been a step backwards. It was difficult with universalist national insurance to maintain sufficient differentiation between well- and poorly paid groups. Improvements for the worst-off should not be brought at the expense of the industrial working class.[69]

In both Denmark and Sweden, social-policy reform was born during a period of major political change and struggle as the child of native social and economic circumstances. The late nineteenth century saw the breakthrough of democratic politics and the coming to power of the broad middle classes, in Scandinavian circumstances primarily farmers and peasants. In this clash, agrarians wrested from the traditional political elites of urban professionals, royal bureaucrats, and aristocratic estate owners that influence to which their growing social and economic importance entitled them. Social-policy reform was colored by its coincidence with this battle. Reforms reflected the strengthened power of farmers and their determination not to be deprived of new forms of statutory benevolence. Socialists were not without a presence during these changes. Vaguely Bonapartist fears encouraged the bourgeois parties to implement some form of statutory social measures. Nevertheless, the content and nature of those finally chosen were determined by the needs of the agrarians, who were emerging as dominant among the bourgeois groups. The occasional and grudging approval by the socialists of those features of social reform for which they would later take and be given credit were responses to demands advanced by agrarians and liberals.

In 1891 Denmark introduced universal, noncontributory, tax-financed pensions. The universalism of these reforms was the result, most generally, of Denmark's agrarian society, more specifically of the farmers' desire to improve their conditions through social measures during the rural crisis. Because their work force included cottagers and small holders as well as landless laborers, attempts to distinguish between the dependently employed and independents, focusing measures on one or the other, made little sense. The agricultural labor force was poorly paid because remuneration was still partly in natura, because rural conditions hindered workers' claims for higher incomes, and because costs were low in the countryside. Contributory social insurance of the sort Bismarck had aimed at the urban worker aristocracy, could help the agricultural labor force only if farmers raised wages. State financing, however, especially in the context of longstanding agrarian demands for tax reform, provided a solution. The tax system of nineteenth-century Denmark had evolved to suit the needs of a predominantly rural nation in which tillers of the soil had not yet developed the political clout to shift burdens elsewhere. Direct taxes on land and its products supplied the local administrations on which the cost of poor relief fell. The manufacturing and industrial classes were treated leniently. Social policy financed through indirect state taxes helped shift the cost of poor relief and local taxes to urban groups. Even though an income tax, long a liberal agrarian demand, was not introduced until after the turn of the century, farmers were convinced that the consumption taxes now used for statutory social policy would afflict urban more than rural workers. Before the era of graduated income taxes, state-financed welfare policy in effect shifted the weight of social risk away from the most progressively assessed levies of the period, cadastral taxes, and onto the shoulders both of the liberals' urban opponents and of those classes supposedly among the direct beneficiaries of the new measures.

In Sweden, matters took a somewhat different course. Well-developed, efficient, and insulated by the rudimentary nature of Swedish politics from outside pressures, the government bureaucracy was initially able to formulate plans for social reform that followed lessons learned from Bismarck more closely than native social circumstances and the wishes of not yet powerful groups. Reformers at first set their sights on contributory social insurance restricted to the working class. But, while capable of formulating reforms in isolation, they could not pass and implement measures that ignored the wishes of important interests.[70] Because antagonisms between liberals and conservatives, and rural and urban groups, were less pronounced than in Denmark, the main dispute in Sweden arose between farmers and the powerful government bureaucracy that was eventually forced to consider their desires. Attempts at reform were stymied for over two decades until, in 1913, Sweden finally implemented universalist, largely tax-financed, pensions. This arrangement rejected Bismarck's legacy, anticipated Beveridge, and embodied the major features later regarded as the essence of the Nordic welfare state. Far from being the realization of demands put forth by the oppressed or the Left, they reflected farmers' wishes not to be deprived of state-subsidized measures that were otherwise targeted at workers only.

In the social interpretation of the welfare state, Bismarck's reforms exemplified social policy used for reactionary, Bonapartist purposes. They were limited to workers, who posed the most immediate threat to social stability. Benefits were differentiated by income to preserve the hierarchies of the marketplace even outside its sphere. Financing was assured through employer and worker premiums with little state financing in order to hold redistribution to a minimum. The Scandinavian welfare states, on the contrary, were qualitatively different in realizing the need of the disadvantaged for solidarity. Nordic social policy supposedly demonstrated that real reform could be wrung form the privileged by the oppressed themselves, on their own terms. It embodied equality, not hierarchy; consensus, not conflict; solidarity, not separatism. Scandinavian measures were universal in their embrace of all citizens. They were financed through taxes that fairly apportioned burdens and had a penchant for being formally egalitarian flat-rate benefits.

The social interpretation anachronistically attributes these features to the power of the social democrats and the working class. Decisions in favor of universalist, tax-financed, egalitarian measures were taken before the socialists had much say in the matter and often against their will. The cornerstone of the unique Nordic welfare edifice was set already during the late nineteenth century, not in the 1930s or after World War II, when the social democrats gained power. Social insurance had been formulated first in Germany to deal with well-paid urban workers. In Scandinavia, these classes could not be the focus. North of the Eider, priorities were defined by the emerging agrarian middle classes. Scandinavian pensions were made universalist because farmers refused to be excluded from these new forms of statutory generosity. They were tax-financed because, in this way, the rural classes expected to gain more than they lost. State-financed social policy is not better than the tax system on which it rests. To attribute the (often dubious) progressivity of twentieth-century measures to an earlier period is to misunderstand the nature of battles then fought out between social groups, in the guise of fiscal and welfare reform. In Scandinavia of the late nineteenth century, government-financed social policy was an element of a drawn-out dispute between rural and urban elites whose resolution allowed farmers to shift social burdens to their urban opponents.

Both of these characteristics – universality and tax financing – did, in fact, later become progressive, solidaristic aspects of welfare policy in the North. When the decision was first made to follow this *Sonderweg* in Scandinavian social policy, however, these features were the result of demands put forth by the emerging agrarian middle classes on their own behalf. Such characteristics were not created, only continued, by the socialists in the 1930s and later. This is not necessarily to denigrate these aspects of Scandinavian social policy. It is, however, to take a realistic look at their genealogies and to make an accurate appraisal of their origins, one that can explain why the Nordic welfare states were unusual without resorting either to the vagueness of supposedly unique Scandinavian social virtues or to the anachronism of socialism's heroic march in these most quintessentially petty bourgeois of European nations. The origins of virtue turn out to be mundane: The solidarity of one age has its roots in the selfishness of another.

Notes

This essay is part of a larger study, 'The Politics of Social Solidarity and the Class Basis of the European Welfare State, 1875–1975,' that will also cover France, Germany, and Britain. I am grateful to Lawrence Stone, Peter Mandler, and other members of the Davis Seminar at Princeton for a thorough working over, and to the American-Scandinavian Foundation for resources to conduct the research. I also owe Daniel Levine a helpful reading of the manuscript.

1 Jean-Jacques Dupeyroux, *Evolution et tendances des systemes de Sécurité sociale des pays membres des communautés européennes et de la Grande-Bretagne* (Luxembourg, 1966), 55–9.
2 Franz-Xaver Kaufmann, *Sicherheit als soziologisches und sozialpolitisches Problem: Untersuchungen zu einer Wertidee hochdifferenzierter Gesellschaften* (Stuttgart, 1970), 18.
3 This is why general histories only of Britain and Sweden seek to define their essence of their current incarnations as welfare states: T. O. Lloyd, *Empire to Welfare State: English History, 1906–1967* (Oxford, 1970); Pauline Gregg, *The Welfare State: An Economic and Social History of Great Britain from 1945 to the Present Day* (London, 1967); Kurt Samuelson, *From Great Power to Welfare State: Three Hundred Years of Swedish Social Development* (London, 1968).
4 Asa Briggs refuses to anoint Bismarck's reforms with the title 'welfare state' because of their Bonapartist intent ('The Welfare State in Historical Perspective,' *Archives européennes de sociologie*, 2:2 [1961], 247–9).
5 An exception is discussed in Daniel Levine, 'The Danish Connection: A Note on the Making of British Old-Age Pensions,' *Albion*, 17:2 (Summer 1985), 181–5.

6 Roland Huntford, *The New Totalitarians* (London, 1971); Marguis Childs, *Sweden: The Middle Way* (New Haven, 1936).

7 On Sweden's career as an ideal type, Arne Ruth, 'The Second New Nation: The Mythology of Modern Sweden,' in *Norden: The Passion for Equality*, Stephen R. Graubard, ed. (Oslo, 1986), 240–82.

8 On the Nordic, institutional model of the welfare state, Richard Titmuss, *Social Policy* (London, 1974), 30–1; Anne-Lise Seip, *Om velferdsstatens fremvekst* (Oslo, 1981), 11–18; Norman Furniss and Timothy Tilton, *The Case for the Welfare State* (Bloomington, 1977), 14–20; Bent Rold Andersen, 'Rationality and Irrationality of the Nordic Welfare State,' in *Norden: The Passion for Equality*, Stephen R. Graubard, ed., 117–21; Michael Shalev, 'The Social-Democratic Model and Beyond: Two "Generations" of Comparative Research on the Welfare State,' *Comparative Social Research*, 6 (1983), 315–51.

9 'The congruence of Scandinavian social-democratic welfare policy,' one recent account would have its readers believe, 'is explained by two critical factors. One was that the parties chose to abandon the ghetto model in favor of parliamentary majoritarianism. They had to cultivate, and fabricate, unity among workers, peasants, and the rising white collar strata. This naturally led to an insistence on universalism' (Gøsta Esping-Andersen, *Politics against Markets: The Social Democratic Road to Power* [Princeton, 1985], 154, 145, 148).

10 Examples of an anachronistic misattribution of the apparent solidarity of early Scandinavian welfare reforms to the socialists: Åke Elmér, *Från Fattigsverige till välfärdsstaten: Sociala föhållanden och socialpolitik i Sverige under nittonhundratalet*, 7th ed. (Stockholm, 1975), 127; Stein Kuhnle, 'The Beginnings of the Nordic Welfare States: Similarities and Differences,' *Acta Sociologica*, 21, supplement (1978), 26; Guy Perrin, 'L'assurance sociale – ses particularités – son role dans le passé, le present et l'avenir,' in *Beiträge zu Geschichte und aktueller Situation der Sozial versicherung*, Peter A. Köhler and Hans F. Zacher, eds. (Berlin, 1983), 40–1; Thomas Wilson, ed., *Pensions, Inflation, and Growth: A Comparative Study of the Elderly in the Welfare State* (London, 1974), 159; Gøsta Esping-Andersen and Walter Korpi, 'From Poor Relief to Institutional Welfare States: The Development of Scandinavian Social Policy,' in *The Scandinavian Model,* John Erikson et al., eds. (Armonk, 1987), 45–6.

11 An explanation of why the universalism of postwar reforms in Scandinavia was not a socialist initiative is given in Peter Baldwin, 'How Socialist is Solidaristic Social Policy? Swedish Postwar Reform as a Case in Point,' *International Review of Social History*, 2 (1988), 121–47.

12 Older, but still useful, accounts include *Danmarks sociallovgivning* (Copenhagen, 1918–20); Harald Jørgensen, *Studier over det offentlige Fattigvæsens historiske Udvikling i Danmark i det 19. aarhundrede* (Copenhagen, 1940); Kjeld Philip, *Staten og Fattigdommen: Fem Kapitler af dansk Kulturpolitik* (Copenhagen, 1947); Cordt Trap, *Om Statens Stilling til Ubemidledes Alderdomsforsørgelse i flere europæiske Lande* (Copenhagen, 1892); Jørgen Dich, 'Kompendium i socialpolitikkens historie: I. Udviklingen indtil 2. Verdenskrig,' manuscript, 2d ed. (1967). Systematizing and expanding the rather schematic works of Dich and others in Jørn Henrik Petersen's recent and extensive account of pension policy in *Den danske adlerdomsforsørgelseslovgivnings udvikling: Bind I. Oprindelsen* (Odense, 1985) (citations from Petersen are to the more detailed, unpublished manuscript of the dissertation of the same title (Odense University, 1985).

13 Dich, 'Kompendium' 19. Petersen, *Den danske alderdomsforsøgelseslovgivnings udvikling,* 143–8.

14 *Betænkning afgiven af den ifølge Kgl. Resolution af 2ode September 1875 til Undersøgelse af Arbeiderforholdene i Danmark nedsatte Kommission* (Copenhagen, 1878), 71–7, 81–3. Background in G. Warmdahl, 'Statens Stilling til Arbejderspørgsmaalet i halvfjerdserne: Arbejderkommissionen af 1875,' in *Sociale studier i dansk historie efter 1857,* Polv Engelstoft and Hans Jensen, eds. (Copenhagen, 1930), 64–81.

15 Rigsarkivet, Copenhagen, PR 404–07–2, Arbejderkommissionen af 1875, Minutes of a meeting 8 December 1875 or 1876. This was the argument put forth by V. Falbe-Hansen. A professor of statistics, he was a conservative deputy at the time, but later joined the upper house in 1909 as a royal appointee and a liberal.

16 *Betænkning,* 87–9.

17 On the complicated negotiations leading up to 1891, Petersen, *Den danske alderdomsforsørgelseslovgivnings udvikling,* ch. 12; Dich, 'Kompendium,' 23–6; Trap, *Statens stilling,* 260–77.

18 N. Neergaard, *Erindringer* (Copenhagen, 1935), 235–40. *Frede Bojsens politiske erindringer,* Kristian Hvidt, ed. (Copenhagen, 1963), 189ff.

19 *Rigsdagstidende,* FT, 14 October 1890, col. 44–6. A general account is Poul Kierkegaard, 'Frede Bojsen som Socialpolitiker,' in *Mænd og Meninger i Dansk Socialpolitik, 1866–1901,* Povl Engelstoft and Hans Jensen, eds. (Copenhagen, 1933), 67–107.

20 *Rigsdagstidende,* FT, 30 October 1890, col. 440–7.

21 Marcus Rubin, 'Hvad koster en Alderdomsforsørgelse for de danske Arbejdere?' *Nationaløkonomisk Tidsskrift,* 26 (1888), 357–8; *idem,* 'Alderdomsforsørgelsesforslaget,' *Nationaløkonomisk Tidsskrift,* 29 (1891),

44–8; Trap, *Statens stilling*, 256; Marcus Rubin, *Om Alderdomsforsørgelsen* (Copenhagen, 1891), 12–16; Letter, Rubin to Edvard Brandes, 9 December 1890, in *Marcus Rubins brevveksling, 1870–1922*, Lorenz Rerup, ed. (Copenhagen, 1963), I, 319–20; Marcus Rubin, *Nogle erindringer* (Copenhagen, 1914), 143–4.

22 In 1890, the government had proposed legislation to reform poor relief by granting it, shorn of its usual demeaning consequences, to the worthy needy, *Rigsdagstidende*, 1890–1, Tillæg A, col. 3393ff.; FT, 11 March 1891, col. 4537–45, 4591–7.

23 The conservatives managed to limit the state's obligation to refund municipal expenses to two million crowns annually. Not until 1902, after the final resolution of the parliamentary battle and liberal victory, was this limit removed.

24 An excellent account of the relation between socialists and their political clientele in Denmark's agrarian society, with important implications for the history of socialism in general, is Hans-Norbert Lahme, *Sozialdemokratie und Landarbeiter in Dänemark (1871–1900)* (Odense, 1982). Also, Henning Grelle, *Socialdemokratie i det danske landbrugssamfund, 1871–ca.1903* (Copenhagen, 1978), and Georg Nørregaard and Hans Jensen, 'Organisationsforsøg blandt Landarbejderne,' in *Bidrag til Arbejderklassens og Arbejderspørgsmaalets Historie i Danmark fra 1864 til 1900*, Povl Engelstoft and Hans Jensen, eds. (Copenhapgen, 1931), 54–202.

25 Thus, for example, socialists rejected the assumption of the Radical Liberals' bill that life was cheaper in rural than urban areas and that differential benefits were necessary. *Rigsdagstidende*, FT, 20 December 1890, col. 1823.

26 Torben Berg Sørensen, *Arbejderklassens organisering og socialpolitikkens dannelse* (Copenhagen, 1978), 104–5, 168–74.

27 This is the argument made, with much supporting evidence on wages and contributions, in P. Knudsen, *Sygeforsikring og Alderdomsforsørgelse: Betænkning afgiven af det paa de københavnske og frederiksbergske Sygekassers Fællesmøde den 29de og 30te August 1883 nedsatte Udvalg* (Copenhagen, 1888), 245–63 *et passim*.

28 Else Rasmussen, 'Socialdemokraternes Stilling til de sociale Spørgsmaal paa Rigsdagen, 1884–1890,' in *Mænd og Meninger i Dansk Socialpolitik, 1866–1901*, Povl Engelstoft and Hans Jensen, eds. (Copenhagen, 1933), 149.

29 Hertha Woolf, *Die Stellung der Sozialdemokratie zur deutschen Arbeiterversicherungsgesetzgebung von ihrer Entstehung an bis zur Reichsversicherungsordnung* (Berlin, 1933), 45–6.

30 The German socialists' interest in contributory financing was tied to the relation between premiums and representation in the social insurance

administrative councils, a motive absent in Denmark, where local authorities
were to run the system.

31 Danes boasted that, whereas among their larger neighbors the cities were
progressive and the countryside reactionary, in Denmark the situation was
reversed (Edvard Brandes, *Fra 85 til 91: En politisk Oversigt* [Copenhagen,
1891], 82).

32 Svend Aage Hansen, *Økonomisk vækst i Danmark* (Copenhagen, 1972), I, chs.
8, 9; Ole Bus Henriksen and Anders Ølgaard, *Danmarks udenrigshandel,
1874–1958* (Copenhagen, 1960). Overviews in English in Michael Tracy,
Agriculture in Western Europe (New York, 1964), and Roy Millward, *Scandinavian Lands* (London, 1964), ch. 8.

33 The comparison between Germany and Denmark in this respect was
memorably drawn by Alexander Gerschenkron in *Bread and Democracy in
Germany* (Berkeley, 1943), 39–40.

34 The tax reforms of 1903 confirmed the political shift of 1901, when liberals
finally replaced conservatives in government. Urban property was drawn into
the distribution of burdens, and a general tax on income and wealth was
introduced. Burdens were markedly shifted from rural to urban areas.
Accounts are in H. C. Henningsen, 'Beskatningsproblemet i Nutiden,' in
Den danske Stat, 2d ed. Even Marstrand et al., eds. (Copenhagen, 1933),
320–64; Sven Røgind, *Danmarks Stats- og Kommuneskatter* (Copenhagen,
1915), 7–12; Michael Koefoed, 'Skattesystemerne af 1802 og 1903,'
Nationaløkonomisk Tidsskrift, 41 (1903), 337–63; K. A. Wieth-Knudsen, *Dansk
Skattepolitik og Finansvæsen* (Copenhagen, 1928), 47–52.

35 Helge Nielsen and Victor Thalbitzer, *Skatter og Skatteforvaltning i ældre Tider*
(Copenhagen, 1948), 127; K., 'Hvorledes fordele Skatterne i Danmark sig
paa de forskellige Samfundsklasser?' *Nationaløkonomisk Tidsskrift,* 32 (1894),
203–5.

36 A. Clausager, 'Godsernes beskatningsforhold,' in *Herregaardene og Samfundet,*
Therkel Mathiassen (Copenhagen, 1943), 283–4.

37 In general, large businesses throughout Europe, especially if protected by
tariffs, feared the increased productive costs of contributory social insurance
least, small businesses most. Free-trading small businessmen, like Danish
farmers, were therefore the strongest supporters of tax-financed social
policy. Where they won, so did it. On business interests elsewhere, see Hans-
Peter Ullmann, 'Industrielle Interessen und die Entstehung der deutschen
Sozialversicherung 1880–1889,' *Historische Zeitschrift,* 229: 3 (December
1979), 574–610; Henri Hatzfeld, *Du paupérisme à la Sécurité sociale* (Paris,
1971), 137–41.

38 The German contributory system worked because it was aimed at the well-paid industrial labor aristocracy. Since Danish legislation focussed first and foremost on agricultural laborers with their lower wages, this would not do.

39 Poul Møller, *Gennembrudsår: Dansk politik i 50' erne* (Copenhagen, 1974), 2.

40 A later account found that rural localities had profited most from the pension legislation. *Rigsdagstidende*, 1896/97, Tillæg B, col. 3101–10.

41 Frede Bojsen, Lovgivningsværket 1890–95 og dets Følger (Copenhagen, 1898), 4–5; L. V. Birck, *Told og Accise* (Copenhagen, 1920), 217; Michael Koefoed, 'Skatterne i Danmark 1870–1900,' *Nationaløkonomisk Tidsskrift*, 40 (1902), 374.

42 Aage Sørensen, 'Om Alderdomsunderstøttelse i Danmark, Australian med Ny Zeland og England,' *Tidsskrift for Arbejderforsikring*, 5 (1909/10), 3–7.

43 The most sustained analysis linking the agricultural crisis, tax policy, and social reform is undertaken in Petersen, *Den danske alderdomsforsørgelses-lovgivnings udvikling*, ch. 10, which fleshes out the hypotheses mentioned, but never developed, in Philip, *Staten og Fattigdommen*, 68–70, and Jørgen Dich, *Den herskende klasse: En kritisk analyse of social udbytning og midlerne imod den*, 4th ed. (Copenhagen, 1973), 25–8. Also, Hans Jensen, 'Landarbejderspørgsmålet Udvikling i Danmark fra ca. 1870 til ca. 1900,' in *Bidrag til Arbejderklassens og Arbejderspørgsmaalets Historie i Danmark fra 1864 til 1900*, Povl Engelstoft and H. Jensen, eds. (Copenhagen, 1931), 48–54.

44 It was no coincidence, Frede Bojsen, leader of the moderate liberals, explained in retrospect, that social reform was concerned with the groups most in need, with the working rural population that had not yet fallen to socialist agitation. The legislation passed was, in the main, aimed to fit rural conditions, without, however, giving other groups reason to complain (Bojsen, *Lovgivningsværket*, 4).

45 Accounts of military and tax reform are in Per Hultqvist, *Försvar och skatter: Studier i svensk riksdagspolitik fråan representationsferormen till kimpromissen 1873* (Göteborg, 1955); idem, *Försvarsorganisationen, värnplikten och skatterna i svensk riksdagspolitik, 1867–1878* (Göteborg, 1959); and Torgny Nevéus, *Ett betryggande försvar: Värnplikten och arméorganisationen i svensk politik, 1880–1885* (Stockholm, 1965).

46 Jörn Svensson, *Jordbruk och depression, 1870–1900: En kritik av statistikens utvecklingsbild* (Malmö, 1965). An overview in English is G. A. Montgomery, *The Rise of Modern Industry in Sweden* (London, 1939), 145ff.

47 Sten Carlsson, *Lantmannapolitiken och industrialismen: Partigruppering och opinionsförskjutningar i svensk politik, 1890–1902* (Stockholm, 1953), 65–81; Arthur Montgomery, *Svensk tullpolitik, 1816–1911* (Stockholm, 1921), ch. 7;

Jan Kuuse, 'Mechanisation, Commercialisation, and the Protectionist Movement in Swedish Agriculture, 1860–1910,' *Scandinavian Economic History Review*, 19: 1 (1971), 23–44.

48 Dankwart A. Rustow, *The Politics of Compromise: A Study of Parties and Cabinet Government in Sweden* (Princeton, 1955), 40–2; Edvard Thermænius, *Rigsdagspartierna*, Vol. XVII of *Sveriges Riksdag* (Stockholm, 1935), ch. 6, esp. pp. 128–30; Per Sundberg, *Ministärerna Bildt och Åkerhielm: En studie i den svenska parlamentarismens förgårdar* (Stockholm, 1961).

49 The standard work on pensions is Åke Elmér, *Folkpensioneringen i Sverige: Med särskild hänsyn till ålderspensioneringen* (Lund, 1960). Detailed accounts of the early phase of Swedish social insurance are Karl Englund, *Arbetarförsäkringsfrågan i svensk politik, 1884–1901* (Uppsala, 1976), and Hans Peter Mensing, *Erscheinungsformen schwedischer Sozialpolitik im ausgehenden 19. Jahrhundert: Adolf Hedin, das Arbeiterversicherungskomitee und die Gewerbeaufsicht nach 1890* (Kiel, 1979). An account in English is in Hugh Heclo, *Modern Social Politics in Britain and Sweden: From Relief to Income Maintenance* (New Haven, 1974), 178–95. The beginnings of the social-insurance debate are surveyed in Arthur Montgomery, *Svensk socialpolitik under 1800-talet*, 2d ed. (Stockholm 1951).

50 *Arbetareförsäkringskomiténs betänkande* (Stockholm, 1889), I, 3, 43–73.

51 *Nya arbetareförsäkringskomiténs betänkande* (Stockholm, 1893), I, 25–107.

52 The working class was defined to include those employed by others and having an income lower than 1,800 crowns annually, but to exclude casual laborers on the fringes between wage earners and the self-employed. These laborers had been included in Germany but with unfortunate results that the Swedes saw no reason to duplicate. To start with, 15 percent of the total population (35 percent of the working population) were to be included.

53 *Ny arbetareförsäkringskomiténs betänkande*, I, 141–8.

54 Prop. 1895: 22, pp. 37–9, 43–58.

55 2SäU 1895: 2, pp. 42–4, 49–50.

56 FK 1895:26, 27 April 1895, pp. 11–12, 45; FK 1895: 27, 27 April 1895, pp. 10–11.

57 Prop. 1898:55, pp. 12–21.

58 Ålderdomsförsäkringskommittén, I *Betänkande och förslag angående allmän pensionsförsäkring* (Stockholm, 1912), 19–21, 40–4.

59 An important cause of the Swedes' concern with costs related to their demographic peculiarities. Blessed by unusual longevity and cursed by high emigration, the population's age profile was markedly skewed toward the older end. In 1900, Sweden had almost twice as many inhabitants over age

seventy as Britain and Germany, and 15 and 20 percent more than even France and Denmark, respectively. Ålderdomsförsäkringskommittén, *Kostnadsberäkningar*, (Stockholm) II, 120; Ålderdomsförsäkringskommittén, *Allmän pensionförsäkring*, 61–3; Riksarkivet, Stockholm, 20/1, Ålderdomsförsäkringskommittén, Letter, Commission to Statsrådet, 9 March 1910; And, Lindstedt, *Förslaget till lag om allmän pensionsförsäkring* (Stockholm, 1913), 8–10.

60 Prop. 1913: 126, pp. 28, 34, 48, 50, 126–7, 186–7.

61 Overviews in Lennart Jörberg, 'The Industrial Revolution in the Nordic Countries,' *The Fontana Economic History of Europe, IV, 2: idem, Growth and Fluctuation of Swedish Industry, 1869–1912* (Lund, 1961); *idem, The Industrial Revolution in Scandinavia, 1850–1914* (London, 1970).

62 This program, formulated by August Palm, was largely a translation of the Danish Gimle program from 1876, in turn a rendition of the German socialists' Gotha program with, as its particular twist, a separate point on the agricultural question: John Lindgren, *Det socialdemokratiska arbetarpartiets uppkomst i Sverige 1881–1889* (Stockholm, 1927), 291–4.

63 In Denmark, agricultural workers were significantly represented in the party; this was not the case in Sweden in the 1890s. Axel Danielsson was the main Kautskien, Hjalmar Branting the reformist in the party (G. Hilding Nordström, *Sveriges socialdemokratiska arbetarparti under gennombrottsåren, 1889–1894* (Stockholm, 1938), 184–5, 256, 261, 388–98, 613–23). On Branting's attitude, his 'Industriarbetarparti eller folkparti?' (1895) in *Tal och skrifter*, 8, (Stockholm, 1929), 48–50.

64 Herbert Tingsten, *The Swedish Social Democrats: Their Ideological Development* (Totawa, N.J., 1973), 115–95. More specifically on agrarian issues, Lars Björlin, 'Jordfrågan i svensk arbetarrörelse 1890–1920,' *Arbetarrörelsens årsbok* (Stockholm, 1974).

65 Seppo Hentilä, *Den svenska arbetarklassen och reformismens genombrott inom SAP före 1914* (Helsinki, 1979), 228–9; Ragnar Edenman, *Socialdemokratiska riksdagsgruppen, 1903–1920* (Uppsala, 1946), 165–99, 278–80.

66 Arbetarrörelsens Arkiv, Stockholm, SAP, Riksdagsgruppen, minutes, 19 February 1913, 28 March 1913, 31 March 1913, 10 April 1913.

67 Arbetarrörelsens Arkiv, Partistyrelsen, minutes, 14 April 1913. The unions wanted public subsidies raised substantially and the question of employer contributions re-examined because, they argued, some way had to be found to allow higher benefits than those foreseen in the 1913 law. LO, *Berättelse*, 1913, p. 10.

68 FK 1913: 34, 21 May 1913, pp. 31–6.

69 AK 1913: 48, 21 May 1913, pp. 44–64; AK 1913: 49, 21 May 1913, pp. 31–6.
70 This is, of course, where the analysis here differs most markedly from that in
   Hugh Heclo, *Modern Social Politics in Britain and Sweden* (New Haven, 1974),
   and in other attempts to 'bring the state back in,' for example, Ann Shola
   Orloff and Theda Skocpol, 'Why Not Equal Protection? Explaining the
   Politics of Public Social Spending in Britain, 1900–1911, and the United
   States, 1880s–1920,' *American Sociological Review*, 49: 6 (December 1984),
   726–50; and, more generally, Peter B. Evans et al., eds., *Bringing the State
   Back In* (Cambridge, 1985).

12

Re-modelling Sweden: The Rise and Demise of the Compromise in a Global Economy

GREGG M. OLSEN

Introduction: Whither the Swedish Model?

The Swedish model has been succinctly characterized as a form of welfare capitalism. For several decades it allowed labor to approximate two of its central goals, full employment and social equality, via a variety of innovative policy instruments. A solidaristic wage policy, active labor-market policies, and an elaborate welfare state were central pillars supporting the model. The foundation for all of this was the existence of an exceptionally well-organized working class, historically, ideologically, and organically linked to the long-incumbent Social Democratic Labor Party (SAP), which was able to reach a compromise with Swedish capital and its equally well-organized and centralized employers' association (SAF).

By the 1980s, however, it was quite evident that the framework of the Swedish model already had begun to deteriorate – developments that were dramatically accelerated under the right-wing coalition government in power from 1991 to 1994 – and its foundation was cracking. Today there is a growing consensus that Sweden is in serious trouble, even if the explanations offered for the nation's economic woes differ quite markedly. Indeed, the 'rise and fall' of the Swedish model is a theme that has been featured prominently in the literature over the past decade by scholars across the political spectrum (De Geer, 1992; Lundberg, 1985; Meidner, 1992, Meyerson, 1991). Most of these studies, however, tend to focus on some particular component of the model, such as collective bargaining, or on specific social programs, rather than on the totality of interrelated policy instruments and strategies that comprise it. Now, with the Swedish Social Democratic Labor Party back in power after a three-year exile, it is an opportune moment to examine closely how much of the model is still intact today and to determine its prognosis in the new, more globalized environment. It will be argued here that new conditions, including a tectonic shift of power from Sweden's labor movement to its increasingly globally oriented capital class, have hastened the erosion of the long-standing Swedish model.

The Rise and Demise of the Compromise

The Swedish model is associated with a variety of policies and procedures that have fostered a measure of equality and social solidarity. Although they all are closely connected, they will be grouped into two broad and separate categories of structural supports, 'industrial relations' and 'social planning/welfare policy,' that roughly correspond to the domains of the industrial and political branches of the labor movement. The former comprises primarily policies and procedures associated with collective bargaining and the workplace, which are of immediate concern to the trade union organizations. By the 1970s, the industrial-relations component of the Swedish model was broadened to include a variety of workplace reforms and a plan to democratize the Swedish economy. 'Social planning/welfare policy,' on the other hand, encompasses the social and economic policies that the SAP introduced to reduce poverty, redistribute income, and maintain full employment, as well as the numerous other programs that constitute the contemporary Swedish welfare state.

1 Swedish Industrial Relations

Sweden's modern industrial relations system was institutionalized in 1938 with the 'Saltsjöbaden' or 'Basic' Agreement reached between Landsorganisation (LO) and Svenska Arbetsgivareföreningen (SAF), which are the dominant blue-collar labor confederation and employers' association, respectively, at Saltsjöbaden, a seaside resort outside of Stockholm. Facing the threat of new restrictive legislation to deal with escalating levels of industrial conflict at a time of political uncertainty, both capital and labor favored a bi-partite accord that would formally exclude the participation of the state. The revisions to the existing industrial relations system generated by the new agreement were clearly circumscribed. In exchange for the establishment of new regulations and procedures for settling disputes and greater employment security – largely an extension of union rights previously achieved through the 1906 LO–SAF December Compromise – LO would have to continue to accept the

FIGURE 1
The Swedish Model

THE SWEDISH MODEL, 1930s – 1970s

INDUSTRIAL RELATIONS	SOCIAL/WELFARE POLICY
Saltsjöbaden Agreement (1938)	*Comprehensive Welfare State* – universal
Centralized Bargaining (1952/1956)*	– generous – public – preventative
Solidaristic Wage Policy (1956)	– decommodifying – coherent
Active Labor Market Policy	*Active Labor Market Policy*
'Societal' Corporatism	*Progressive Income Tax Policy*
'Labor Peace'	*Regulation of Capital*

LABOR OFFENSIVE, 1970s

INDUSTRIAL RELATIONS	SOCIAL PLANNING/WELFARE POLICY
'New' Solidaristic Wage Policy (late 1960s)	*Welfare Programs Expanded*
'Administrative' Corporatism (1970s–80s)	*Active Labor Market Policy Continued*
Socio-technical Changes (1970s–80s)	*Income Taxes Become More Progressive*
'Legislative Offensive' (1970s–80s)	*New Forms of Capital Regulation Introduced*
Wage-Earner Funds (1970s–80s)	

* Although the first peak-level LO-SAF agreement was reached in 1952, centralized bargaining was not firmly established until 1956.

employers' right to 'hire and fire and direct and distribute work.' This was palatable to labor leaders concerned that union loyalty might be undermined by existing proposals that called for increased 'worker participation' in decision making in workplace issues. The agreement also required a 'peace obligation' that prohibited strikes during the term of a collective agreement, although unions were not constrained from striking over issues not covered in the agreement.[1] Thus, as Klas Åmark (1992: 75) notes, the Saltsjöbaden Accord 'became a symbol for cooperation between SAF and LO [and] one of the most important components of the "Swedish model."' Less than 40 years later, it would serve also as a catalytic focal point for radical reform.

The second major development in the Swedish industrial relations system occurred almost 20 years later, with the official launching of centralized wage bargaining in 1956 and the implementation of the solidaristic wage policy. It was the development of this 'tri-level centralized bargaining system' – in which broad 'framework' collective agreements were reached at the central level between LO and SAF but detailed at the local (industry and plant) levels – that allowed for the adoption of LO's celebrated solidaristic wage policy (SWP) in the late 1950s.[2] The SWP was the cornerstone of the Rehn–Meidner model developed by LO economists Gösta Rehn and Rudolf Meidner. By requiring firms to pay 'equal wages for equal work,' irrespective of their level of profitability, the SWP was intended to foster economic equality and solidarity among workers. It was also designed to promote structural change by squeezing profits, while leaving control over the allocation of capital to market forces. Expansion in the most dynamic sectors of the economy and the introduction of a variety of active labor market policies served to offset the job loss resulting from the collapse of firms unable to pay solidaristic wages and kept unemployment levels very low by international standards (LO 1953; Olsen, 1988).

By the latter half of the 1960s, a more egalitarian form of the SWP involving a general wage-levelling across sectors and occupations began to displace LO's earlier compromise position based on 'equal pay for equal work.' This first, modest departure from the Swedish model marked a return to the more radical formulation originally proposed by Rehn and Meidner in the 1940s (Hibbs, 1990; Pontusson, 1992). Throughout the 1960s and 1970s, the SWP functioned as an 'extra-governmental' alternative to the divisive incomes policies common in other capitalist nations, dramatically decreasing the wage dispersion among blue-collar and private-sector white-collar workers. Between 1965 and 1975, wage dispersion declined by 74 percent among blue-collar workers and by 40 percent among private-sector white-collar workers. Between 1970 and 1982, wages were further compressed by 55 percent among blue-collar workers.

A by-product of the SWP was a dramatic reduction in the wage gap between men and women. By the early 1980s, a significant narrowing of wage discrepancies between blue-collar men and women already had occurred, and full-time female industrial laborers were earning 91 percent of the income received by their male counterparts. Differences in pay between white-collar men and women were reduced substantially also, if not as dramatically, as a result of parallel wage developments between the public sector, where women are highly segregated, and the male-dominated private sector. Female state employees, municipal employees, and salaried employees in industry received only 89 percent, 85 percent, and 72 percent, respectively, of the earnings of males in these three areas of the labor market. However, these figures were quite impressive by international standards.

In addition to setting wage scales, LO and SAF determined the penalties for those who failed to comply with the rules they set out. For several decades both capital and labor preferred this form of 'societal corporatism' to the tripartite structures that had emerged in many other Western European nations. It was characterized by self-regulation and informal state intervention largely limited to adjusting the labor supply to corporate investment decisions. However, by the 1970s and 1980s, a network of tripartite administrative bodies was created at the central and county levels. Labor and capital representatives sought membership on these new governing boards and agencies in order to influence the formation and implementation of government policies and work out compromise positions. This new 'administrative' form of corporatism already had become well entrenched by the early 1980s when 'SAF had about 5,000 persons and LO over 1,000 persons appointed to over 600 public boards, committees and councils' (Ahrne and Clement, 1992: 467).

For nearly three decades, the Swedish industrial relations system worked rather well in many ways, and Sweden's level of industrial conflict – one of the highest in the world with respect to the frequency and duration of strikes as well as the numbers of workers involved (in relative terms) – declined dramatically, transforming it into one of the most 'peaceful' nations during this 'golden era.' However, both labor and capital would come to reject central elements of the Swedish model's industrial relations system.

Labor's dissatisfaction with the long-established practices was manifest in a wave of illegal strikes of an unprecedented magnitude in the late 1960s. This renewed radicalism was accompanied by high rates of absenteeism and turnover in Swedish factories, which were facilitated by a panoply of generous and 'decommodifying' welfare and labor-market policies. All of this compelled capitalists to address labor's dissatisfaction with boring, stressful, and alienating industrial jobs and its growing demands for greater control in the workplace. This meant a departure from the Saltsjöbaden Agreement, which had specifically excluded production issues and limited collective bargaining to matters concerning distribution.

At the shop-floor level, job redesign and new 'flexible' technologies were introduced that gave employees more control over the work process in an attempt to increase worker satisfaction as well as economic efficiency. These socio-technical innovations were most conspicuously, if not exclusively, promoted and adopted by Swedish automobile producers (Volvo and Saab), and epitomized in Volvo's so-called new factories. Volvo's widely celebrated plants, which were opened in Kalmar in 1974 and Uddevalla in 1989, replaced the assembly line with work stations and multifunctional robots, and utilized teams of 'reskilled' workers with rotating jobs and leaders to build entire automotive systems (Kalmar) or complete automobiles (Uddevalla) (Berggren, 1992).

The employer's prerogatives enshrined in paragraph 32 of the Saltsjöbaden Agreement and the tradition of bi-partite, 'societal corporatism' were further challenged when a series of government acts were introduced in the 1970s and early 1980s that: increased labor's control and influence in the workplace over issues of job security and promotion, health and safety, gender equality, and educational leave; promoted 'co-determination'; and placed union representatives on company boards (LO, 1982; Swedish Ministry of Labour, 1985). The most radical divergence from the Swedish model at this time was an LO proposal, devised by Rudolf Meidner, to create economic democracy through the establishment of employee investment funds (Meidner, 1978). The 'Meidner plan' called for the 'socialization' of private firms through the establishment of capital-accumulating 'wage-earner funds' (WEF) from levies on the profits of corporations. In addition to providing labor with an instrument with which to influence investment and gain greater control over the workplace, and thereby discourage capital flight and preserve jobs, wage-earner funds would compensate workers for lost wages and counteract the concentration in the Swedish economy that had resulted from the SWP.[3]

Labor's offensive was short-lived. By the early 1980s, most of the procedures and policies that had characterized the industrial relations system for decades, as well as labor's more recent modifications and gains, were overhauled or eliminated as part of a new 'capital offensive.' Centralized bargaining and the attendant SWP were the first casualties. Many employers argued that the conditions that had made centralized bargaining and the SWP attractive in the 1950s no longer obtained. The increasingly stringent interpretation of the SWP (a general wage leveling) had become far too restrictive for some employers, such as VF (Verkstadsföreningen), the powerful Engineering Employers' Association that first broke away from centralized wage bargaining in 1983, although it had been one of the strongest supporters of centralized bargaining at the outset in the 1950s. SAF later jumped on board, maintaining that centralized bargaining no longer produced either wage restraint – as wage ceilings set at the national level became wage floors routinely exceeded in industry and plant level agreements – or labor peace. These concerns, and a desire to weaken labor, brought the era of centralized bargaining and the SWP to a close (Ahlén, 1989; Martin, 1992; SAF, 1993).[4] Today the SAF and many Swedish employers, such as Volvo and Asea Brown-Boveri (ABB), seek to replace industry-level bargaining with firm-level negotiations.

The collapse of centralized bargaining and the consequent disabling of the SWP set in motion a reversal of the considerable wage compression that had been under way for more than 20 years. By 1990, the variance in wages already had increased to the level of the mid-1970s (Hibbs and Locking, 1991). Wage differentials between men and women also began to increase among some groups by the mid-1980s and has continued into the 1990s (Persson, 1990; SCB, 1990).

In 1990, the SAF formally closed down its bargaining department and soon afterward ceased collecting the wage statistics necessary to calculate solidaristic wages. The following year, it abandoned corporatism, withdrawing its members from most of the tripartite boards with which it had been involved, including the National (and County) Labor Market Board (AMS), the National Board of Occupational Safety and Health (ASSI), Labor Inspection Boards, the Working Life Fund (ALF), and numerous Social Insurance Committees (SAF, 1992). Union representatives, consequently, were not reappointed to many of these boards.

For the most part, the apparent commitment of Swedish employers to 'industrial democracy,' or at least to some type of 'workplace humanization,' has faded also. Volvo's two automotive 'showpieces' have, tellingly, been shut down as the automotive giant contemplates further expansion of its truck operations in Europe and Asia. And, while much of the workplace legislation introduced and extended throughout the 1970s and early 1980s has remained largely intact, there have been a number of important setbacks here as well. These include funding cuts for retraining and union education, and the elimination of tax breaks for union dues (but no corresponding cuts for employers' associations); amendments that weaken rights related to seniority and arbitrary dismissal; an increase in the duration of probationary employment periods and fixed-term contracts (from six months to one year in each case); and stricter qualification rules for disability insurance.

Given the variety of restrictions imposed before their eventual introduction in a very diluted form in 1984, the wage-earner funds were not expected to democratize the Swedish economy (see Olsen, 1992). However, they did provide other benefits, such as generating revenue to strengthen the ATP pension system *(allmän tilläggspension)*. These advantages were eliminated when the 'bourgeois' government carried out its long-standing threat to dismantle all five of the funds. The fund capital has since been placed in a pool to fund research projects and help out small- and medium-size businesses. All of the changes to the industrial relations system outlined above have served to weaken labor and unhinge the Swedish model.

2 Social Planning/Welfare Policy

As occurred in the industrial relations sphere, a compromise was struck between capital and labor in the 'political' domain. The counterpart to the rights sought under the Saltsjöbaden Agreement was the SAP's commitment to social equality. Demand management, indicative planning, taxation policy, currency regulations, price controls, and the gradual implementation of the variety of tax and transfer policies and social services that came to comprise Sweden's widely admired, 'cradle-to-grave' welfare state were the major tools of social and economic engineering. The quid pro quo was the SAP's virtual abandonment of its remaining ambitions to directly or decisively control investment through 'socialization.' By the end of the 1940s, it had adopted an entirely pragmatic approach, promoting nationalization as only one of many strategies that might be used in a particular instance as a means to other ends, such as ensuring full employment (Hancock, 1972; Pontusson, 1988).

Taxation policy and the regulation of capital were two key aspects of the SAP's alternative planning and co-ordination strategy. With regard to the former, it is useful to separate corporate- from income-tax policies. In keeping with the tenor and integrity of the welfare state and its commitment to economic and social equality, the SAP ensured that the Swedish income tax system became increasingly progressive. Important tax reforms carried out in 1938, 1947, and over the next few decades marked the SAP's concern with redistribution (Gustafsson, 1983). By 1980, the top marginal rate of taxation was near 85 percent, and almost three-quarters of full-time employees paid marginal tax rates in excess of 50 percent. This supported the expansion of a variety of public welfare programs that are provided in the private sector in other countries. However, the low corporate tax rate in Sweden also necessitated the internationally high rate of income tax (McLure Jr. and Norrman, 1993; Södersten, 1984)

Despite high statutory corporate tax rates throughout the post-war period in Sweden, *effective* corporate tax rates remained rather low by international standards due to the gradual construction of an elaborate system of investment and depreciation allowances, inventory rules, tax equalization funds, and other deductions. Perhaps the most important and best known of these was the investment reserve fund system (IF). Although it was created in 1938, the IF system did not play an important role in the Swedish economy until the late 1950s, when it was first revised (Bergström and Södersten, 1984). It allowed firms to place a portion of their profits with the Central Bank (Riksbank) which could be withdrawn tax-free if invested in Sweden at times specified by the government. While this did not allow the government to influence the *allocation* of investment, it did provide it with a counter-cyclical mechanism with which it could influence the *timing* of investment.

The SAP also introduced a variety of general and selective regulations in the financial market that afforded considerable influence over credit and monetary policy. These included cash reserve requirements, which directed banks to maintain a percentage of their deposits in accounts at the central bank, and liquidity ratio requirements, which forced banks to invest in government securities or housing bonds. These and other policies afforded the government, through the Riksbank, a greater measure of control over the volume, sectoral allocation, and price of credit in Sweden. These credit market controls were, in turn, bolstered by strict exchange control regulations, which restricted the possibility for capital movement across national borders and allowed the SAP more freedom to pursue counter-cyclical monetary policies.

An integral part of the Swedish model, and justifiably the most renowned of its various components is, of course, the welfare state. The onset of the Depression in the 1930s and, later, the Second World War sparked the growth of the public sector and social welfare, which developed into a web of publicly provided, universal social services and insurance-based benefits ('transfers') designed to maintain the income levels of new parents, the sick, the disabled, and the unemployed. By the 1980s, few welfare states were as comprehensive (including sickness insurance, parental insurance, refugee assistance, and high-quality, near-universal day care provision, in addition to more familiar programs such as unemployment insurance and health care); as generous (providing 90 per cent replacement level for most programs, including more than five weeks of statutory vacation); or as well-funded (Sweden's expenditures on various programs and services exceeded 25 percent of GDP by 1983, making it a top spender among the OECD countries) (Olsen, 1994; Olsson, 1993). Preventative health care programs ensured high life expectancy and low mortality rates in Sweden, while a solid commitment to full employment through active labor market policies, rather than the passive unemployment insurance programs emphasized in many other Western nations, was largely responsible for record-low levels of unemployment. Sweden's average rate of *open* unemployment between 1960 and 1985 was only 2.1 percent (OECD, 1987; Olsen, 1988).

Another impressive achievement of the Swedish model has been its dramatic success in reducing wage inequality and in virtually eliminating poverty. It is common knowledge that, unlike many other industrial nations, Swedish society has not been marked by inner city slums or the presence of a large, homeless, indigent 'underclass' for many decades. By 1980, for example, Sweden's rate of poverty was only 5 percent while that in most other countries, such as Canada (12.1 percent), Germany (7.2 percent), Israel (14.5 percent), the U.K. (8.8 percent), and the United States (16.9 percent), was higher, often approaching or exceeding double-digit levels (Hedström and Ringen, 1987). Moreover, because the annual earnings of the lowest income-earners in Sweden more closely approximate the average (median) income, and because the poor have access to numerous benefits and services, these groups have higher living standards than their counterparts in most other advanced nations. According to Björklund and Freeman (1993: 2), Sweden's system of tax and transfer policies were 'the major cause of Sweden's distributional record,' although they also acknowledge the impact of the solidaristic wage policy and the SAP's commitment to full employment.

As in the field of industrial relations, it was quite evident by the mid-1980s that Sweden's socio-economic planning and welfare measures were under reconstruction. The Swedish credit market, for example, was rapidly deregulated throughout the 1980s. By the end of the decade, Sweden's long-standing system of controls over foreign investment and exchange and the financial sector were effectively eliminated (Englund, 1990; Jonung, 1986; Myhrman and Sundberg, 1986). Finance houses proliferated during this period, and money flooded into office buildings and real estate, both in Sweden and abroad. However, the speculative boom ended in short order. The Swedish credit system foundered by the end of 1991, forcing the government to divert tax revenues to bail out several of its major banks at a cost of 3 percent of GDP. The near collapse of the key banks and insurance companies that comprise the financial industry helped to bring the international recession to Sweden.

A fundamental reform of the taxation system was also undertaken in 1988 and continued through the early 1990s. High marginal tax rates were dramatically lowered from 85 percent to 50 percent and the income tax on dividends was eliminated. Indirect, regressive taxes, such as the value-added sales tax (VAT), were extended and increased, while corporate and property taxes remained low. These taxes were lower in Sweden than in any other OECD country by the early 1990s (OECD, 1991). In addition, the IF tax system, which previously had allowed the government some limited control over the timing of capital investment, was abolished as part of the tax reform in 1990, and proposals were put forward to reduce taxes on wealth (OECD, 1991).[6]

Although they garnered much less attention than wage-earner funds because they were not geared toward the issue of ownership, 'renewal funds' were introduced by the SAP in 1984. As with the IF investment system, companies were encouraged to place a portion of their profits in interest-free accounts at the Riksbank. These accounts would be exempt from corporate taxation when withdrawn, but the resultant funds were to be used for investment in research and development and employee education and retraining rather than in fixed capital. However, labor lost yet another opportunity to influence corporate investment when the SAP failed to extend the legislation past 1985 (Pontusson, 1992).

By far the most shocking new development in Sweden was the emergence of mass unemployment in the early 1990s. Sweden has been widely admired for maintaining internationally low rates of unemployment, but its double-digit level in 1993 indicated that full employment was not a top priority for the conservative coalition government. Consequently, expenditures on unemployment insurance eclipsed those on preventive, active labor market policies for the first time in decades. In a blatant attempt to weaken workers' connections to the unions, the same government also introduced a compulsory, state-controlled unemployment insurance program as an alternative to the long-standing system administered by union-linked benefit societies (see Rothstein, 1992).

A number of other attacks on the welfare state occurred in the 1990s, including reductions in the levels of income-related replacement benefits for parental, unemployment and sickness insurance from 90 percent to 80 percent of income, and an increase in the retirement age from 65 to 66. In 1993, displaced workers were no longer immediately eligible to collect benefits but were required to wait one week for unemployment insurance and one day for sickness insurance. Moreover, employers were made responsible for the first 14 days of sickness insurance payments in order to give them more control over 'abuse.' Costs were increased for prescription drugs, dental care, and visits to the physician, while annual grants to municipalities to provide various public services were cut, leading to reductions in the number of full-time workers and a consequent reduction in staff–client ratios in nurseries, day care centers, primary schools, and homes for seniors. In the area of housing, the government enforced a deregulation of housing norms and weakened rent controls – leading to rent increases in large cities – and cut housing subsidies (Olsson and McMurphy, 1993). Many more far-reaching changes were proposed or scheduled to take place but were scrapped or put on hold with the SAP's return to power in September 1994.

While the breadth of these modifications is both startling and significant, it is relatively minor when compared with the dramatic restructuring that has occurred in other nations such as the United Kingdom, especially given Sweden's advanced level of development. Means or income tests were not introduced, and universality maintained its status as the central feature of the welfare state. More worrisome is the recent development of private and corporate welfare programs, like those found in the United States. These include the creation of a voucher system through which parents can choose to send their children to one of hundreds of new private schools and kindergartens, the creation of private alternatives in health care, and the provision of public funding for private day care. While the emergence and proliferation of such private alternatives are not necessarily unwarranted in some cases, they do increase the likelihood of differential access, two-tier provision, and increased inequality.

Throughout the 1970s and early 1980s, Sweden gained a reputation as one of the most egalitarian nations in the capitalist world, largely as a result of its welfare state and other redistributive policies (Ringen and Uusitalo, 1992). However, by the mid-1980s, concomitant with the emergence of the first chinks in the Swedish model, a reversal was set in motion that began to accelerate in the late 1980s. Changes to the taxation system helped promote an upward trend in factor income (labor and capital market earnings) inequality. Björklund and Freeman (1993) note that the differential in factor incomes between the lowest and highest deciles of earners in Sweden increased by almost 50 percent between 1987 and 1991. Given the more muted nature of the reforms to various insurance programs during this period, the increase in disposable income (after taxes and transfers) inequality was much more modest (Björklund and Freeman, 1993; Fritzell, 1993; Ringen and Uusitalo, 1992). Poverty rates, however, rose fairly steadily throughout the 1980s. In 1978, the poverty rate in Sweden was only 3.6 percent, but by 1992 it had reached 7.2 percent (Jansson, 1994). While the poverty rate in Sweden is still low by international standards, its doubling over the past 15 years signals a disturbing new trend.

The Foundation Cracks: The Swedish Model in a Global Economy

The most definitive characteristic of the current period is the increasingly global orientation of the world economy.[7] The transition from a 'capitalist world economy' to a 'world capitalist economy' involves the transformation of multinational corporations (MNCs) into transnational corporations (TNCs), 'defined by the expanding internationalization of their production and the decline of a meaningful home base or domestic market' (Teeple, 1995: 63–4). In this period, international foreign exchange and capital markets and newly created or modified supranational agreements and organizations, such as the North American Free Trade Agreement (NAFTA), the European Union (EU, formerly the EEC), and the World Trade Organization (WTO, formerly GATT), play an increasingly central role in liberalizing world trade. All of this and the demands of the new global order have meant an erosion of the power of national states. Consequently, Keynesianism, social planning, and the welfare state often have given way to monetarist policies, even under Social Democratic governments (cf. Bonefeld and Holloway, 1991; Burrows and Loader, 1994; Goodman and Pauly, 1993). Given the compass of these developments, the reconstruction of the Swedish model documented earlier should come as no surprise.

Three different explanations recently have been proffered to account for the unraveling of the Swedish model in the 1980s, emphasizing what might be referred to as political, economic, and sociological ('balance of power') factors, respectively.

Political Factors

The most superficial, but not irrelevant, account provides a *political* explanation that highlights the role that governments have played. One version puts the blame squarely on the right-wing coalition government that came to power in 1991. As the nation's first genuinely neo-liberal government, it deliberately set out to radically transform the Swedish model. Thus, in addition to the welfare cuts and credit market and tax reforms, it deregulated, privatized, and introduced a variety of other measures to encourage greater competition and 'restore' the market. For example, the broadcasting and telecommunications monopolies, telephone company, postal services, and state alcohol authority and retail company have all experienced deregulation, while municipal cleaning services and parts of the public transportation systems, including the bus service in Sweden's third-largest city (Malmö), have been contracted out. Many of these changes, of course, were hastened by the prospect of membership in a European Union (EU) which encouraged such developments. The government's new approach was epitomized in the establishment of the Swedish Competition Authority (Konkurrensverket) in 1992 and in the introduction of a new Competition Act the following year (Konkurrensverket, 1993). Enhancing competition, especially within the public sector, was openly declared as one of the new organization's central tasks. However, many of the most important changes outlined here were initiated or accelerated by the SAP before it lost power in 1991. For example, although the right-wing coalition government of 1976–82 began to deregulate the credit market (abolishing controls on bank deposit rates and removing the regulatory limits on interest rates for private bonds), it was the SAP that radically transformed the capital market upon its return to power in 1982 by eliminating almost all of the remaining controls in the domestic financial sector and removing long-standing restraints on foreign investment and the movement of capital. It was also the SAP that engineered the 'great tax reform' in 1991, although its fiscal proclivities were enthusiastically pursued by the conservative coalition government that returned to power that same year.

While the attacks on the Swedish model made by the 'non-socialist' coalition governments are not hard to understand, it is somewhat more

difficult to explain the SAP's cutbacks and reforms from this narrow
political perspective. Some accounts point to the takeover in the early
1980s of key positions within the party by a contingent of right-wing
politicians who abandoned the model and 'betrayed' its supporters (e.g.,
Canova, 1994). Kjell-Olof Feldt, finance minister, and Bengt Dennis,
head of the central bank, were the most high-profile and influential
among the prime minister's economic advisors who sought to ensure
that neo-liberalism would take root in Sweden. Be that as it may, the fact
that many of the most dramatic changes outlined here – such as the
decline of centralized bargaining (Katz, 1993) – also took place in a
variety of other nations suggests that the actions of incumbent political
parties or blocs in Sweden, whether of the left or right, can not fully
explain why the model began to break down in the 1980s. Rather, the
actions of Swedish governments of the left and right represented a response to the demands of internationalized capital in the new, more
globally oriented world economy.

Economic Factors

A second explanation for the demise of the Swedish model emphasizes
economic factors. While this account has both a left-wing variant, focusing
on the 'fiscal crisis' of the state (O'Connor, 1973; Offe, 1985), and a
right-wing version, it is the latter that is routinely popularized in the
media. This account highlights impairments to the efficiency of market
mechanisms as the main cause of the current crisis – reflected in declining long-term productivity growth, double-digit unemployment, and a
record-high budget deficit and national debt – and suggests that the
Swedish model has been crumbling under its own weight over the past
20 years. It is best summarized in a report from the conservative coalition government in 1994:

The underlying reasons for the current deep economic crisis in Sweden go back
a long way ... [P]ublic monopolies ... resulted in poorer efficiency and higher
costs than necessary and, thereby, 'crowding-out' effects ... The growth in public
spending resulted in a high and rising tax pressure ... which caused distortions in
the economy. High marginal taxes ... resulted in an unreasonable and arbitrary
redistribution of wealth ... [C]ostly regulatory systems ... contributed to the inefficient allocation of resources, poorer efficiency and high costs to the economy.
(Ministry of Finance, 1994: 15–17).

A recent OECD study (1994: 88) tentatively concurs: 'Sweden's comparatively slow growth and poor productivity record during the last couple of decades might at least to some extent be due to the country's large and growing public sector' (cf. Meyerson, 1982, 1985).

Other accounts (Eklund et al., 1993; Lindbeck, 1993; Lindbeck et al., 1994) place more emphasis on the deleterious effects that the 'excesses' of the tax and transfer programs are said to have upon the choices Swedes make. Thus, high marginal taxation rates, for example, are seen as encouraging workers to choose leisure over educational upgrading and retraining, thereby creating labor shortages. High tax rates also lead to tax avoidance, from this perspective, because 'honesty is too expensive.' Overly generous, universal benefits with few restrictions governing eligibility, such as sickness insurance, are considered to encourage program abuse and are held responsible for the internationally high rates of absenteeism found in Sweden. By severing the relationship between effort and reward, welfare programs are believed to destroy the work ethic and create disincentives to saving and entrepreneurship. And various programs that provide income and personal services to women and families are viewed as 'undermining' the family.

In the industrial relations sphere, strict regulations purportedly create similar problems. Mandated employer contributions that largely fund various social insurance programs and tight labor laws make it expensive to hire (or fire) workers. And job security legislation, which enforces priority rules based on seniority rather than skill or expertise for grounded dismissals, sometimes forces employers facing a shortage of work to lay off their most valuable and productive employees (Eklund et al., 1993; Lindbeck, 1993; Lindbeck et al., 1994).

This 'crumbling under its own weight' argument is, of course, not unrelated to the political explanation initially set out here. In fact, many politicians from both the 'bourgeois' and 'socialist' camps maintain that these critical conditions forced them to abandon key elements of the traditional Swedish model. Liposuction and radical surgery were the only way to deal with a 'bloated and inefficient' public sector and many other long-standing rigidities. Yet, the relationship between the size of the public sector and economic growth is far from clear (cf. Cameron, 1978, 1982; Hicks, 1988; Hicks and Patterson, 1989; Löfgren, 1994). And many suggest that the current budget deficit has much more to do with the neo-liberal policies embraced in the 1980s than with size of the public sector. A number of nations with much less developed public sectors than Sweden's are facing very similar problems. Moreover, as recently as 1990, when the public sector was still in full bloom, the budget deficit and unemployment levels were practically non-existent – a fact largely ignored in the popular media at that time.

Sociological Factors

A third and much broader explanation focuses on *structural developments* and their impact on the *balance of power* between class forces. In the late 1970s and 1980s, 'power resources theorists' usefully demonstrated that welfare states were much more developed and inequality much lower in nations like Sweden, where labor movements were strong, well organized, and well represented by incumbent social democratic or labor parties (cf. Esping-Andersen, 1985; Korpi, 1983; Stephens, 1980). However, because they tended to overlook capital, they were hard-pressed to account for the attack on the welfare state and rising inequality seen in Scandinavia and elsewhere.

Studies that appeared in the late 1980s and early 1990s provided a useful corrective to the then-dominant view that the Swedish model was largely, if not solely, the product of a powerful labor movement by refocusing attention upon the strength, strategies, and organizations of Swedish capital (Olsen, 1991, 1992; Pontusson, 1987, 1992; Swenson, 1989, 1991). Thus, contrary to the received wisdom, it was pointed out that centralized bargaining, like other key components of the Swedish model, was initiated by the employers as a means of promoting wage restraint during the 'Fordist' era (Fulcher, 1991). The SWP, in turn, was the quid pro quo necessary 'to obtain the consent of low-pay unions reluctant to give up their bargaining autonomy and power in a full-employment economy unless they received some distributional payoff' (Swenson, 1989: 65).

It should not be concluded, however, that Swedish capitalists were united over the introduction of the various components of the Swedish model or completely in charge of its construction, either. Indeed, the engineering sector, which was largely geared toward production for export, fairly consistently and quite vehemently opposed the introduction of most of what came to constitute the central pillars of the Swedish model. In the 1930s, for example, the Directors' Club, a pressure group comprising the managing directors of five of the largest engineering/ export industries, unsuccessfully attacked the SAP's plans to introduce welfare-Keynesianism because it believed there would be little benefit for them. In the early 1960s, the Kamarilla, an organization of seven employers' associations, including the Engineering Employers' Association (VF), made another failed attempt to scuttle centralized bargaining. Export-oriented, engineering capital was thwarted in these endeavors not least because the home-market faction of capital was willing to ally with labor and accommodate the wishes of the unions and the SAP.[8] After all, given its greater dependence upon domestic consumption and the Swedish labor force, home-market capital would stand to benefit from a more quiescent, high-wage workforce and the demand-oriented, Keynesian welfare state. It was able to engineer such a compromise with labor through its control over SAF.

By the 1970s, however, the traditional export sector – now joined by a number of formerly home-market (primarily) companies (such as Volvo) that had become markedly more internationally oriented throughout the preceding decade – was fast becoming the clearly dominant force in Sweden. Spurred on by the solidaristic wage policy, these firms had grown very large and powerful, and Sweden's economy had become highly concentrated. By 1986, 61 percent of Swedish workers were employed in firms employing 500 or more, an extraordinarily high rate from a comparative perspective. The corresponding figure for the European Community, for example, was only half as large, as indicated in table 1.

By 1983, foreign sales greatly exceeded domestic sales for 19 of Sweden's 20 largest multinationals, and the majority of these firms were

TABLE 1
The Distribution of Employment as a Percentage of Total Workforce in Selected European Countries according to Firm Size, 1986

	Number of employees in firm			
	1–9	10–99	100–499	500+
Sweden	9.5	17.3	12.6	60.6
EC	20.9	48.7*		30.4
Germany	18.2	27.3	18.7	35.8
France	15.1	28.6	16.7	39.6
U.K.	23.2	23.9	22.9	30.0
Netherlands	14.0	27.7	17.1	41.3
Denmark	16.8	42.4	23.2	17.6

* 10–499 employees.
Note: Firms with no employees are excluded.
Source: SOU 1992 19: 308.

TABLE 2
Recent Employment Trends in the 21 Largest Swedish Companies

Company	Employment abroad		Employment in Sweden	
	Number employed	% Change 1987–96	Number employed	% Change 1987–96
Ericsson	50,100	54	43,900	23
Volvo	27,000	36	43,300	–19
ABB	188,674	631	26,200	–30
Saab-Scania	11,247	17	26,000	–31
Skanska	17,745	128	20,500	3
Electrolux	98,200	–2	13,900	–53
Stora	10,600	188	12,100	–11
NCC	4,600	47	11,300	–41
Sandvik	20,100	49	10,300	–3
Tetra Laval	28,900	11	8,900	8
SAS	15,700	–32	7,900	–8
SCA	26,400	317	7,700	–35
Moda	2,800	6	7,100	–38
Assidomän	6,800	166	6,900	–43
Trelleborg	5,600	137	6,800	175
Astra	13,200	280	6,600	101
SKF	36,100	–3	6,400	–19
Pharmacia & Upjohn	25,700	765	6,000	23
Securitas	31,654	1,000+	5,000	5
BTL	5,500	227	5,000	0
Akzo Nobel	66,000	1,000+	4,700	–65
Total/Average % Change	692,620	159	286,500	–3

Source: Affärsvärlden No. 1–3, 1998: 31.

employing far greater numbers of workers outside than within the Swedish border (Olsen, 1991, 1992). At the end of the decade, following deregulation, Swedish firms were investing far more capital abroad than within Sweden. These trends have continued apace, as indicated in table 2.

Stronger, much more unified, and considerably less dependent upon Swedish labor and the domestic scene, Swedish capital has been able to pursue new strategies more suited to the emerging global order.

Verkstadsföreningen (VF; now called Verkstadsindustrier or VI), for example, stated that the employers in the engineering sector had to be free to offer high wages in order to attract and keep the highly skilled and educated workers required by the new, more flexible workplace. It also made the familiar case favoring lower wages for less-skilled workers in order to decrease labor costs and remain competitive in the new global environment (Lash, 1985; Pontusson and Swenson, 1993). No longer useful, centralized wage bargaining and the solidaristic wage policy were unceremoniously discarded. The Swedish model and the 'politics of compromise' had become somewhat of an embarrassment to Swedish capital and, having outlived their usefulness, had to be methodically dismantled. New times called for new strategies.

Of course, old tried-and-true strategies have not been abandoned, and Swedish capital has taken every opportunity to flex its muscles. Thus, Volvo closed its taxpayer-financed, state-of-the-art plant in Uddevalla in 1993 after only four years of operation, and its plant in Kalmar the following year. The new Volvo leadership apparently favors 'Toyotaism' and traditional Fordist methods of production over its own experiments with extended worker autonomy and a more humane workplace, even though these two plants were quite profitable (Berggren, 1993; Sandberg, 1994).[9]

Taking the same tack, the CEOs of some of Sweden's largest engineering/export companies made a habit of appearing in the media in 1994 to ensure that their pro–European Union position was embraced in the referendum in November of that year. Sweden has been part of a free trade agreement (EFTA) with the European Community since 1960. Moreover, since joining the European Economic Area (EEA) in 1994, it has enjoyed all of the 'four freedoms of movement' (goods, services, capital, and labor) set out in the EEC Treaty of Rome in 1957 and adopted new rules on competition, research, and consumer policy. However, none of this was enough for the Swedish business community. It wanted to be able to influence policy from within the European Union and feared that the EEA arrangement might be terminated at any time following the requisite one-year notice period.

While very concerned with gaining influence within the EU, Swedish capital has not abandoned its mission to effect change domestically. Thus, SAF, the central employers association, was recently restructured and reoriented.[10] Its secretariat was dramatically reduced in size, and most of its 36 member associations, representing some 43,000 companies, reorganized into nine branches according to economic activity (engineering, mining/metal, insurance and finance, and so on). The rather significant reduction in fees for association members, from 0.41 percent to 0.14 percent of each employer's total wage bill, indicated that a number of important developments had transpired. First, given its international orientation, Swedish capital had largely outgrown SAF. Moreover, several large employers' associations, such as VF, have even built up separate insurance funds, further decreasing their reliance upon SAF. However, they retain their membership in SAF in order to maintain some influence over the home-market sub-contractors they are reliant upon for just-in-time production. Second, the 'war against socialism' had been decisively won. The defeat of the wage-earner fund program symbolized the end of labor's 'dominance' and the beginning of a new period. And, finally, with the end of centralized bargaining, SAF's activities were dramatically curtailed and refocused. SAF representatives candidly admit that the organization's main task now is to influence public opinion. This was clearly indicated by SAF chair, Ulf Laurin, in an open letter published in SAF's internal organ, *SAF Tidningen*, in 1990:

After a protracted period of sickness the so-called 'Swedish model' is dead ... The centre of gravity in SAF's work [now] shifts to idea and opinion building. If SAF can ... successfully guide tomorrow's thoughts its role will be larger than ever before ... A new SAF is taking form. (*SAF Tidningen*, 1990: 11, author's translation; cf. Pestoff, 1995)

SAF's new publishing houses now routinely disseminate articles and books attacking the public sector, the welfare state, and 'collectivism,' in favor of the market economy, the 'free and good society,' and membership in the EU. Recent publications celebrate the 'system-shift' that has taken place in New Zealand (e.g., Jilmstad, 1993). Today it is held up as an even better model for Sweden to emulate than was the United States. There is more to learn from a nation like New Zealand, which has had to deal with strong unions, a developed welfare state, and other market rigidities. 'New Zealand shows the way to change,' proclaimed a recent article in the SAF paper (*SAF Tidningen*, 1994; author's translation).

If capital has grown stronger over the past 20 years, labor has become much weaker during this same period as a result of fragmentation. The growing ideological divide between the central blue-collar federation (LO) and the labor party (SAP) was only most dramatically demonstrated through the wrangle over the wage-earner fund issue. Since then, the organic link between the two bodies has been all but severed. The practice of 'collective affiliation,' whereby LO members became members of the SAP, was officially ended in 1990. Moreover, by the late 1980s, support for the SAP among LO members had dropped from around 75 percent to only 50 percent (Olsson, 1991). The widening gulf between these two bodies, once considered 'branches of the same tree,' has been dubbed the 'war of the roses.'

Equally significant is the growing tension within the union movement itself, related to the emergence of 'post-industrialism.' Up until the 1960s, wage bargaining in Sweden was a relatively simple process dominated by two major economic actors, the blue-collar confederation (LO) and the employers' association (SAF). However, the expansion of the white-collar unions and the public sector undermined the privileged LO-SAF axis. Throughout the 1970s and 1980s, bargaining became an increasingly complex undertaking, characterized by shifting and, in recent years, cross-sectoral alliances. This situation was accelerated when the public sector unions (Kommunal and SF) replaced the Metalworkers Union (Metall) as the most powerful unit within the LO. The union system thus has fragmented into several blocs of relatively equal strength, sometimes blurring the old blue-collar/white-collar divide. This has made it somewhat easier for employers to foster competition between unions or federations (Kjellberg, 1992; Mahon, 1994b). Intra-federation tensions have also arisen of late, evidenced, for example, when the various branches within Metall provided little by way of protest or support for their brethren when the Uddevalla plant was selected for shutdown. The very high levels of unionization that Swedish workers still enjoy thus mask underlying problems that dramatically weaken the position of labor vis-à-vis capital.

Conclusion

It should be abundantly evident from the present discussion that the 'Swedish model' has undergone serious reconstruction over the past decade. Almost all of what is presented in figure 1 under the 'Industrial Relations' heading has been eliminated or dramatically altered. And, although the welfare state is still largely intact, serious restructuring has also taken place in the 'Social Planning/Welfare Policy' sphere. It should also be clear that the conditions that originally encouraged and allowed the model to exist no longer obtain. The SAP's return to power in September 1994 has enabled it to reverse some of the changes made to labor legislation, taxation policy (such as the restoration of taxes on dividends and higher marginal tax rates for high-income earners), and the welfare state, and to put a halt to some of the cutbacks and 're-modelling' that the coalition government had planned for 1995. However, the SAP's actions are much more severely circumscribed in a neo-liberal environment dominated by TNCs and global financial markets. Thus, the devaluation of the Swedish Krona by unregulated, speculative international money markets, the demands made by credit-rating agencies, threats made by Swedish TNCs and business organizations, and the convergence rules of the European Union's Maastricht Treaty concerning deficits, inflation, and interest rates, virtually ensured that the SAP would introduce a 'Supplementary Budget Bill' in April 1995 calling for deeper cuts to the welfare state. The April 'mini-budget' further decreased compensation levels for sickness, unemployment, and parental insurance from 80 percent to 75 percent, lowered pension payments, and introduced the first reduction in child benefits since they were initiated in 1948 (Ministry of Finance, 1995).

Swedish labor now must develop new strategies and policies to fit the new more globally oriented environment. Some of this has already begun. Unions have been promoting the idea of 'solidaristic work for solidaristic wages' to counteract employers' attempts to introduce greater wage discrepancies and to divide workers. This plan calls for a general increase in skill levels and the rotation of 'rewarding' and higher-paying jobs among members of production teams (Mahon, 1991, 1994a). Sweden's membership in the EU as of January 1995 greatly intensifies the need to strengthen cross-national alliances with other labor movements and parties within the EU. It will be increasingly difficult for Sweden to maintain its commitment to the welfare state and social equality as an EU member. Optimistic suggestions that the EU can be 'Swedenized' appear far-fetched, given the demonstrated preference for inflation-fighting over job creation in Western Europe – even by incumbent social-democratic governments, as in Spain.

One of the greatest strengths of Swedish labor has been its ability to creatively adapt to new situations not of its own making. The imposition of centralized bargaining in the 1950s, for example, led to the implementation of the solidaristic wage policy. Unless labor can meet the challenges posed by the new environment, the 'Swedish model' may become little more than a museum piece studied and debated by historians.

Notes

The author would like to thank Rudolf Meidner, Joan Durrant and the anonymous reviewers for Social Problems for helpful comments. The generosity of the

362   Gregg M. Olsen

Institute for Arbetslivforskning and the Sociology Department of the University
of Umeå is acknowledged gratefully also.

1 The conditions set out by the 1906 December compromise had been
   extended to white-collar unions in the mid-1930s. State employees did not
   receive full rights to engage in collective bargaining and to strike until 1965.
2 The roots of the SWP date back to discussions at LO congresses in the 1920s
   and a 1938 LO publication written by Albin Lind. A more detailed discussion of the SWP than that presented here can be found in Meidner 1974
   and Hibbs 1990.
3 As noted, the SWP stipulated that the wages of the lowest-paid workers
   would rise faster than 'average' wage rates, thereby promoting 'equal pay for
   equal work' and, eventually, rendering wages more equal across industries
   and regions. Moreover, it eliminated unproductive firms unable to pay
   solidaristic wages. However, the SWP also stimulated the growth of those
   dynamic and profitable firms that were paying 'average' wages by restraining
   demands for higher wages and thereby led to greater concentration in the
   Swedish economy.
4 After 1983, bargaining shifted between the central and industry levels a
   number of times until the end of the decade, when the government
   effectively enforced centralized bargaining in an attempt to secure wage
   moderation through the Rehnberg Agreement. However, industry-level
   bargaining resumed in 1993 after the settlement had expired.
5 Asia is now Volvo's first priority for geographic expansion according to the
   chief executive of Volvo Truck, Karl-Erling Trogen. Plans for a joint venture
   in China and a feasibility study concerning production in India are already
   under way.
6 While the overall redistributive impact of these changes to the taxation
   system mainly benefited the wealthy, the previous system was somewhat less
   progressive than often is assumed, due to the existence of a variety of tax
   loopholes.
7 Various authors have suggested that the current era reflects the ongoing
   shift from 'Fordism,' characterized by the dominance of giant multinational
   corporations, mass production/mass consumption, and U.S. hegemony, to
   'post-Fordism,' based on new patterns of consumption, distribution, and
   production favoring 'flexible specialization' and the emergence of
   transnational corporations (for an overview, see Brenner and Glick, 1991;
   and Hirst and Zeitlin, 1991). However, it may be premature to announce
   the birth of post-Fordism or conduct post-mortem analyses of the Fordist
   period. While there have been some marked trends and tendencies toward

post-Fordism – especially in the sphere of production – they are often of a highly contingent nature and open to interruption or reversal. Furthermore, these changes in patterns of accumulation have not been accompanied by a new, coherent, and stable mode of social regulation. Welfare states, for example, remain as central components of the mode of regulation, at least for the moment, however severe their retrenchment over the past decade (Tickell and Adam, 1995; Burrows and Loader, 1994). More importantly, as the discussion here indicates, many recent developments in Sweden suggest that Fordism has been simply heightened and internationalized (neo-Fordism), not superseded (post-Fordism). The focus here is thus on the 'globalization of the world economy,' rather than on post-Fordism.

8 In contrast to the position taken here, Swenson (1991) points to an alliance between workers and employers in the export sector as crucial to the creation of the historical compromise that became the basis of the Swedish model. (Cf. Olsen, 1991, 1992.)

9 A joint venture between Volvo and Britain's TRW has led to the reopening of the Volvo Uddevalla plant recently.

10 This section is based on interviews conducted with various representatives of SAF and other employer associations and research institutes cited in the references.

References

Affärsvärlden. 1993. 'De Svenska Storföretagen.' *Affärsvärlden* 26/32: 22–37.

Ahlén, Kristina. 1989. 'Swedish collective bargaining under pressure: Inter-union rivalry and incomes policies.' *British Journal of Industrial Relations* 27: 330–44.

Ahrne, Göran, and Wallace Clement. 1992. 'A new regime?: Class representation within the Swedish state.' *Economic and Industrial Democracy* 13: 455–79.

Åmark, Klas. 1992. 'Social democracy and the trade union movement: Solidarity and the politics of self-interest.' In *Creating Social Democracy: A Century of the Social Democratic Labor Party in Sweden,* ed. Klas Misgeld, Karl Molin, and Klas Åmark, 67–96. University Park: Pennsylvania State University Press.

Andersson, Krister. 1987. 'Sweden.' In *Comparative Tax Systems: Europe, Canada, and Japan,* ed. Joseph A. Pechman, 33–90. New York and Washington, D.C.: The Brookings Institution.

Berggren, Christian. 1993. 'The Volvo plant: Why the decision to close it is mistaken.' *Journal of Industry Studies* 1: 175–81.

– 1992. *Alternatives to Lean Production: Work Organization in the Swedish Auto Industry.* Ithaca, N.Y.: ILR Press.

Bergström, Villy, and Jan Södersten. 1984. 'Do tax allowances stimulate invest-ment?' *Scandinavian Journal of Economics* 86: 244–68.

Björklund, Anders, and Richard B. Freeman. 1993. 'Reforming the welfare state: The Swedish model in transition.' Unpublished paper presented at the NBER–SNS Conference on 'Reforming the Swedish Welfare State,' Stockholm.

Bonefeld, Werner, and John Holloway, eds. 1991. *Post-Fordism and Social Form: A Marxist Debate on the Post-Fordist State*. London: Macmillan.

Brenner, Robert, and Mark Glick. 1991. 'The regulation approach: Theory and history.' *New Left Review* 188: 45–119.

Burrows, Roger, and Brian Loader, eds. 1994. *Towards a Post-Fordist Welfare State?* London: Routledge.

Cameron, David R. 1978. 'The expansion of the public economy: A comparative analysis.' *American Political Science Review* 72: 1243–61.

– 1982. 'On the limits of the public economy.' *Annals of the American Association of Political and Social Science* 459: 46–62.

Canova, Timothy A. 1994. 'The Swedish model betrayed.' *Challenge* 37: 36–40.

De Geer, Hans. 1992. *The Rise and Fall of the Swedish Model*. Chichester: Carden.

Eklund Klas, Assar Lindbeck, Mats Persson, Hans Tson Söderström, and Staffan Viotti. 1993. *Sweden's Economic Crisis: Diagnosis and Cure*. Stockholm: Studieförbundet Näringsliv och Samhälle.

Englund, Peter. 1990. 'Financial deregulation in Sweden.' *European Economic Review* 34: 385–93.

Esping-Andersen, Gøsta. 1985. *Politics against Markets*. Princeton: Princeton University Press.

– 1990. *The Three Worlds of Welfare Capitalism*. Princeton: Princeton University Press.

Fritzell, Johan. 1993. 'Income Inequality Trends in the 1980s: A Five-Country Comparison.' *Acta Sociologica* 36: 47–62.

Fulcher, James. 1991. *Labour Movements, Employers and the State: Conflict and Cooperation in Britain and Sweden*. Oxford: Clarendon Press.

Goodman, John B., and Louis W. Pauly. 1993. 'The obsolescence of capital controls? Economic management in an age of global markets.' *World Politics* 46: 50–82.

Gustafsson, Bo. 1983. 'The Causes of the Expansion of the Public Sector in Sweden during the 20th Century.' Report No. 1: Uppsala Papers in Economic History.

Hancock, M. Donald. 1972. *Sweden: The Politics of Postindustrial Change*. Hinsdale: Dryden Press.

Hedström, Peter, and Stein Ringen. 1987. 'Age and Contemporary society: A research note.' *Journal of Social Policy* 16: 227–39.

Hibbs, Douglas A. 1990. 'Wage dispersion and trade union action in Sweden.' In *Generating Equality in the Welfare State: The Swedish Experience,* ed. Inga Persson, 181–201. Oslo: Norwegian University Press.

Hibbs, Douglas A., and Håkan Locking. 1991. *Wage Compression, Wage Drift, and Wage Inflation in Sweden.* Stockholm: FIEF.

Hicks, Alexander. 1988. 'Social democratic corporatism and economic growth.' *Journal of Politics* 50: 677–704.

Hicks, Alexander, and William David Patterson. 1989. 'On the robustness of the left corporatist model of economic growth.' *Journal of Politics* 51: 662–75.

Hirst, Paul, and Jonathan Zeitlin. 1991. 'Flexible specialization versus post-Fordism: Theory, evidence and policy implications.' *Economy and Society* 20: 1–57.

Jansson, Kjell. 1994. *Inkomstfördelningen i Sverige, 1975–1992, med en Speciell Redovisning av Perioden 1989–1992.* Örebro: SCB.

Jilmstad, Lars. 1993. *Nya Zeeland: Från Kris Till Systemskifte.* Stockholm: Timbro.

Jonung, Lars. 1986. 'Financial deregulation in Sweden.' *Skandinaviska Enskilda Banken Quarterly Review* 4: 109–19.

Katz, Harry C. 1993. 'The decentralization of collective bargaining: A literature review and comparative analysis.' *Industrial and Labor Relations Review* 47: 3–22.

Kjellberg, Anders. 1992. 'Sweden: Can the model survive?' In *Industrial Relations in the New Europe,* ed. Anthony Ferner and Richard Hyman, 88–142. Oxford: Basil Blackwell.

Konkurrensverket. 1993. *1992/93 Årsredovisning.* Stockholm: Konkurrensverket.

Korpi, Walter. 1983. *The Democratic Class Struggle.* London: Routledge and Kegan Paul.

Lash, Scott. 1985. 'The end of neo-corporatism? The breakdown of centralised bargaining in Sweden.' *British Journal of Industrial Relations* 23: 215–39.

Lindbeck, Assar. 1993. *The Welfare State: The Selected Essays of Assar Lindbeck,* Volume II. Aldershot: Edward Elgar.

Lindbeck, Assar, Per Molander, Torsten Persson, Olof Petersson, Agnar Sandmo, Birgitta Swedenborg, and Niels Thygesen. 1994. *Turning Sweden Around.* Cambridge, Mass.: MIT Press.

LO (Landsorganisation). 1953. *Trade Unions and Full Employment.* Stockholm: LO.

– 1982. *Co-determination through Collective Agreements and Legislation.* Stockholm: LO.

– 1993. *The Trade Unions in Figures.* Stockholm: LO.

Löfgren, Christer. 1994. 'Tillväxt och offentlig sektor i OECD-länderna.' Unpublished manuscript.

Lundberg, Erik. 1985. 'The rise and fall of the Swedish model.' *Journal of Economic Literature* 23: 1–36.

Mahon, Rianne. 1991. 'From solidaristic wages to solidaristic work: A post-historic compromise for Sweden?' *Economic and Industrial Democracy* 12: 295–325.

366   Gregg M. Olsen

- 1994a. 'Wage earners and/or co-workers? Contested identities.' *Economic and Industrial Democracy* 15: 355–83.
- 1994b. 'Yesterday's "modern times" are no longer modern Swedish unions confront the double shift.' Unpublished manuscript.
Martin, Andrew. 1992. *Wage Bargaining and Swedish Politics: The Political Implications of the End of Central Negotiations.* Stockholm: FIEF.
McLure, Charles E., and Erik Norrman. 1993. 'Tax Policy in Sweden.' Unpublished paper presented at the NBER–SNS Conference on 'Reforming the Swedish Welfare State,' Stockholm.
Meidner, Rudolf. 1974. *Co-ordination and Solidarity: An Approach to Wages Policy.* Stockholm: Prisma/ LO.
- 1978. *Employee Investment Funds: A Collective Approach to Capital Formation.* London: George Allen and Unwin.
- 1992. 'The rise and fall of the Swedish model.' *Studies in Political Economy* 39: 159–71.
Meyerson, Per-Martin. 1982. *The Welfare State in Crisis.* Stockholm: Federation of Swedish Industries.
- 1985. *Eurosclerosis: The Case of Sweden.* Stockholm: Caslon Press.
- 1991. *Den Svenska Modellens Uppgång Och Fall.* Stockholm: SNS Förlag.
Ministry of Finance. 1994. *Economic Policy Statement by the Swedish Government.* Stockholm: Ministry of Finance.
- 1995. *Extract of Supplementary Budget Bill 1995/96.* Stockholm: Ministry of Finance.
Myhrman, Johan, and Jan Sundberg. 1986. 'The credit market in transformation.' *Skandinaviska Enskilda Banken Quarterly Review* 2: 30–8.
O'Connor, James. 1973. *The Fiscal Crisis of the State.* New York: St. Martin's Press.
OECD. 1987. *Historical Statistics.* Paris: OECD.
- 1991. *Taxing Profits in a Global Economy: Domestic and International Issues.* Paris: OECD.
- 1994. *OECD Economic Surveys, 1993–1994.* Paris: OECD.
Offe, Claus. 1985. *Contradictions of the Welfare State.* Cambridge, Mass.: MIT Press.
Olsen, Gregg M. 1991. 'Labour mobilization and the strength of capital: The rise and stall of economic democracy in Sweden.' *Studies in Political Economy* 34: 109–45.
- 1992. *The Struggle for Economic Democracy in Sweden.* Aldershot, England: Avebury/Gower.
- 1994. 'Locating the Canadian welfare state: Family policy and health care in Canada, Sweden and the United States.' *The Canadian Journal of Sociology* 19: 1–20.

Olsen, Gregg M., ed. 1988. *Industrial Change and Labour Adjustment in Sweden and Canada*. Toronto: Garamond.

Olsson, Sven E. 1993. *Social Policy and Welfare State in Sweden*, Second Edition. Lund: Arkiv.

Olsson, Sven E., and Suzanne McMurphy. 1993. 'Social policy in Sweden: The Swedish model in transition.' *Social Policy Review* 5: 248–69.

Olsson, Ulf. 1991. 'Planning in the Swedish welfare state.' *Studies in Political Economy* 34: 147–71.

Persson, Inga. 1990. 'The third dimension – equal status between Swedish women and men.' In *Generating Equality in the Welfare State: The Swedish Experience*, ed. Inga Persson, 223–44. Oslo: Norwegian University Press.

Pestoff, Victor. 1995. 'Towards a new Swedish model of collective bargaining.' In *Organisations in the Labour Market – What Future?* ed. Colin Crouch and Franz Traxler, 151–82. London: Avebury.

Pontusson, Jonas. 1987. 'Radicalization and retreat in Swedish social democracy.' *New Left Review* 165: 5–33.

– 1988. 'The triumph of pragmatism: Nationalisation and privatisation in Sweden.' *West European Politics* 11: 129–45.

– 1992. *The Limits of Social Democracy: Investment Politics in Sweden*. Ithaca, N.Y.: Cornell University Press.

Pontusson, Jonas, and Peter Swenson. 1993. 'Employers on the offensive: Wage bargaining, pay practices and new production strategies in Sweden.' Unpublished manuscript.

Ringen, Stein, and Hannu Uusitalo. 1992. 'Income distribution and redistribution in the Nordic welfare states.' In *The Study of Welfare Regimes*, ed. Jon Eivind Kolberg, 69–91. Armonk: M.E. Sharpe.

Rothstein, Bo. 1992. 'Labor-market institutions and working-class strength.' In *Structuring Politics: Historical Institutionalism in Comparative Analysis*, ed. Sven Steinmo, Kathleen Thelen, and Frank Longstreth, 33–56. Cambridge: Cambridge University Press.

SAF. 1992. *SAF's Decision to Leave the Governing Boards of State Authorities*. Document No. 1097. Stockholm: SAF.

– 1993. *The Swedish Employers' Confederation – An Influential Voice in Public Affairs*. Stockholm: SAF.

SAF Tidningen. 1990. 'Ett nya SAF tar form.' *SAF Tidningen* 6: 10–11.

– 1994. 'Nya Zeeland visar väg till förändring.' *SAF Tidningen* 7: 12.

Sandberg, Åke. 1994. '"Volvoism" at the end of the road?' *Studies in Political Economy* 45: 170–82.

SCB. 1990. *Women and Men in Sweden Equality of the Sexes*. Stockholm: SCB.

Södersten, Jan. 1984. 'Sweden.' In The Taxation of Income From Capital, ed. M.A. King and D. Fullerton, 87–148. Chicago: University of Chicago Press.

SOU. 1992. *Långtidsutredningen 1992*. Stockholm: Allmanna Förlaget.

Stephens, John. 1980. *The Transition from Capitalism to Socialism*. Atlantic Highlands, N.J.: Humanities Press.

Swedish Ministry of Labour. 1985. *The Swedish Act on Co-determination at Work*. Stockholm: Ministry of Labor.

Swenson, Peter. 1989. *Fair Shares: Unions, Pay and Politics in Sweden and West Germany*. Ithaca, N.Y. Cornell University Press.

– 1991. 'Bringing capital back in, or social democracy reconsidered.' *World Politics* 43: 513–44.

Teeple, Gary. 1995. *Globalization and the Decline of Social Reform*. Toronto: Garamond.

Tickell, Adam, and Jamie A. Peck. 1995. 'Social regulation after Fordism: Regulation theory, neo-liberalism and the global-local nexus.' *Economy and Society* 24: 357–86.

Interviews

De Geer, Hans. 1987/1994. Director, Fa Rådet (Swedish Institute for Management and Work Life Issues), Stockholm.

Jilmstad, Lars. 1994. Head of Information Department, SAF, Stockholm.

Larsson, Janerik. 1987. Senior Vice-President, SAF, Stockholm.

Meyerson, Per-Martin. 1988/1994. Director, SI (Federation of Swedish Industries) /currently retired, Stockholm.

Schager, Nils Henrik. 1987. Researcher, IUI (Industrial Institute for Economic and Social Research), Stockholm.